LLOYD'S

MARITIME ATLAS

OF WORLD PORTS AND SHIPPING PLACES

Eighteenth Edition

Lloyd's of London Press Ltd
Sheepen Place, Colchester, Essex CO3 3LP
United Kingdom
Tel +44 (1206) 772277
Fax +44 (1206) 772118

Lloyd's of London Press Inc.
611 Broadway, Suite 308
New York, NY 10012, USA
Tel +1 (212) 529 9500
Fax +1 (212) 529 9826

Lloyd's of London Press (Germany) GmbH
Ehrenbergstrasse 59
22767 Hamburg
Germany
Tel +49 (40) 38 97 23
Fax +49 (40) 38 78 69

Lloyd's of London Press (Far East) Ltd
Room 1101, Hollywood Centre
233 Hollywood Road
Hong Kong
Tel +852 854 3222
Fax +852 854 1538

Cartography:
Department of Maritime Studies
University of Wales College of Cardiff (UWCC)
Cardiff CF1 3YP

Map preparation
Cook Hammond & Kell Ltd
Mitcham, Surrey CR4 3XR

Editorial Research:
Chris Holmes, Paul Aldworth, Jan Waters

The editorial work on the sixteenth edition of A. K. C. Beresford
and H. W. Dobson is gratefully acknowledged

Production Editor:
Stan Dover

Index Origination:
Facsimile Graphics Ltd, Coggeshall, Essex CO6 1SX

Cover Design:
Michael Walsh, Colchester, Essex CO6 5LP

Distance Tables:
BP Shipping Marine Distance Tables

Printed & bound in Great Britain by:
Butler & Tanner Ltd
Frome and London

Every care has been taken to ensure the accuracy of this Atlas at the time of publication.
However, the publishers do not accept responsibility for errors or omissions or any
consequences arising therefrom.

British Library Cataloguing in Publication Data:
Lloyd's Maritime Atlas of world ports and shipping places — 18th ed.
    1. Harbours — maps
    912.13871   G1046.P55

ISBN 1 85978 004 0
ISSN 0076-020X

CONTENTS i

Geographic Index

Index to ports and shipping places by geographic sequence around the world, incorporating latitudes and longitudes and a code to facilities available at primary ports.

The Geographic Index is arranged in columns which are divided into four sections so that each entry may be quickly and easily located.

The appropriate map number, which refers to the most detailed map on which an entry is featured, is also provided.

PORT FACILITY INFORMATION

P Petroleum	**Q** Other Liquid Bulk	**Y** Dry Bulk
G General Cargo	**C** Containers	**R** Ro-Ro
B Bunkers	**D** Dry Dock	**T** Towage
A Airport (within 100 Km)	**L** Lloyd's Agent (not including sub-agents)	

Alphabetical Index

An alphabetical index of the world's ports and shipping places with references to relevant map page numbers and Geographic Index column number and section.

Lloyd's Book of Ports and Shipping Places
A geographical listing
of Ports and Shipping Places
of the World
with complete Index.
Edited by the Shipping Editor of Lloyd's.
Published by the Corporation of Lloyd's, London.

Published from July 1937
approximately every other year until 1950.

Lloyd's Maritime Atlas
A geographical listing
of Ports and Shipping Places of the World,
Alphabetical Index of all ports and places listed.
First edition published with maps.
Published by the Corporation of Lloyd's, London.

First Edition 1951
Second Edition 1953
Third Edition 1958
Fourth Edition 1961
Fifth Edition 1964
Sixth Edition 1966
Seventh Edition 1969
Eighth Edition 1971

Lloyd's Maritime Atlas
Published by Lloyd's of London Press Limited, Colchester.

Ninth Edition 1973
Tenth Edition 1975
Eleventh Edition 1977
Twelfth Edition 1979
Thirteenth Edition 1981
Fourteenth Edition 1983

Lloyd's Maritime Atlas of World Ports and Shipping Places.
Published by Lloyd's of London Press Limited, Colchester.

Fifteenth Edition 1987
Sixteenth Edition 1989
Seventeenth Edition 1993
Eighteenth Edition 1995

The first edition of *Lloyd's Maritime Atlas* was published in 1951 when maps were added to the *Lloyd's Book of Ports and Shipping Places*. A new edition has been published approximately every two years since then, ending before this with the Seventeenth edition in 1993.

In this, the Eighteenth edition, all the new country borders and the new country and port names are shown, although the final position of the former Yugoslavia has still to be established. New ports and terminals have been added as they have opened and an extensive revision of those parts of the world now re-opening to international traffic has been undertaken.

The port facilities for the major ports have all been revised and this provides the link to *Lloyd's Ports of the World*, where greater details on these ports may be found.

Each regional map features distance tables and those ports in bold type appear on the world table at the front. All have authoritative figures, in nautical miles, extracted from *BP Marine Distance Tables*.

The alphabetical index is cross indexed to both the geographic index and the maps. Alternative place names and spellings, along with recent renamings, are shown in both indices; however, the spelling of names usually conforms to the general practice in Lloyd's publications.

Once again, following this revision, Lloyd's Maritime Atlas maintains its position as the most comprehensive, accurate and up to date maritime atlas available anywhere, and continues to be the standard reference book for anyone in the shipping, insurance and related fields.

La première édition du *Lloyd's Maritime Atlas* (Atlas Maritime du Lloyd) parut en 1951 lorsque des cartes furent ajoutées au *Lloyd's Book of Ports and Shipping Places (Journal des Ports et des Lieux de Navigation du Lloyd)*. Une nouvelle édition est, depuis, parue à peu près tous les deux ans, la dernière en date étant la dix-septième édition de 1993.

La présente édition, qui est la dix-huitième, incorpore toutes les nouvelles frontières de pays et fait mention des nouveaux noms de pays et de ports, bien que l'emplacement définitif de l'ancienne Yougoslavie soit encore indéterminé. Des nouveaux ports et terminaux y ont été ajoutés au fur et à mesure de leur ouverture et une révision détaillée de ces parties du monde accueillant à nouveau le trafic international a été entreprise.

Tous les équipements des principaux ports ont été revus, ce qui a permis de donner naissance au *Lloyd's Ports of the World (Ports Mondiaux du Lloyd)*, qui renferme de plus amples détails sur ces ports.

Des tables de distances figurent sur chaque carte régionale et

les ports susmentionnés apparaissent en caractères gras dans la table mondiale donnée en première page. Toutes les cartes sont accompagnées de mesures officielles, indiquées en milles marins, extraites des *BP Marine Distance Tables (Tables des Distances Marines de la B.P.)*.

La table alphabétique fait référence à la fois à la table géographique et aux cartes. Les noms et orthographes de rechange de certains lieux ainsi que ceux récemment rebaptisés sont indiqués dans les deux tables; toutefois, l'orthographe adoptée pour ces noms est généralement celle utilisée dans les autres publications du Lloyd.

Une fois de plus, suite à cette édition revue et corrigée, le *Lloyd's Maritime Atlas* reste l'atlas maritime le plus complet, le plus exact et le plus récent disponible à l'heure actuelle ainsi que l'ouvrage de base de ceux appartenant aux secteurs de la navigation et des assurances et aux domaines qui s'y rattachent.

La primera edición del *Lloyd's Maritime Atlas* (el Atlas Marítimo de Lloyds) fue publicada en 1951, cuando se añadió una sección de mapas al *Lloyd's Book of Ports and Shipping Places (El Libro de Puertos y Sitios de Embarque, de Lloyds)*. Desde entonces, se ha publicado una edición nueva cada dos años, aproximadamente, y la última edición antes de esta ha sido la decimoséptima en 1993.

En esta, la decimoctavo edición, se indican todas las nuevas fronteras y los nombres de los países y de los puertos nuevos, aunque todavía no se han establecido los de que antes era la Yugoslavia. Cuando se han inaugurado, se han añadido los nuevos puertos y terminales, y se ha realizado una extensa revisión de esas partes del mundo donde se ha reiniciado el tráfico internacional.

Se han revisado también todas las facilidades de los puertos principales, vinculando el Atlas con el *Lloyd's Ports of the World, (Los Puertos del Mundo, de Lloyds)* en donde se pueden encontrar más detalles sobre estos puertos.

Cada plano regional incluye tablas de distancias y los puertos impresos en negrita aparecen en la tabla mundial en la parte delantera. Todos los planos contienen cifras autoritativas, en millas náuticas, obtenidas de las *BP Marine Distance Tables (Las Tablas BP de Distancias Marinas)*.

El índice alfabético tiene referencias cruzadas tanto con el índice geográfico como los planos. Ambos índices indican alternativas de nombres y de ortografía y los cambios recientes de nombre; sin embargo, la ortografía de los nombres generalmente conforma con la que se acostumbra en las publicaciones de Lloyds.

Seguido a esta revisión, *Lloyds Maritime Atlas* una vez más mantiene su posición como el atlas marítimo más exacto y actualizado disponible, y continúa siendo la obra de referencia estándar para cualquier persona o entidad en los sectores del transporte marítimo, los seguros y en los sectores asociados con ellos.

Distance (nautical miles) / **Voyage Time at 15 knots (days-hours)**

Region	Port	Mombasa	Algiers	Port Said	Dubai	Lagos	Cape Town	Bombay	Calcutta	Singapore	Hong Kong	Manila	Tokyo	Shanghai	Fremantle	Adelaide	Sydney	Hobart	Wellington
AFRICA & MIDDLE EAST	Mombasa		•4492	•2989	2413	5064	2509	2400	3701	3985	5441	5322	6885	6218	4564	5708	6505	6171	7409
	Algiers	12-11		1503	•4394	3506	5502	•4549	•6194	•6517	•7973	•7854	•9417	•8750	•7804	•9002	•9799	•9465	•10703
	Port Said	8-7	4-4		•2891	5007	•5346	•3046	•4691	•5014	•6470	•6351	•7914	•7247	•6301	•7499	•8296	•7962	•9200
	Dubai	6-17	12-5	8-1		7309	4754	1122	3107	3430	4886	4767	6330	5663	4976	6208	7005	6671	7909
	Lagos	14-2	9-18	13-22	20-7		2566	7154	8044	8166	9472	9246	10918	10254	7270	8361	9158	8824	9750
	Cape Town	6-23	15-7	14-20	13-5	7-3		4599	5489	5611	6917	6691	8363	7699	4715	5766	6563	6229	7467
ASIA	Bombay	6-16	12-15	8-11	3-3	19-21	12-19		2112	2435	3891	3772	5335	4668	3982	5220	6017	5683	6921
	Calcutta	10-7	17-5	13-1	8-15	22-8	15-6	5-21		1650	3106	2987	4550	3883	3684	4957	5754	5420	6658
	Singapore	11-2	18-2	13-22	9-13	22-16	15-14	6-18	4-14		1460	1341	2904	2237	2220	3504	4273	3967	5205
	Hong Kong	15-3	22-4	17-23	13-14	26-7	19-5	10-19	8-15	4-1		632	1596	845	3504	4799	4511	5128	5266
	Manila	14-19	21-20	17-15	13-6	25-16	18-14	10-13	8-7	3-17	1-18		1770	1128	2971	4266	3964	4581	4755
	Tokyo	19-3	26-4	22-0	17-14	30-8	23-6	14-20	12-15	8-2	4-10	4-22		1048	4500	5299	4343	4960	5041
	Shanghai	17-7	24-4	20-3	15-18	28-12	21-9	12-23	10-19	6-5	2-8	3-3	2-22		4037	5332	4632	5249	5358
AUSTRALASIA	Fremantle	12-16	21-16	17-12	13-20	20-5	13-2	11-1	10-6	6-4	9-18	8-6	12-12	11-5		1343	2140	1806	3044
	Adelaide	15-21	25-0	20-20	17-6	23-5	16-0	14-12	13-18	9-18	13-8	11-20	14-17	14-19	3-18		973	756	1884
	Sydney	18-2	27-5	23-1	19-11	25-11	18-6	16-17	16-0	11-21	12-13	11-0	12-2	12-21	5-23	2-17		638	1236
	Hobart	17-3	26-7	22-3	18-13	24-12	17-7	15-19	15-1	11-0	14-6	12-17	13-19	14-14	5-0	2-2	1-19		1293
	Wellington	20-14	29-18	25-13	21-23	27-2	20-18	19-5	18-12	14-11	14-15	13-5	14-0	14-21	8-11	5-6	3-10	3-14	
	Suva	22-16	30-19	26-18	22-10	29-7	22-20	19-16	17-17	13-4	12-12	11-5	11-0	12-10	10-13	7-7	4-20	6-2	4-2
SOUTH AMERICA	La Guaira	22-12	11-7	15-11	23-12	11-18	15-14	23-22	28-12	29-9	27-23	28-10	23-19	26-6	28-3	25-11	23-18	23-15	20-11
	Recife	16-2	9-20	14-0	22-1	6-20	9-5	21-22	24-9	24-17	28-8	27-17	30-7	30-12	22-5	25-6	25-2	24-14	21-17
	Buenos Aires	17-3	15-20	20-0	23-9	11-23	10-8	22-23	25-10	25-18	29-9	28-18	29-15	31-0	23-6	21-6	19-22	19-10	16-14
	Punta Arenas	18-15	18-20	23-0	24-21	14-10	11-20	24-10	26-22	26-8	26-22	25-13	25-18	27-3	20-8	17-9	16-1	15-14	12-17
	Valparaiso	22-14	20-13	24-17	28-20	18-9	15-19	28-10	31.21	27-18	28-9	26-22	25-20	28-4	21-18	18-19	17-11	16-23	14-2
	Callao	26-0	17-0	21-4	29-5	17-19	19-5	29-15	33-16	29-15	27-14	27-9	23-10	25-20	23-15	20-16	19-7	18-20	15-21
NORTH AMERICA	Montreal	22-11	9-23	14-4	22-4	14-6	19-18	22-15	27-4	28-2	32-3	31-19	30-9	32-19	31-16	32.0	30-7	30-4	27-0
	Halifax	21-4	8-16	12-20	20-21	12-13	18-1	21-8	25-21	26-19	30-20	30-12	27-21	30-7	30-9	29-13	27-19	27-17	24-13
	New York	22-13	10-1	14-5	22-6	13-13	18-21	22-16	27-6	28-4	31-3	31-14	26-23	29-9	31-7	28-15	26-22	26-19	23-15
	New Orleans	26-7	13-20	18-0	26-1	16-0	20-7	26-12	31-21	31-22	29-13	30-0	25-9	27-20	29-17	27-1	25-8	25-5	22-1
	San Francisco	31-12	22-7	26-11	29-23	23-3	26-23	27-4	25-0	20-10	16-19	17-7	12-16	15-0	23-15	20-10	17-22	19-6	16-10
	Vancouver	30-18	24-11	28-15	29-5	25-6	29-3	26-10	24-6	19-16	16-0	16-13	11-21	14-5	23-10	21-12	18-23	20-10	17-23
	Honolulu	27-9	26-7	30-6	25-20	27-3	29-12	23-2	20-22	16-8	13-10	13-6	9-11	12-17	18-2	14-20	12-7	13-17	11-10
CENTRAL AMERICA	Balboa	24-20	13-6	17-10	25-11	14-2	17-23	25-22	30-11	29-4	25-13	26-0	21-9	23-19	26-0	23-1	21-8	21-5	18-1
	Port of Spain	21-16	10-15	14-19	22-20	10-22	14-18	23-6	27-20	28-17	28-20	29-6	24-16	27-2	27-19	26-7	24-14	24-12	21-7
	Salina Cruz	28-2	16-13	20-17	28-17	17-8	21-5	29-4	30-14	26-0	22-10	22-21	18-6	20-16	25-4	21-23	19-20	20-9	16-20
	Tampico	27-3	14-15	18-19	26-20	16-17	20-20	27-6	31-20	32-18	29-18	30-4	25-14	28-0	29-22	27-6	25-12	25-10	22-6
	Kingston	24-8	12-0	16-4	24-5	13-9	17-11	24-15	29-5	30-3	27-5	27-15	23-1	25-11	27-9	24-16	22-23	22-21	19-16
EUROPE	London	17-7	4-19	9-0	17-0	11-11	17-0	17-11	22-0	22-22	26-23	26-15	30-23	29-3	26-12	29-19	32-1	31-2	31-9
	Rotterdam	17-10	4-22	9-2	17-3	11-14	17-3	17-13	22-3	23-1	27-2	26-18	31-2	29-5	26-14	29-22	32-3	31-5	31-11
	Hamburg	18-2	5-15	9-19	17-20	12-7	17-20	18-6	22-20	23-17	27-18	27-11	31-19	29-22	27-7	30-15	32-20	31-22	32-4
	Stockholm	20-2	7-15	11-19	19-20	14-7	19-20	20-6	24-20	25-17	29-18	29-11	33-19	31-22	29-7	32-15	34-20	33-22	33-14
	Marseilles	12-12	1-3	4-5	12-6	10-12	16-1	12-16	17-6	18-3	22-4	21-20	26-4	24-8	21-17	25-1	27-6	26-8	29-18
	Gibraltar	13-15	1-3	5-8	13-8	8-15	14-4	13-19	18-8	19-6	23-7	22-23	27-7	25-11	22-20	26-3	28-9	27-10	30-4
	Piraeus	9-23	2-23	1-16	9-16	12-17	16-12	10-3	14-16	15-14	19-15	19-7	23-15	21-19	19-4	22-11	24-17	23-18	27-5

× Via Kiel Canal   + Via Panama Canal
• Via Suez Canal

WORLD DISTANCE TABLES | V |

	Recife	Buenos Aires	Punta Arenas	Valparaiso	Callao	Montreal	Halifax	New York	New Orleans	San Francisco	Vancouver	Honolulu	Balboa	Port of Spain	Salina Cruz	Tampico	Kingston	London	Rotterdam	Hamburg	Stockholm	Marseilles	Gibraltar	Piraeus
					SOUTH AMERICA				**NORTH AMERICA**					**CENTRAL AMERICA**					**EUROPE**					
094	5794	6168	6706	8133	9361	•8082	•7616	•8108	•9472	•11337	11063	9858	+8942	•7793	+10115	•9759	8758	•6222	•6263	•6516	•7236	×4501	×4902	•3582
064	3540	5701	+6774	+7391	+6116	3592	3126	3618	4982	+8022	+8801	+9464	+4776	3823	+5949	5269	4325	1732	1773	2026	2746	410	412	1071
565	5041	7202	+8275	+8892	+7617	5093	4627	5119	6483	+9523	+10302	•10887	+6277	5324	+7450	6770	5826	3233	3274	3527	4247	1512	1913	593
456	7932	8413	8951	10378	•10508+	•7984	•7518	•8010	•9374	10782	10508	9303	•9168	•8215	•10341	•9661	•8717	•6124	•6165	•6418	•7138	×4403	×4804	•3484
230	2453	4304	5186	6613	+6412	5130	4512	4870	5754	+8318	+9097	+9760	+5072	3929	+6245	6018	4821	4130	4171	4424	5144	3784	3098	4575
617	3318	3718	4256	5683	6911	•7115	6489	6789	7306	+9710	10489	10626	+6464	5315	+7637	7498	6279	6122	6163	6416	7136	5780	5094	5939
611	7884	8258	8796	10223	+10663	•8139	•7673	•8165	•9529	9787	9513	8308	•9323	•8370	•10496	•9816	•8872	•6279	•6320	•6573	•7293	×4558	×4959	•3639
256	8774	9148	9686	11113	12115	•9784	•9318	•9810	•11174	9002	8728	7523	•10968	•10015	11008	•11461	•10517	•7924	•7965	•8218	•8938	•6203	•6604	•5284
579	8896	9270	9482	9988	10662	•10107	•9641	•10133	•11497	7356	7082	5877	10495	•10338	9362	•11784	•10840	•8247	•8288	•8541	•9261	•6526	•6927	•5607
069	10202	10576	9708	10214	9929	•11563	•11097	•11207	+10638	6044	5760	4837	9196	+10375	8070	+10708	+9790	•9703	•9744	•9997	•10717	•7982	•8383	•7063
228	9976	10350	9202	9689	9849	•11444	•10978	•11366	+10797	6223	5950	4769	9355	•10534	8229	+10867	+9949	•9584	•9625	•9878	•10598	•7863	•8264	•6944
572	10911	10666	9271	9294	8424	+10928	+10036	+9710	+9141	4559	4276	3402	7699	+8878	6569	+9211	+8293	•11147	•11188	•11441	•12161	•9426	•9827	•8507
444	10984	11163	9768	10134	9304	+11800	+10908	+10582	+10013	5398	5114	4572	8571	9750	7443	+10083	+9165	•10480	•10521	•10774	•11494	•8759	•9160	•7840
130	8000	8374	7321	7827	8501	•11394	•10928	+11268	+10699	8501	8428	6503	9357	+9999	9065	+10769	+9851	•9534	•9575	•9828	•10548	•7813	•8214	•6894
165	9091	7651	6256	6762	7436	+11521	+10629	+10303	+9734	7356	7745	5336	8292	+9471	7898	+9804	+8886	•10732	•10773	•11026	•11746	•9011	•9412	•8092
546	9027	7174	5779	6281	6944	+10902	+10010	+9684	+9115	6456	6822	4427	7673	+8852	7142	+9185	+8267	•11529	•11570	•11823	•12543	•9808	•10209	•8889
509	8848	6995	5603	6106	6780	+10865	+9973	+9647	+9078	6930	7346	4931	7636	+8815	7331	+9148	+8230	•11195	•11236	•11489	•12209	•9474	•9875	•8555
365	7818	5965	4570	5069	5717	+9721	+8829	+8503	+7934	5909	6459	4114	6492	+7671	6059	+8004	+7086	•11291	•11332	•11585	•12097	•10712	•10860	•9793
185	8617	6764	5369	5758	5980	+9541	+8649	+8323	+7754	4760	5187	2783	6312	+7491	5521	+7824	+6906	•11111	•11152	•11405	•11917	•11147	•10680	•10228
	2464	4535	+4810	+3488	+2213	2933	2058	1848	1838	+4119	+4898	+5561	+873	329	+2046	+1945	730	4193	4234	4487	5071	4342	3656	5133
20		2177	3248	4675	+4552	4269	3540	3670	4052	+6458	+7237	+7900	+3212	2063	+4385	4246	3027	4133	4174	4427	×4942	3818	3132	4609
14	6-1		1395	2822	4050	6440	5715	5845	6223	7596	8403	7765	+5383	4238	5868	6419	5198	6300	6341	6594	7314	5979	5293	6770
9	9-1	3-21		1427	2655	7515	6786	6916	7298	6201	7008	6370	3937	5309	4473	7492	+4531	7375	7416	+7669	8389	7052	6336	7843
17	13-0	7-20	3-23		1299	+5844	+4952	+4626	+4057	5146	5919	5917	2615	+3794	3247	+4127	+3209	+7414	+7455	+7708	+8220	+7669	+6983	+8460
4	12-15	11-6	7-9	3-15		+4569	+3677	+3351	+2782	3988	4767	5157	1340	+2519	2011	+2852	+1934	+6139	+6180	+6433	+6945	+6394	+5708	+7185
4	11-21	17-21	20-21	16-6	12-17		958	1516	3069	+6475	+7254	+7917	+3229	2895	+4402	3354	2690	3249	3290	3412	3889	3870	3184	4661
17	9-20	15-21	18-20	13-18	10-5	2-16		593	2148	+5583	+6362	+7025	+2337	2055	+3510	2438	1795	2741	2782	2975	3452	3404	2718	4195
3	10-5	16-6	19-5	12-20	9-7	4-5	1-16		1707	+5257	+6036	+6699	+2011	1932	+3184	1999	1472	3342	3303	3620	4097	3896	3210	4687
3	11-6	17-7	20-7	11-6	7-17	8-13	5-23	4-18		+4688	+5467	+6130	+1442	2065	+2615	733	1155	4813	4854	5064	5541	5260	4574	6051
11	17-23	21-2	17-5	14-7	11-2	18-0	15-12	14-14	13-1		816	2095	3246	+4425	2122	+4758	+3840	+8045	+8086	+8339	+8851	+8300	+7614	+9091
15	20-2	23-8	19-11	16-11	13-6	20-4	17-16	16-18	15-4	2-7		2423	4025	+5204	2920	+5537	+4619	+8824	+8865	+9118	+9630	+9079	+8393	+9870
11	21-23	21-14	17-17	16-10	14-8	22-0	19-12	18-15	17-1	5-20	6-18		4688	+5867	3578	+6200	+5282	+9487	+9528	+9781	+10293	+9742	9056	+10533
10	8-22	14-23	10-22	7-6	3-17	9-6	6-12	5-14	4-0	9-0	11-4	13-1		+1179	1173	+1512	+594	+4799	+4840	+5093	+5605	+5054	+4368	+5845
22	5-18	11-19	14-18	10-13	7-0	8-1	5-17	5-9	5-18	12-7	14-11	16-7	3-7		+2352	2220	999	4010	4051	4304	4928	4101	3415	4892
16	12-4	16-7	12-10	9-0	5-14	12-5	9-18	8-20	7-6	5-21	8-3	9-23	3-6	6-13		+2685	+1767	+5972	+6013	+6266	+6778	+6277	+5541	+7018
10	11-19	17-20	20-19	11-11	7-22	9-8	6-19	5-13	2-1	13-5	15-9	17-5	4-5	6-4	7-11		1263	5101	5142	5352	5829	5547	4861	6338
1	8-10	14-11	12-14	8-22	5-9	7-11	5-0	4-2	3-5	10-16	12-20	14-16	1-16	2-19	4-22	3-12		4271	4312	4565	5068	4603	3917	5394
16	11-12	17-12	20-12	20-14	17-1	9-1	7-15	9-7	13-9	22-8	24-12	26-8	13-8	11-3	16-14	14-4	11-21		187	428	×943	2010	1324	2801
18	11-14	17-15	20-14	20-17	17-4	9-3	7-17	9-10	13-12	22-11	24-15	26-11	13-11	11-6	16-17	14-7	11-23	0-12		305	×820	2051	1365	2842
11	12-7	18-8	21-8	21-10	17-21	9-11	8-6	10-1	14-2	23-4	25-8	27-4	14-4	11-23	17-10	14-21	12-16	1-5	0-20		×587	2304	1618	3095
2	13-17	20-8	23-7	22-20	19-7	10-19	9-14	11-9	15-9	24-14	26-18	28-14	15-14	13-17	18-20	16-5	14-2	2-15	2-7	1-16		3024	2338	3815
1	10-15	16-15	19-14	21-7	17-18	10-18	9-11	10-20	14-15	23-1	25-5	27-1	14-1	11-9	17-10	15-10	12-19	5-14	5-17	6-10	8-10		690	1065
4	8-17	14-17	17-16	19-10	15-21	8-20	7-13	8-22	12-17	21-4	23-8	25-4	12-3	9-12	15-9	13-12	10-21	3-16	3-19	4-12	6-12	1-22		1481
6	12-19	18-19	21-19	23-12	19-23	12-23	11-16	13-0	16-19	25-6	27-10	29-6	16-6	13-14	19-12	17-15	15-0	7-19	7-21	8-14	10-14	2-23	4-3	

LLOYD'S

MARITIME ATLAS

OF WORLD PORTS AND SHIPPING PLACES

SYMBOLS

·	Port
▼	Anchorage/Roadstead Port
▪	Offshore Terminal
□	Oil Field in Production
⊙	Gas Field in Production
——	Oil Pipeline
——	Gas Pipeline
♦	Pipeline Landfall
∗	Signal Station (Suez Canal)
®	Research Station (Antarctic)
◉	Capital City
•	Major City or Town

International Boundary	——
State/Province Boundary	----
Median Line	----
International Dateline	——
River	
Seasonal River	
Seasonal Lake	
Limit of Permanent Pack Ice	
Ice Shelf	
Canal	
Lock (Panama Canal)	
Dam/Barrage	
Area Covered by Inset	

LETTERING

Port, Major City or Town	Rotterdam	Birmingham
Capital City	LONDON	MOSCOW
Country	UNITED KINGDOM	
Dependency / Territory	Society Islands (FRANCE)	
State / Province	CALIFORNIA	
Ocean	ATLANTIC OCEAN	
Sea	Caribbean Sea	
River, Canal	Thames	Kiel Canal
Physical Feature	Land's End	Tierra del Fuego
Island	Jersey	

ABBREVIATIONS

loa	—	Length Overall
N/A	—	Not Applicable
Km	—	Kilometres
Nm	—	Nautical Miles
dwt	—	Deadweight Tonnage

GLOSSARY

Beam .... Overall vessel width.
Draught .... Vertical distance between a vessel's lowest point and adjacent sea level.
Air Draught................ Vertical distance between a vessel's highest point and adjacent sea level.
Seasonal Draught ..... Variations in draught according to season and geographical region.
Elevation .... Height above mean sea level.

Ports in **bold type** on regional distance tables are included on the World Distance Table. All distances are in Nautical Miles, except on Fact Panels where kilometres are also provided where relevant.

Scale varies between each individual map and is indicated on the appropriate scale bar.

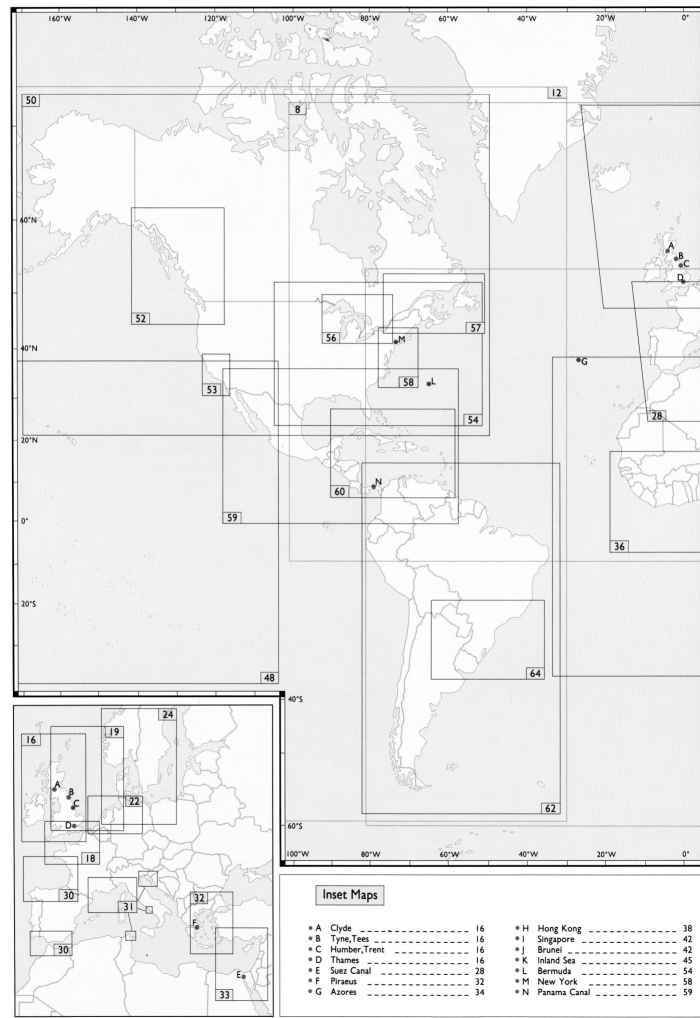

160°W	140°W	120°W	100°W	80°W	60°W	40°W	20°W	0°

50

8

12

60°N

A

B
C

D

52

57

56

40°N

M

G

58

L

53

28

54

20°N

59

N

36

0°

20°S

48

40°S

16

24

19

22

A
B
C

D

18

30

31

30

32

F

33

E

62

60°S

64

100°W	80°W	60°W	40°W	20°W	0°

Inset Maps

• A	Clyde	16		• H	Hong Kong	38
• B	Tyne, Tees	16		• I	Singapore	42
• C	Humber, Trent	16		• J	Brunei	42
• D	Thames	16		• K	Inland Sea	45
• E	Suez Canal	28		• L	Bermuda	54
• F	Piraeus	32		• M	New York	58
• G	Azores	34		• N	Panama Canal	59

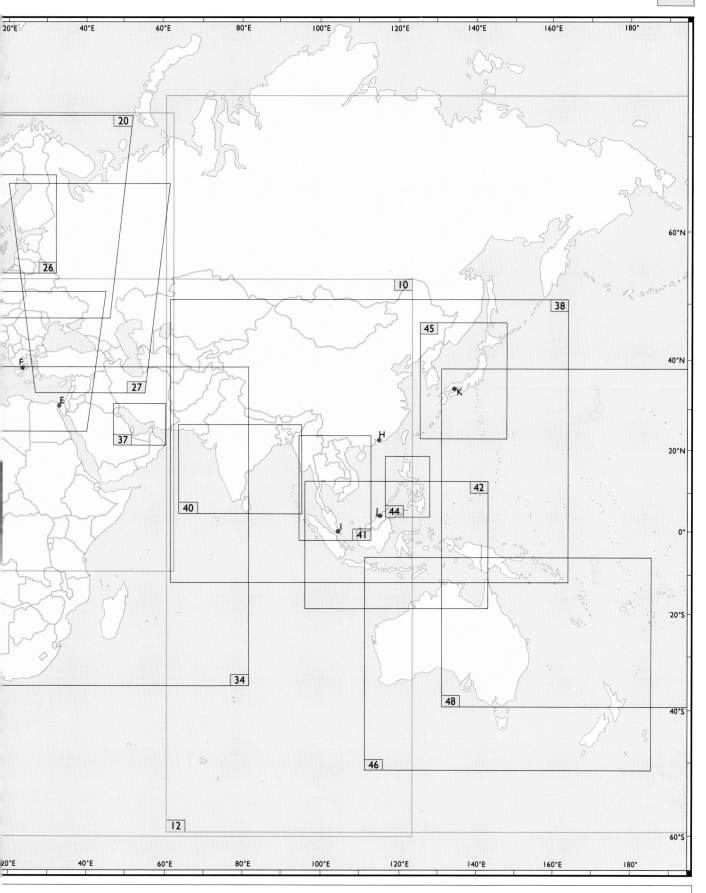

Fact Panels

World and Ocean Maps

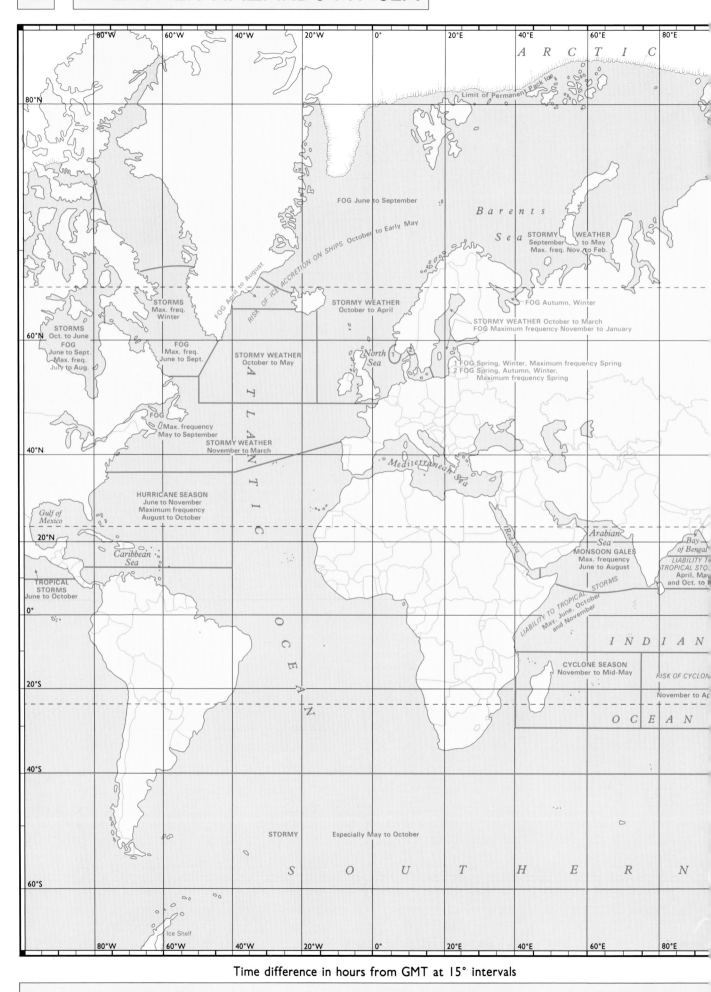

Time difference in hours from GMT at 15° intervals

| −6 | −5 | −4 | −3 | −2 | −1 | GMT | +1 | +2 | +3 | +4 | +5 | +6 |

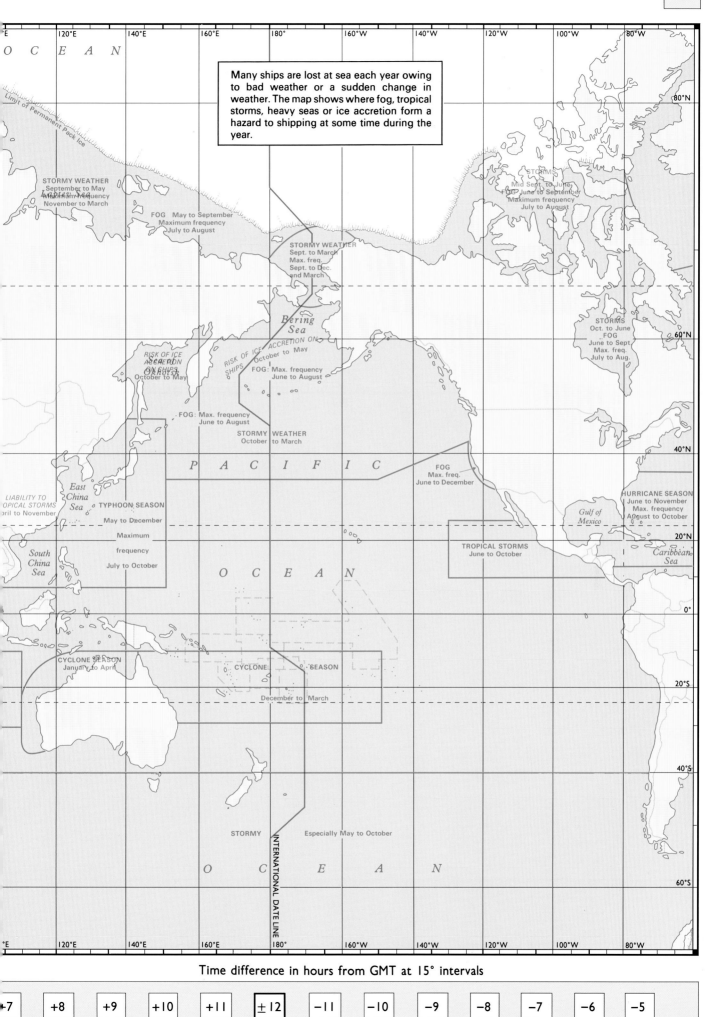

Many ships are lost at sea each year owing to bad weather or a sudden change in weather. The map shows where fog, tropical storms, heavy seas or ice accretion form a hazard to shipping at some time during the year.

Time difference in hours from GMT at 15° intervals

| +7 | +8 | +9 | +10 | +11 | ± 12 | −11 | −10 | −9 | −8 | −7 | −6 | −5 |

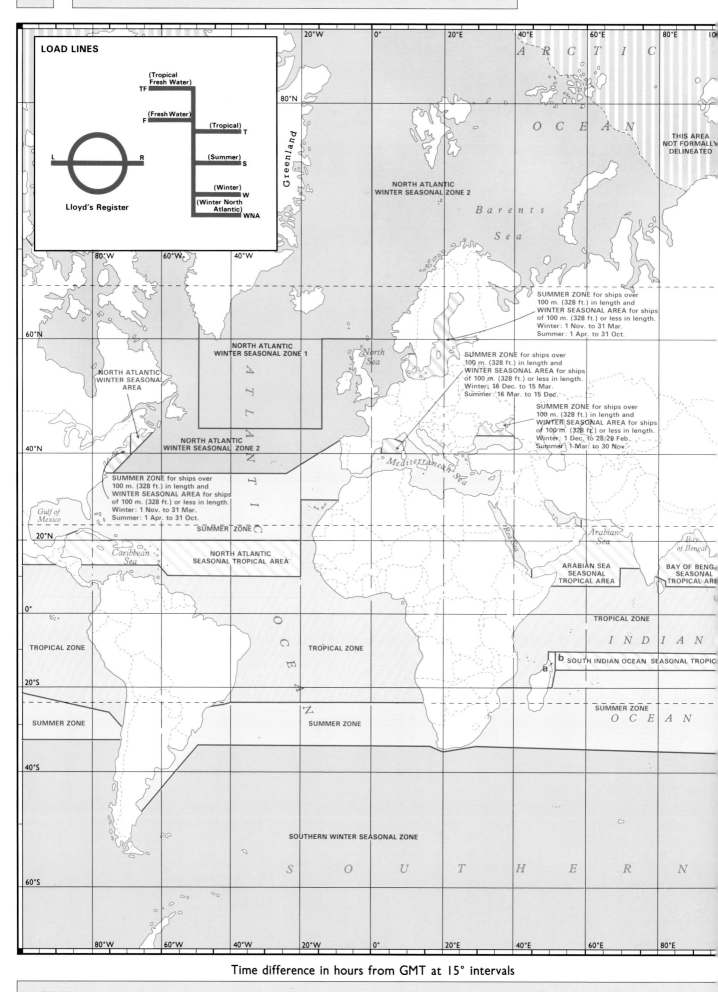

LOAD LINES

TF (Tropical Fresh Water)
F (Fresh Water)
T (Tropical)
S (Summer)
W (Winter)
WNA (Winter North Atlantic)

L | R

Lloyd's Register

Greenland

ARCTIC OCEAN

THIS AREA NOT FORMALLY DELINEATED

NORTH ATLANTIC WINTER SEASONAL ZONE 2

Barents Sea

North Sea

NORTH ATLANTIC WINTER SEASONAL ZONE 1

NORTH ATLANTIC WINTER SEASONAL AREA

SUMMER ZONE for ships over 100 m. (328 ft.) in length and WINTER SEASONAL AREA for ships of 100 m. (328 ft.) or less in length. Winter: 1 Nov. to 31 Mar. Summer: 1 Apr. to 31 Oct.

SUMMER ZONE for ships over 100 m. (328 ft.) in length and WINTER SEASONAL AREA for ships of 100 m. (328 ft.) or less in length. Winter: 16 Dec. to 15 Mar. Summer: 16 Mar. to 15 Dec.

SUMMER ZONE for ships over 100 m. (328 ft.) in length and WINTER SEASONAL AREA for ships of 100 m. (328 ft.) or less in length. Winter: 1 Dec. to 28/29 Feb. Summer: 1 Mar. to 30 Nov.

NORTH ATLANTIC WINTER SEASONAL ZONE 2

A T L A N T I C

Mediterranean Sea

Red Sea

Arabian Sea

Bay of Bengal

Gulf of Mexico

SUMMER ZONE for ships over 100 m. (328 ft.) in length and WINTER SEASONAL AREA for ships of 100 m. (328 ft.) or less in length. Winter: 1 Nov. to 31 Mar. Summer: 1 Apr. to 31 Oct.

SUMMER ZONE

Caribbean Sea

NORTH ATLANTIC SEASONAL TROPICAL AREA

ARABIAN SEA SEASONAL TROPICAL AREA

BAY OF BENG. SEASONAL TROPICAL AREA

TROPICAL ZONE

TROPICAL ZONE

TROPICAL ZONE

O C E A N

TROPICAL ZONE

I N D I A N

b SOUTH INDIAN OCEAN SEASONAL TROPIC

a

SUMMER ZONE

SUMMER ZONE

SUMMER ZONE

O C E A N

SOUTHERN WINTER SEASONAL ZONE

S O U T H E R N

Time difference in hours from GMT at 15° intervals

| −6 | −5 | −4 | −3 | −2 | −1 | GMT | +1 | +2 | +3 | +4 | +5 | +6 |

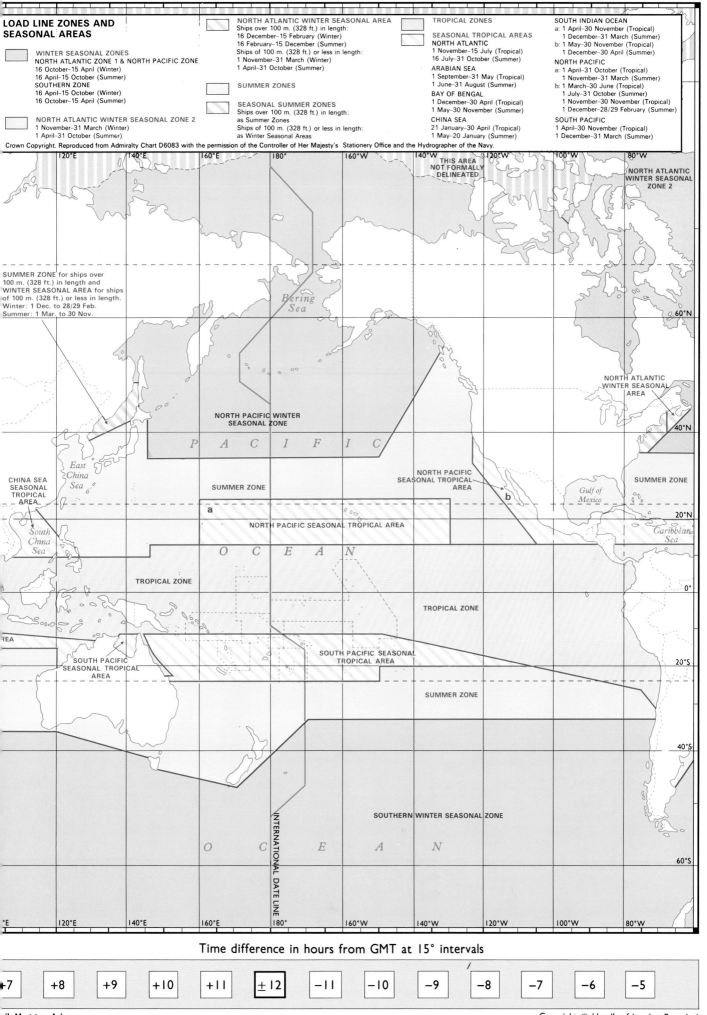

LOAD LINE ZONES AND SEASONAL AREAS

WINTER SEASONAL ZONES
NORTH ATLANTIC ZONE 1 & NORTH PACIFIC ZONE
16 October–15 April (Winter)
16 April–15 October (Summer)
SOUTHERN ZONE
16 April–15 October (Winter)
16 October–15 April (Summer)

NORTH ATLANTIC WINTER SEASONAL ZONE 2
1 November–31 March (Winter)
1 April–31 October (Summer)

NORTH ATLANTIC WINTER SEASONAL AREA
Ships over 100 m. (328 ft.) in length:
16 December–15 February (Winter)
16 February–15 December (Summer)
Ships of 100 m. (328 ft.) or less in length:
1 November–31 March (Winter)
1 April–31 October (Summer)

SUMMER ZONES

SEASONAL SUMMER ZONES
Ships over 100 m. (328 ft.) in length:
as Summer Zones
Ships of 100 m. (328 ft.) or less in length:
as Winter Seasonal Areas

TROPICAL ZONES

SEASONAL TROPICAL AREAS
NORTH ATLANTIC
1 November–15 July (Tropical)
16 July–31 October (Summer)
ARABIAN SEA
1 September–31 May (Tropical)
1 June–31 August (Summer)
BAY OF BENGAL
1 December–30 April (Tropical)
1 May–30 November (Summer)
CHINA SEA
21 January–30 April (Tropical)
1 May–20 January (Summer)

SOUTH INDIAN OCEAN
a: 1 April–30 November (Tropical)
   1 December–31 March (Summer)
b: 1 May–30 November (Tropical)
   1 December–30 April (Summer)
NORTH PACIFIC
a: 1 April–31 October (Tropical)
   1 November–31 March (Summer)
b: 1 March–30 June (Tropical)
   1 July–31 October (Summer)
   1 November–30 November (Tropical)
   1 December–28/29 February (Summer)
SOUTH PACIFIC
1 April–30 November (Tropical)
1 December–31 March (Summer)

Crown Copyright. Reproduced from Admiralty Chart D6083 with the permission of the Controller of Her Majesty's Stationery Office and the Hydrographer of the Navy.

SUMMER ZONE for ships over
100 m. (328 ft.) in length and
WINTER SEASONAL AREA for ships
of 100 m. (328 ft.) or less in length.
Winter: 1 Dec. to 28/29 Feb.
Summer: 1 Mar. to 30 Nov.

Bering Sea

THIS AREA
NOT FORMALLY
DELINEATED

NORTH ATLANTIC
WINTER SEASONAL
ZONE 2

NORTH PACIFIC WINTER
SEASONAL ZONE

NORTH ATLANTIC
WINTER SEASONAL
AREA

P A C I F I C

East China Sea

CHINA SEA
SEASONAL
TROPICAL
AREA

SUMMER ZONE

NORTH PACIFIC
SEASONAL TROPICAL
AREA

SUMMER ZONE

South China Sea

a

NORTH PACIFIC SEASONAL TROPICAL AREA

b

Gulf of Mexico

Caribbean Sea

O C E A N

TROPICAL ZONE

TROPICAL ZONE

SOUTH PACIFIC SEASONAL
TROPICAL AREA

SOUTH PACIFIC
SEASONAL TROPICAL
AREA

SUMMER ZONE

SOUTHERN WINTER SEASONAL ZONE

INTERNATIONAL DATE LINE

O C E A N

Time difference in hours from GMT at 15° intervals

| +7 | +8 | +9 | +10 | +11 | ±12 | −11 | −10 | −9 | −8 | −7 | −6 | −5 |

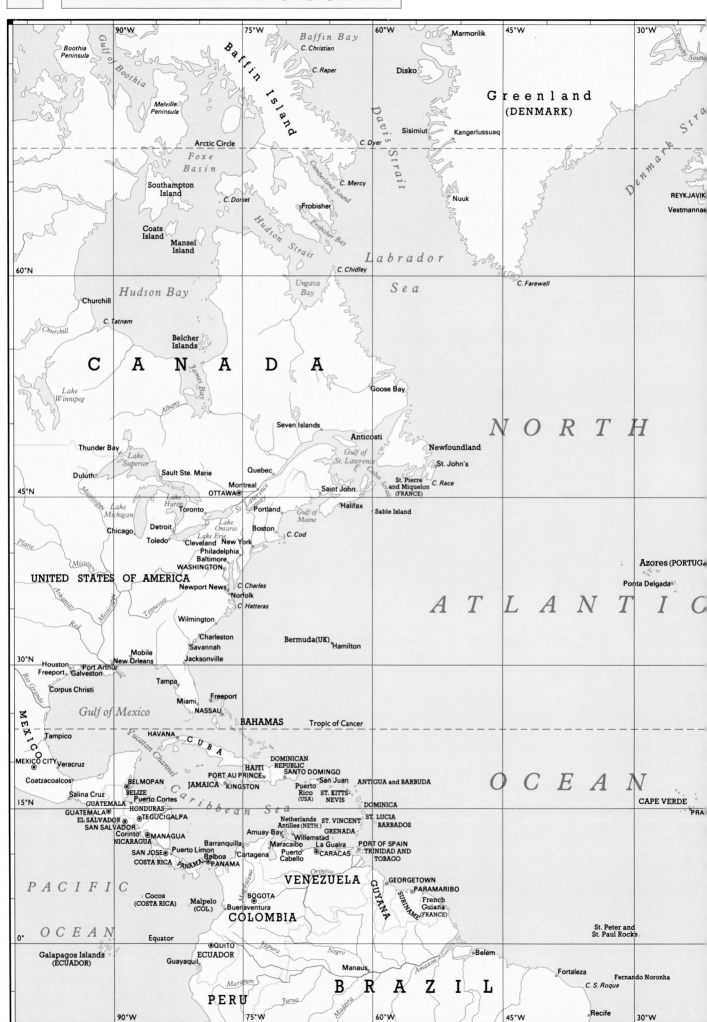

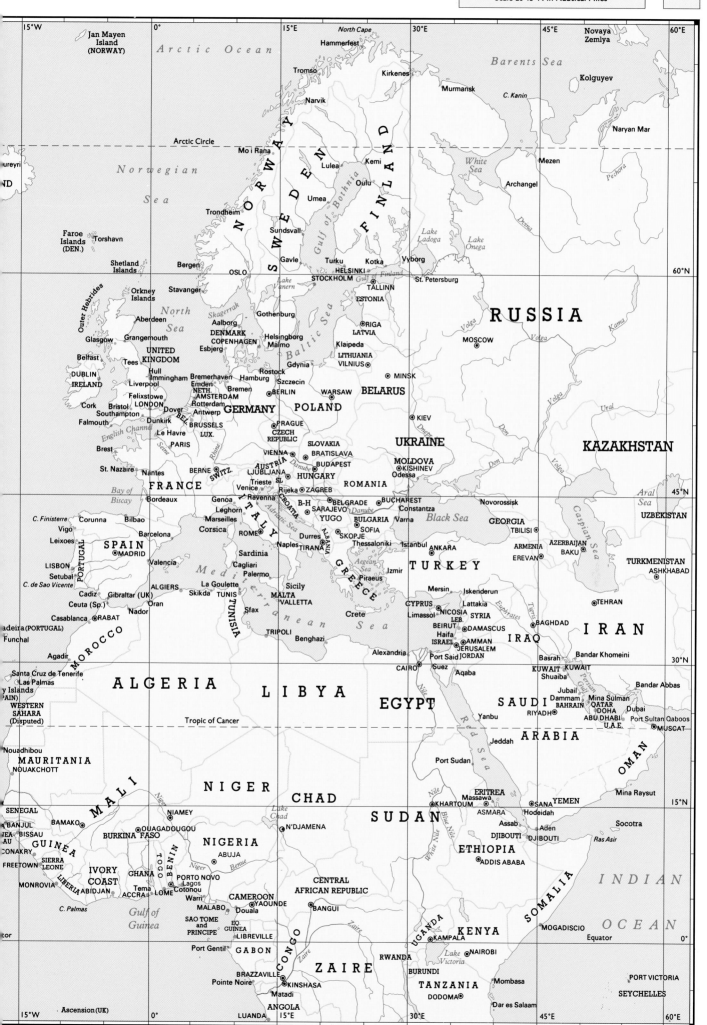

0   720
Scale at 45°N in Nautical Miles

15°W   0°   15°E   30°E   45°E   60°E

Jan Mayen
Island
(NORWAY)

Arctic Ocean

North Cape
Hammerfest

Tromso   Kirkenes

Barents Sea

Narvik   Murmansk   C. Kanin   Kolguyev

Naryan Mar

Arctic Circle

*Norwegian
Sea*

Mo i Rana   Lulea   Kemi   *White
Sea*   Mezen

ureyri   Trondheim   Umea   Oulu   Archangel

ND   Sundsvall

Faroe
Islands
(DEN.)   Torshavn   Bergen   Gavle   Turku   Kotka   Vyborg

Shetland
Islands   OSLO   HELSINKI   St. Petersburg   60°N
STOCKHOLM   *Gulf of Finland*

Orkney
Islands   Stavanger   *Lake
Vanern*   TALLINN   *Lake
Ladoga*   *Lake
Onega*

Outer Hebrides   Aberdeen   Gothenburg   ESTONIA   *Volga*

*North
Sea*   *Skagerrak*   Helsingborg   RIGA   RUSSIA

Glasgow   Grangemouth   Aalborg   LATVIA   MOSCOW
DENMARK   Malmo   Klaipeda
Belfast   COPENHAGEN   LITHUANIA   *Volga*   *Kama*
Tees   Esbjerg   Rostock   VILNIUS
UNITED   Hull   Hamburg   Gdynia   MINSK   KAZAKHSTAN
DUBLIN   KINGDOM   Immingham   Bremerhaven   Szczecin   WARSAW
IRELAND   Liverpool   NETH.   Bremen   BERLIN   BELARUS   *Volga*
Cork   Felixstowe   AMSTERDAM   POLAND   *Ural*
Bristol   LONDON   Rotterdam   GERMANY   KIEV
Southampton   Antwerp   PRAGUE   UKRAINE
Falmouth   Dunkirk   BEL.   CZECH   *Dnieper*
        Dover   BRUSSELS   REPUBLIC   *Don*
English Channel   Le Havre   LUX.   SLOVAKIA
Brest   PARIS   VIENNA   BRATISLAVA   MOLDOVA
        Seine   AUSTRIA   BUDAPEST   KISHINEV
St. Nazaire   Nantes   BERNE   SWITZ.   LJUBLJANA   HUNGARY   Odessa
        Rhine   SL.   *Danube*   ROMANIA   *Aral
Sea*
FRANCE   Trieste   Venice   CROATIA   ZAGREB   *Don*   UZBEKISTAN
        *Bay of
Biscay*   Bordeaux   Genoa   Ravenna   B-H   BELGRADE   BUCHAREST   Novorossisk   *Caspian
Sea*
C. Finisterre   Corunna   Bilbao   Leghorn   SARAJEVO   *Danube*   Constantza   GEORGIA
Vigo   Marseilles   YUGO   BULGARIA   Varna   *Black Sea*   TBILISI
Leixoes   Barcelona   Corsica   ROME   SOFIA   ARMENIA   AZERBAIJAN
SPAIN   Durres   SKOPJE   Thessaloniki   Istanbul   EREVAN   BAKU   TURKMENISTAN
LISBON   MADRID   Sardinia   Naples   ALBANIA   TIRANA   ANKARA   ASHKHABAD
Setubal   Valencia   Cagliari   Palermo   *Aegean
Sea*   Izmir   TURKEY   Mersin   Iskenderun
C. de Sao Vicente   PORTUGAL   Sicily   GREECE   Piraeus   TEHRAN
adeira (PORTUGAL)   Cadiz   Gibraltar (UK)   ALGIERS   La Goulette   MALTA   Crete   CYPRUS   Lattakia   SYRIA   BAGHDAD   IRAN
Funchal   Ceuta (Sp.)   Skidka   TUNIS   VALLETTA   Limassol   NICOSIA   BEIRUT   DAMASCUS
        Nador   Oran   TUNISIA   Sfax   *Mediterranean Sea*   LEB.   IRAQ
Casablanca   RABAT   TRIPOLI   Benghazi   Haifa   AMMAN   Basrah   Bandar Khomeini
Agadir   MOROCCO   ISRAEL   JERUSALEM   30°N
        Alexandria   Port Said   JORDAN   KUWAIT   KUWAIT
Santa Cruz de Tenerife   CAIRO   Suez   Aqaba   Shuaiba
Las Palmas   ALGERIA   LIBYA   EGYPT   SAUDI   Jubail   Dammam   Bandar Abbas
y Islands   Tropic of Cancer   *Nile*   Yanbu   RIYADH   BAHRAIN   Mina Sulman   Dubai
WESTERN   ARABIA   ABU DHABI   Port Sultan Qaboos
SAHARA   QATAR   DOHA   U.A.E.   MUSCAT
(Disputed)   *Red Sea*   Jeddah   Port Sudan   OMAN
Nouadhibou   MAURITANIA   MALI   NIGER   CHAD   ERITREA   Massawa   Mina Raysut
NOUAKCHOTT   *Lake
Chad*   SUDAN   KHARTOUM   SANA   YEMEN   Socotra
SENEGAL   NIAMEY   ASMARA   Assab   Ras Asir
BANJUL   BAMAKO   N'DJAMENA   Hodeidah
EA-BISSAU   OUAGADOUGOU   NIGERIA   *Blue Nile*   DJIBOUTI   DJIBOUTI
CONAKRY   BURKINA FASO   ABUJA   ETHIOPIA   Aden
GUINEA   *Niger*   *Benue*   ADDIS ABABA
FREETOWN   SIERRA   IVORY   GHANA   TOGO   BENIN   PORTO NOVO   CENTRAL
LEONE   COAST   Tema   Lagos   AFRICAN REPUBLIC
MONROVIA   LIBERIA   ABIDJAN   ACCRA   LOME   Cotonou   CAMEROON   BANGUI   UGANDA   Socotra
C. Palmas   *Gulf of
Guinea*   Warri   YAOUNDE   KENYA
        SAO TOME   MALABO   Douala   MOGADISCIO   *INDIAN*
        and   EQ. GUINEA   *Zaire*   KAMPALA   NAIROBI   *OCEAN*
        PRINCIPE   LIBREVILLE   *Lake
Victoria*   Equator   0°
tor   Port Gentil   GABON   *Congo*   RWANDA
        ZAIRE   BURUNDI   Mombasa   PORT VICTORIA
Ascension (UK)   BRAZZAVILLE   KINSHASA   TANZANIA   Dar es Salaam   SEYCHELLES
        Pointe Noire   DODOMA
        ANGOLA
15°W   0°   LUANDA   15°E   30°E   45°E   60°E

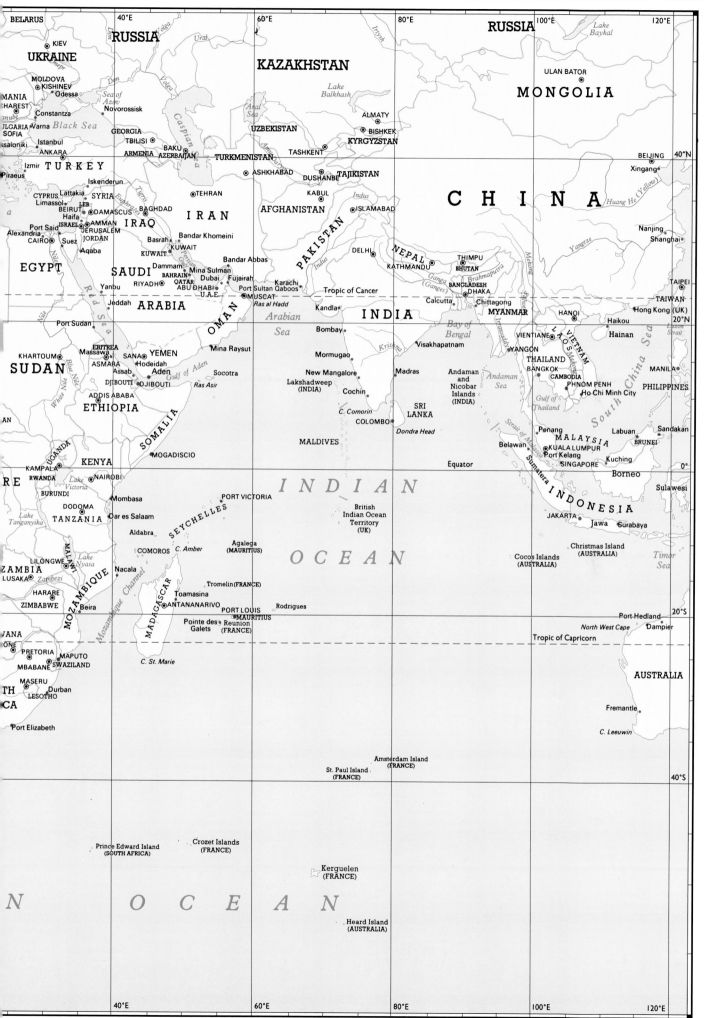

Scale at 0° in Nautical Miles
0   1200

11

BELARUS
40°E   60°E   80°E   RUSSIA   100°E   120°E
KIEV
UKRAINE   RUSSIA
Volga   KAZAKHSTAN
Ural   Irtysh   Lake
Baykal
MOLDOVA
KISHINEV
MANIA   Odessa   Lake   ULAN BATOR
HAREST   Novorossisk   Balkhash   MONGOLIA
Danube   Sea of
Azov   Aral   ALMATY
JLGARIA Varna   Black Sea   GEORGIA   Sea   BISHKEK   40°N
SOFIA   UZBEKISTAN   KYRGYZSTAN   BEIJING
ssaloniki Istanbul   TBILISI   Amu Darya   Xingang
ANKARA   ARMENIA BAKU   TASHKENT
Izmir TURKEY   AZERBAIJAN   TURKMENISTAN
Piraeus   ASHKHABAD   DUSHANBE TAJIKISTAN   CHINA
Iskenderun   TEHRAN   KABUL
CYPRUS Lattakia SYRIA   Euphrates   AFGHANISTAN   ISLAMABAD   Huang He (Yellow)
Limassol LEB.   DAMASCUS   Tigris   IRAN   Nanjing
BEIRUT   BAGHDAD   Indus   DELHI   Yangtze   Shanghai
Haifa   AMMAN   IRAQ   PAKISTAN   NEPAL   THIMPU
Alexandria ISRAEL JORDAN   Bandar Khomeini   KATHMANDU BHUTAN
Port Said JERUSALEM   BASRAH   Indus   BANGLADESH   TAIPEI
CAIRO Suez Aqaba   KUWAIT   Bandar Abbas   DHAKA   TAIWAN
EGYPT   KUWAIT   Dammam Mina Sulman   Karachi   Ganga   Calcutta   Chittagong   Hong Kong (UK)
SAUDI   BAHRAIN Dubai Fujairah   Port Sultan Qaboos   (Ganges)   MYANMAR   20°N
Yanbu   RIYADH QATAR ABU DHABI   Kandla   Tropic of Cancer   HANOI
ARABIA   U.A.E.   MUSCAT   INDIA   Haikou
Port Sudan   Jeddah   OMAN   Ras al Hadd   Arabian   Bombay   Bay of   VIENTIANE   Hainan
Sea   Sea   Bengal   YANGON   South China
ERITREA SANA   Mina Raysut   Mormugao   Visakhapatnam   VIETNAM   Sea
KHARTOUM   Massawa   YEMEN   THAILAND
ASMARA Hodeidah   Socotra   New Mangalore   Madras   Andaman   BANGKOK   MANILA
SUDAN   Aden   Ras Asir   Lakshadweep   Cochin   and   CAMBODIA
DJIBOUTI Assab   Gulf of Aden   (INDIA)   Nicobar   PHNOM PENH   PHILIPPINES
DJIBOUTI   C. Comorin   SRI   Islands   Ho Chi Minh City
ADDIS ABABA   LANKA   (INDIA)   Gulf of
ETHIOPIA   COLOMBO   Thailand   Penang   Labuan Sandakan
AN   SOMALIA   Dondra Head   MALAYSIA   BRUNEI
UGANDA   KENYA   MALDIVES   Strait of Malacca   KUALA LUMPUR   Kuching
KAMPALA   Equator   Belawan Port Kelang   0°
RWANDA Lake   MOGADISCIO   SINGAPORE   Borneo
RE BURUNDI Victoria NAIROBI   Sumatera INDONESIA   Sulawesi
DODOMA   Mombasa   PORT VICTORIA   INDIAN
Lake   SEYCHELLES   British   JAKARTA   Jawa Surabaya
ZAMBIA Tanganyika TANZANIA   Dar es Salaam   Indian Ocean
LUSAKA Zambezi   Aldabra   Territory   Christmas Island
COMOROS C. Amber   Agalega   (UK)   Cocos Islands   (AUSTRALIA)   Timor
ZAMBIA Lake   (MAURITIUS)   OCEAN   (AUSTRALIA)   Sea
LILONGWE Nyasa   Nacala   Tromelin(FRANCE)   Port-Hedland
HARARE MALAWI   Toamasina   PORT LOUIS   North West Cape Dampier
ZIMBABWE Beira   ANTANANARIVO MAURITIUS Rodrigues   Tropic of Capricorn   20°S
VANA   Pointe des Reunion
ONE   C. St. Marie   Galets (FRANCE)   AUSTRALIA
PRETORIA MAPUTO
MBABANE SWAZILAND
MASERU   Durban   Fremantle
LESOTHO
TH
CA   Port Elizabeth   C. Leeuwin
40°S
Amsterdam Island
(FRANCE)
St. Paul Island
(FRANCE)

N   O   C   E   A   N

Prince Edward Island   Crozet Islands
(SOUTH AFRICA)   (FRANCE)

Kerguelen
(FRANCE)

Heard Island
(AUSTRALIA)

40°E   60°E   80°E   100°E   120°E

Maritime Atlas   Copyright © Lloyd's of London Press Ltd.

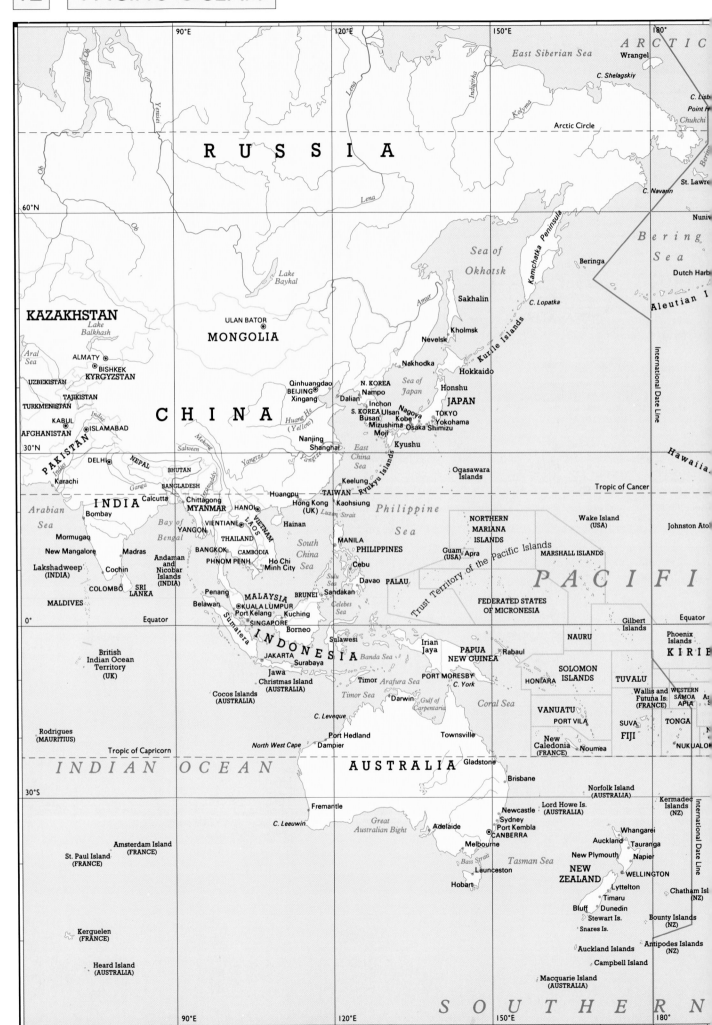

Scale at 20°N in Nautical Miles
0   1800

CEAN
Point Barrow
Beaufort Sea
C. Bathurst
Tuktoyaktuk
Amundsen Gulf
Banks Island
Victoria Island
Gulf of Boothia
Baffin Bay
Baffin Island
Greenland
(DENMARK)

Arctic Circle
Foxe Basin

ALASKA
Yukon
U.S.A.
Great Bear Lake
Southampton Island
Hudson Strait
Davis Strait

Anchorage
Valdez
Great Slave Lake
Labrador
C. Chidley
Ungava Bay
Sea
C. Farewell
60°N

Skagway
Peace
Hudson Bay
Nelson

Alaska Peninsula
Bristol Bay
Kodiak Island
Gulf of Alaska
C A N A D A

Prince Rupert
Athabasca
Saskatchewan

Queen Charlotte Islands
Lake Winnipeg
Lake Superior
Gulf of St. Lawrence
Newfoundland
St. John's

Vancouver Island
Vancouver
New Westminster
Nanaimo
Seattle
Tacoma
Duluth
Missouri
Lake Michigan
Lake Huron
Quebec
Saint John
Lake Ontario
Montreal
⊙OTTAWA
Boston
Halifax

Portland
Toronto Detroit
Lake Erie
New York
Philadelphia

Coos Bay
Chicago
Toledo
NORTH

UNITED STATES OF AMERICA
Ohio WASHINGTON
Baltimore

San Francisco
Oakland
Colorado
Norfolk
ATLANTIC

Los Angeles
Long Beach
Rio Grande
Wilmington
Charleston
Savannah
Bermuda (UK)

Houston
Mobile
Jacksonville
OCEAN

Guadalupe
Gulf de California
Galveston
New Orleans
Tampa
Miami
30°N

Gulf of Mexico
BAHAMAS
Tropic of Cancer

ds (USA)
nolulu
Hawaii
Mazatlan
MEXICO
Tampico
HAVANA
CUBA

MEXICO CITY⊙
Manzanillo
Coatzacoalcos
HAITI
DOMINICAN REPUBLIC

Revillagigedo Islands
Salina Cruz
BELIZE
JAMAICA
KINGSTON
San Juan
Lesser Antilles

OCEAN
GUATEMALA
HONDURAS
Caribbean Sea

Clipperton (FRANCE)
EL SALVADOR
Corinto
NICARAGUA
Barranquilla
Maracaibo
La Guaira

COSTA RICA
Balboa
⊙CARACAS
Orinoco

Cocos (COSTA RICA)
PANAMA
VENEZUELA
GEORGETOWN
PARAMARIBO
French Guiana (FRANCE)

Buenaventura
Malpelo (COLOMBIA)
BOGOTA⊙
GUYANA
SURINAME

Galapagos Islands (ECUADOR)
COLOMBIA
Amazon
Equator
0°

Guayaquil
QUITO⊙
ECUADOR
Amazon (Solimoes)
Manaus
Belem

Line Islands
C. S. Roque
Recife

Marquesas Islands
PERU
⊙LIMA
BRAZIL

Society Islands
Callao
Salvador

Papeete
Tuamotu Archipelago
LA PAZ⊙
⊙BRASILIA

ok
nds
Z)
French Polynesia
(FRANCE)
BOLIVIA
Vitoria
C. de Sao Tome

Australes Islands
Pitcairn Islands (UK)
Tropic of Capricorn
PARAGUAY
Rio de Janeiro
Santos

Easter Island (CHILE)
Sala y Gomez (CHILE)
San Felix Is.
Antofagasta
San Ambrosio Is. (CHILE)
ASUNCION
Paranagua

30°S

Valparaiso
Rosario
URUGUAY
Rio Grande

Juan Fernandez Islands (CHILE)
⊙SANTIAGO
BUENOS AIRES⊙
MONTEVIDEO
River Plate

CHILE
ARGENTINA
Bahia Blanca
SOUTH

ATLANTIC

OCEAN

Punta Arenas
Tierra del Fuego
Falkland Islands (UK)
South Georgia (UK)

C. Horn
Drake Passage

150°W
120°W
90°W
60°W

OCEAN

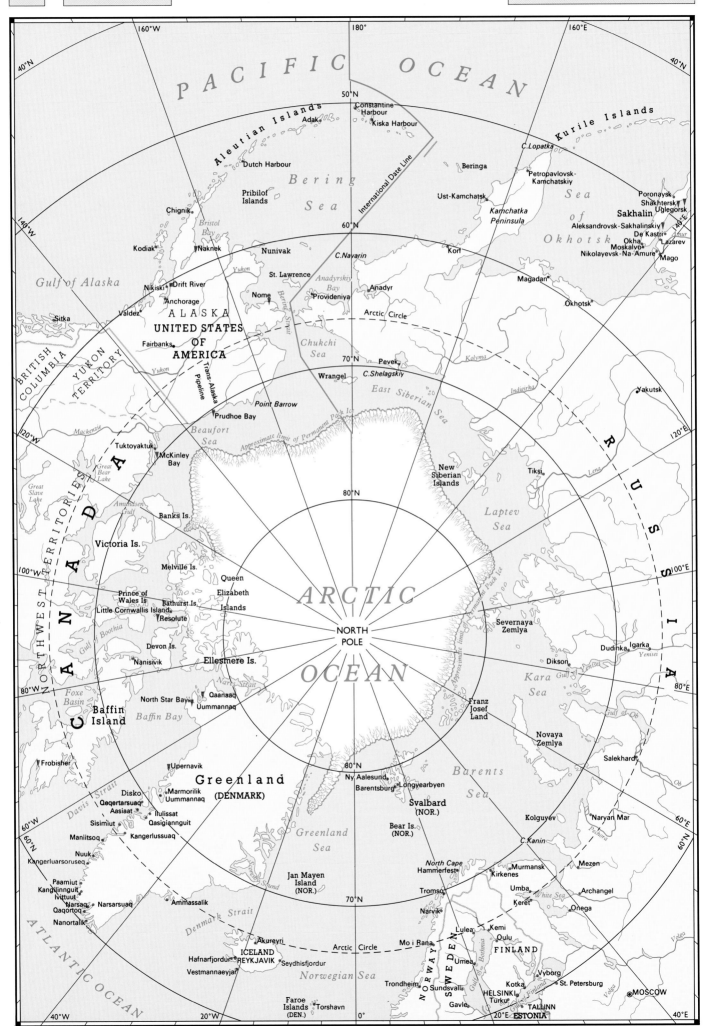

0   720
Scale at 70°N in Nautical Miles

PACIFIC OCEAN

40°N

50°N

160°W   180°   160°E

Aleutian Islands

Kurile Islands

Constantine Harbour
Adak
Kiska Harbour

Dutch Harbour

Beringa

C.Lopatka

Petropavlovsk-Kamchatskiy

Poronaysk
Shakhtersk
Uglegorsk

Bering Sea

International Date Line

Ust-Kamchatsk

Sea of Okhotsk

Sakhalin

Pribilof Islands

60°N

Aleksandrovsk-Sakhalinskiy
De Kastri

Chignik

Bristol Bay

Naknek

Nunivak

C.Navarin

Kamchatka Peninsula

Korf

Okha
Moskalvo
Lazarev

Kodiak

St. Lawrence

Nikolayevsk-Na-Amure
Mago

Gulf of Alaska

Yukon

Nome

Anadyrskiy Bay

Providenlya

Anadyr

Magadan

140°E

Nikiski
Drift River

Bering Strait

Okhotsk

Anchorage

Valdez

Sitka

ALASKA
UNITED STATES OF AMERICA

Arctic Circle

Chukchi Sea

Kolyma

140°W

Fairbanks

70°N

Pevek

C.Shelagskiy

Yakutsk

YUKON TERRITORY

Yukon

Trans-Alaska Pipeline

Wrangel

East Siberian Sea

Indigirka

BRITISH COLUMBIA

Point Barrow

Approximate limit of Permanent Pack Ice

120°E

Prudhoe Bay

Beaufort Sea

RUSSIA

Mackenzie

120°W

Tuktoyaktuk

McKinley Bay

New Siberian Islands

Tiksi

Lena

Great Bear Lake

NORTHWEST TERRITORIES

Banks Is.

80°N

Laptev Sea

Great Slave Lake

Amundsen Gulf

Victoria Is.

100°E

Melville Is.

Queen
Elizabeth
Islands

CANADA

Prince of Wales Is
Bathurst Is.
Little Cornwallis Island
Resolute

ARCTIC

Severnaya Zemlya

100°W

Gulf of Boothia

Devon Is.

NORTH POLE

Dudinka Igarka

Nanisivik

Ellesmere Is.

OCEAN

Dikson

Yenisei

Kara Sea

80°E

Nares Strait

Franz Josef Land

Gulf of Ob

Foxe Basin

80°W

North Star Bay
Qaanaaq
Uummannaq

Baffin Bay

Novaya Zemlya

Frobisher

Baffin Island

Salekhard

Upernavik

Greenland
(DENMARK)

Ny Aalesund
Barentsburg

Longyearbyen

Barents Sea

Kolguyev

Naryan Mar

60°E

Disko

Davis Strait

Marmorilik
Uummannaq

Svalbard
(NOR.)

C.Kanin

Qeqertarsuaq
Aasiaat
Ilulissat
Qasigianguit

Bear Is.
(NOR.)

Mezen

Sisimiut

Kangerlussuaq

60°W

Maniitsoq

60°N

Greenland Sea

North Cape
Hammerfest

Murmansk

Archangel

Kangerluarsoruseq

Nuuk

Kirkenes

Umba
Keret

White Sea

Onega

Paamiut
Kangilinnguit
Ivittuut
Narsaq
Qaqortoq
Narsarsuaq

Ammassalik

Jan Mayen Island
(NOR.)

70°N

Tromsø

Pechora

40°E

Nanortalik

Narvik

NORWAY

ATLANTIC OCEAN

Denmark Strait

Akureyri

Arctic Circle

Mo i Rana

Luleå
Kemi
Oulu

FINLAND

Volga

Hafnarfjordur
ICELAND
REYKJAVIK
Vestmannaeyjar

Seydhisfjordur

Norwegian Sea

SWEDEN

Umeå

Gulf of Bothnia

Trondheim
Sundsvall

Vyborg
St. Petersburg

Gavle

HELSINKI
Turku

MOSCOW

40°W   20°W   0°   20°E   40°E

Faroe Islands
(DEN.)
Torshavn

Kotka
TALLINN
ESTONIA

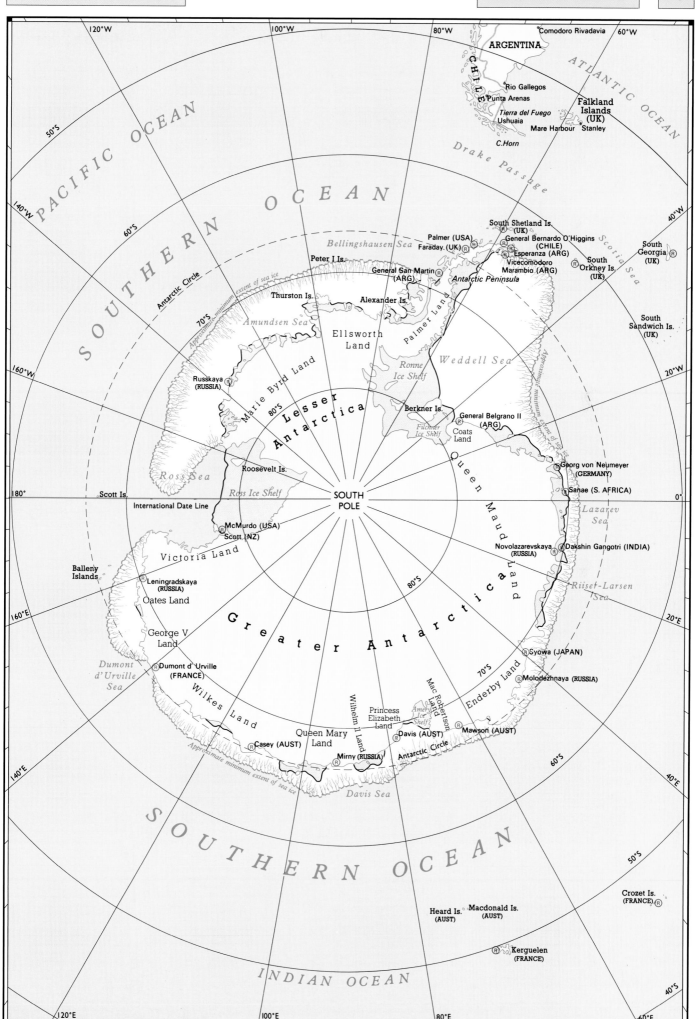

0 ——— 720
Scale at 60°S in Nautical Miles

ARGENTINA

Comodoro Rivadavia

ATLANTIC OCEAN

CHILE

Rio Gallegos
Punta Arenas
Tierra del Fuego
Ushuaia

Falkland
Islands
(UK)
Mare Harbour Stanley

C. Horn

Drake Passage

PACIFIC OCEAN

SOUTHERN   OCEAN

50°S
60°S
Antarctic Circle

Bellingshausen Sea

South Shetland Is.
(UK)
Palmer (USA)
Faraday. (UK)
General Bernardo O'Higgins
(CHILE)
Esperanza (ARG)
Vicecomodoro
Marambio (ARG)
Antarctic Peninsula

South
Georgia
(UK)

South
Orkney Is.
(UK)

Scotia Sea

South
Sandwich Is.
(UK)

Peter I Is.
General San Martin
(ARG)

Thurston Is.

Alexander Is.

Palmer Land

Amundsen Sea

Ellsworth
Land

Weddell Sea

Ronne
Ice Shelf

Russkaya
(RUSSIA)

Marie Byrd Land

Lesser
Antarctica

Berkner Is.

Filchner
Ice Shelf

Coats
Land

General Belgrano II
(ARG)

Queen Maud Land

Georg von Neumeyer
(GERMANY)

Sanae (S. AFRICA)

Roosevelt Is.

Ross Sea

Ross Ice Shelf

SOUTH
POLE

Lazarev
Sea

Scott Is.

International Date Line

McMurdo (USA)
Scott (NZ)

Victoria Land

Novolazarevskaya
(RUSSIA)

Dakshin Gangotri (INDIA)

Balleny
Islands

Leningradskaya
(RUSSIA)

Oates Land

Riiser-Larsen
Sea

George V
Land

Greater Antarctica

Syowa (JAPAN)

Molodezhnaya (RUSSIA)

Enderby Land

Dumont
d'Urville
Sea

Dumont d' Urville
(FRANCE)

Wilkes Land

Wilhelm II Land

Mac Robertson Land

Amery
Ice Shelf

Princess
Elizabeth
Land

Davis (AUST)

Mawson (AUST)

Queen Mary
Land

Casey (AUST)

Mirny (RUSSIA)

Antarctic Circle

Approximate minimum extent of sea ice

Davis Sea

SOUTHERN   OCEAN

Crozet Is.
(FRANCE)

Heard Is.
(AUST)

Macdonald Is.
(AUST)

Kerguelen
(FRANCE)

INDIAN OCEAN

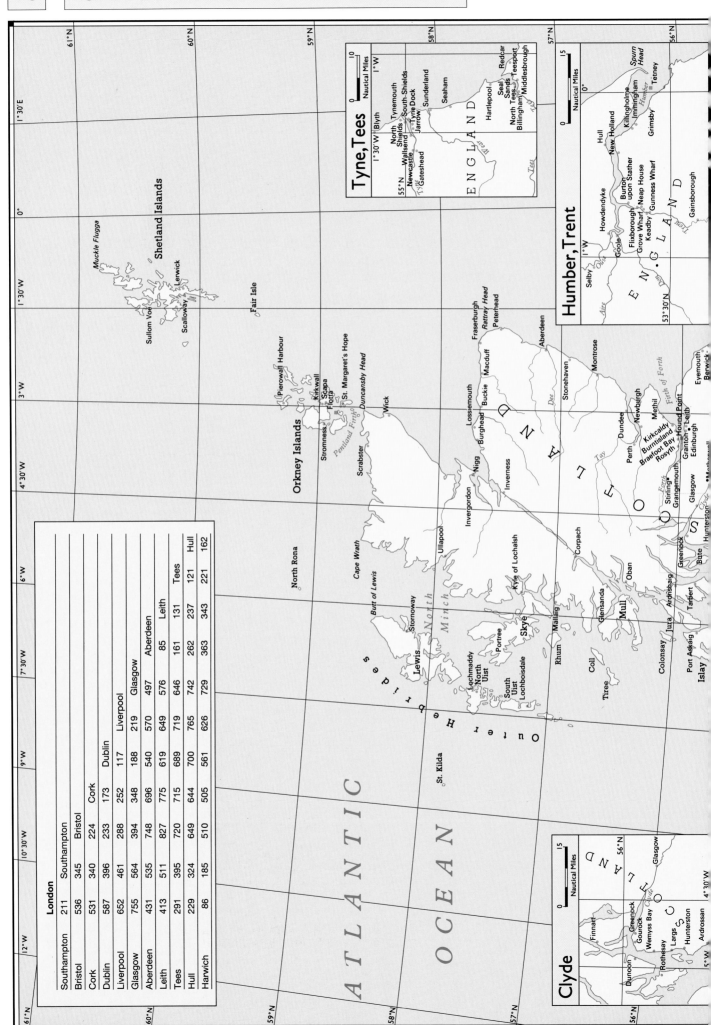

London

	London	Southampton	Bristol	Cork	Dublin	Liverpool	Glasgow	Aberdeen	Leith	Tees	Hull
Southampton	211										
Bristol	536	345									
Cork	531	340	224								
Dublin	587	396	233	173							
Liverpool	652	461	288	252	117						
Glasgow	755	564	394	348	188	219					
Aberdeen	431	535	748	696	540	570	497				
Leith	413	511	827	775	619	649	576	85			
Tees	291	395	720	715	689	719	646	161	131		
Hull	229	324	649	644	700	765	742	262	237	121	
Harwich	86	185	510	505	561	626	729	363	343	221	162

Tyne, Tees

Nautical Miles

North Tynemouth
Blyth
Wallsend · North · South Shields
Newcastle · Shields
Gateshead · Jarrow · Tyne Dock
Sunderland
Seaham
Hartlepool
Seal · Redcar
Sands
North Tees · Teesport
Billingham · Middlesbrough

ENGLAND

Wear

Tees

Humber, Trent

Spurn
Head
Killingholme
Immingham · Tetney
Hull · Grimsby
New Holland

Selby
Goole
Howdendyke
Burton
upon Stather
Flixborough · Neap House
Grove Wharf
Keadby · Gunness Wharf
Gainsborough

ENGLAND

Ouse
Trent
Aire

Clyde

Nautical Miles

Finnart
Greenock
Gourock · Glasgow
Wemyss Bay
Rothesay · Largs
Hunterston
Ardrossan

SCOTLAND

Muckle Flugga

Shetland Islands

Sullom Voe
Lerwick
Scalloway

Fair Isle

Pierowall Harbour
Kirkwall
Orkney Islands
Stromness · Scapa · Flotta
St. Margaret's Hope
Pentland Firth · *Duncansby Head*
Scrabster
Wick

Fraserburgh
Rattray Head
Peterhead
Lossiemouth
Buckie · Macduff
Burghead
Aberdeen

Nigg

S C O T L A N D

Dee
Stonehaven
Montrose

Invergordon
Inverness

Ullapool

Tay
Newburgh
Perth
Dundee
Kirkcaldy
Braefoot Bay
Burntisland · Hound Point
Rosyth
Firth of Forth
Granton · Leith
Stirling · Edinburgh
Grangemouth
Eyemouth
Berwick

Cape Wrath

Kyle of Lochalsh

Corpach

North Rona

Butt of Lewis

Stornoway
Lewis

N o r t h   M i n c h

Portree
Skye
Maliaig

Mallaig
Rhum
Coll
Tiree
Mull
Oban

Glensanda

Co11
Colonsay
Jura
Port Askaig
Islay

Greenock
Bute
Hunterston
Tarbert
Ardrishaig

Lochmaddy
North
Uist
South
Uist
Lochboisdale

O u t e r   H e b r i d e s

St. Kilda

A T L A N T I C

O C E A N

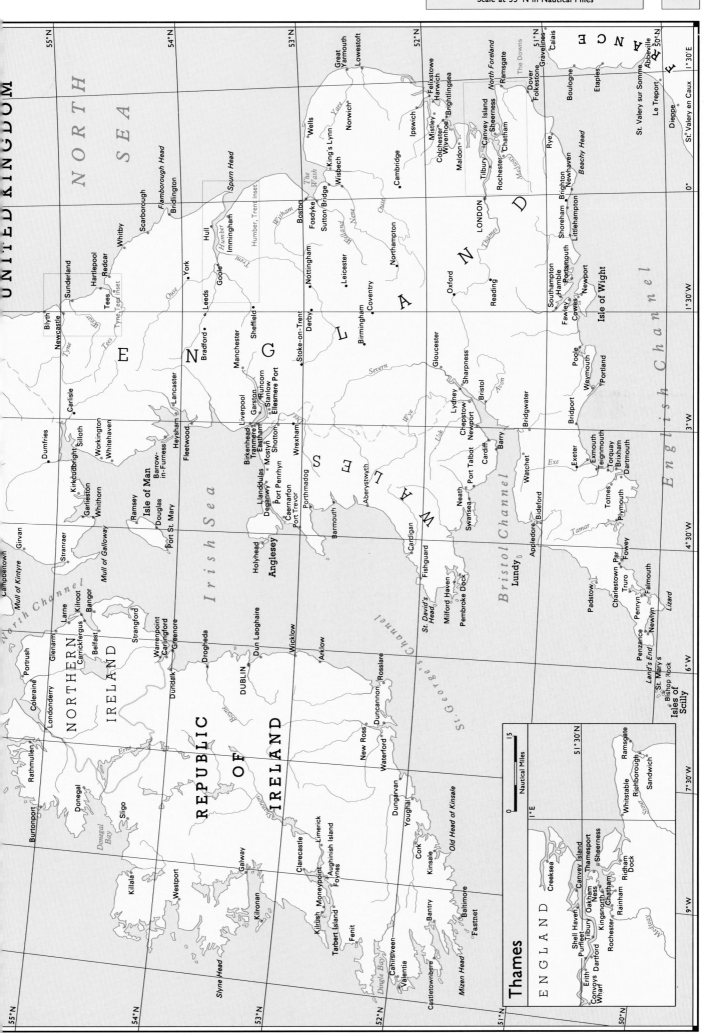

0   90
Scale at 55°N in Nautical Miles

UNITED KINGDOM

NORTH SEA

ENGLAND

WALES

NORTHERN IRELAND

REPUBLIC OF IRELAND

Irish Sea

North Channel

St. George's Channel

Bristol Channel

English Channel

55°N   54°N   53°N   52°N   51°N   50°N

55°N
54°N
53°N
52°N

1°30'W   0°   1°30'E

3°W   4°30'W   6°W   7°30'W   9°W

Thames

ENGLAND

0   15
Nautical Miles

51°30'N
51°N
50°N

7°30'W   9°W

Creeksea
Canvey Island
Thamesport
Ridham Dock
Sheerness
Chatham
Rochester
Kingsnorth
Oakham Ness
Tilbury
Purfleet
Dartford
Erith
Convoys Wharf
Shell Haven
Rainham

Whitstable
Richborough
Sandwich
Ramsgate

Campbeltown
Mull of Kintyre
Girvan
Stranraer
Mull of Galloway
Portrush
Coleraine
Londonderry
Portstewart
Rathmullen
Burtonport
Donegal
Donegal Bay
Killala
Westport
Sligo
Glenarm
Larne
Carrickfergus
Belfast
Bangor
Kilroot
Strangford
Warrenpoint
Carlingford
Greenore
Dundalk
Drogheda
Dublin
Dun Laoghaire
Wicklow
Arklow
Rosslare
Duncannon
Wexford
New Ross
Waterford
Youghal
Dungarvan
Cork
Kinsale
Old Head of Kinsale
Baltimore
Fastnet
Fenit
Aughinish Island
Foynes
Limerick
Clarecastle
Kilrush
Moneypoint
Tarbert Island
Kilronan
Galway
Bantry
Castletownbere
Kingsnorth
Cahirsiveen
Valentia
Mizen Head
Dingle Bay
Slyne Head

Girvan
Stranraer
Dumfries
Kirkcudbright
Silloth
Workington
Whitehaven
Carlisle
Newcastle
Blyth
Sunderland
Hartlepool
Redcar
Tees
Tyne
Wear
Tyne, Tees inset
Whitby
Scarborough
Flamborough Head
Bridlington
Spurn Head
Hull
Immingham
Goole
Leeds
York
Bradford
Manchester
Liverpool
Birkenhead
Tranmere
Garston
Runcorn
Stanlow
Eastham
Ellesmere Port
Mostyn
Shotton
Wrexham
Sheffield
Stoke-on-Trent
Derby
Nottingham
Leicester
Coventry
Birmingham
Gloucester
Sharpness
Lydney
Chepstow
Newport
Cardiff
Barry
Port Talbot
Neath
Swansea
Llanelli
Carmarthen
Milford Haven
Pembroke Dock
St. David's Head
Fishguard
Cardigan
Aberystwyth
Barmouth
Porthmadog
Port Trevor
Caernarfon
Anglesey
Holyhead
Llanddulas
Deganwy
Port Penrhyn
Heysham
Fleetwood
Lancaster
Barrow-in-Furness
Isle of Man
Douglas
Ramsey
Port St. Mary
Preston

Boston
Fosdyke
Sutton Bridge
Wisbech
King's Lynn
The Wash
Wells
Great Yarmouth
Lowestoft
Norwich
Ipswich
Cambridge
Northampton
Reading
Oxford
Felixstowe
Harwich
Mistley
Colchester
Wivenhoe
Brightlingsea
Maldon
Tilbury
Canvey Island
Sheerness
Chatham
Rochester
LONDON
Medway
Thames
North Foreland
Ramsgate
The Downs
Dover
Folkestone
Gravelines
Calais
Boulogne
Etaples
Le Treport
St. Valery sur Somme
Abbeville
St. Valery en Caux
Dieppe
Rye
Beachy Head
Brighton
Newhaven
Shoreham
Littlehampton
Southampton
Hamble
Fawley
Cowes
Portsmouth
Newport
Isle of Wight
Poole
Weymouth
Portland
Bridport
Exmouth
Exeter
Teignmouth
Torquay
Brixham
Dartmouth
Totnes
Plymouth
Fowey
Charlestown
Par
Truro
Newlyn
Penzance
Penryn
Falmouth
Land's End
St. Mary's
Bishop Rock
Isles of Scilly
Lizard
Padstow
Appledore
Bideford
Barnstaple
Watchet
Bridgwater
Lundy

FRANCE

51°N
50°30'N

1°30'E

Severn
Avon
Wye
Usk
Trent
Ouse
Witham
Welland
Nene
Yare
Exe
Tamar

Humber, Trent inset

Lloyd's Maritime Atlas

Copyright © Lloyd's of London Press Ltd.

0   90

Scale at 49°N in Nautical Miles

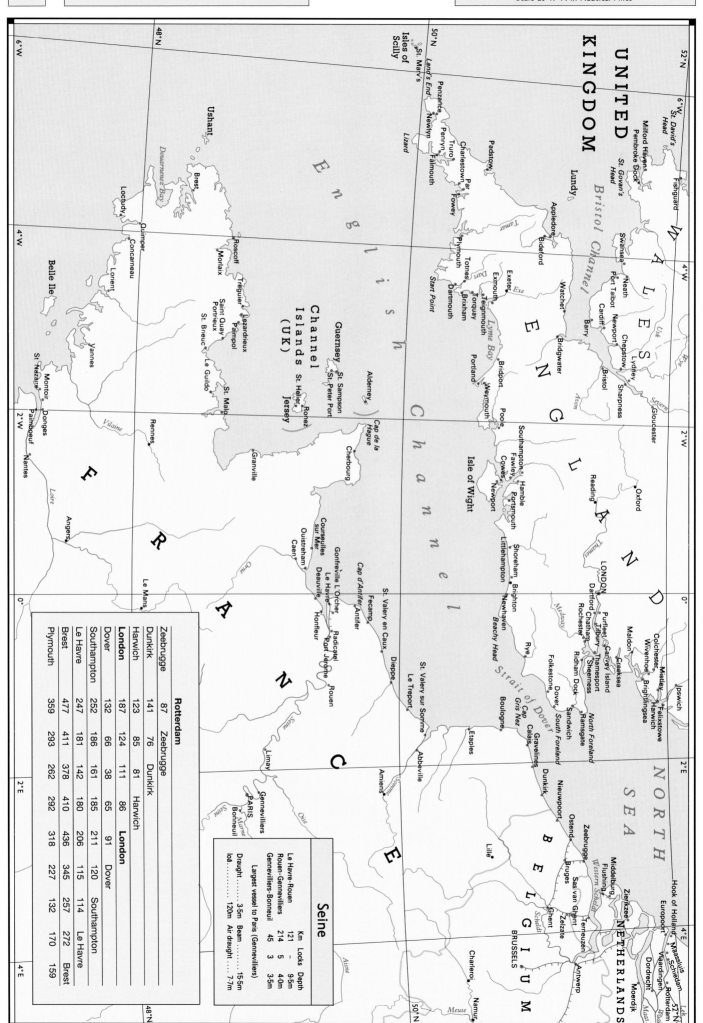

Rotterdam

	Zeebrugge	Dunkirk	Harwich	London	Dover	Southampton	Le Havre	Brest	Plymouth
Rotterdam	87	141	123	187	132	252	247	477	359
Zeebrugge		76	85	124	66	186	181	411	293
Dunkirk			81	111	38	161	142	378	262
Harwich				86	65	185	180	410	292
London					91	211	206	436	318
Dover						120	115	345	227
Southampton							114	257	132
Le Havre								272	170
Brest									159

Seine

	Km	Locks	Depth
Le Havre-Rouen	121	–	9·5m
Rouen-Gennevilliers	214	5	4·0m
Gennevilliers-Bonneuil	45	3	3·5m

Largest vessel to Paris (Gennevilliers)
Draught........3·5m   Beam..........15·5m
loa............120m   Air draught....7·7m

Lloyd's Maritime Atlas

Copyright © Lloyd's of London Press Ltd.

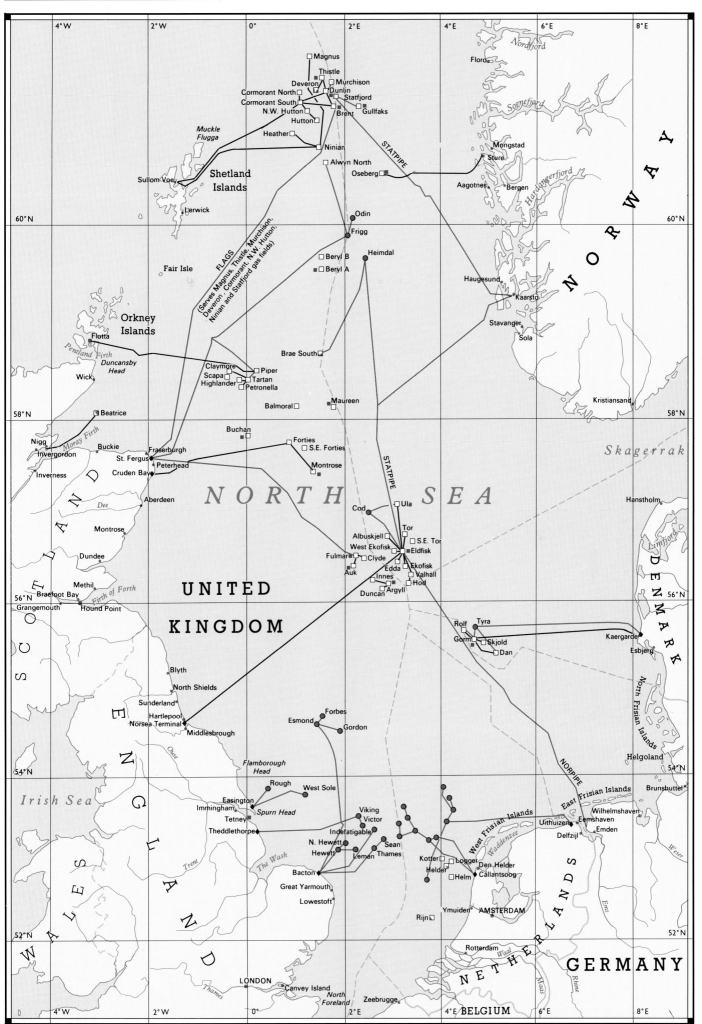

0 — 120
Scale at 57°N in Nautical Miles

Magnus
Thistle
Deveron Murchison
Cormorant North Dunlin
Cormorant South Statfjord
N.W. Hutton Brent Gullfaks
Hutton
Heather
Ninian
Muckle Flugga
Shetland Islands
Sullom Voe
Lerwick
Alwyn North
Oseberg
STATPIPE
Nordfjord
Floro
Sognefjord
Mongstad
Sture
Aagotnes
Bergen
Hardangerfjord

NORWAY

Odin
Frigg
Fair Isle
FLAGS (Serves Magnus, Thistle, Murchison, Deveron, Cormorant, N.W. Hutton, Ninian and Statfjord gas fields)
Beryl B
Beryl A
Heimdal
Haugesund
Kaarsto
Stavanger
Sola

Orkney Islands
Flotta
Pentland Firth
Duncansby Head
Wick
Beatrice
Nigg Moray Firth
Invergordon
Inverness
Buckie
Fraserburgh
St. Fergus
Peterhead
Cruden Bay
Aberdeen

Claymore Piper
Scapa Tartan
Highlander Petronella
Balmoral
Brae South
Maureen

Kristiansand

Skagerrak
Hanstholm
Limfjord

DENMARK

NORTH   SEA

Buchan
Forties
S.E. Forties
Montrose
Cod Ula
Tor
Albuskjell S.E. Tor
West Ekofisk Eldfisk
Fulmar Edda Ekofisk
Auk Clyde Valhall
Innes Hod
Duncan Argyll
STATPIPE

UNITED

KINGDOM
SCOTLAND
Dee
Montrose
Dundee
Methil
Braefoot Bay
Grangemouth Firth of Forth
Hound Point

Rolf Tyra
Gorm Skjold
Dan
Kaergarde
Esbjerg

North Frisian Islands

Blyth
North Shields
Sunderland
Hartlepool
Norsea Terminal
Middlesbrough

Esmond Forbes
Gordon

NORPIPE

Helgoland
Brunsbuttel

Flamborough Head
Irish Sea
ENGLAND
Ouse
Trent
The Wash

Rough West Sole
Easington
Immingham Spurn Head
Tetney
Theddlethorpe
Viking
Victor
Indefatigable
N. Hewett
Hewett Leman Thames
Sean
Bacton
Great Yarmouth
Lowestoft

West Frisian Islands Waddenzee East Frisian Islands
Uithuizen
Delfzijl
Emden
Ems
Wilhelmshaven
Eemshaven
Weser

Kotter Logger
Helder Den Helder
Helm Callantsoog

Rijn
Ymuiden AMSTERDAM

NETHERLANDS

GERMANY

WALES
LONDON
Thames
Canvey Island
North Foreland
Zeebrugge
BELGIUM
Rotterdam
Waal
Maas
Rhine

Lloyd's Maritime Atlas

Copyright © Lloyd's of London Press Ltd.

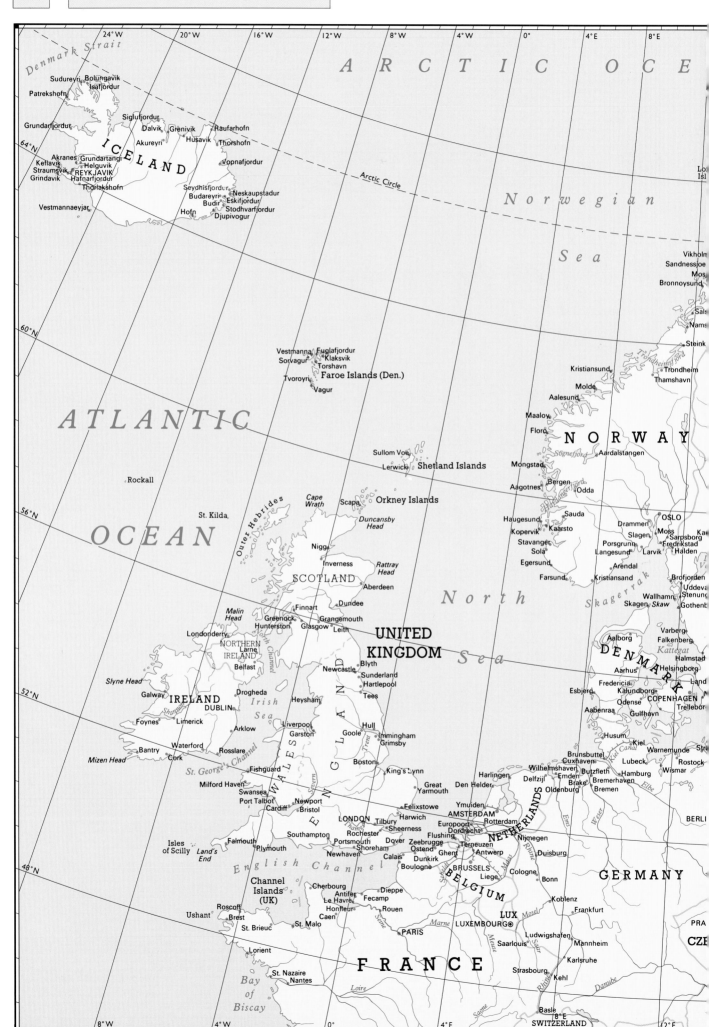

A R C T I C   O C E

Denmark Strait

ICELAND

Sudureyri Bolungavik
Patrekshofn Isafjordur
Siglufjordur
Grundarfjordur Dalvik Grenivik Raufarhofn
Akureyri Husavik Thorshofn
64°N Vopnafjordur
Akranes Grundartangi
Keflavik Helguvik
Straumsvik REYKJAVIK
Grindavik Hafnarfjordur
Thorlakshofn Seydhisfjordur
Budareyri Neskaupstadur
Vestmannaeyjar Budir Eskifjordur
Hofn Stodhvarfjordur
Djupivogur

Arctic Circle

Norwegian

Sea

Vikholm
Sandnessjoe
Mos
Bronnoysund

60°N

Sals
Nams

Steink

Vestmanna Fuglafjordur
Sorvagur Klaksvik
Torshavn
Tvoroyri Faroe Islands (Den.)
Vagur

ATLANTIC

Kristiansund Trondheim
Thamshavn
Molde
Aalesund

Maalov
Floro N O R W A Y

Rockall

OCEAN

Sullom Voe
Lerwick Shetland Islands
Cape
Wrath Scapa Orkney Islands
Duncansby
Head

Mongstad
Aagotnes Bergen
Odda
Sauda
Haugesund
Kopervik Kaarsto
Stavanger Drammen OSLO
Sola Porsgrunn Moss
Slagen Sarpsborg
Langesund Fredrikstad
Egersund Larvik Halden
Farsund Arendal
Kristiansand Brofjorden
Uddeva
Wallhamn Stenung
Skagen Skaw Gothenb

56°N

St. Kilda

Outer Hebrides

Nigg
Inverness
SCOTLAND Rattray
Aberdeen Head

North

Varberg
Falkenberg
Kattegat
Aalborg Halmstad
DENMARK Helsingborg
Aarhus
Fredericia
Esbjerg Kalundborg
Odense COPENHAGEN
Aabenraa Gulfhavn Trellebor
Husum

Dundee

Malin
Head Greenock Grangemouth
Londonderry Hunterston Leith
NORTHERN Larne Glasgow
IRELAND
Belfast Newcastle Blyth
Sunderland
Hartlepool
Tees

Sea

52°N

Slyne Head

Galway IRELAND Drogheda
Foynes DUBLIN
Limerick Irish
Arklow Sea
Bantry Waterford
Mizen Head Cork Rosslare

Heysham

Liverpool
Garston
Hull
Goole
Immingham
Grimsby
Boston

King's Lynn

UNITED
KINGDOM

Kiel
Brunsbuttel Warnemunde Str
Cuxhaven
Wilhelmshaven Lubeck
Delfzijl Emden Butzfleth Bremerhaven Rostock
Harlingen Brake Wismar
Den Helder Oldenburg Bremen
Fishguard
Milford Haven
Swansea Newport
Port Talbot Cardiff
Bristol

Great
Yarmouth

St. George's Channel

WALES
ENGLAND

Isles
of Scilly Land's
End

Falmouth Southampton
Plymouth Portsmouth
Shoreham
Newhaven

Felixstowe
Harwich
Ymuiden AMSTERDAM
Europoort Rotterdam
Flushing Dordrecht
Tilbury Zeebrugge Terneuzen
LONDON Ostend Ghent Antwerp
Rochester
Sheerness
Dover
Calais
Dunkirk
Boulogne BELGIUM

NETHERLANDS
Nijmegen Duisburg

Rhine

Brussels
Liege Cologne
Bonn

GERMANY

English Channel

Channel
Islands
(UK)

Ushant

Cherbourg
Antifer
Roscoff Le Havre Dieppe
Brest Honfleur Fecamp
Caen Rouen
St. Brieuc St. Malo

Lorient

Bay
of
Biscay

St. Nazaire
Nantes

F R A N C E

Seine

PARIS

Marne LUXEMBOURG
LUX

Koblenz
Frankfurt
Ludwigshafen
Saarlouis Mannheim

Meuse

Karlsruhe

Loire

Strasbourg
Kehl

Saone Rhine
Basle
SWITZERLAND

Danube

PRA
CZE

BERLI

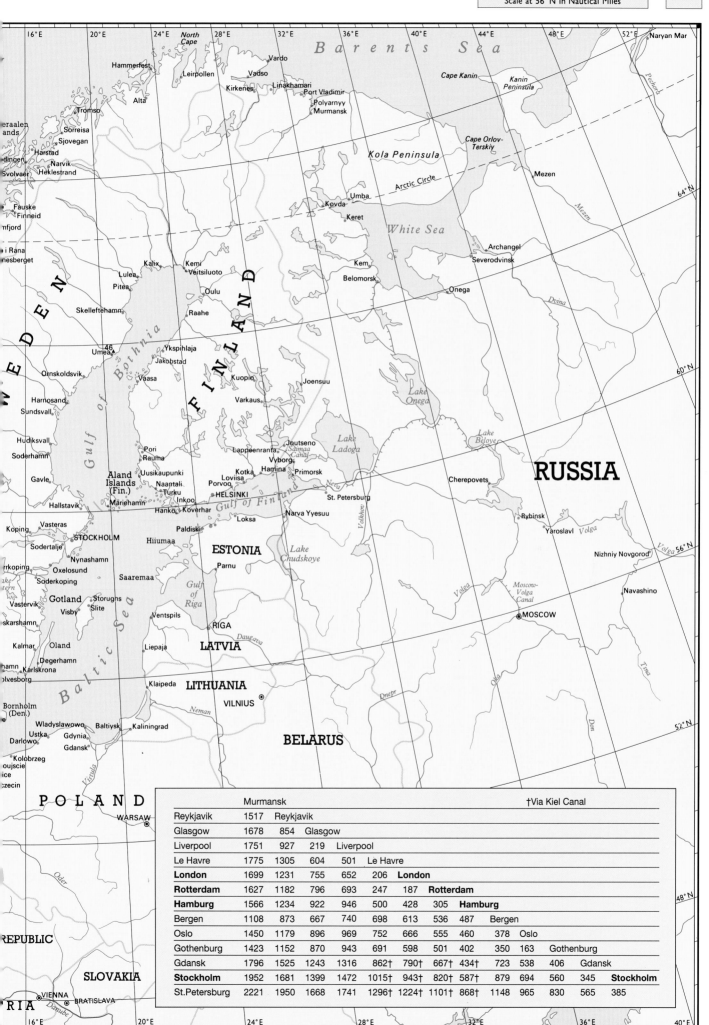

0 — 180
Scale at 56°N in Nautical Miles

	Murmansk													†Via Kiel Canal
Reykjavik	1517	Reykjavik												
Glasgow	1678	854	Glasgow											
Liverpool	1751	927	219	Liverpool										
Le Havre	1775	1305	604	501	Le Havre									
London	1699	1231	755	652	206	**London**								
Rotterdam	1627	1182	796	693	247	187	**Rotterdam**							
Hamburg	1566	1234	922	946	500	428	305	**Hamburg**						
Bergen	1108	873	667	740	698	613	536	487	Bergen					
Oslo	1450	1179	896	969	752	666	555	460	378	Oslo				
Gothenburg	1423	1152	870	943	691	598	501	402	350	163	Gothenburg			
Gdansk	1796	1525	1243	1316	862†	790†	667†	434†	723	538	406	Gdansk		
Stockholm	1952	1681	1399	1472	1015†	943†	820†	587†	879	694	560	345	**Stockholm**	
St.Petersburg	2221	1950	1668	1741	1296†	1224†	1101†	868†	1148	965	830	565	385	St.Petersburg

's Maritime Atlas

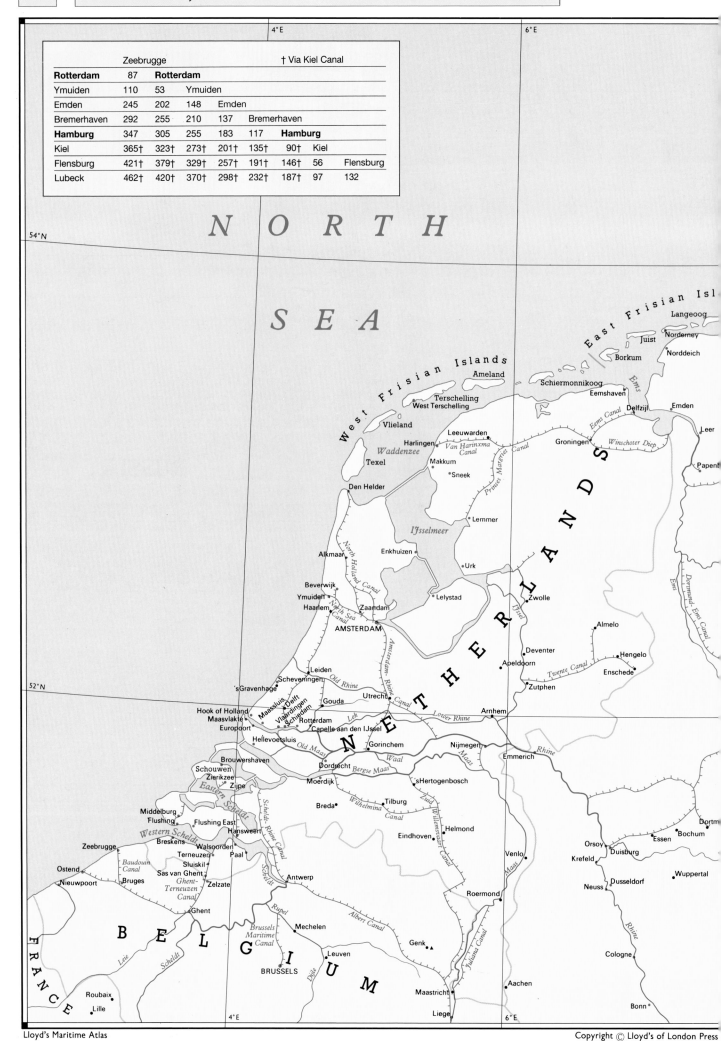

	Zeebrugge			† Via Kiel Canal			
Rotterdam	87	**Rotterdam**					
Ymuiden	110	53	Ymuiden				
Emden	245	202	148	Emden			
Bremerhaven	292	255	210	137	Bremerhaven		
Hamburg	347	305	255	183	117	**Hamburg**	
Kiel	365†	323†	273†	201†	135†	90†	Kiel
Flensburg	421†	379†	329†	257†	191†	146†	56	Flensburg
Lubeck	462†	420†	370†	298†	232†	187†	97	132

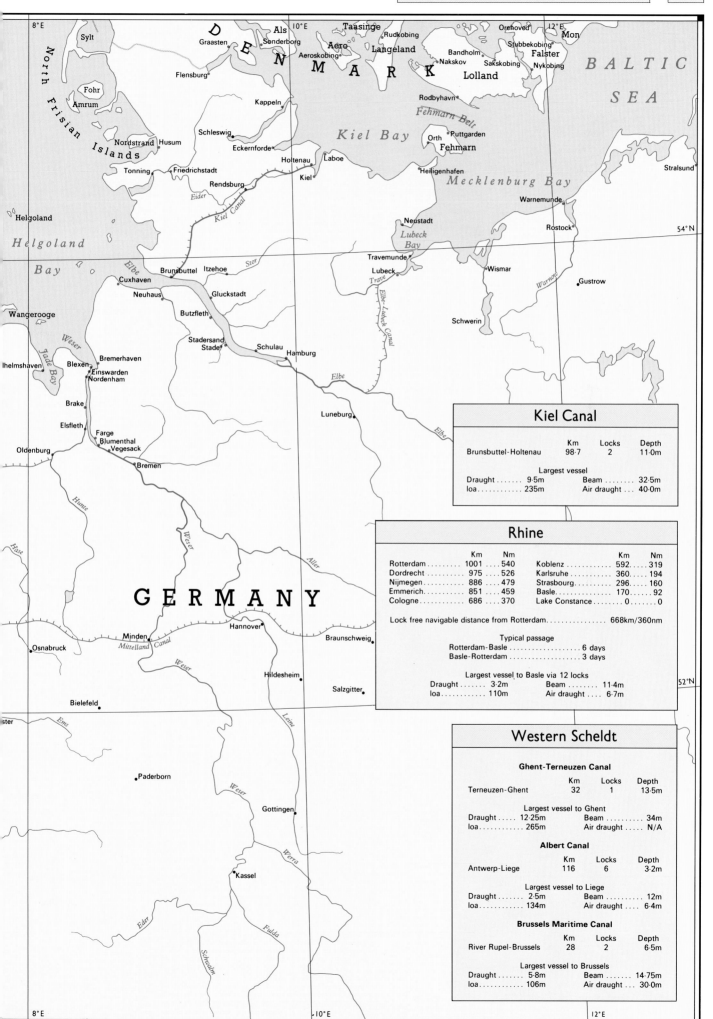

0 — 60
Scale at 53°N in Nautical Miles

North Frisian Islands

DENMARK

Sylt
Graasten
Als
Sonderborg
Taasinge
Aeroskobing
Aero
Rudkobing
Langeland
Orehoved
Mon
Stubbekobing
Bandholm
Nakskov
Saksobing
Falster
Nykobing
Lolland
Rodbyhavn

Flensburg
Fohr
Amrum
Kappeln
Schleswig

BALTIC SEA

Fehmarn Belt
Kiel Bay
Orth
Puttgarden
Fehmarn

Nordstrand
Husum
Eckernforde
Tonning
Friedrichstadt
Holtenau
Laboe
Heiligenhafen
Stralsund

Rendsburg
Kiel
Eider
Kiel Canal

Mecklenburg Bay

Warnemunde
Rostock
54°N

Helgoland

Helgoland Bay

Brunsbuttel
Itzehoe
Stor
Neustadt
Lubeck Bay
Travemunde
Lubeck
Wismar
Gustrow

Cuxhaven
Neuhaus
Gluckstadt
Butzfleth
Trave
Warnow

Wangerooge
Stadersand
Stade
Schulau
Hamburg
Elbe-Lubeck Canal
Schwerin

Ihelmshaven
Jade Bay
Bremerhaven
Blexen
Einswarden
Nordenham
Weser
Elbe

Brake
Luneburg

Elsfleth
Farge
Blumenthal
Vegesack

Oldenburg
Bremen

Hunte
Hase

GERMANY

Weser

Osnabruck
Minden
Mittelland Canal
Hannover
Braunschweig

Weser
Hildesheim

Bielefeld
Salzgitter
Leine
52°N

Ems

Paderborn

Weser

Gottingen

Werra
Fulda

Kassel

Eder
Schwalm

Kiel Canal

	Km	Locks	Depth
Brunsbuttel-Holtenau	98·7	2	11·0m

Largest vessel

Draught	9·5m	Beam	32·5m
loa	235m	Air draught	40·0m

Rhine

	Km	Nm		Km	Nm
Rotterdam	1001	540	Koblenz	592	319
Dordrecht	975	526	Karlsruhe	360	194
Nijmegen	886	479	Strasbourg	296	160
Emmerich	851	459	Basle	170	92
Cologne	686	370	Lake Constance	0	0

Lock free navigable distance from Rotterdam 668km/360nm

Typical passage
Rotterdam-Basle . . . . 6 days
Basle-Rotterdam . . . . 3 days

Largest vessel to Basle via 12 locks

Draught	3·2m	Beam	11·4m
loa	110m	Air draught	6·7m

Western Scheldt

Ghent-Terneuzen Canal

	Km	Locks	Depth
Terneuzen-Ghent	32	1	13·5m

Largest vessel to Ghent

Draught	12·25m	Beam	34m
loa	265m	Air draught	N/A

Albert Canal

	Km	Locks	Depth
Antwerp-Liege	116	6	3·2m

Largest vessel to Liege

Draught	2·5m	Beam	12m
loa	134m	Air draught	6·4m

Brussels Maritime Canal

	Km	Locks	Depth
River Rupel-Brussels	28	2	6·5m

Largest vessel to Brussels

Draught	5·8m	Beam	14·75m
loa	106m	Air draught	30·0m

8°E   10°E   12°E

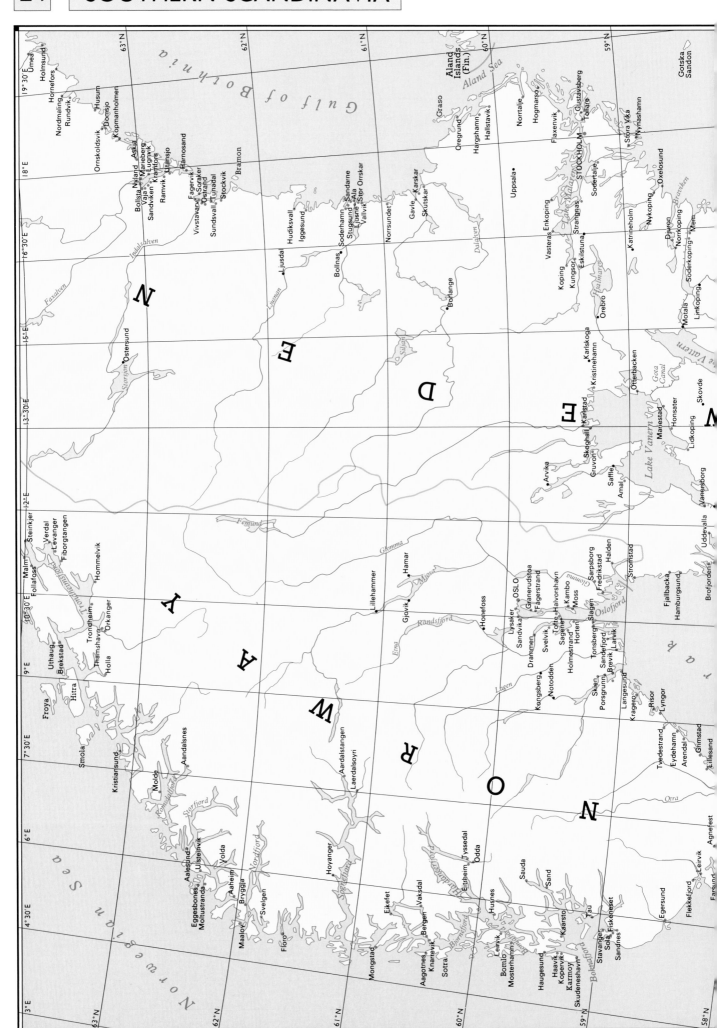

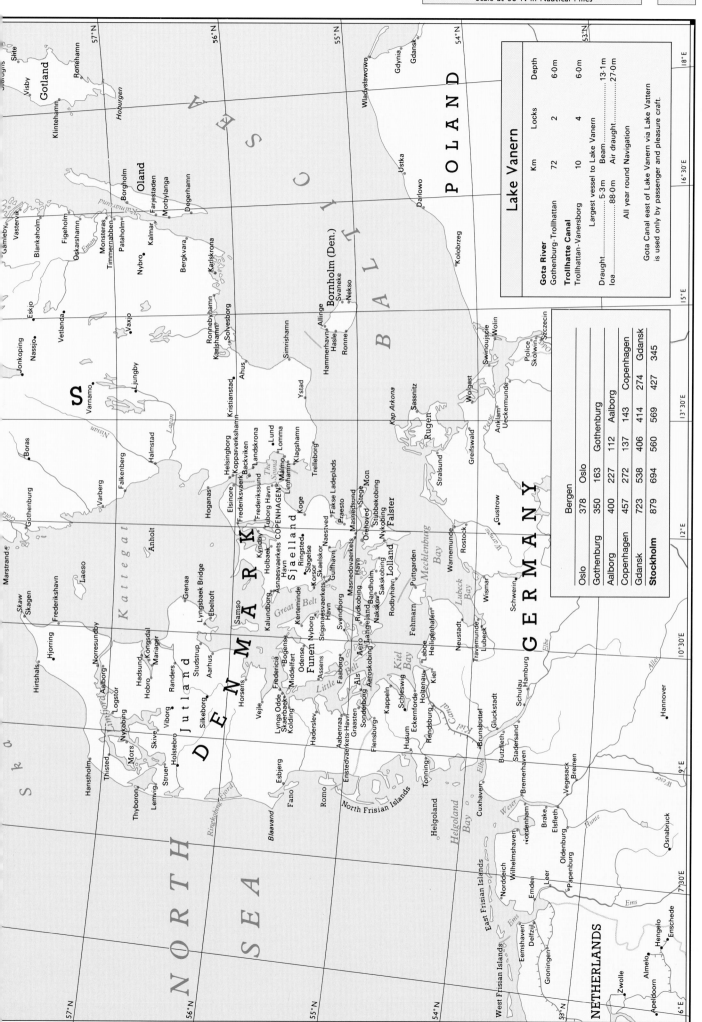

0 ————————————— 90
Scale at 58°N in Nautical Miles

NORTH SEA

BALTIC SEA

KATTEGAT

Skagerrak

Lake Vanern

	Km	Locks	Depth
Gota River			
Gothenburg-Trollhattan	72	2	6·0m
Trollhatte Canal			
Trollhattan-Vanersborg	10	4	6·0m

Largest vessel to Lake Vanern
Draught.....................5·3m   Beam................13·1m
loa.............................88·0m   Air draught.........27·0m

All year round Navigation

Gota Canal east of Lake Vanern via Lake Vattern
is used only by passenger and pleasure craft.

	Bergen	Oslo				
Oslo	378					
Gothenburg	350	163	Gothenburg			
Aalborg	400	227	112	Aalborg		
Copenhagen	457	272	137	143	Copenhagen	
Gdansk	723	538	406	414	274	Gdansk
Stockholm	879	694	560	569	427	345

POLAND

GERMANY

DENMARK

Jutland

Sjaelland

Funen

Lolland

Falster

Gotland

Oland

Bornholm (Den.)

NETHERLANDS

Maritime Atlas

Copyright © Lloyd's of London Press Ltd.

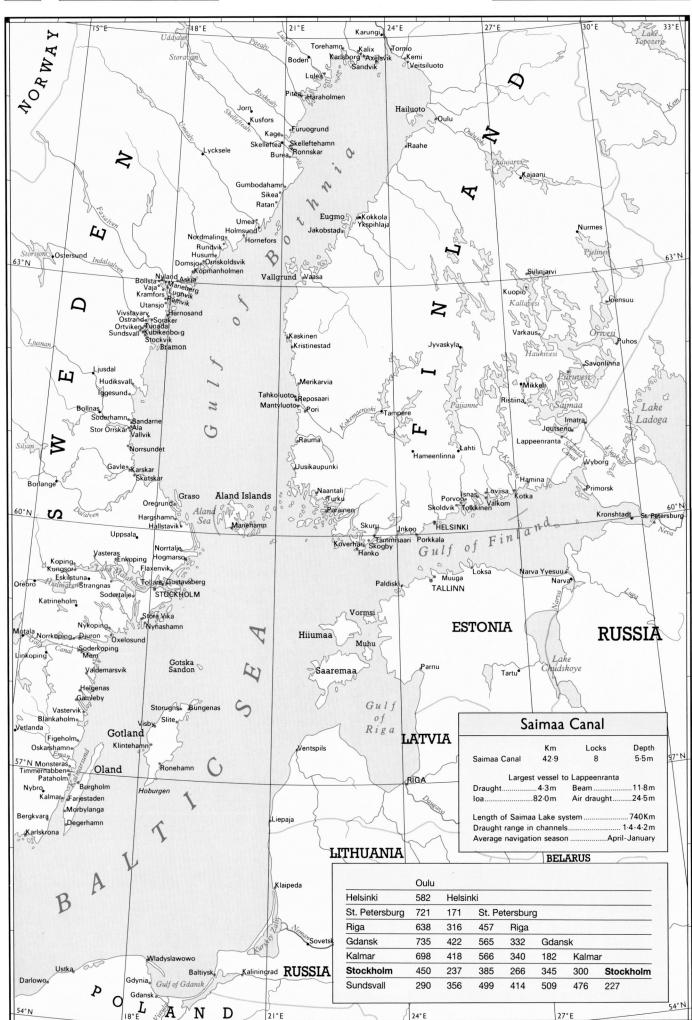

0   120
Scale at 60°N in Nautical Miles

Saimaa Canal

	Km	Locks	Depth
Saimaa Canal	42·9	8	5·5m

Largest vessel to Lappeenranta

Draught................4·3m	Beam..................11·8m
Ioa.......................82·0m	Air draught..........24·5m

Length of Saimaa Lake system 740Km
Draught range in channels..........................1·4-4·2m
Average navigation season ....April-January

	Oulu						
Helsinki	582	Helsinki					
St. Petersburg	721	171	St. Petersburg				
Riga	638	316	457	Riga			
Gdansk	735	422	565	332	Gdansk		
Kalmar	698	418	566	340	182	Kalmar	
Stockholm	450	237	385	266	345	300	**Stockholm**
Sundsvall	290	356	499	414	509	476	227

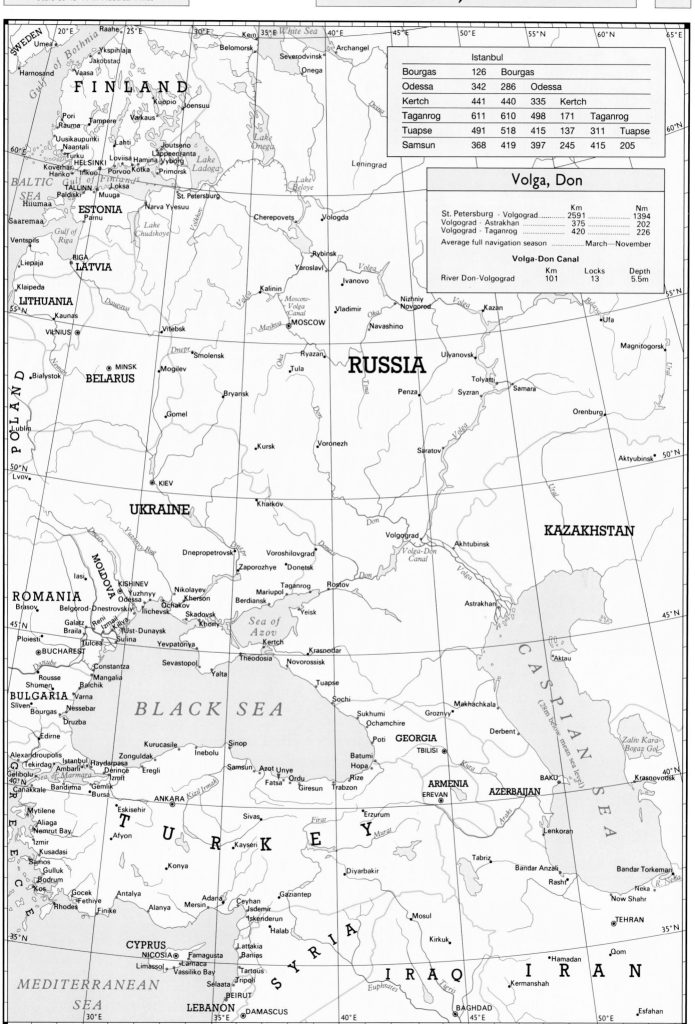

Scale at 45°N in Nautical Miles
0　　　300

Istanbul					
Bourgas	126	Bourgas			
Odessa	342	286	Odessa		
Kertch	441	440	335	Kertch	
Taganrog	611	610	498	171	Taganrog
Tuapse	491	518	415	137	311	Tuapse
Samsun	368	419	397	245	415	205

Volga, Don

	Km	Nm
St. Petersburg - Volgograd	2591	1394
Volgograd - Astrakhan	375	202
Volgograd - Taganrog	420	226
Average full navigation season	March—November	

Volga-Don Canal

	Km	Locks	Depth
River Don-Volgograd	101	13	5.5m

Lloyd's Maritime Atlas   Copyright © Lloyd's of London Press Ltd.

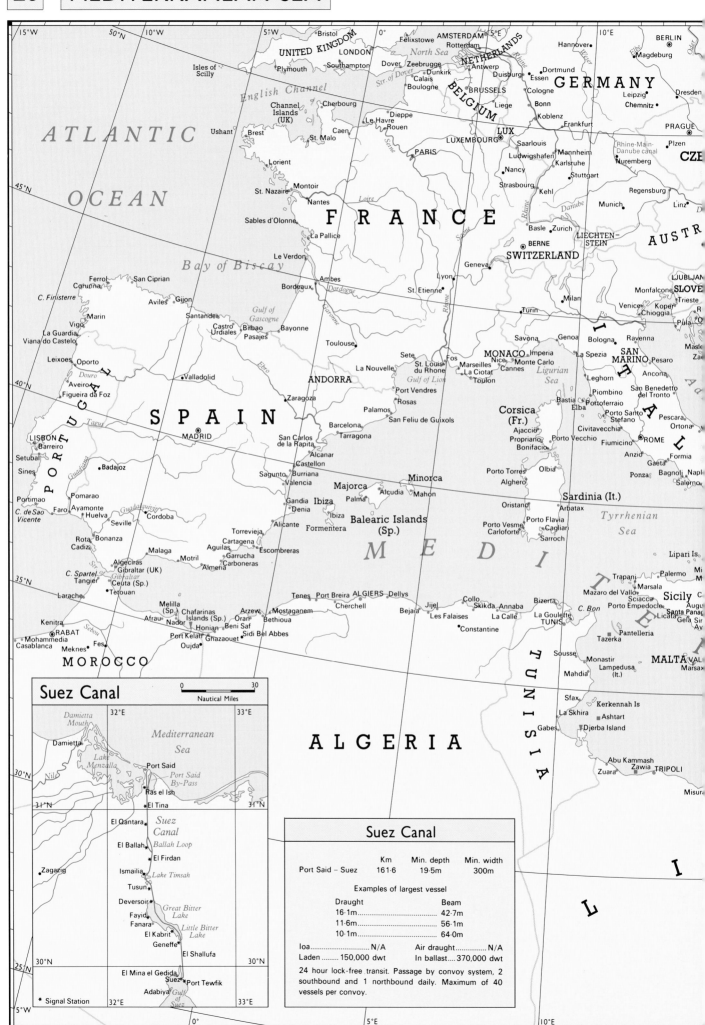

Suez Canal

0   30
Nautical Miles

Suez Canal

	Km	Min. depth	Min. width
Port Said – Suez	161·6	19·5m	300m

Examples of largest vessel

Draught		Beam
16·1m		42·7m
11·6m		56·1m
10·1m		64·0m

loa	N/A	Air draught	N/A
Laden	150,000 dwt	In ballast	370,000 dwt

24 hour lock-free transit. Passage by convoy system, 2 southbound and 1 northbound daily. Maximum of 40 vessels per convoy.

* Signal Station

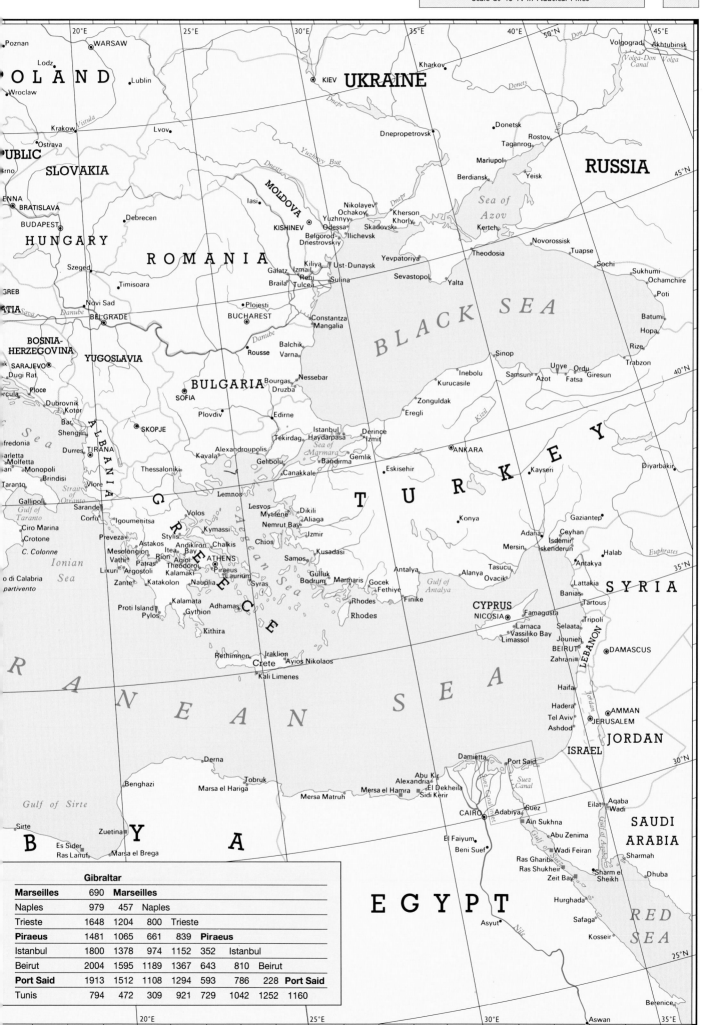

Scale at 40°N in Nautical Miles

	Gibraltar							
Marseilles	690	**Marseilles**						
Naples	979	457	Naples					
Trieste	1648	1204	800	Trieste				
Piraeus	1481	1065	661	839	**Piraeus**			
Istanbul	1800	1378	974	1152	352	Istanbul		
Beirut	2004	1595	1189	1367	643	810	Beirut	
Port Said	1913	1512	1108	1294	593	786	228	**Port Said**
Tunis	794	472	309	921	729	1042	1252	1160

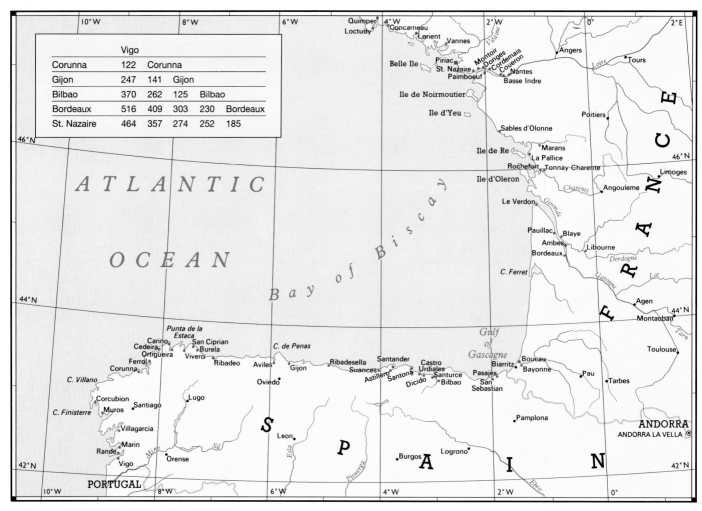

0					100

Scale at 44°N in Nautical Miles

	Vigo				
Corunna	122	Corunna			
Gijon	247	141	Gijon		
Bilbao	370	262	125	Bilbao	
Bordeaux	516	409	303	230	Bordeaux
St. Nazaire	464	357	274	252	185

STRAIT of GIBRALTAR

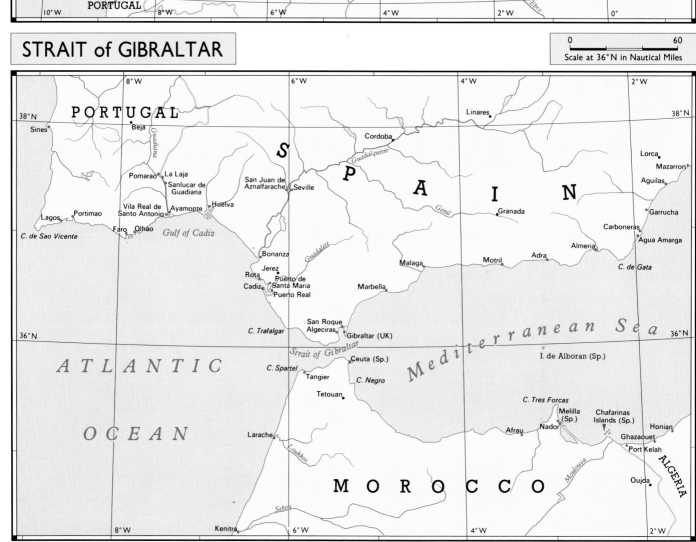

0		60

Scale at 36°N in Nautical Miles

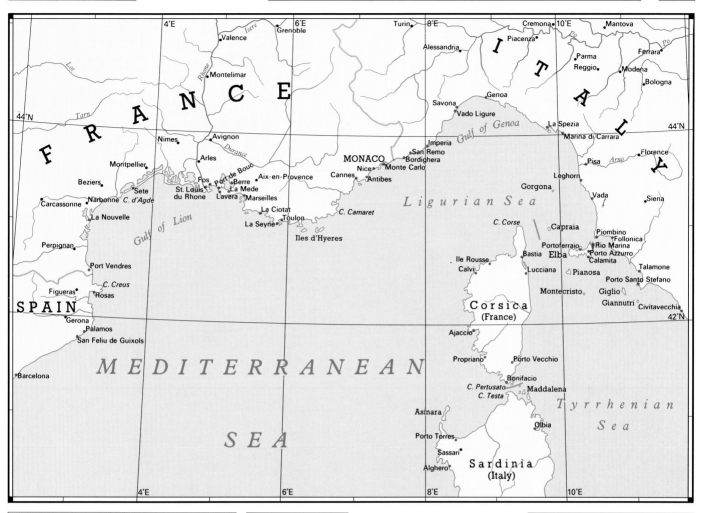

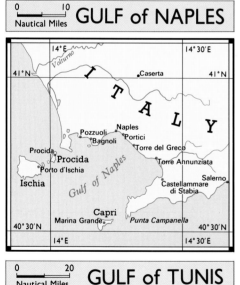

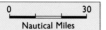

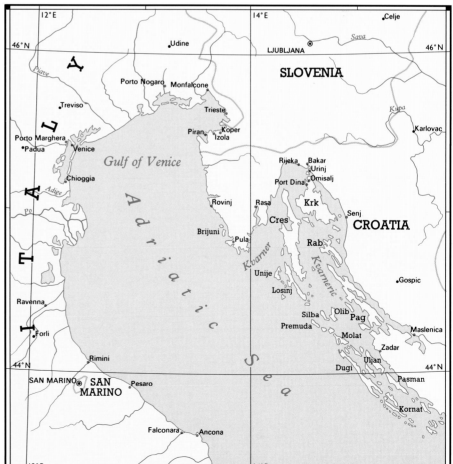

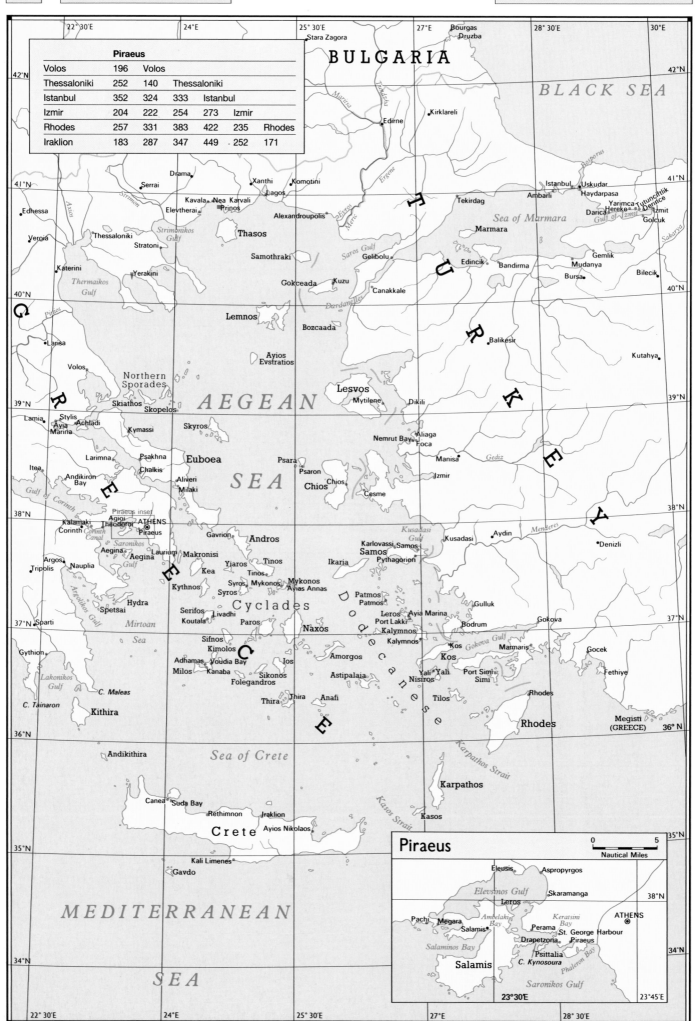

Piraeus					
Volos	196	Volos			
Thessaloniki	252	140	Thessaloniki		
Istanbul	352	324	333	Istanbul	
Izmir	204	222	254	273	Izmir
Rhodes	257	331	383	422	235	Rhodes
Iraklion	183	287	347	449	252	171

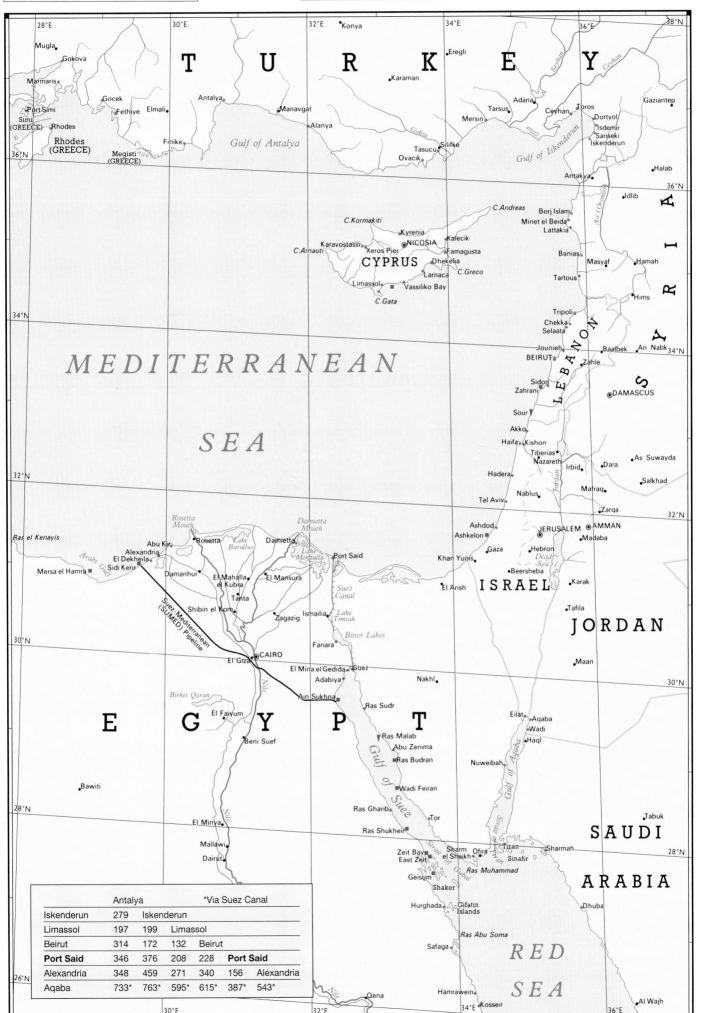

0 ——————— 120
Scale at 32°N in Nautical Miles

TURKEY

Mugla
Gokova
Marmaris
Port Simi
Simi (GREECE)
Rhodes
Rhodes (GREECE)
Gocek
Fethiye
Elmali
Megisti (GREECE)
Finike
Antalya
Manavgat
Alanya
Gulf of Antalya
Konya
Eregli
Karaman
Tasucu
Ovacik
Silifke
Mersin
Tarsus
Adana
Ceyhan
Toros
Goksu
Scyhan
Ceyhan
Dortyol
Isdemir
Sariseki
Iskenderun
Gulf of Iskenderun
Gaziantep
Halab
Antakya
Idlib

C.Kormakiti
C.Andreas
Kyrenia
Kalecik
Karavostassi
NICOSIA
Famagusta
Xeros Pier
C.Arnauti
CYPRUS
Dhekelia
C.Greco
Larnaca
Limassol
Vassiliko Bay
C.Gata

Borj Islam
Minet el Beida
Lattakia
Banias
Masyaf
Hamah
Tartous
Hims
Tripoli
Chekka
Selaata
Jounieh
BEIRUT
Baalbek
An Nabk
Zahle
Sidon
Zahrani
DAMASCUS
Sour
Akko
Haifa
Kishon
Tiberias
Nazareth
Dara
As Suwayda
Irbid
Salkhad
Hadera
Matraq
Nablus
Tel Aviv
Zarqa

MEDITERRANEAN

SEA

SYRIA
LEBANON

Asi (Orontis)

Ras el Kenayis
Rosetta Mouth
Damietta Mouth
Abu Kir
Rosetta
Lake Burullus
Damietta
Lake Menzalla
Port Said
Ashdod
Ashkelon
JERUSALEM
AMMAN
Madaba
Alexandria
El Dekheila
Sidi Kerir
Arabs Gulf
Mersa el Hamra
Damanhur
El Mahalla el Kubra
Tanta
El Mansura
Gaza
Hebron
Dead Sea
Beersheba
Khan Yunis
El Arish
Karak
Tafila
Suez Canal
Shibin el Kom
Zagazig
Ismailia
Lake Timsah
Suez-Mediterranean (SUMED) Pipeline
Birket Qarun
El Faiyum
El Giza
CAIRO
Nile
Fanara
Bitter Lakes
El Mina el Gedida
Adabiya
Suez
Nakhl
Maan
Ain Sukhna
Ras Sudr
Eilat
Aqaba
Wadi
Haql
Beni Suef
Ras Malab
Abu Zenima
Ras Budran
Nuweibah
Bawiti
Wadi Feiran
El Minya
Ras Gharib
Tor
Tabuk
Mallawi
Ras Shukheir
Dairut
Zeit Bay
East Zeit
Sharm el Sheikh
Ofira
Sinafir
Sharmah
Geisum
Tiran
Ras Muhammad
Shaker
Hurghada
Gifatin Islands
Dhuba
Ras Abu Soma
Safaga
Al Wajh
Qena
Hamrawein
Kosseir

EGYPT

Gulf of Suez
Strait of Gubal
Strait of Tiran
Gulf of Aqaba

ISRAEL
JORDAN

SAUDI
ARABIA

RED SEA

	Antalya	*Via Suez Canal			
Iskenderun	279	Iskenderun			
Limassol	197	199	Limassol		
Beirut	314	172	132	Beirut	
Port Said	346	376	208	228	**Port Said**
Alexandria	348	459	271	340	156	Alexandria
Aqaba	733*	763*	595*	615*	387*	543*	Aqaba

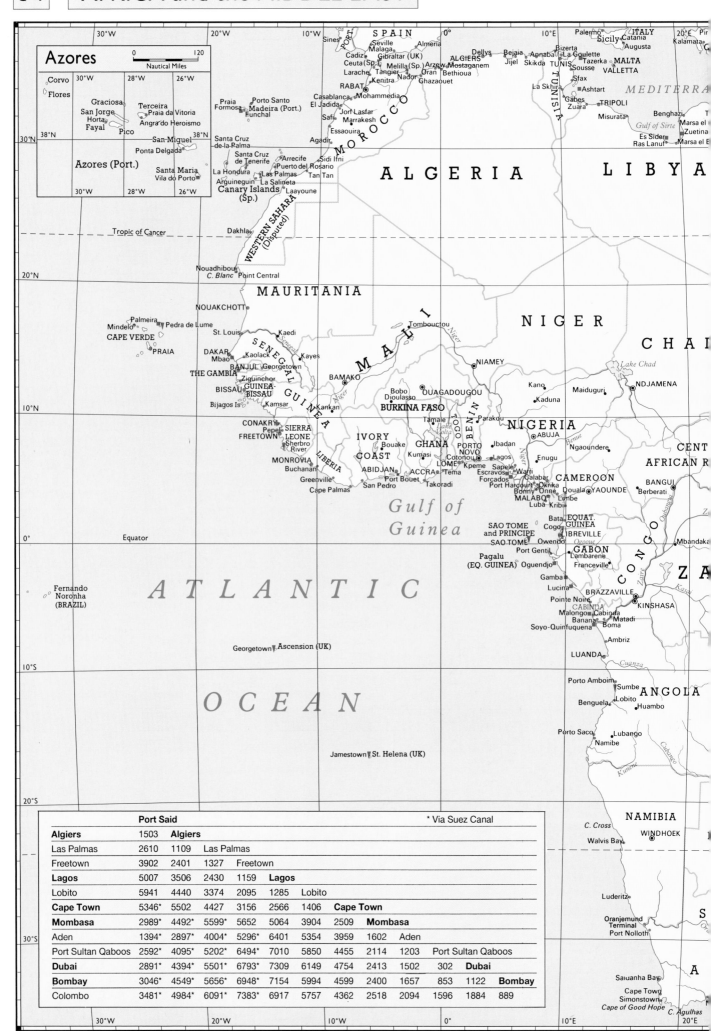

	Port Said	Algiers	Las Palmas	Freetown	Lagos	Lobito	Cape Town	Mombasa	Aden	Port Sultan Qaboos	Dubai	Bombay	Colombo
Algiers	1503	**Algiers**											
Las Palmas	2610	1109	Las Palmas										
Freetown	3902	2401	1327	Freetown									
Lagos	5007	3506	2430	1159	**Lagos**								
Lobito	5941	4440	3374	2095	1285	Lobito							
Cape Town	5346*	5502	4427	3156	2566	1406	**Cape Town**						
Mombasa	2989*	4492*	5599*	5652	5064	3904	2509	**Mombasa**					
Aden	1394*	2897*	4004*	5296*	6401	5354	3959	1602	Aden				
Port Sultan Qaboos	2592*	4095*	5202*	6494*	7010	5850	4455	2114	1203	Port Sultan Qaboos			
Dubai	2891*	4394*	5501*	6793*	7309	6149	4754	2413	1502	302	**Dubai**		
Bombay	3046*	4549*	5656*	6948*	7154	5994	4599	2400	1657	853	1122	**Bombay**	
Colombo	3481*	4984*	6091*	7383*	6917	5757	4362	2518	2094	1596	1884	889	Colombo

* Via Suez Canal

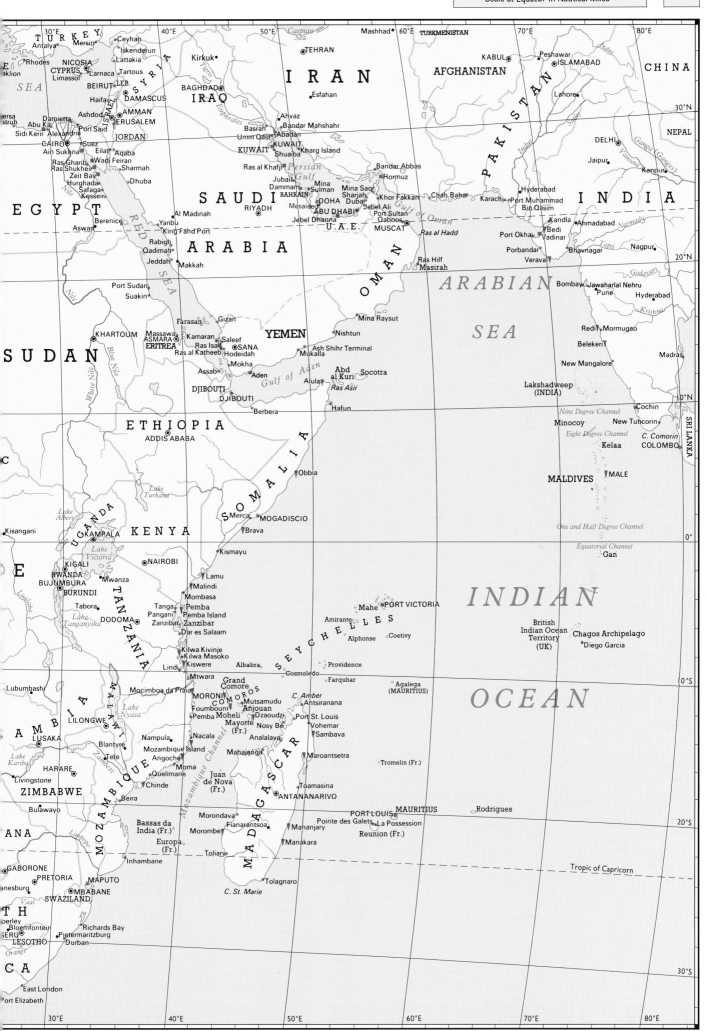

0   720
Scale at Equator in Nautical Miles

TURKEY
Antalya 30°E Mersin
Rhodes   Iskenderun 40°E   Mashhad 60°E **TURKMENISTAN** 70°E   80°E
Iraklion **NICOSIA** Larnaca Lattakia   Kirkuk   **TEHRAN**
CYPRUS Limassol Tartous   **I R A N**   KABUL Peshawar ISLAMABAD
SEA LEB. **BEIRUT** **SYRIA** **BAGHDAD**   Esfahan   **AFGHANISTAN**   **CHINA**
Haifa **DAMASCUS** **IRAQ**   Lahore
Mersa Damietta Ashdod **ISRAEL** **AMMAN** Ahvaz   30°N
Sidi Kerir Abu Kir Port Said **JERUSALEM**   Bandar Mahshahr   **P** DELHI **NEPAL**
Alexandria **CAIRO** Suez **JORDAN** Basrah Abadan   **A**
Ain Sukhna Eilat Umm Qasr   **K**   Jaipur Kanpur
Ras Gharib Wadi Feiran **KUWAIT** **KUWAIT** Kharg Island   **I** Hyderabad
Ras Shukheir Sharmah Ras al Khafji Shuaiba **Persian**   **S** Karachi Port Muhammad
Zeit Bay Dhuba   Jubail **Gulf** Mina Bandar Abbas   **T** Bin Qasim
Hurghada   Dammam Sulman Hormuz Khor Fakkan Chah Bahar **A**
Safaga Kosseir **SAUDI** Al Madinah **BAHRAIN** Mesaieed Mina Saqr **N** **INDIA**
                RIYADH **DOHA** Dubai Jebel Ali   Kandla Ahmadabad
E G Y P T Berenice   **ABU DHABI** Port Sultan   Port Okha Bedi Narmada
        Aswan **ARABIA** Jebel Dhanna **U.A.E.** Qaboos   Vadinar 20°N
                MUSCAT   Porbandar Bhavnagar Nagpur
Rabigh Qadimah   **O** Ras al Hadd   Veraval
        Yanbu   **M**   Godavari
Jeddah Makkah   **A** Ras Hilf   Bombay Jawaharlal Nehru
        N Masirah   **A R A B I A N** Pune Hyderabad
Port Sudan   **SEA**
Suakin   Krishna
        Farasan Gizan   Mina Raysut   Redi Mormugao
KHARTOUM Massawa Kamaran **YEMEN** Nishtun   Belekeri
        ASMARA Saleef   Ash Shihr Terminal   New Mangalore Madras
SUDAN **ERITREA** Ras Isa **SANA** Mukalla
        Ras al Katheeb Hodeidah   Lakshadweep
        Assab Mokha   (INDIA)   Cochin 0°N
                Aden Abd   Socotra   Nine Degree Channel   New Tuticorin
        DJIBOUTI Alula al Kuri   Minicoy   **SRI**
        DJIBOUTI   Ras Asir   Eight Degree Channel Kelaa C. Comorin **LANKA**
        Berbera Hafun   **COLOMBO**
ETHIOPIA   **MALDIVES** **MALE**
ADDIS ABABA
                        Obbia   One and Half Degree Channel   0°
Lake
Turkana   Equatorial Channel
Kisangani Lake **UGANDA**   Merca **MOGADISCIO**   Gan
        Albert **KAMPALA** **KENYA** Brava
KIGALI Lake   Kismayu   **I N D I A N**
RWANDA Victoria **NAIROBI**
BUJUMBURA Mwanza   Lamu
BURUNDI   Malindi   Mahe **PORT VICTORIA**
Tabora **TANZANIA** Mombasa   Amirante   British
        Tanga Pemba   Coetivy   Indian Ocean Chagos Archipelago
Lake **DODOMA** Pangani Pemba Island   Alphonse   Territory Diego Garcia
Tanganyika   Zanzibar Zanzibar   (UK)
        Dar es Salaam   Providence   **S**
        Kilwa Kivinje   Gosmoledo Farquhar   **E**
Lubumbashi   Kilwa Masoko   **Y** Agalega **O C E A N**
        Lindi Kiswere Albabra   **C** (MAURITIUS)
        Mtwara   **H**
        Mocimboa da Praia Grand   **E**
        MORONI Comore Mutsamudu C. Amber   **L**
AMBIA Foumbouni **COMOROS** Anjouan Ahtsiranana   **L**
LUSAKA Pemba Moheli Dzaoudzi Nosy Be   **E**
        LILONGWE Lake Mayotte Vohemar   **S**
        MALAWI Nyasa (Fr.) Sambava
Nampula   Analalava
Mozambique Island   Tromelin (Fr.)
Blantyre Angoche Mahajanga
HARARE Tete Moma   Maroantsetra
Livingstone Quelimane
        Chinde Juan
ZIMBABWE **MOZAMBIQUE** de Nova **MADAGASCAR**
        Beira (Fr.) Toamasina
Bulawayo   Morondava **ANTANANARIVO**   Rodrigues   10°S
        Bassas da Pointe des Galets **PORT LOUIS** **MAURITIUS**
ANA India (Fr.) Morombe Fianarantsoa Mahanjary La Possession
        Europa Manakara Reunion (Fr.)
GABORONE (Fr.) Toliary
PRETORIA **MAPUTO** Inhambane
nesburg **MBABANE**
SWAZILAND   C. St. Marie   Tolagnaro   Tropic of Capricorn
TH Vaal
CA   20°S
nberley **LESOTHO**
ERU Bloemfontein Richards Bay
Orange Pietermaritzburg
East London
ort Elizabeth Durban   30°S

30°E   40°E   50°E   60°E   70°E   80°E

Scale at 5°N in Nautical Miles
0 — 360

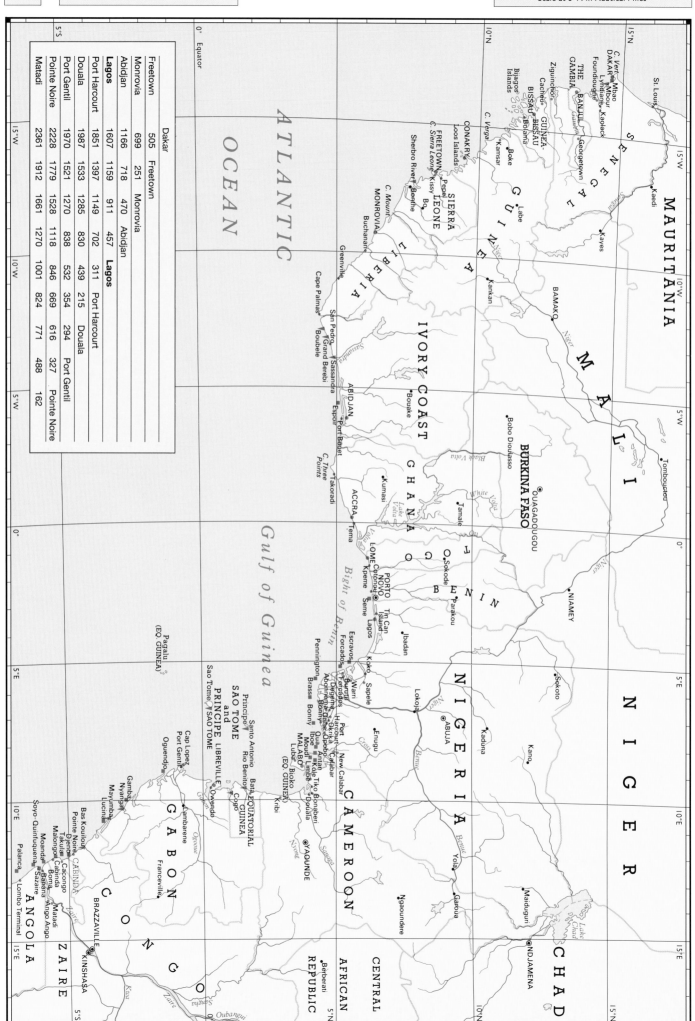

Distance table (nautical miles):

	Dakar	Freetown	Monrovia	Abidjan	Lagos	Port Harcourt	Douala	Port Gentil	Pointe Noire
Freetown	505								
Monrovia	699	251							
Abidjan	1166	718	470						
Lagos	1607	1159	911	457					
Port Harcourt	1851	1397	1149	702	311				
Douala	1987	1533	1285	838	439	215			
Port Gentil	1970	1521	1270	830	532	354	294		
Pointe Noire	2228	1779	1528	1118	846	669	616	327	
Matadi	2361	1912	1661	1270	1001	824	771	488	162

0   120
Scale at 26°N in Nautical Miles

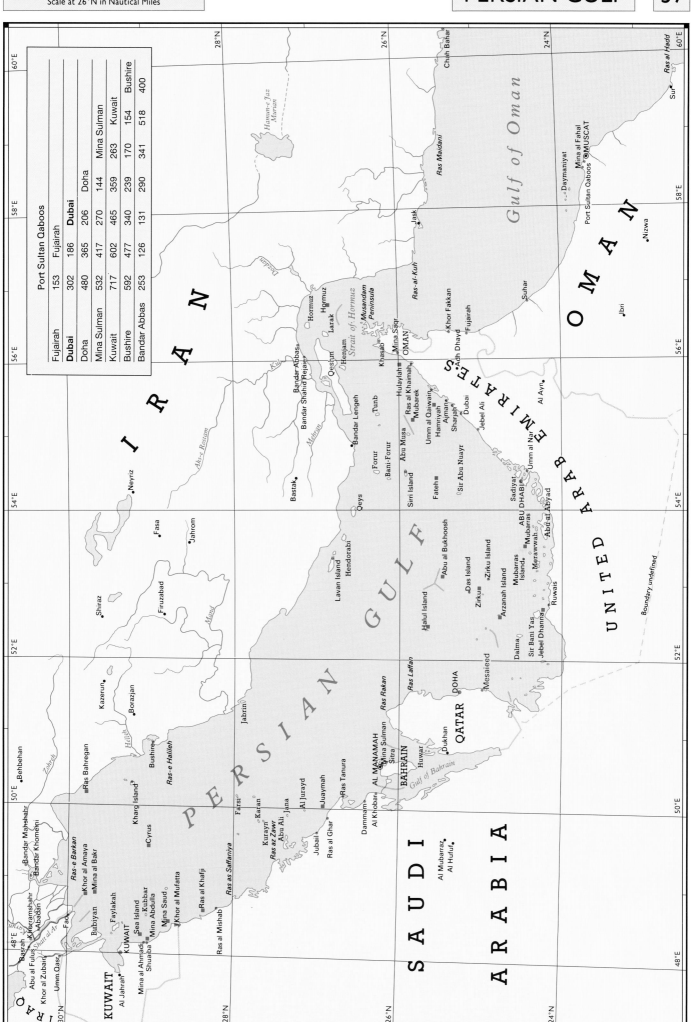

	Port Sultan Qaboos	Fujairah	Dubai	Doha	Mina Sulman	Kuwait	Bushire
Fujairah	153						
Dubai	302	186					
Doha	480	365	206				
Mina Sulman	532	417	270	144			
Kuwait	717	602	465	359	263		
Bushire	592	477	340	239	170	154	
Bandar Abbas	253	126	131	290	341	518	400

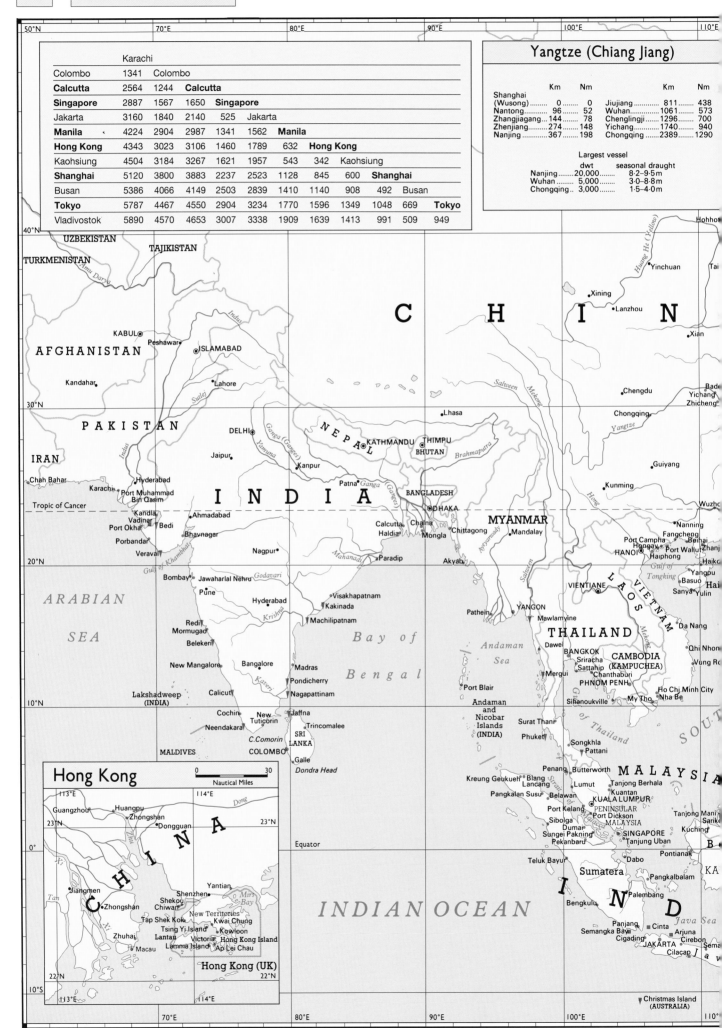

	Karachi								
Colombo	1341	Colombo							
Calcutta	2564	1244	**Calcutta**						
Singapore	2887	1567	1650	**Singapore**					
Jakarta	3160	1840	2140	525	Jakarta				
Manila	4224	2904	2987	1341	1562	**Manila**			
Hong Kong	4343	3023	3106	1460	1789	632	**Hong Kong**		
Kaohsiung	4504	3184	3267	1621	1957	543	342	Kaohsiung	
Shanghai	5120	3800	3883	2237	2523	1128	845	600	**Shanghai**
Busan	5386	4066	4149	2503	2839	1410	1140	908	492 Busan
Tokyo	5787	4467	4550	2904	3234	1770	1596	1349	1048 669 **Tokyo**
Vladivostok	5890	4570	4653	3007	3338	1909	1639	1413	991 509 949

Yangtze (Chiang Jiang)

	Km	Nm		Km	Nm
Shanghai					
(Wusong)........	0	0	Jiujiang	811	438
Nantong	96	52	Wuhan	1061	573
Zhangjiagang..	144	78	Chenglingji	1296	700
Zhenjiang	274	148	Yichang	1740	940
Nanjing	367	198	Chongqing	2389.......	1290

Largest vessel

	dwt	seasonal draught
Nanjing	20,000.......	8·2–9·5m
Wuhan	5,000.......	3·0–8·8m
Chongqing ..	3,000.......	1·5–4·0m

Hong Kong

Nautical Miles 0 — 30

Hong Kong (UK)

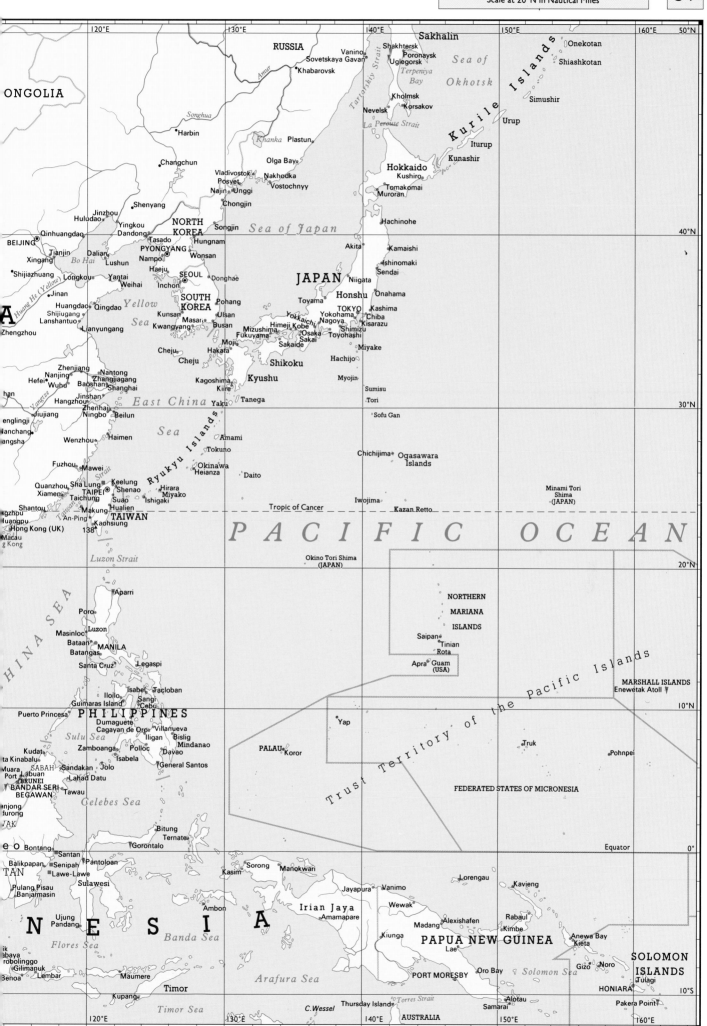

Scale at 20°N in Nautical Miles
0   720

Lloyd's Maritime Atlas

Copyright © Lloyd's of London Press Ltd.

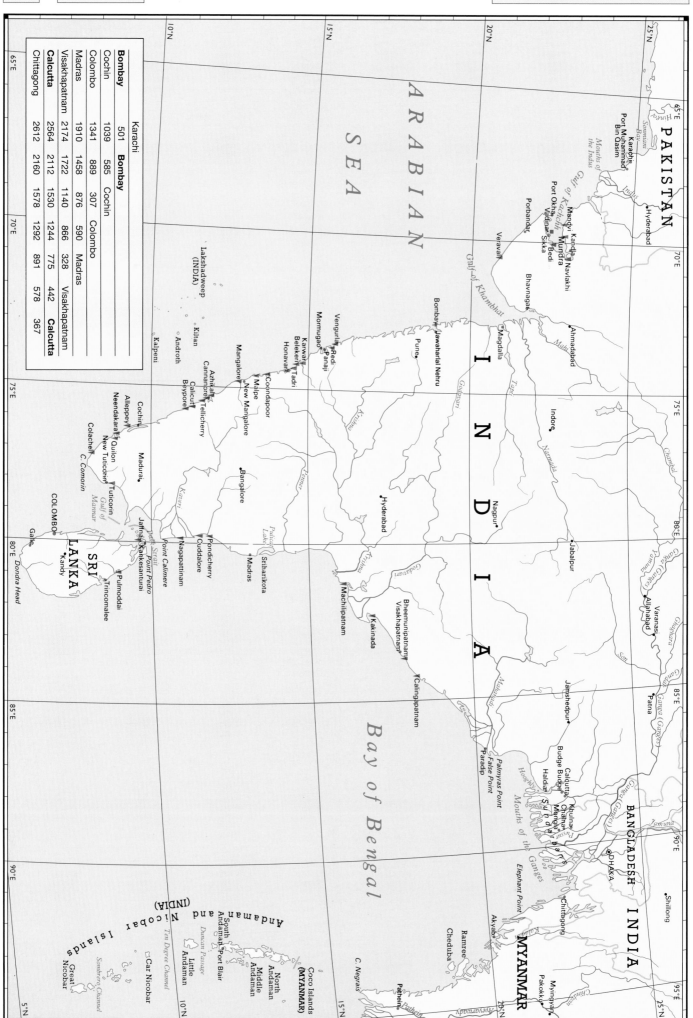

Scale at 20°N in Nautical Miles

0 — 300

Karachi							
Bombay	501	**Bombay**					
Cochin	1039	585	**Cochin**				
Colombo	1341	889	307	**Colombo**			
Madras	1910	1458	876	590	**Madras**		
Visakhapatnam	2174	1722	1140	866	328	**Visakhapatnam**	
Calcutta	2564	2112	1530	1244	775	442	**Calcutta**
Chittagong	2612	2160	1578	1292	891	578	367

0 _____ 240
Scale at 10°N in Nautical Miles

	Yangon				
Port Kelang	911	Port Kelang			
Singapore	1117	210	**Singapore**		
Bangkok	1944	1037	831	Bangkok	
Ho Chi Minh City	1759	852	646	681	Ho Chi Minh City
Da Nang	2144	1237	1031	1082	518	Da Nang
Haiphong	2435	1528	1322	1374	803	308	Haiphong

CHINA

Wuzhou

Xi

Nanning Yu

Hong (Red)

Da (Black)

Fangcheng
Beihai Zhanjiang
Port Wallut
Campha
HANOI Hongay
Haiphong Haikou

Gulf of
Tongking Yangpu
Hainan
Basuo

20°N

Paracel Islands
(Disputed)

Sanya Yulin

Luang Prabang

Mekong

Chieng Mai

MYANMAR

Salween

Mekong

VIENTIANE

L
A
O
S

V
I
E
T
N
A
M

Hue
Da Nang

Pathein YANGON

Salween

Tak

Mawlamyine

Ubon Ratchathani

15°N

THAILAND

Chao Phraya

Mouths of the Irrawaddy

Gulf of
Martaban

Dawei

Qui Nhon

Dawei Point

BANGKOK

Ko Sichang Sriracha
Bight
of Sattahip
Bangkok

Battambang

Chanthaburi

CAMBODIA
(KAMPUCHEA)

Vung Ro

Tonle Sap

Mergui

Kompong Cham

A
n
d
a
m
a
n

Mergui Archipelago

PHNOM PENH

Mekong

Ho Chi Minh City
Nha Be
My Tho

Nha Trang

S
e
a

Sihanoukville

Phu Quoc

10°N

Phangan

Samui

Khanom

Gulf of

Mui Bai Bung

Con Son

Spratly Islands
(Disputed)

Surat Thani

T h a i l a n d

Phuket
Phuket

S
O
U
T
H

Kantang

Songkhla

Pattani

C
H
I
N
A

Butang
Group

Teluk Ewa

Langkawi
Islands

Tapis

S
E
A

Sabang

Penang

Uleelheue
Kruengraya

Butterworth

Kuala Terengganu **MALAYSIA**

5°N

Blang Lancang
Kruenggeukueh Lhokseumawe

Kuala Beukah

Dungun
Kerteh

Kualalangsa

Ipoh

Tanjong Berhala

Pangkalan Susu

Lumut

Kuantan

PENINSULAR

Belawan

Teluk Intan

Udang

Medan
Kuala Tanjung

MALAYA

Tapaktuan

Telok Nibung

Kepulauan
Natuna

I
N
D
O

Port Kelang

KUALA LUMPUR

Tioman

Kepulauan
Anambas

(INDONESIA)

MALAYSIA

Simeulue

Tanjung Balai

Port Dickson
Tanjong Bruas
Melaka

Sibu
Sarikel
Tanjong Mani Binatang

Bagan Si Api Api

Muar
Batu Pahat

Lundu Kuching **SARAWAK**
Sijingkat Lingga

Sibolga

Dumai Bengkalis
Sungei Pakning
Lalang

Pasir Gudang
SINGAPORE
Telok Ramunia

Sambas
Pemangkat Singkawang

Gunung Sitoli

Siak

Pekanbaru

Singapore Inset
Tanjung Uban
Kijang

Kepulauan
Tambelan

N
E
S

KALIMANTAN

Nias

Kampar

Kepulauan Riau

Equator

Pontianak Landai

Telok Ayer

Kapuas

0° Equator

Batu Islands

Inaragiri

Kepulauan
Lingga

Penuba

Dabo

I
A

Siberut

Teluk Bayur
Padang

Selat Berhala

Sumatera

95°E 100°E 105°E 110°E

MYANMAR

Mergui
Sattahip
Chanthaburi

CAMBODIA
(KAMPUCHEA)

VIETNAM

Vung Ro

Gulf

PHNOM PENH

Phangan
Samui
Khanom

of

Sihanoukville
Phu Quoc
Ho Chi Minh City
Nha Be
My Tho

Andaman

Thailand

SOUTH

Sea

Mui Bai Bung
Con Son

CHINA

Phuket
Phuket

Kantang

Songkhla

Pattani

Spratly Islands
(Disputed)

SEA

Sabang
Uleelheue
Kruengraya
Kruenggeukueh
Blang Lancang
Lhokseumawe
Kuala Beukah

Teluk Ewa
Alor Setar

Penang
Butterworth

PENINSULAR

Kuala
Terengganu
Tapis

MALAYSIA

Balab
Palaw

Balabac Strait

Kudat
Tembungo
Ca
Sandak
Sapangar
Bay
Kota Kinabalu

SABAH

Kualalangsa
Pangkalan
Susu
Belawan

Ipoh
Teluk Intan

MALAYSIA

KUALA
LUMPUR

Dungun
Kerteh
Tanjong Berhala
Kuantan

Udang

BANDAR SERI BEGAWAN
BRUNEI
Lumut
Lutong Miri
Kuala Belait

Muara Port

Labuan

Limbang
Ku
Sen
Wallace Bay
Sebuk
Pulau Bunyu

Tapaktuan
Simeulue

Medan

Kuala Tanjung
Telok Nibung
Tanjung Balai

Port Kelang
Port Dickson
Tanjong Bruas
Melaka

Tioman

Kepulauan
Anambas

Kepulauan
Natuna

Brunei inset

Tanjong Kidurong

Bintulu

SARAWAK

Gunung Sitoli
Nias
Sibolga

Bagan Si Api Api

Dumai
Bengkalis
Sungei Pakning
Pekanbaru

Lalang

Pasir Gudang
Batu Pahat
Muar

SINGAPORE
Tanjung Uban
Kijang

Kepulauan
Riau

Kepulauan
Tambelan

Singkawang

Tanjong Mani
Sijingkat
Sambas
Pemangkat
Lundu

Sibu
Binatang
Sarikei
Lingga

Kuching

Rajang

Berau

Tanjungredeb

Batu
Islands
Padang
Teluk Bayur

Penuba
Dabo

Kepulauan
Lingga

Pontianak

Borneo

KALIMANTAN

Kapuas

Sangatta
Bontang

Siberut

Sipura

Jambi

Bangka

Telok Ayer

Ketapang

Samarinda
Senipah
Be
Balikpapa
Lawe-Law

Pagai
Utara

Pagai
Selatan

Muntok
Pangkalbalam

Palembang
Plaju

Bengkulu

Pulau Baai

Tanjung
Pandan

Manggar

Belitung

Sampit

Pulang
Pisau

Kuala Kapuas
Banjarmasin

Kota Baru
Laut

Enggano

Java Sea

Semangka Bay

Panjang
Tanjung
Sekong
Cigading
Prointal

Cinta
Bima
Arjuna

JAKARTA

Balongan
Cirebon

Bawean

Poleng

Kangean

Bandung

Tegal

Tuban

Semarang
Cilacap
Surakarta
Pasuruan
Meneng
Probolinggo
Banyuwangi

Gresik
Surabaya

Kalianget

Madura

Bali Sea

Panarukan

Gilimanuk
Celukan
Bawang
Bali
Benoa

Lombok
Lembar

Sum
Kemp

Christmas Island
(AUSTRALIA)

INDIAN

OCEAN

SINGAPORE

0   15
Nautical Miles

MALAYSIA

103°45'E
1°30'N

104°E
1°30'N

J'hore
Bahru

Sembawang
Pasir Gudang

SINGAPORE

Telok Ramunia

Jurong Port
Pulau Merlimau
Pulau Ayer
Chawan

Pasir
Panjang

SINGAPORE

1°15'N

Pulau Bukom

Singapore Strait

Selat Sinki

INDONESIA

Pulau Sambu
Pulau Batam

103°45'E   104°E

0 300
Scale at 0° in Nautical Miles

43

BRUNEI

0 45
Nautical Miles

114°E   115°E

SOUTH CHINA
SEA

Labuan   10°N

Muara Port   *Brunei Bay*   SABAH

5°N   BANDAR SERI BEGAWAN   Lawas   5°N
Limbang   Tanjong Salirong

Seria   Lumut
Baram   Kuala Belait   BRUNEI
Lutong   Miri   BRUNEI
Baram   MALAYSIA

4°N   SARAWAK   4°N

114°E   115°E   INDONESIA

MALAYSIA

120°E   Tandoc   125°E   130°E   135°E   140°E

Luzon
Batangas
Calapan   Santa Cruz
Mindoro   Tabaco   Legaspi
San Jose

PHILIPPINES

Masbate   Samar
Masbate   Catbalogan
Panay   Isabel   Tacloban
Iloilo   Cebu   Leyte
Guimaras Island   Sangi
Negros   Cebu
Buluta   Bohol
Bais   Bohol
Bacong   Sea
Dumaguete
Roxas   Villanueva
Cagayan de Oro
Iligan   Quinalang
Cove   Bislig
Zamboanga   Mindanao
Isabela   Polloc   Mati
Basilan   Datu Piang   Davao
Jolo   General Santos

Sulu
Sea

PACIFIC

Kepulauan
Talaud

Celebes
Sea

Sangihe   Tahuna

OCEAN

Manado
Bitung   Halmahera
Minahassa Peninsula   Ternate
Gorontalo   Gebe Island   Waigeo   Biak
Kepulauan Togian   Biak
Teluk   Bacan   *Halmahera*   Salawati   Sorong   Manokwari   Biak
Tomini   Obi   *Sea*   Salawati   Kasim   Yapen
Pantoloan   Peleng   Misool   Steenkool   Muturi
Palu   Kepulauan Sula   *Teluk Berau*   *Teluk*   Jayapura   Vanimo
Poso   *Cenderawasih*
Teluk   *Seram Sea*   Fak Fak
Towori   Seram   Bula   *Memberamo*
Malili   Buru   Seram   Adi   **Irian Jaya**   5°S
Mangkasa   Ambon   Amamapare
Pare Pare   *Teluk*   **PAPUA**
Pomalaa   *Bone*   Kepulauan   Kiunga   **NEW**
Ujung Pandang   Buton   Kai
Banda Sea   Kepulauan   **GUINEA**
Aru

Flores Sea   Damar   Merauke
Wetar   Roma
Flores   Moa   Babar   Kepulauan   10°S
Maumere   Dili   Tanimbar   *Torres Strait*
Timor   Thursday Island
Sumba   *Savu Sea*   C. York
Savu   *Arafura Sea*
Kupang   C. Wessel
Roti   Wessel
Timor Sea   Gove
Jabiru   Melville   *Gulf of Carpentaria*   Weipa   15°S
Bathurst   *Van Diemen*
Beagle Gulf   *Gulf*
Darwin

C. Londonderry   *Joseph Bonaparte*
Gulf

Wyndham

Yampi Sound
C. Leveque   **AUSTRALIA**

120°E   125°E   130°E   135°E   140°E

Singapore							
Belawan	375	Belawan					
Jakarta	525	861	Jakarta				
Surabaya	759	1130	386	Surabaya			
Darwin	1887	2254	1532	1200	Darwin		
Davao	1510	1881	1510	1246	1240	Davao	
Balikpapan	1055	1426	765	481	1169	771	Balikpapan
Sandakan	1040	1411	1248	1072	1444	568	605	Sandakan
Labuan	735	1106	935	1081	1804	884	997	412

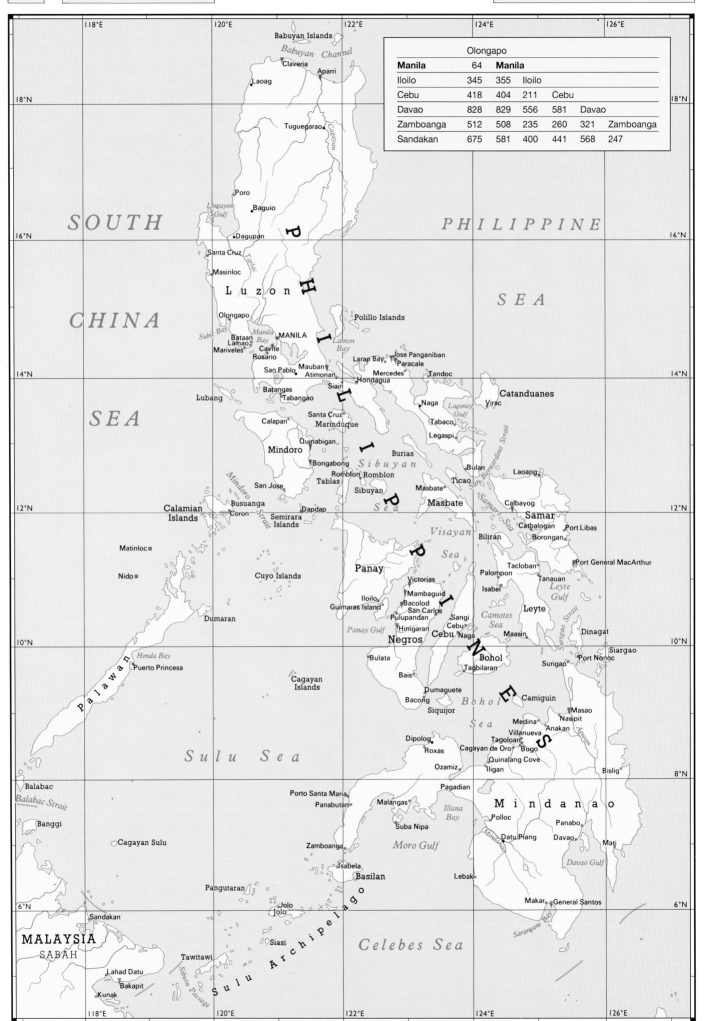

Scale at 12°N in Nautical Miles

0   150

Olongapo					
Manila	64	**Manila**			
Iloilo	345	355	Iloilo		
Cebu	418	404	211	Cebu	
Davao	828	829	556	581	Davao
Zamboanga	512	508	235	260	321	Zamboanga
Sandakan	675	581	400	441	568	247

SOUTH

CHINA

SEA

Babuyan Channel

Babuyan Islands

Claveria

Aparri

Laoag

Tuguegarao

Cagayan

PHILIPPINE

SEA

Poro

Baguio

Lingayen Gulf

Dagupan

Santa Cruz

Tarlac

Masinloc

Luzon

Olongapo

Subic Bay

Manila Bay

MANILA

Bataan

Lamao

Mariveles

Cavite

Rosario

San Pablo

Mauban

Atimonan

Mercedes

Hondagua

Siain

Polillo Islands

Lamon Bay

Larap Bay

Jose Panganiban

Paracale

Tandoc

PHILIPPINES

Lubang

Batangas

Tabangao

Calapan

Santa Cruz

Marinduque

Quinabigan

Mindoro

Naga

Lagonoy Gulf

Virac

Catanduanes

Tabaco

Legaspi

Burias

Bongabong

Romblon

Romblon

Tablas

Sibuyan

Sibuyan Sea

Ticao

Bulan

Laoang

San Bernardino Strait

San Jose

Masbate

Masbate

Samar Sea

Calbayog

Samar

Catbalogan

Port Libas

Calamian Islands

Busuanga

Coron

Mindoro Strait

Dapdap

Semirara Islands

Visayan Sea

Biliran

Borongan

Matinloc

Nido

Cuyo Islands

Panay

Victorias

Tacloban

Palompon

Port General MacArthur

Tanauan

Leyte Gulf

Isabel

Leyte

Dumaran

Iloilo

Guimaras Island

Mambaguid

Bacolod

San Carlos

Pulupandan

Sangi

Cebu

Naga

Hinigaran

Cebu

Maasin

Camotes Sea

Dinagat

Negros

Bulata

Bais

Bohol

Tagbilaran

Surigao

Siargao

Port Nonoc

Palawan

Honda Bay

Puerto Princesa

Cagayan Islands

Dumaguete

Bacong

Siquijor

Bohol Sea

Camiguin

Masao

Nasipit

Anakan

Medina

Villanueva

Tagoloan

Dipolog

Roxas

Cagayan de Oro

Bugo

Quinalang Cove

Ozamiz

Iligan

Bislig

Sulu Sea

Balabac

Balabac Strait

Banggi

Mindanao

Pagadian

Porto Santa Maria

Panabutan

Malangas

Suba Nipa

Illana Bay

Polloc

Panabo

Davao

Mati

Cagayan Sulu

Zamboanga

Isabela

Moro Gulf

Datu Piang

Mindanao

Davao Gulf

Pangutaran

Basilan

Lebak

MALAYSIA

SABAH

Sandakan

Sulu Archipelago

Celebes Sea

Siasi

Tawitawi

Sibutu Passage

Jolo

Jolo

Makar

General Santos

Sarangani Bay

Lahad Datu

Bakapit

Kunak

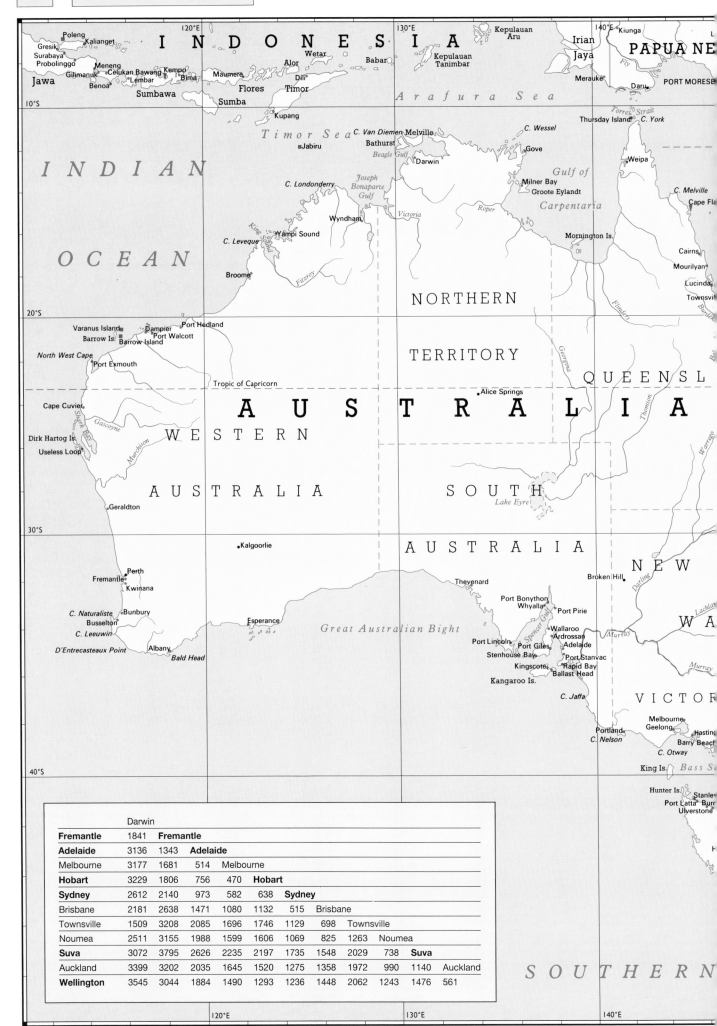

	Darwin									
Fremantle	1841	**Fremantle**								
Adelaide	3136	1343	**Adelaide**							
Melbourne	3177	1681	514	Melbourne						
Hobart	3229	1806	756	470	**Hobart**					
Sydney	2612	2140	973	582	638	**Sydney**				
Brisbane	2181	2638	1471	1080	1132	515	Brisbane			
Townsville	1509	3208	2085	1696	1746	1129	698	Townsville		
Noumea	2511	3155	1988	1599	1606	1069	825	1263	Noumea	
Suva	3072	3795	2626	2235	2197	1735	1548	2029	738	**Suva**
Auckland	3399	3202	2035	1645	1520	1275	1358	1972	990	1140	Auckland
Wellington	3545	3044	1884	1490	1293	1236	1448	2062	1243	1476	561

Scale at 30°S in Nautical Miles
0   480

JINEA
Solomon Sea
Anewa Bay
Bougainville Kieta
Lofung Choiseul
ro Bay
Kiriwina   Gizo Noro New   Santa Isabel
Viru Harbour   Georgia   SOLOMON
Woodlark   Yandina Tulagi Auki Malaita   ISLANDS
D'Entrecasteaux   HONIARA Aola Bay
Islands   Guadalcanal
Alotau   Pakera Point
Samarai   San Cristobal   Ndeni   Santa Cruz
Tagula   Rennell   Islands
                                      Paeu Vanikolo

Coral
CORAL SEA
Coringa
ISLANDS TERRITORY   Torres Islands
                                            Banks
Sea   Islands
                              Espiritu Santo
                              Santo Palikulo Bay
ot Point   Malakula Pentecost
                                      VANUATU
Hay Point   PORT VILA Efate
C. Townshend
                              Erromango
Rockhampton   Cato   Tanna
Port Alma Gladstone   Aneityum
Bundaberg Sandy Cape   Paagoumene
           Fraser Is.   Gomen
D   C. Moreton   Baie Ugue Poro
                                       Moueo Kouaoua
Brisbane   New Bourail Nakety
Toowoomba   Caledonia   Thio
                             (FRANCE) Noumea
                                          Ile des Pins

Rotuma
TUVALU Nukufetau Atoll
        FUNAFUTI
Nanumea Atoll

                    Wallis and
                    Futuna Islands Wallis
                    (FRANCE)   Uvea
                    Futuna
                             Alofi

Vanua Levu Malau
            Labasa
Savusavu
Lautoka Vatia   Lau
Vuda Point Levuka Group
Viti Levu SUVA FIJI
                                20°S

Matthew
Hunter
Walpole
Tropic of Capricorn

P A C I F I C

O C E A N

Norfolk Island
(AUSTRALIA)   Kermadec
                           Islands
                           (NZ)
                                30°S

Lord Howe Is.
(AUSTRALIA)

Newcastle
Catherine Hill Bay
Sydney   Three Kings Islands
Botany Bay   North Cape
Port Kembla   Whangaroa
                           Opua Whangarei
CANBERRA   Portland Marsden Point
AUSTRALIAN   Great Barrier Is.
PITAL TERRITORY   Auckland
Eden   Onehunga Bay of Plenty
                        Raglan Tauranga Mount Maunganui
C. Howe   Taharoa Hamilton East Cape
                              North Island
T a s m a n   S e a   New Plymouth Gisborne
                        Napier Hawke
nders Is.   Wanganui Bay
                                40°S

ddystone Point
                        C. Farewell Palmerston North
                   Tarakohe Nelson WELLINGTON
TASMANIA   Westport Picton
                                    NEW
g Bay   Greymouth   ZEALAND

                   Christchurch Lyttelton   Chatham
                   South Island Akaroa   Islands
                                                 (NZ)
                        Timaru

                   C. Providence Port Chalmers
                              Dunedin
                   Invercargill
                   Bluff   Bounty
                   Oban   Islands
                   Stewart Is.   (NZ)

OCEAN   Snares Is.

150°E   160°E   170°E   180°

	Guam									
Rabaul	1190	Rabaul								
Townsville	2566	1246	Townsville							
Sydney	3005	1844	1129	**Sydney**						
Auckland	3492	2357	1972	1275	Auckland					
Noumea	2530	1380	1263	1069	990	Noumea				
Suva	2805	1786	2029	1735	1140	738	**Suva**			
Apia	3068	2229	2620	2357	1583	1361	644	Apia		
Papeete	4332	3524	3873	3306	2215	2500	1835	1303	Papeete	
Honolulu	3333	3359	4252	4427	3820	3368	2783	2262	2380	**Honolulu**
San Francisco	5055	5399	6313	6456	5689	5467	4760	4167	3669	2095

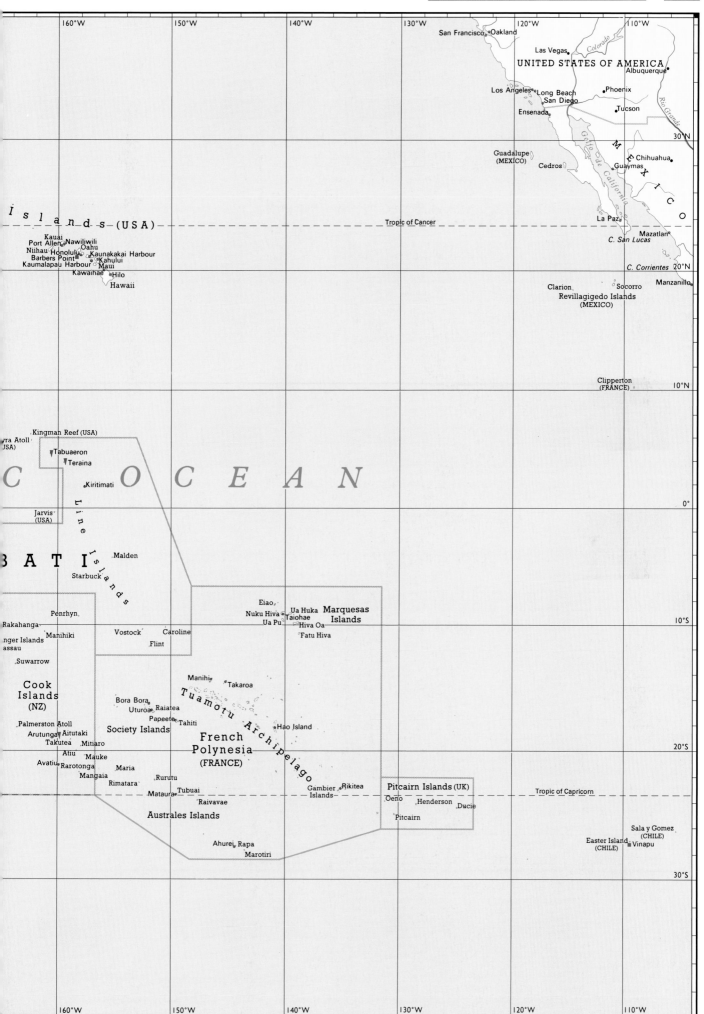

0   960
Scale at 0° in Nautical Miles

UNITED STATES OF AMERICA

San Francisco •Oakland

Las Vegas

Los Angeles• •Long Beach
   •San Diego
Ensenada•

•Albuquerque

•Phoenix

•Tucson

30°N

M E X I C O

Guadalupe
(MEXICO)
   Cedros

•Chihuahua
•Guaymas

Golfo de California

La Paz

C. San Lucas

Mazatlan

C. Corrientes   20°N

Manzanillo

Tropic of Cancer

I s l a n d s (USA)

Kauai
Port Allen •Nawiliwili
Niihau •Honolulu •Oahu
Barbers Point• •Kaunakakai Harbour
Kaumalapau Harbour• •Kahului
   •Maui
Kawaihae• •Hilo
  Hawaii

Clarion
  •Socorro
Revillagigedo Islands
(MEXICO)

Clipperton
(FRANCE) •   10°N

Kingman Reef (USA)

yra Atoll
JSA)

▼Tabuaeron

▼Teraina

•Kiritimati

C   O C E A N

Line Islands

Jarvis
(USA)

0°

B A T I

•Malden

Starbuck•

Penrhyn•

•Vostock   •Caroline

•Flint

Eiao•
Nuku Hiva• Ua Huka   **Marquesas**
 •Taiohae   **Islands**
Ua Pu• •Hiva Oa

•Fatu Hiva

10°S

Rakahanga•
nger Islands •Manihiki
assau

•Suwarrow

Manihi•
  •Takaroa

Tuamotu Archipelago

**Cook
Islands**
(NZ)

Bora Bora•
 Uturoa• •Raiatea
  Papeete• Tahiti
•Palmerston Atoll   **Society Islands**
Arutunga• •Aitutaki
Takutea• •Mitiaro
 Atiu• •Mauke
Avatiu• •Rarotonga •Maria
  Mangaia• •Rurutu
  Rimatara•
Mataura• •Tubuai

**French
Polynesia
(FRANCE)**

•Hao Island

20°S

Gambier •Rikitea
Islands

Pitcairn Islands (UK)
Oeno•
  •Henderson •Ducie
•Pitcairn

Tropic of Capricorn

•Raivavae

Australes Islands

Ahurei• Rapa
  •Marotiri

Sala y Gomez
  •(CHILE)
Easter Island• ■Vinapu
(CHILE)

30°S

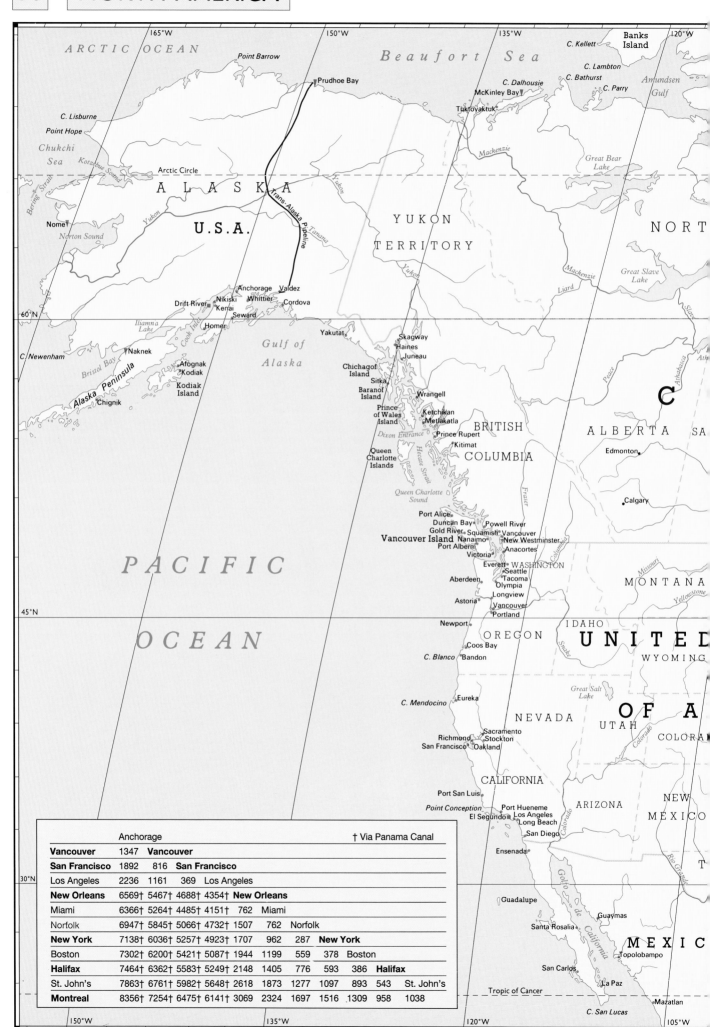

ARCTIC OCEAN

Beaufort Sea

Banks Island

C. Kellett

C. Lambton

C. Bathurst

Point Barrow

C. Dalhousie

Prudhoe Bay

C. Parry

McKinley Bay

Amundsen Gulf

Tuktoyaktuk

C. Lisburne

Point Hope

Mackenzie

Great Bear Lake

Chukchi Sea

Korzebue Sound

Arctic Circle

A L A S K A

Nome

Norton Sound

Yukon

U.S.A.

Trans-Alaska Pipeline

Tanana

Y U K O N

T E R R I T O R Y

N O R T

Yukon

Mackenzie

Great Slave Lake

Liard

Ath

60°N

Iliamna Lake

Anchorage

Valdez

Drift River

Nikiski

Whittier

Cordova

Kenai

Seward

Homer

Cook Inlet

Naknek

Gulf of Alaska

Yakutat

Skagway

Haines

Juneau

Chichagof Island

Sitka

Baranof Island

Wrangell

Ketchikan

Metlakatla

Prince Rupert

Kitimat

B R I T I S H

C O L U M B I A

Edmonton

A L B E R T A

SA

C

C. Newenham

Bristol Bay

Alaska Peninsula

Afognak

Kodiak

Kodiak Island

Chignik

Prince of Wales Island

Dixon Entrance

Hecate Strait

Queen Charlotte Islands

Queen Charlotte Sound

Fraser

Calgary

P A C I F I C

Port Alice

Duncan Bay

Powell River

Gold River

Squamish

Vancouver

Vancouver Island

Nanaimo

New Westminster

Port Alberni

Anacortes

Victoria

Everett

WASHINGTON

Seattle

Tacoma

Aberdeen

Olympia

Astoria

Longview

Vancouver

Portland

M O N T A N A

Columbia

Missouri

Yellowstone

45°N

O C E A N

Newport

O R E G O N

Coos Bay

C. Blanco

Bandon

I D A H O

U N I T E D

WYOMING

Snake

Great Salt Lake

C. Mendocino

Eureka

N E V A D A

U T A H

O F A

COLORA

Colorado

Sacramento

Stockton

Richmond

San Francisco

Oakland

C A L I F O R N I A

Port San Luis

Point Conception

El Segundo

Port Hueneme

Los Angeles

Long Beach

San Diego

A R I Z O N A

N E W

M E X I C O

Ensenada

30°N

Golfo de California

Guadalupe

Guaymas

Santa Rosalia

M E X I C

San Carlos

La Paz

Tropic of Cancer

Mazatlan

Topolobampo

C. San Lucas

	Anchorage				† Via Panama Canal				
Vancouver	1347	**Vancouver**							
San Francisco	1892	816	**San Francisco**						
Los Angeles	2236	1161	369	Los Angeles					
New Orleans	6569†	5467†	4688†	4354†	**New Orleans**				
Miami	6366†	5264†	4485†	4151†	762	Miami			
Norfolk	6947†	5845†	5066†	4732†	1507	762	Norfolk		
New York	7138†	6036†	5257†	4923†	1707	962	287	**New York**	
Boston	7302†	6200†	5421†	5087†	1944	1199	559	378	Boston
Halifax	7464†	6362†	5583†	5249†	2148	1405	776	593	386	**Halifax**
St. John's	7863†	6761†	5982†	5648†	2618	1873	1277	1097	893	543	St. John's
Montreal	8356†	7254†	6475†	6141†	3069	2324	1697	1516	1309	958	1038

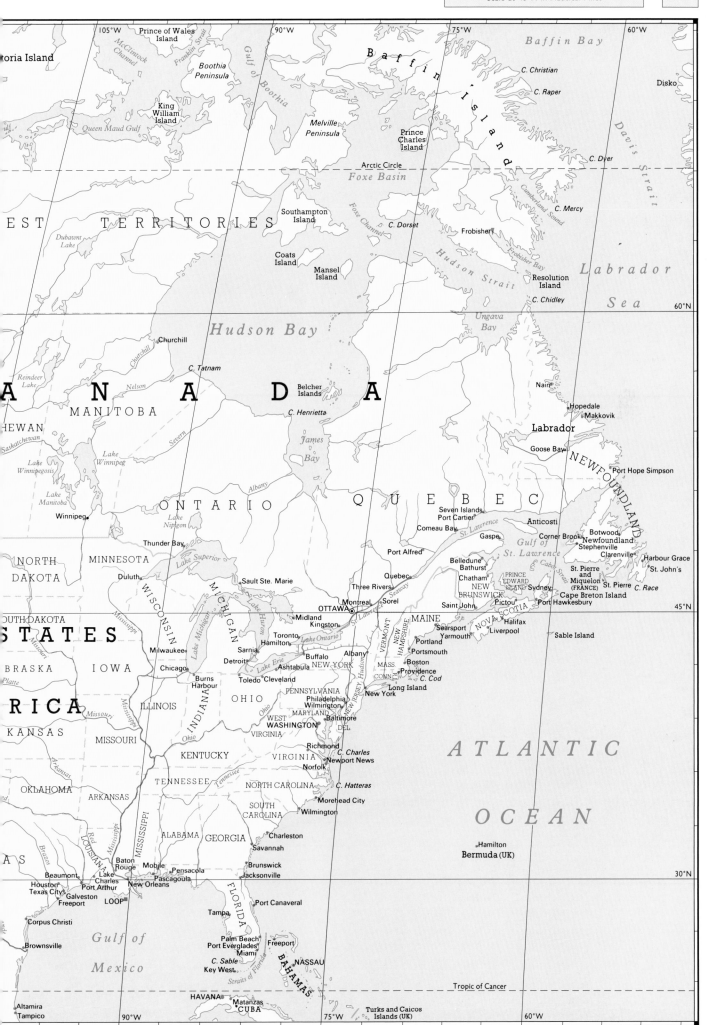

0 540
Scale at 45°N in Nautical Miles

Baffin Bay

105°W   Prince of Wales Island   90°W   75°W   60°W

McClintock Channel

Boothia Peninsula

Gulf of Boothia

Baffin Island

C. Christian
C. Raper

Disko

King William Island

Melville Peninsula

Prince Charles Island

Queen Maud Gulf

Arctic Circle

Foxe Basin

C. Dyer

Davis Strait

EST   TERRITORIES

Southampton Island

C. Dorset

Foxe Channel

Cumberland Sound

C. Mercy

Dubawnt Lake

Frobisher

Labrador

C. Chidley

Sea

Coats Island

Mansel Island

Hudson Strait

Frobisher Bay

Resolution Island

60°N

Hudson Bay

Ungava Bay

Reindeer Lake

Churchill   Churchill

Nelson

C. Tatnam

Nain

ANADA

HEWAN

MANITOBA

Saskatchewan

Severn

Belcher Islands

C. Henrietta

Hopedale
Makkovik

Labrador

Lake Winnipegosis

Lake Winnipeg

James Bay

Goose Bay

Port Hope Simpson

NEWFOUNDLAND

Lake Manitoba

Albany

ONTARIO

QUEBEC

Winnipeg

Lake Nipigon

Seven Islands
Port Cartier

Anticosti

Corner Brook

Botwood
Newfoundland
Stephenville
Clarenville

Harbour Grace

Thunder Bay

Lake Superior

Comeau Bay

St. Lawrence

Gulf of
St. Lawrence

NORTH DAKOTA

MINNESOTA

Duluth

Sault Ste. Marie

Port Alfred

Gaspe

St. Pierre and Miquelon (FRANCE)

St. John's

STATES

WISCONSIN

Lake Michigan

Lake Huron

Three Rivers

Quebec

Belledune
Bathurst

Chatham   NEW
BRUNSWICK

PRINCE
EDWARD
ISLAND

Sydney

Cabot Strait

St. Pierre   C. Race

SOUTH DAKOTA

Milwaukee

Sarnia

Toronto

Sorel

Seaway

Saint John

Pictou   Cape Breton Island

Port Hawkesbury

45°N

BRASKA

IOWA

Chicago

Detroit

Hamilton

Lake Ontario

Montreal

OTTAWA

St. Lawrence

Midland
Kingston

MAINE

NOVA SCOTIA

Halifax

RICA

ILLINOIS

INDIANA

Burns Harbour

Toledo   Cleveland

Lake Erie

Buffalo

Ashtabula

Albany

NEW YORK

VERMONT
NEW HAMPSHIRE

Searsport
Yarmouth

Portland

Liverpool

Sable Island

KANSAS

MISSOURI

OHIO

Ohio

PENNSYLVANIA

Philadelphia

NEW JERSEY

Hudson

MASS.
CONN.

Portsmouth

Boston
Providence

C. Cod

Long Island

New York

WEST
VIRGINIA

WASHINGTON

Baltimore

MARYLAND

DEL.

KENTUCKY

VIRGINIA

Richmond

C. Charles
Newport News
Norfolk

ATLANTIC

TENNESSEE

Tennessee

NORTH CAROLINA

C. Hatteras

OKLAHOMA

ARKANSAS

SOUTH
CAROLINA

Morehead City

Wilmington

OCEAN

Arkansas

ALABAMA   GEORGIA

Charleston

Savannah

AS

Red

LOUISIANA

MISSISSIPPI

Baton Rouge

Mobile

Pensacola
Pascagoula

Brunswick

Jacksonville

Hamilton

Bermuda (UK)

Brazos

Beaumont
Houston
Texas City
Galveston
Freeport

Port Arthur
Lake Charles

New Orleans

LOOP

FLORIDA

Port Canaveral

30°N

Corpus Christi

Tampa

Brownsville

Gulf of

Palm Beach
Port Everglades
Miami

Freeport

NASSAU

BAHAMAS

Mexico

C. Sable
Key West

Straits of Florida

Tropic of Cancer

Altamira
Tampico

90°W

HAVANA

Matanzas
CUBA

75°W

Turks and Caicos
Islands (UK)

60°W

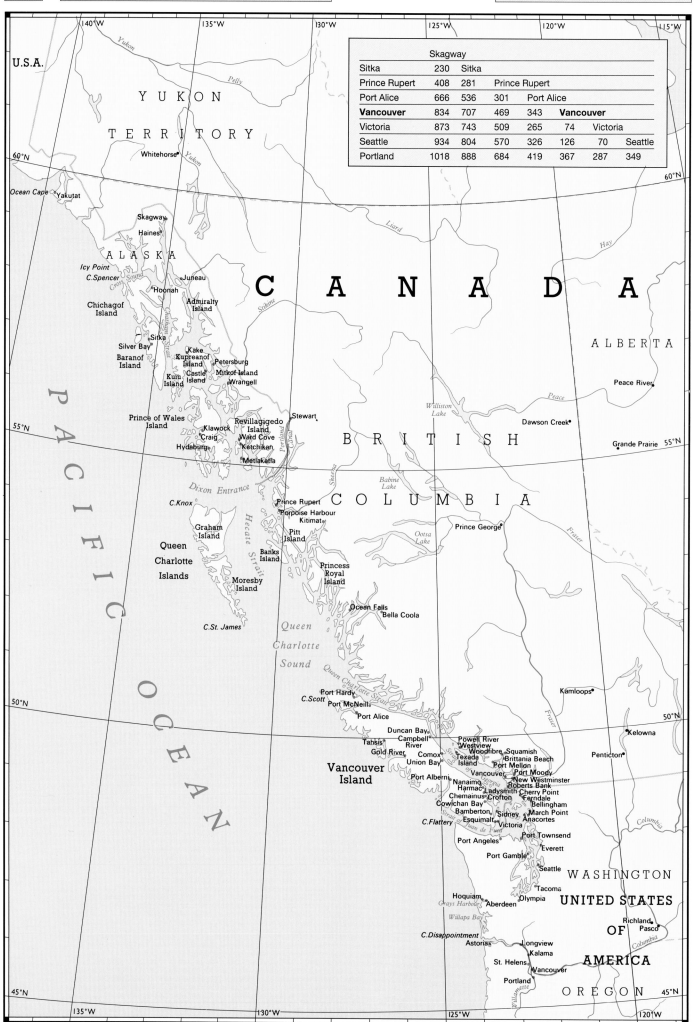

Skagway						
Sitka	230	Sitka				
Prince Rupert	408	281	Prince Rupert			
Port Alice	666	536	301	Port Alice		
Vancouver	834	707	469	343	**Vancouver**	
Victoria	873	743	509	265	74	Victoria
Seattle	934	804	570	326	126	70	Seattle
Portland	1018	888	684	419	367	287	349

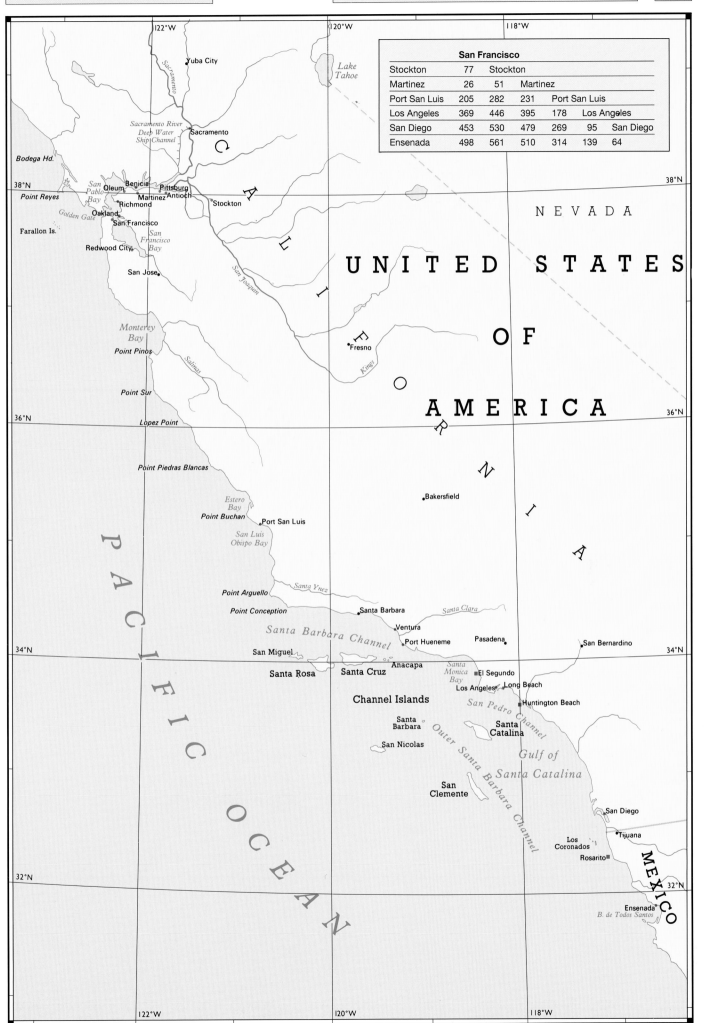

San Francisco					
Stockton	77	Stockton			
Martinez	26	51	Martinez		
Port San Luis	205	282	231	Port San Luis	
Los Angeles	369	446	395	178	Los Angeles
San Diego	453	530	479	269	95	San Diego
Ensenada	498	561	510	314	139	64

Yuba City

Lake Tahoe

Sacramento River Deep Water Ship Channel

Sacramento

Bodega Hd.

38°N

Benicia
Oleum
Martinez Pittsburg
Antioch
Stockton

San Pablo Bay
Point Reyes
Richmond
Oakland
Golden Gate
San Francisco
Farallon Is.
San Francisco Bay
Redwood City

San Jose

N E V A D A

U N I T E D   S T A T E S

C A L I F O R N I A

San Joaquin

Monterey Bay
Point Pinos

O F

Fresno

Point Sur

Salinas

Kings

A M E R I C A

36°N

Lopez Point

Point Piedras Blancas

Bakersfield

Estero Bay
Point Buchan
Port San Luis
San Luis Obispo Bay

Point Arguello
Santa Ynez
Point Conception
Santa Clara
Santa Barbara

Ventura
Pasadena
San Bernardino
Port Hueneme

34°N

San Miguel

Santa Barbara Channel

Santa Monica Bay
El Segundo
Long Beach
Los Angeles
Huntington Beach

San Pedro Channel

Santa Rosa
Santa Cruz
Anacapa

Channel Islands

Santa Barbara

San Nicolas

Santa Catalina

Gulf of Santa Catalina

Outer Santa Barbara Channel

San Clemente

San Diego
Tijuana

Los Coronados

Rosarito

MEXICO

32°N

Ensenada
B. de Todos Santos

P A C I F I C   O C E A N

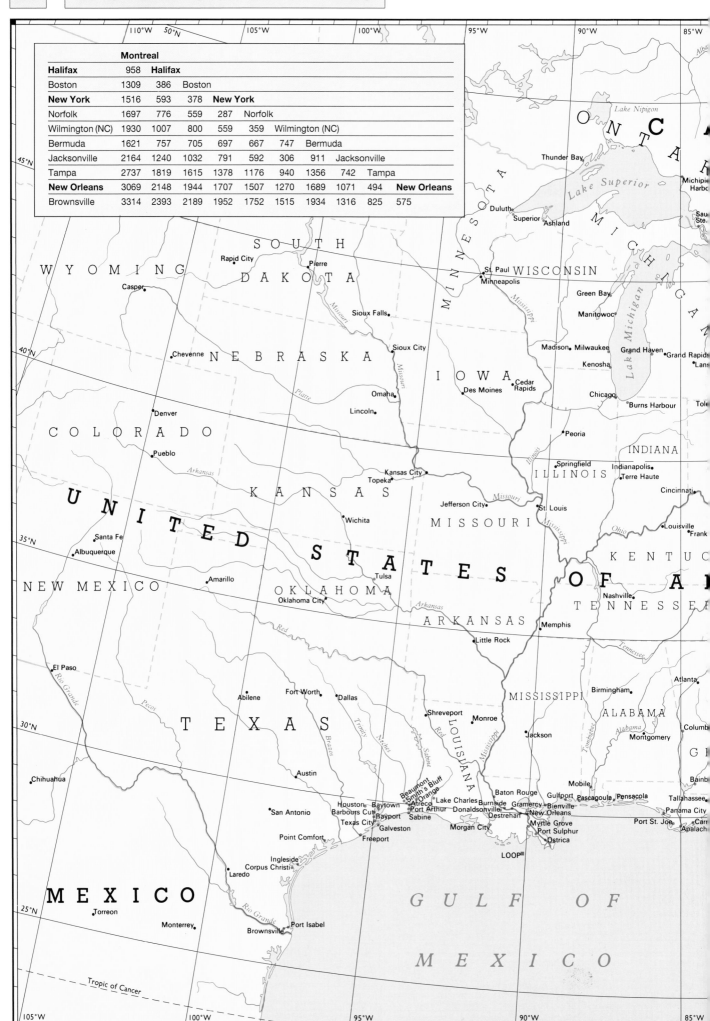

	Montreal	Halifax	Boston	New York	Norfolk	Wilmington (NC)	Bermuda	Jacksonville	Tampa	New Orleans	Brownsville
Halifax	958	Halifax									
Boston	1309	386	Boston								
New York	1516	593	378	New York							
Norfolk	1697	776	559	287	Norfolk						
Wilmington (NC)	1930	1007	800	559	359	Wilmington (NC)					
Bermuda	1621	757	705	697	667	747	Bermuda				
Jacksonville	2164	1240	1032	791	592	306	911	Jacksonville			
Tampa	2737	1819	1615	1378	1176	940	1356	742	Tampa		
New Orleans	3069	2148	1944	1707	1507	1270	1689	1071	494	**New Orleans**	
Brownsville	3314	2393	2189	1952	1752	1515	1934	1316	825	575	Brownsville

QUEBEC

CANADA

NEWFOUNDLAND
Stephenville

Seven Islands
Port Cartier
Anticosti
Gulf of St. Lawrence
Gaspé
Grand Bank
St. Pierre and Miquelon (FRANCE)
St. Pierre
C. Race

Comeau Bay
Magdalen Islands
C. North

Chicoutimi
Belledune
Bathurst
PRINCE EDWARD ISLAND
North Sydney
Sydney

Port Alfred
Gros Cacouna
Chatham
NEW
Charlottetown
Little Narrows

Quebec
BRUNSWICK
Port Hawkesbury
Point Tupper

Pictou
NOVA

Three Rivers
Saint John
Hantsport
SCOTIA
Sable Island

Sorel
MAINE
Halifax

Contrecoeur
Eastport
Meteghan
Lunenburg

Montreal
Searsport
Bucksport
Yarmouth
Liverpool

Valleyfield
Gulf of Maine

OTTAWA
Cornwall

Parry Sound
Bath
Portland

Midland
Collingwood
Kingston
Portsmouth
Gloucester

Toronto
Oswego
VERMONT
Boston

Hamilton
Port Weller
Albany
Troy
MASSACHUSETTS
Plymouth

Port Colborne
Buffalo
NEW YORK
CONNECTICUT
Providence
C. Cod
New Bedford

Erie
New Haven
New London

Ashtabula
Scranton
Long Island

Cleveland
NEW JERSEY
New York

PENNSYLVANIA
Trenton

Harrisburg
Philadelphia

Pittsburgh
Wilmington
Camden

Columbus
Baltimore
C. May

WEST VIRGINIA
WASHINGTON
Cambridge

Charleston
Piney Point

VIRGINIA
Richmond
C. Charles

Newport News
Norfolk
Portsmouth

ERICA
ATLANTIC OCEAN

Greensboro
Raleigh

NORTH CAROLINA
C. Hatteras

Charlotte
Morehead City

Greenville
C. Lookout

SOUTH
Columbia
Wilmington

CAROLINA
C. Fear
Bermuda
Hamilton
(UK)

Augusta
Georgetown

Charleston

Port Royal

Savannah

GIA
B.unswick

Fernandina

Jacksonville

LORIDA
Tropic of Cancer

Orlando
Port Canaveral

Tampa
St. Petersburg
Fort Pierce

Port Manatee

Boca Grande
Grand Bahama
Palm Beach

Port Everglades
Freeport
South Riding Point
Great Abaco

Miami
BAHAMAS
Eleuthera

C. Sable
NASSAU

Florida Keys
New Providence

Key West
Andros

Bermuda

0 ———— 5
Nautical Miles

64°50'W   64°40'W

St. George's Island
St. George's
St. David's Island

32°20'N
32°20'N

Ireland Island
Somerset Island
Freeport

Hamilton

Main Island

Bermuda (UK)

64°50'W   64°40'W

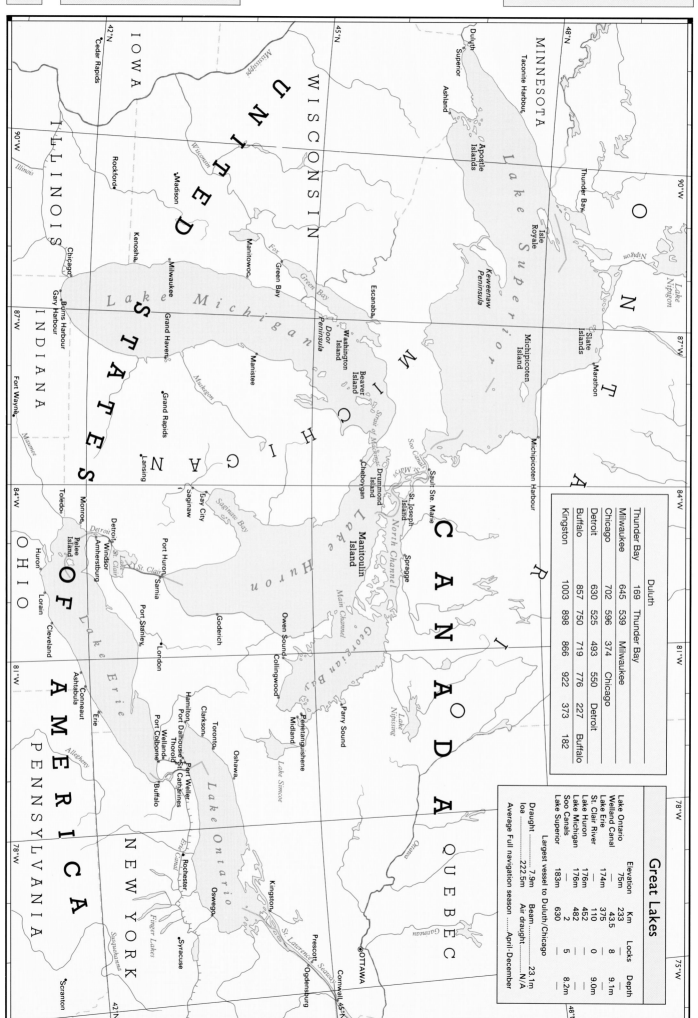

0 ————————— 120
Scale at 45°N in Nautical Miles

Distance table

	Duluth	Thunder Bay	Milwaukee	Chicago	Detroit	Buffalo
Thunder Bay	169					
Milwaukee	645	539				
Chicago	702	596	374			
Detroit	630	525	493	550		
Buffalo	857	750	719	776	227	
Kingston	1003	898	866	922	373	182

Great Lakes

	Elevation	Km	Locks	Depth
Lake Ontario	75m	233		
Welland Canal		43.5	8	9.1m
Lake Erie	174m	375		
St. Clair River		110	0	
Lake Huron	176m	452		
Lake Michigan	176m	482		
Soo Canals		2	5	9.0m
Lake Superior	183m	630		8.2m

Largest vessel to Duluth/Chicago

Draught	7.9m	Beam	23.1m
loa	222.5m	Air draught	N/A

Average Full navigation season ....April-December

Lloyd's Maritime Atlas

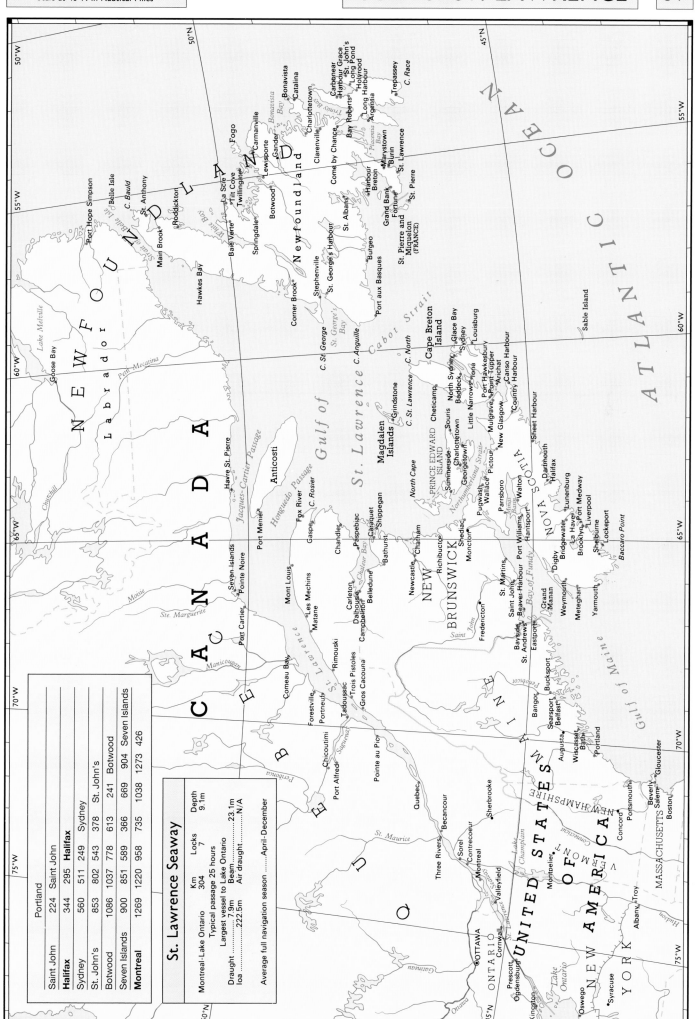

Distance table

	Portland	Saint John	Halifax	Sydney	St. John's	Botwood	Seven Islands
Saint John	224						
Halifax	344	295					
Sydney	560	511	249				
St. John's	853	802	543	378			
Botwood	1086	1037	778	613	241		
Seven Islands	900	851	589	366	669	904	
Montreal	1269	1220	958	735	1038	1273	426

St. Lawrence Seaway

	Km	Locks	Depth
Montreal–Lake Ontario	304	7	9.1m

Typical passage 25 hours

Largest vessel to Lake Ontario
Draught ....7.9m   Beam..........23.1m
loa ....222.5m   Air draught....N/A

Average full navigation season ......April–December

Lloyd's Maritime Atlas

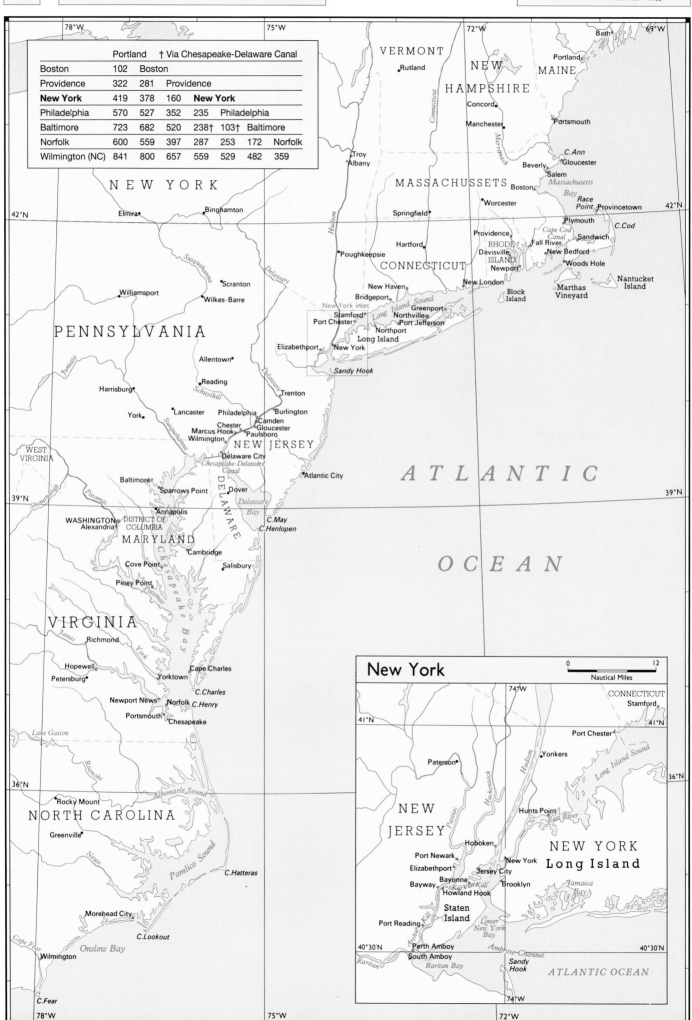

Scale at 39°N in Nautical Miles

0   90

	Portland	† Via Chesapeake-Delaware Canal				
Boston	102	Boston				
Providence	322	281	Providence			
New York	419	378	160	**New York**		
Philadelphia	570	527	352	235	Philadelphia	
Baltimore	723	682	520	238†	103†	Baltimore
Norfolk	600	559	397	287	253	172	Norfolk
Wilmington (NC)	841	800	657	559	529	482	359

New York

0   12
Nautical Miles

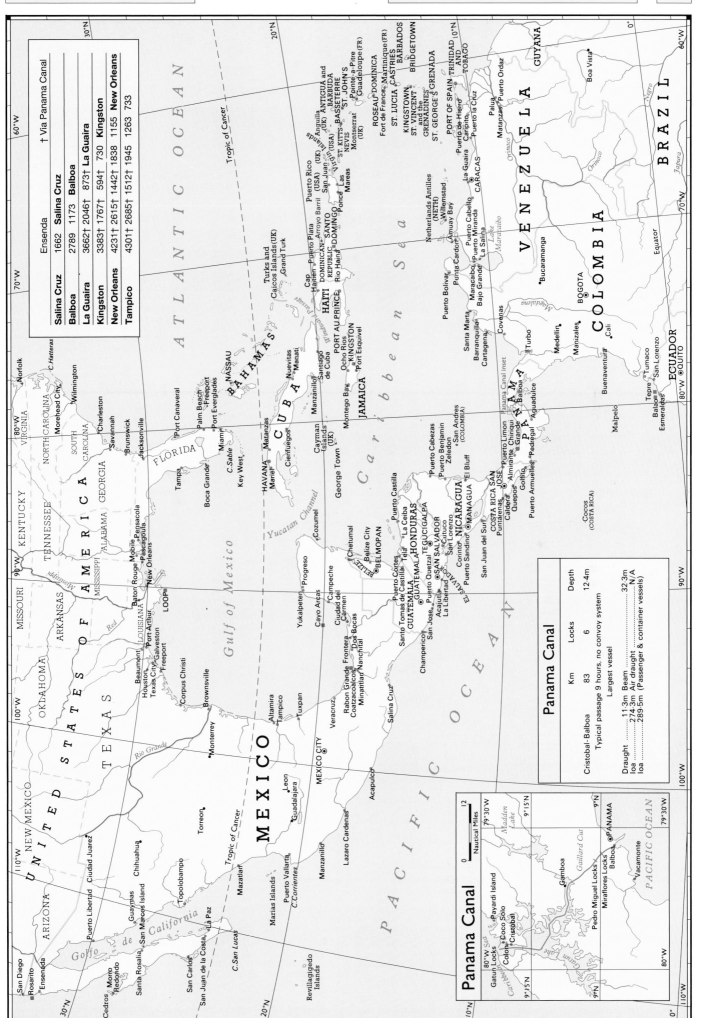

Scale at 20°N in Nautical Miles
0 480

	Ensenda	Salina Cruz	Balboa		
					†Via Panama Canal
Salina Cruz	1662	1173			
Balboa	2789	2046†	873†	La Guaira	
La Guaira	3662†	1767†	594†	730	Kingston
Kingston	3383†	2615†	1442†	1838	1155	New Orleans
New Orleans	4231†	2685†	1512†	1945	1263	733
Tampico	4301†				

Panama Canal

	Km	Locks	Depth
Cristobal–Balboa	83	6	12·4m

Typical passage 9 hours, no convoy system

Largest vessel

Draught .... 11·3m Beam .... 32·3m
loa .... 274·3m Air draught ... N/A
loa .... 289·5m (Passenger & container vessels)

Panama Canal

Nautical Miles
0 12

0 — 180
Scale at 18°N in Nautical Miles

	Cristobal									
Belize City	798	Belize City								
Havana	990	523	Havana							
Kingston	555	696	743	**Kingston**						
Port au Prince	766	930	657	278	Port au Prince					
Santo Domingo	800	1092	939	428	444	Santo Domingo				
San Juan	992	1302	969	635	549	230	San Juan			
Castries	1158	1603	1358	952	938	587	412	Castries		
Port of Spain	1140	1624	1478	999	1035	678	575	222	**Port of Spain**	
La Guaira	834	1321	1281	730	790	500	538	404	329	**La Guaira**
Cartagena	276	901	1075	483	642	606	776	924	905	598

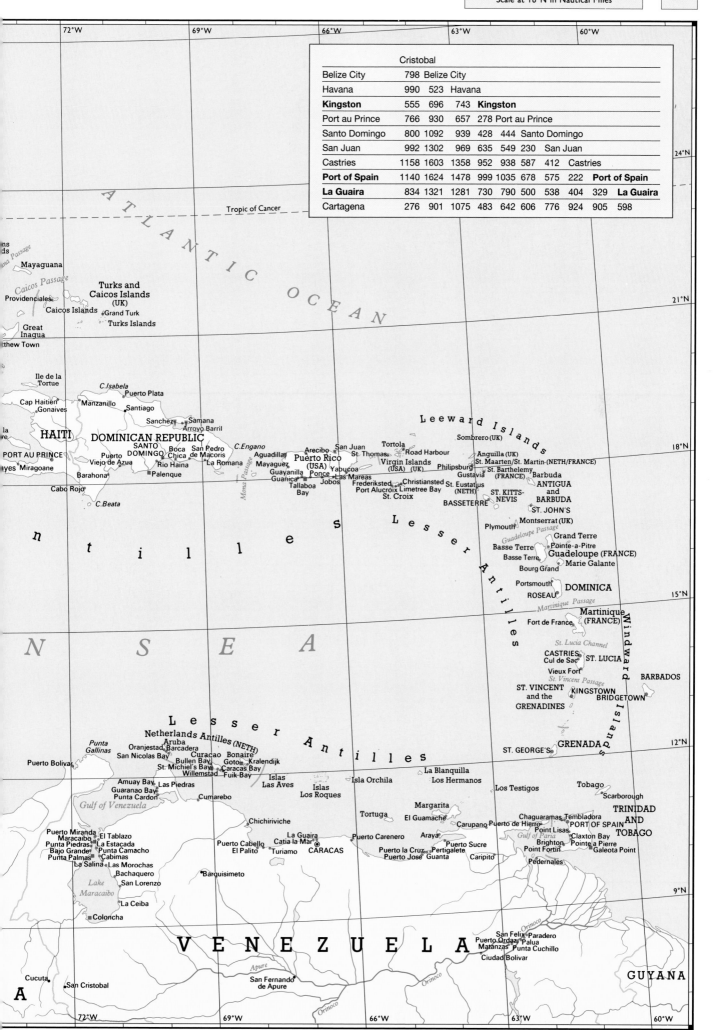

Maritime Atlas

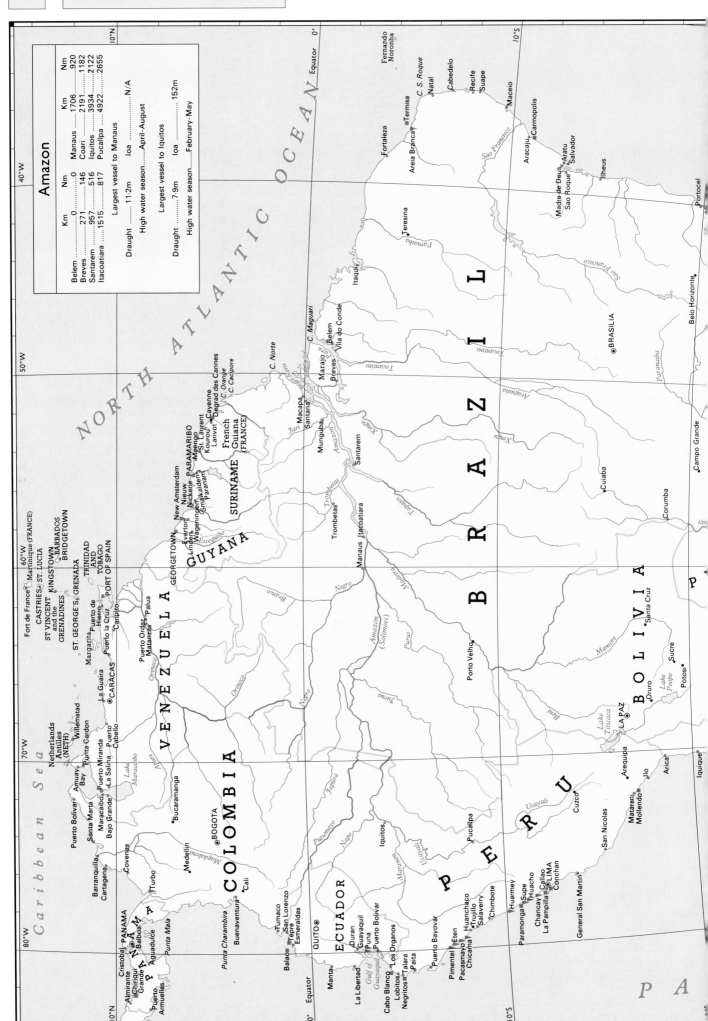

Amazon

	Km	Nm		Km	Nm
Belem	0	0	Manaus	1706	920
Breves	271	146	Coari	2191	1182
Santarem	957	516	Iquitos	3934	2122
Itacoatiara	1515	817	Pucallpa	4922	2655

Largest vessel to Manaus

Draught	11·2m	loa	N/A

High water season......April-August

Largest vessel to Iquitos

Draught	7·9m	loa	152m

High water season......February-May

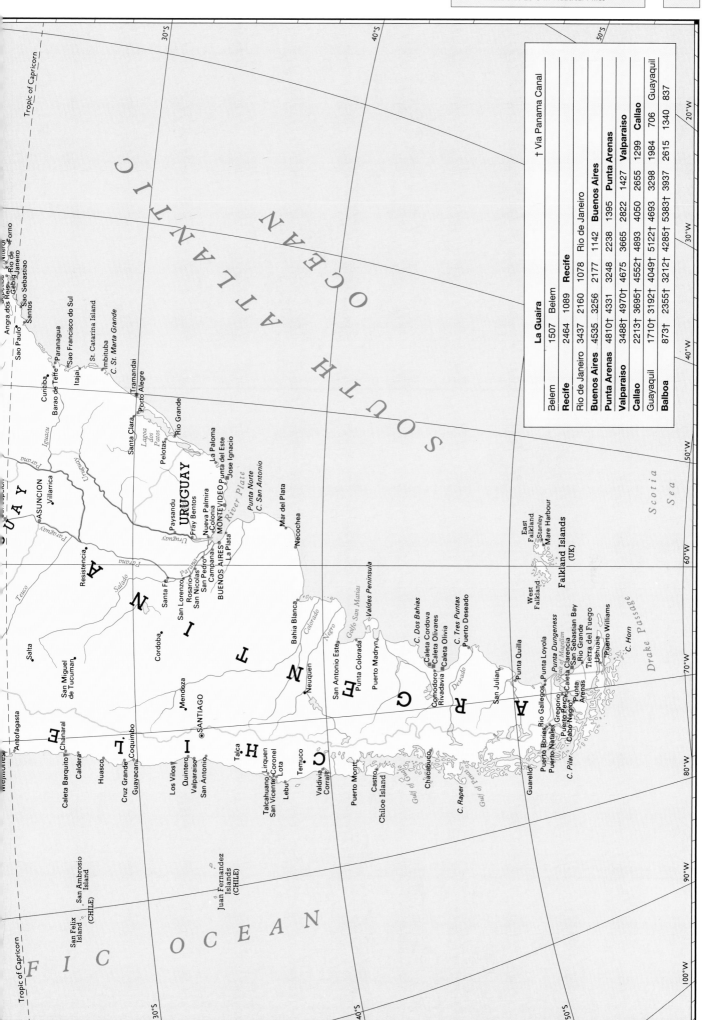

0   480
Scale at 20°S in Nautical Miles

	La Guaira	Belem									† Via Panama Canal
Belem	1507	Belem									
Recife	2464	1089	**Recife**								
Rio de Janeiro	3437	2160	1078	Rio de Janeiro							
Buenos Aires	4535	3256	2177	1142	**Buenos Aires**						
Punta Arenas	4810†	4331	3248	2238	1395	**Punta Arenas**					
Valparaiso	3488†	4970†	4675	3665	2822	1427	**Valparaiso**				
Callao	2213†	3695†	4552†	4893	4050	2655	1299	**Callao**			
Guayaquil	1710†	3192†	4049†	5122†	4693	3298	1984	706	Guayaquil		
Balboa	873†	2355†	3212†	4285†	5383†	3937	2615	1340	837		

SOUTH ATLANTIC OCEAN

Tropic of Capricorn

URUGUAY

ARGENTINA

CHILE

PARAGUAY

ASUNCION

MONTEVIDEO

BUENOS AIRES

SANTIAGO

Falkland Islands (UK)
East Falkland
West Falkland
Stanley
Mare Harbour

Scotia Sea

Drake Passage
C. Horn

PACIFIC OCEAN

Tropic of Capricorn

Juan Fernandez Islands (CHILE)

San Ambrosio Island (CHILE)
San Felix Island (CHILE)

0   240

Scale at 26°S in Nautical Miles

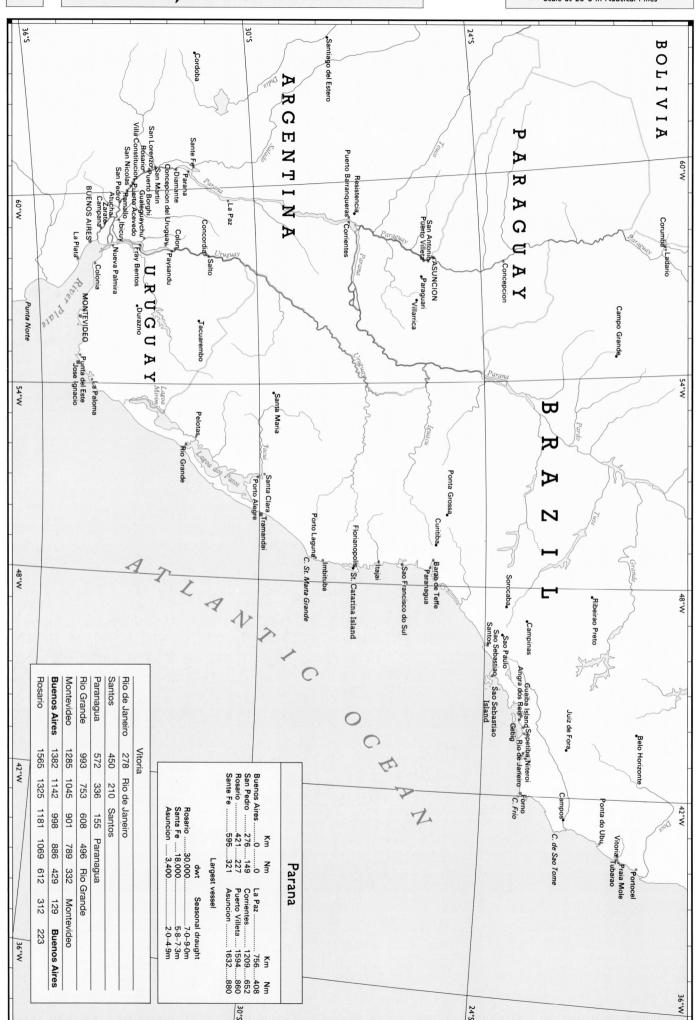

Vitoria							
278	Rio de Janeiro						
450	210	Santos					
572	336	155	Paranagua				
993	753	608	496	Rio Grande			
1285	1045	901	789	332	Montevideo		
1382	1142	998	886	429	129	Buenos Aires	
1565	1325	1181	1069	612	312	223	Rosario

Parana

	Km	Nm		Km	Nm
Rosario	0	0	La Paz	756	408
San Pedro	276	149	Corrientes	1209	652
Rosario	421	227	Puerto Villeta	1594	860
Santa Fe	595	321	Asuncion	1632	880

Largest vessel

	dwt	Seasonal draught
Rosario	30,000	7.0-9.0m
Santa Fe	18,000	5.8-7.3m
Asuncion	3,400	2.0-4.9m

GEOGRAPHIC INDEX

UNITED KINGDOM   1A

ENGLAND

River Thames   p.16/17
  London 51 30 N 0 04 W

| P | Q | Y | G | C | R | B | T | A | L | | |

  Convoys Wharf 51 29 N 0 01 W
  Greenwich 51 29 N 0 00
  Dagenham 51 31 N 0 09 E
  Erith 51 29 N 0 11 E
  Woolwich 51 30 N 0 04 E
  Barking 51 31 N 0 05 E
  Purfleet 51 28 N 0 15 E
  Dartford 51 27 N 0 16 E
  Greenhithe 51 27 N 0 17 E
  Grays 51 28 N 0 18 E
  Tilbury 51 27 N 0 20 E

| Y | G | C | R | B | T | A | L | | | |

  Gravesend 51 27 N 0 22 E
  Cliffe 51 29 N 0 28 E
  Shell Haven 51 30 N 0 31 E
  Coryton 51 31 N 0 32 E
  Hole Haven 51 30 N 0 33 E
  Canvey Island 51 31 N 0 38 E
  Chapman Anchorage 51 30 N 0 38 E
  Leigh 51 33 N 0 39 E
  Southend-on-Sea 51 32 N 0 43 E
River Medway   1B
  Medway

| P | Q | Y | G | C | R | B | D | T | A | |

  Isle of Grain 51 26 N 0 43 E
  Thamesport 51 26 N 0 42 E

| Y | G | C | T | A | | | | | | |

  Kethole Anchorage 51 26 N 0 40 E
  Bee Ness 51 26 N 0 39 E
  Oakham Ness 51 25 N 0 39 E
  Kingsnorth 51 25 N 0 36 E
  Upnor 51 25 N 0 32 E
  Strood 51 23 N 0 30 E
  Rochester 51 24 N 0 30 E
  Halling 51 21 N 0 27 E
  Snodland 51 20 N 0 27 E
  Chatham 51 24 N 0 33 E
  Gillingham 51 29 N 0 33 E
  Rainham 51 23 N 0 37 E
  Otterham Quay 51 23 N 0 38 E
  Stangate Creek 51 23 N 0 42 E
  Queenborough 51 25 N 0 44 E
  Sheerness 51 26 N 0 44 E
Ridham Dock 51 23 N 0 46 E   1C
Grovehurst Jetty 51 22 N 0 46 E
Sittingbourne 51 21 N 0 44 E
Milton Creek 51 22 N 0 46 E
Faversham 51 20 N 0 54 E
Whitstable 51 22 N 1 02 E

| Y | G | B | A | | | | | | | |

Herne Bay 51 23 N 1 08 E
Margate 51 23 N 1 23 E
North Foreland 51 22 N 1 27 E
Ramsgate 51 20 N 1 25 E

| Y | G | C | R | B | T | A | | | | |

River Stour
  Richborough 51 18 N 1 21 E

| P | G | B | A | | | | | | | |

  Sandwich 51 16 N 1 20 E
  Deal 51 13 N 1 24 E
The Downs 51 13 N 1 27 E   1D
South Foreland 51 08 N 1 23 E
Dover 51 07 N 1 20 E

| Y | G | C | R | B | T | A | L | | | |

Folkestone 51 05 N 1 12 E

| G | R | A | | | | | | | | |

Sandgate 51 04 N 1 06 E
Hythe 51 04 N 1 04 E
Dungeness 50 55 N 0 59 E
Rye 50 56 N 0 46 E

| Y | G | B | T | A | | | | | | |

Hastings 50 51 N 0 35 E
Royal Sovereign Light 50 43 N 0 26 E
Beachy Head 50 44 N 0 15 E
Seaford 50 46 N 0 07 E

Newhaven 50 47 N 0 04 E   2A

| Y | G | C | R | B | T | A | | | | |

Brighton 50 49 N 0 06 W
Shoreham 50 50 N 0 15 W

| P | Q | Y | G | R | B | D | T | A | | |

Worthing 50 48 N 0 23 W
Littlehampton 50 48 N 0 32 W

| Y | G | A | | | | | | | | |

Owers Light 50 40 N 0 41 W
Selsey Bill 50 43 N 0 47 W
Chichester Harbour
  Bosham 50 48 N 0 54 W
  Nab Tower 50 40 N 0 57 W
Langstone Harbour
  Bedhampton 50 50 N 1 00 W
Portsmouth 50 48 N 1 06 W

| Q | Y | G | C | R | B | T | A | | | |

Fareham 50 51 N 1 11 W
Gosport 50 48 N 1 07 W
Fort Gilkicker 50 46 N 1 08 W
Stokes Bay 50 47 N 1 09 W
Isle of Wight   2B
  Ryde 50 44 N 1 09 W
  St. Helen's 50 42 N 1 05 W
  Bembridge 50 41 N 1 05 W
  Niton 50 35 N 1 17 W
  St. Catherine's Point 50 34 N 1 18 W
  Freshwater Bay 50 40 N 1 31 W
  Needles 50 40 N 1 35 W
  Yarmouth 50 42 N 1 30 W
  Cowes 50 46 N 1 18 W

| P | Y | G | R | B | T | A | | | | |

  River Medina
    Newport 50 42 N 1 17 W

| Y | G | B | | | | | | | | |

Southampton Water
  Hamble 50 49 N 1 18 W

| P | A | | | | | | | | | |

  River Itchen 50 54 N 1 22 W
  Southampton 50 54 N 1 24 W

| Y | G | C | R | B | D | T | A | L | | |

  Redbridge 50 56 N 1 28 W
  River Test
    Totton 50 55 N 1 29 W
    Eling 50 54 N 1 28 W
  Hythe 50 52 N 1 23 W
  Fawley 50 49 N 1 20 W

| P | Q | B | T | | | | | | | |

Calshot Light Vessel 50 48 N 1 17 W   2C
Lymington 50 45 N 1 32 W
Christchurch 50 44 N 1 45 W
Bournemouth 50 43 N 1 54 W
Poole 50 43 N 1 59 W

| P | Q | Y | G | C | R | B | T | A | | |

Swanage 50 37 N 1 58 W
Weymouth 50 37 N 2 27 W

| Y | G | R | B | A | | | | | | |

Portland 50 34 N 2 26 W

| Q | G | B | T | A | | | | | | |

Portland Bill 50 31 N 2 27 W

CHANNEL ISLANDS   2D

Casquets 49 44 N 2 23 W   p.18
Alderney 49 43 N 2 12 W

| P | G | A | | | | | | | | |

Guernsey
  St. Peter Port 49 27 N 2 32 W

| P | Q | Y | G | C | R | B | A | L | | |

  St. Sampson 49 29 N 2 31 W
Sark 49 26 N 2 22 W
Jersey
  Corbiere Point 49 11 N 2 15 W
  St. Aubin 49 11 N 2 10 W
  St. Helier 49 11 N 2 07 W

| P | Q | Y | G | C | R | B | T | A | L | |

  Gorey 49 12 N 2 01 W
  Ronez 49 15 N 2 08 W

Les Minquiers   3A
  Maitresse Island 48 58 N 2 04 W

ENGLAND

Lyme Bay   p.16/17
  Bridport 50 43 N 2 46 W

| G | B | A | | | | | | | | |

  Lyme Regis 50 43 N 2 56 W
  Sidmouth 50 41 N 3 15 W
  River Exe
    Exmouth 50 37 N 3 25 W
    Topsham 50 41 N 3 38 W
    Exeter 50 43 N 3 31 W
  Teignmouth 50 33 N 3 30 W

| Y | G | R | B | A | | | | | | |

Tor Bay
  Torquay 50 27 N 3 32 W

| Y | G | B | T | A | | | | | | |

  Brixham 50 24 N 3 30 W

| B | T | A | | | | | | | | |

Berry Head 50 24 N 3 29 W   3B
River Dart
  Dartmouth 50 21 N 3 35 W

| G | B | T | A | | | | | | | |

  Tuckenhay 50 24 N 3 40 W
  Totnes 50 26 N 3 41 W

| Y | G | B | A | | | | | | | |

Start Point 50 13 N 3 39 W
Prawle Point 50 12 N 3 43 W
Salcombe 50 14 N 3 46 W
Kingsbridge 50 17 N 3 47 W
Bolt Head 50 13 N 3 47 W
Plymouth Sound
  Plymouth 50 22 N 4 11 W

| P | Y | G | R | B | T | A | L | | | |

  Devonport 50 22 N 4 10 W
  River Tamar
    Saltash 50 24 N 4 12 W
  St. Germans River
    St. Germans 50 24 N 4 20 W
  Torpoint 50 22 N 4 12 W
Eddystone Light 50 11 N 4 16 W
Looe 50 21 N 4 27 W
Fowey 50 20 N 4 38 W

| Y | G | B | T | A | | | | | | |

Par 50 21 N 4 42 W

| P | Y | G | B | | | | | | | |

Charlestown 50 20 N 4 45 W   3C

| Y | G | B | A | | | | | | | |

Pentewan 50 17 N 4 47 W
Mevagissey 50 16 N 4 47 W
River Fal
  Truro River
    Truro 50 10 N 5 02 W

| Y | G | B | A | | | | | | | |

    Woodbury 50 11 N 5 01 W
  Penryn River
    Penryn 50 10 N 5 06 W

| Y | G | B | A | | | | | | | |

Falmouth 50 10 N 5 03 W

| P | G | B | D | T | A | L | | | | |

Helford River   3D
  Porth Navas 50 06 N 5 08 W
  Gweek 50 05 N 5 12 W
Porthoustock 50 03 N 5 04 W
Dean Quarry 50 02 N 5 05 W
Coverack 50 01 N 5 06 W
Lizard 49 57 N 5 12 W
Mount's Bay
  Porth Mellin 50 01 N 5 15 W
  Poldhu 50 02 N 5 16 W
  Porthleven 50 05 N 5 19 W
  Marazion 50 07 N 5 29 W
  Penzance 50 08 N 5 32 W

| Y | G | B | D | T | A | L | | | | |

  Newlyn 50 08 N 5 33 W

| G | B | A | | | | | | | | |

GEOGRAPHIC INDEX

ENGLAND *continued* — 4A

Mousehole 50 05 N 5 32 W
Porthcurno 50 02 N 5 38 W
Wolf Rock 49 57 N 5 48 W
Land's End 50 04 N 5 43 W
Longships Light 50 04 N 5 45 W
Isles of Scilly
  St. Mary's Island
    St. Mary's 49 55 N 6 19 W
`[G][A]`

St. Agnes Island 49 53 N 6 20 W
Bishop Rock 49 52 N 6 27 W
Cape Cornwall 50 08 N 5 43 W
Pendeen 50 10 N 5 40 W
St. Ives 50 13 N 5 29 W
Hayle 50 11 N 5 26 W
Portreath 50 16 N 5 17 W
St. Agnes Head 50 19 N 5 14 W
Newquay 50 25 N 5 05 W
Trevose Head 50 33 N 5 02 W
River Camel
  Padstow 50 33 N 4 56 W
`[Y][G][B][A]`

Wadebridge 50 31 N 4 50 W
Portquin 50 35 N 4 52 W
Port Isaac 50 36 N 4 50 W
Boscastle 50 42 N 4 42 W
Bude 50 50 N 4 33 W
Hartland Point 51 01 N 4 32 W
Lundy Island 51 10 N 4 39 W
River Torridge
  Appledore 51 03 N 4 12 W
  Instow 51 03 N 4 10 W
  Westleigh 51 02 N 4 11 W
  Northam 51 02 N 4 13 W
  Bideford 51 01 N 4 12 W
`[G][B][A]`

4B

River Taw
  Yelland 51 04 N 4 09 W
  Fremington 51 05 N 4 08 W
  Barnstaple 51 05 N 4 04 W
Ilfracombe 51 12 N 4 07 W
Lynmouth 51 14 N 3 50 W
Minehead 51 13 N 3 28 W
Watchet 51 11 N 3 20 W
`[G][B][A]`

4C

River Parrett
  Combwich 51 11 N 3 03 W
  Dunball 51 10 N 2 59 W
  Bridgwater 51 10 N 3 00 W
`[Y][G][R][B][A]`

Highbridge 51 13 N 2 59 W
Burnham 51 15 N 3 00 W
Walton Bay 51 28 N 2 49 W
Portishead 51 29 N 2 46 W
King Road 51 30 N 2 46 W
River Avon
  Portbury 51 30 N 2 44 W
  Avonmouth 51 30 N 2 43 W
  Bristol 51 27 N 2 38 W
`[P][Q][Y][G][C][R][B][D][T][A][L]`

River Severn
  Lydney 51 43 N 2 32 W
`[G][A]`

Sharpness 51 43 N 2 29 W
`[Y][G][C][R][B][D][T][A]`

Gloucester 51 52 N 2 13 W

WALES — 4D

River Wye
  Chepstow 51 39 N 2 40 W
River Usk
  Newport 51 34 N 2 59 W
`[Y][G][C][R][B][D][T][A][L]`

Cardiff 51 28 N 3 11 W
`[P][Y][G][C][R][B][T][A][L]`

Penarth 51 26 N 3 10 W
Barry 51 24 N 3 16 W
`[P][Q][Y][G][R][B][D][A]`

Barry Island 51 23 N 3 16 W

5A

Porthcawl 51 28 N 3 42 W
Port Talbot 51 35 N 3 43 W
`[Y][B][T][A]`

River Neath
  Briton Ferry 51 37 N 3 50 W
  Neath 51 38 N 3 50 W
`[P][G][B][T][A]`

Swansea 51 37 N 3 56 W
`[P][Q][Y][G][C][R][B][D][T][A][L]`

Mumbles 51 34 N 3 58 W
Llanelli 51 40 N 4 10 W
Burry Port 51 40 N 4 15 W
River Towy
  Carmarthen 51 51 N 4 18 W
Saundersfoot 51 43 N 4 42 W
Tenby 51 42 N 4 43 W
Caldy Island 51 38 N 4 41 W
St. Govan's Head 51 36 N 4 55 W
Milford Haven
`[P][Q][G][R][B][T][A]`

Angle Bay 51 41 N 5 05 W
Pembroke Dock 51 42 N 4 57 W
`[Y][G][C][B][D][T]`

West Cleddau River
  Haverfordwest 51 48 N 4 58 W
  Neyland 51 42 N 4 57 W
Milford Docks 51 43 N 5 02 W
`[G][B][D][T][A]`

5B

Dale Roads 51 42 N 5 09 W
St. Ann's Head 51 41 N 5 10 W
Smalls Light 51 43 N 5 40 W
St. Bride's Bay
  Solva 51 52 N 5 12 W
St. David's Head 51 54 N 5 19 W
Fishguard 52 01 N 4 59 W
`[G][C][R][B][T][A]`

Newport 52 01 N 4 50 W
Cardigan 52 05 N 4 39 W
New Quay 52 13 N 4 22 W
Aberaeron 52 15 N 4 15 W
Aberystwyth 52 24 N 4 06 W
River Dovey
  Aberdovey 52 32 N 4 03 W
Barmouth 52 43 N 4 03 W
Porthmadog (Portmadoc) 52 55 N 4 08 W

5C

`[P][Q][G][R]`

Pwllheli 52 53 N 4 25 W
Llanbedrog 52 51 N 4 28 W
Abersoch 52 50 N 4 30 W
St. Tudwal's Roads 52 48 N 4 28 W
Bardsey Island 52 45 N 4 48 W
Porth Dinllaen 52 57 N 4 34 W
Porth Nefyn 52 55 N 4 31 W
Carreg-y-Llam 52 58 N 4 28 W
Porth y Nant 52 58 N 4 28 W
Port Rivals 52 59 N 4 28 W
Port Trevor 53 00 N 4 25 W
Clynnog 53 01 N 4 22 W
Menai Strait
  Caernarfon 53 09 N 4 16 W
`[G][B]`

Port Dinorwic 53 11 N 4 13 W
Anglesey
  South Stack 53 18 N 4 42 W
  Holyhead 53 19 N 4 37 W
`[Y][G][R][T][L]`

5D

Skerries Light 53 25 N 4 36 W
Cemaes Bay 53 25 N 4 27 W
Amlwch 53 25 N 4 20 W
Point Lynas 53 25 N 4 17 W
Moelfre Roads 53 21 N 4 14 W
Redwharf Bay 53 19 N 4 12 W
Dinmor 53 18 N 4 03 W
Beaumaris 53 16 N 4 05 W
Bangor 53 14 N 4 08 W
Port Penrhyn 53 14 N 4 06 W
`[Y][G][R][B]`

Penmaenmawr 53 16 N 3 57 W
Conwy 53 18 N 3 51 W
Deganwy 53 18 N 3 50 W
Great Ormes Head 53 21 N 3 52 W

6A

Llandudno 53 19 N 3 49 W
Llanddulas 53 18 N 3 39 W
`[Y][A]`

Rhyl 53 19 N 3 29 W
River Dee
  Point of Air 53 21 N 3 19 W
  Mostyn 53 19 N 3 14 W
`[Y][G][B][T][A]`

Flint 53 15 N 3 08 W
Connah's Quay 53 14 N 3 04 W
Shotton 53 12 N 3 02 W
`[G][A]`

Queensferry 53 12 N 3 01 W

ENGLAND — 6B

Saltney 53 11 N 2 56 W
Chester 53 12 N 2 54 W
Bar Light 53 32 N 3 19 W
River Mersey
  Wallasey 53 25 N 3 03 W
  Birkenhead 53 24 N 3 01 W
  Tranmere 53 22 N 3 00 W
  Rock Ferry 53 21 N 3 00 W
  Bromborough 53 21 N 2 59 W
Manchester Ship Canal
`[P][Q][Y][G][C][R][B][D][T][A]`

Eastham 53 21 N 2 58 W
Ellesmere Port 53 17 N 2 54 W
Stanlow 53 17 N 2 52 W
Ince 53 17 N 2 51 W
Frodsham 53 18N 2 44W
River Weaver
  Northwich 53 16 N 2 32 W
Weston Church Wall 53 19 N 2 45 W
Weston Point 53 20 N 2 46 W
Runcorn 53 21 N 2 44 W
Acton Grange 53 22 N 2 38 W
Warrington 53 24 N 2 36 W
Latchford 53 23 N 2 34 W
Cadishead 53 24 N 2 27 W
Partington 53 26 N 2 26 W
Irlam 53 26 N 2 25 W
Barton 53 28 N 2 22 W
Irwell 53 28 N 2 21 W
Weaste 53 28 N 2 20 W
Mode Wheel 53 27 N 2 20 W
Manchester 53 28 N 2 17 W
River Mersey

6C

  Widnes 53 21 N 2 44 W
  Garston 53 21 N 2 54 W
`[Q][Y][G][R][B][T][A]`

Dingle 53 22 N 2 58 W
Liverpool 53 25 N 3 00 W
`[P][Q][Y][G][C][R][B][D][T][A][L]`

Seaforth 53 28 N 3 01 W
Southport 53 39 N 3 01 W
River Ribble
  Preston 53 45 N 2 42 W
Blackpool 53 50 N 3 03 W
River Wyre
  Fleetwood 53 56 N 3 00 W
`[R][B][T][A]`

River Lune
  Glasson Dock 54 00 N 2 50 W
  Lancaster 54 00 N 2 51 W
Heysham 54 02 N 2 56 W
`[G][C][R][B][A]`

6D

Morecambe Bay
  Morecambe 54 04 N 2 53 W
Ulverston 54 12 N 3 05 W
Piel 54 04 N 3 10 W
Barrow-in-Furness 54 06 N 3 13 W
`[Q][Y][G][R][B][A][L]`

Millom 54 11 N 3 16 W
Isle of Man
  Point of Ayre 54 25 N 4 22 W
  Ramsey 54 19 N 4 23 W
`[Y][G][C][B][A]`

Douglas 54 09 N 4 28 W
`[P][Q][Y][G][C][R][B][A][L]`

P Petroleum Q Other Liquid Bulk Y Dry Bulk G General Cargo
C Containers R Ro-Ro B Bunkers D Dry Dock T Towage
A Airport (within 100km) L Lloyd's Agent (not including sub-agents)

7A

Castletown 54 04 N 4 39 W
G A

Port St. Mary 54 04 N 4 44 W
G B A

Port Erin 54 05 N 4 45 W
Peel 54 14 N 4 42 W
P G B A

Ravenglass 54 21 N 3 25 W
Whitehaven 54 33 N 3 35 W
Q G B

Harrington 54 37 N 3 34 W
Workington 54 39 N 3 34 W
P Q Y G R B A

Maryport 54 43 N 3 30 W
Silloth 54 52 N 3 24 W
Q Y G B A

7B

NORTHERN IRELAND

Lough Foyle
Lisahally 55 02 N 7 16 W
Londonderry 54 59 N 7 19 W
P Y G C B T A L

Coleraine 55 08 N 6 40 W
P Y G C B A

Port Stewart 55 11 N 6 43 W
Portrush 55 13 N 6 40 W
G

Rathlin Island 55 17 N 6 10 W
Ballycastle 55 13 N 6 14 W
Carnlough 54 59 N 6 00 W
Glenarm 54 57 N 5 57 W
Lough Larne
Larne 54 51 N 5 47 W
P Y G C R B T A

Ballylumford 54 50 N 5 47 W
Magheramorne 54 49 N 5 46 W
Belfast Lough
Kilroot 54 43 N 5 45 W
P Y

Carrickfergus 54 39 N 5 53 W
P Y G B T A

Belfast 54 36 N 5 56 W
P Q Y G C R B D T A L

Bangor 54 40 N 5 40 W
G B A

7C

Groomsport Bay 54 41 N 5 36 W
Donaghadee 54 39 N 5 32 W
Ballywalter 54 33 N 5 29 W
Portavogie 54 27 N 5 26 W
Strangford Lough
Portaferry 54 23 N 5 33 W
Killyleagh 54 24 N 5 39 W
G

Quoile Quay 54 21 N 5 41 W
Strangford 54 23 N 5 36 W
G R B A

Ardglass 54 16 N 5 37 W
Dundrum 54 16 N 5 51 W
Newcastle 54 12 N 5 53 W
Annalong 54 06 N 5 54 W
Ballymartin 54 05 N 5 56 W
Kilkeel 54 04 N 6 00 W

7D

Carlingford Lough
Warrenpoint 54 06 N 6 15 W
Y G C R B A L

Newry 54 11 N 6 20 W

REPUBLIC OF IRELAND (EIRE)

Carlingford 54 03 N 6 11 W
Greenore 54 02 N 6 08 W
Y G C B A

8A

Dundalk 54 00 N 6 23 W
P Y G B A

River Boyne
Drogheda 53 43 N 6 21 W
P Q Y G C B T A

Balbriggan 53 37 N 6 11 W
Skerries 53 35 N 6 06 W
Howth 53 23 N 6 04 W
Dublin 53 21 N 6 13 W
P Q Y G C R B D T A L

Dun Laoghaire 53 18 N 6 08 W
G R B A

Bray 53 12 N 6 06 W
Wicklow 52 59 N 6 02 W
Y G B T A

Arklow 52 48 N 6 09 W
P Q Y G B D T A

8B

Cahore Point 52 34 N 6 11 W
Wexford 52 20 N 6 25 W
Rosslare 52 15 N 6 20 W
R B T A

Tuskar Light 52 12 N 6 12 W
Carnsore Point 52 10 N 6 22 W
Kilmore 52 11 N 6 35 W
Bannow Bay 52 12 N 6 49 W
Waterford Harbour
Duncannon 52 13 N 6 55 W
New Ross 52 24 N 6 57 W
P Q Y G C R B D T A

Waterford 52 07 N 6 55 W
P Q Y G C R B T A L

Passage East 52 14 N 6 59 W
Dunmore East 52 09 N 6 59 W
B D A

Tramore 52 10 N 7 09 W
Dungarvan 52 05 N 7 36 W
G B

Youghal 51 56 N 7 50 W
Y G B T A

8C

Cork Harbour
Whitegate 51 50 N 8 15 W
Ballinacurra 51 53 N 8 10 W
Cobh 51 51 N 8 17 W
Haulbowline Island 51 50 N 8 18 W
Passage West 51 52 N 8 20 W
Cork 51 54 N 8 28 W
P Q Y G C R B D T A L

Daunt Rock Light 51 43 N 8 15 W
River Bandon
Kinsale 51 42 N 8 30 W
Y G B T A

Kilmacsimon 51 45 N 8 44 W
Old Head of Kinsale 51 36 N 8 32 W
Courtmacsherry 51 38 N 8 43 W
Clonakilty 51 37 N 8 52 W
Galley Head 51 32 N 8 57 W
Glandore 51 34 N 9 07 W
Union Hall 51 34 N 9 08 W

8D

Castletownsend 51 31 N 9 11 W
Baltimore 51 27 N 9 24 W
G T A

Skibbereen 51 33 N 9 16 W
Fastnet Rock 51 23 N 9 36 W
Skull (Schull) 51 31 N 9 32 W
Crookhaven 51 29 N 9 42 W
Mizen Head 51 27 N 9 49 W
Bantry Bay
Whiddy Island 51 41 N 9 32 W
Bantry 51 42 N 9 28 W
P G A

Glengariff 51 45 N 9 32 W
Bear Haven
Lawrence Cove 51 38 N 9 49 W
Castletonbere 51 39 N 9 54 W
G

9A

Kenmare 51 52 N 9 36 W
Portmagee 51 53 N 10 23 W
Valentia 51 56 N 10 18 W
G B A

Cahirsiveen 51 58 N 10 20 W
G B A

Dingle Bay
Dingle 52 08 N 10 16 W
Tralee Bay
Tralee 52 16 N 9 42 W
Fenit 52 17 N 9 53 W
Q Y G B A

Shannon River
Ballylongford 52 33 N 9 28 W
Tarbert Island 52 35 N 9 22 W
Foynes Island 52 37 N 9 07 W
Foynes 52 37 N 9 06 W
P Q Y G B T A

Aughinish Island 52 38 N 9 03 W
Beagh Castle 52 40 N 8 57 W
Dernish Island 52 41 N 8 55 W
Limerick 52 40 N 8 38 W
P Q Y G C B T A L

Clarecastle 52 49 N 8 57 W
Killadysert 52 40 N 9 06 W
Moneypoint 52 36 N 9 24 W
Kilrush 52 38 N 9 30 W
G B T A

9B

Galway Bay
Black Head 53 09 N 9 16 W
Galway 53 16 N 9 03 W
P G B T A L

Aran Islands
Inishmore Island
Kilronan 53 07 N 9 40 W
G A

Slyne Head 53 24 N 10 14 W
Clifden 53 29 N 10 01 W
Killary Bay
Leenaun 53 36 N 9 42 W
Clew Bay
Westport 53 48 N 9 32 W
G A

9C

Newport 53 53 N 9 33 W
Blacksod Bay
Belmullet 54 13 N 9 59 W
Blacksod 54 06 N 10 04 W
Broadhaven 54 17 N 9 52 W
Killala Bay
Killala 54 13 N 9 13 W
Ballina 54 07 N 9 10 W
G

Sligo 54 16 N 8 28 W
Y G B A

Donegal Bay
Ballyshannon 54 30 N 8 12 W
Donegal 54 39 N 8 07 W
G

Killybegs 54 38 N 8 23 W
Y G B

9D

Burtonport 55 00 N 8 26 W
G B A

Bunbeg 55 03 N 8 19 W
Tory Island 55 16 N 8 15 W
Mulroy Bay
Port Millford 55 06 N 7 42 W
Lough Swilly
Portsalon 55 13 N 7 32 W
Rathmullen 55 06 N 7 32 W
G B

Ramelton 55 02 N 7 38 W
Letterkenney 54 57 N 7 45 W
Buncrana 55 08 N 7 27 W
Malin Head 55 23 N 7 24 W
Inishtrahull Island 55 26 N 7 14 W
Lough Foyle
Moville 55 11 N 7 02 W

GEOGRAPHIC INDEX

P Petroleum **Q** Other Liquid Bulk **Y** Dry Bulk **G** General Cargo
C Containers **R** Ro-Ro **B** Bunkers **D** Dry Dock **T** Towage
A Airport (within 100km) **L** Lloyd's Agent (not including sub-agents)

UNITED KINGDOM — 10A

SCOTLAND

Annan 54 59 N 3 16 W
River Nith
  Glencaple 55 01 N 3 35 W
  Dumfries 55 04 N 3 37 W
River Urr
  Kippford 54 53 N 3 49 W
  Palnackie 54 53 N 3 51 W
  Dalbeattie 54 56 N 3 49 W
Kirkcudbright 54 50 N 4 03 W
`[G][B][A][ ][ ][ ][ ][ ][ ]`

Creetown 54 54 N 4 22 W
Wigtown 54 52 N 4 26 W
Garlieston 54 48 N 4 22 W
`[G][A][ ][ ][ ][ ][ ][ ][ ]`

Isle of Whithorn 54 42 N 4 22'W
`[G][ ][ ][ ][ ][ ][ ][ ][ ]`

Port William 54 46 N 4 35 W
Drummore 54 41 N 4 53 W
Mull of Galloway 54 38 N 4 51 W
Port Logan 54 42 N 4 57 W
Portpatrick 54 50 N 5 07 W
Corsewall Point 55 00 N 5 09 W
Stranraer 54 55 N 5 02 W — 10B
`[G][R][B][A][ ][ ][ ][ ][ ]`

Cairn Ryan 54 58 N 5 01 W
Ballantrae 55 06 N 5 00 W
Girvan 55 15 N 4 52 W
`[Q][Y][G][B][A][ ][ ][ ][ ]`

Firth of Clyde
  Ayr 55 28 N 4 38 W
`[Q][Y][G][B][T][A][ ][ ][ ]`

Troon 55 33 N 4 41 W
`[G][B][D][A][ ][ ][ ][ ][ ]`

Irvine 55 36 N 4 41 W
`[G][B][T][A][ ][ ][ ][ ][ ]`

Ardrossan 55 38 N 4 49 W — 10C
`[P][Y][G][C][R][B][T][A][ ]`

Hunterston 55 45 N 4 53 W
`[Y][B][A][ ][ ][ ][ ][ ][ ]`

Fairlie 55 46 N 4 52 W
Largs 55 48 N 4 52 W
`[G][R][A][ ][ ][ ][ ][ ][ ]`

Wemyss Bay 55 53 N 4 53 W
`[G][R][A][ ][ ][ ][ ][ ][ ]`

Inverkip 55 55 N 4 52 W
Gourock 55 57 N 4 48 W
`[G][R][A][ ][ ][ ][ ][ ][ ]`

Tail of the Bank 55 57 N 4 45 W
River Clyde
  Greenock 55 57 N 4 44 W
`[Y][G][C][R][B][D][A][ ][ ]`

Port Glasgow 55 56 N 4 41 W
`[G][B][A][ ][ ][ ][ ][ ][ ]`

River Cart
  Paisley 55 51 N 4 26 W
  Renfrew 55 52 N 4 24 W
  Glasgow 55 52 N 4 17 W — 10D
`[Y][G][R][B][D][T][A][L][ ]`

Dalmuir 55 54 N 4 26 W
Old Kilpatrick 55 55 N 4 27 W
Bowling 55 56 N 4 30 W
Forth and Clyde Canal (W. Entrance)
Dunglass 55 56 N 4 31 W
Dumbarton 55 56 N 4 34 W
Gareloch
  Shandon 56 03 N 4 49 W
  Faslane Dock 56 04 N 4 49 W
  Garelochhead 56 05 N 4 50 W
  Rosneath 56 01 N 4 48 W
Kilcreggan 55 59 N 4 49 W
Loch Long
  Finnart 56 07 N 4 50 W
`[P][A][ ][ ][ ][ ][ ][ ][ ]`

Column 2 — 11A

Glenmallan 56 07 N 4 49 W
Glenmallan 56 07 N 4 49 W
Holy Loch
  Strone Point 55 59 N 4 54 W
Dunoon 55 56 N 4 55 W
`[G][R][A][ ][ ][ ][ ][ ][ ]`

Toward Point 55 52 N 4 59 W
Ardyne Point 55 52 N 5 02 W
Loch Striven 55 57 N 5 05 W
Isle of Bute
  Kames Bay
    Port Bannatyne 55 52 N 5 04 W
  Rothesay 55 50 N 5 03 W
`[G][R][B][A][ ][ ][ ][ ][ ]`

Loch Fyne
  Portavadie 55 52 N 5 18 W
  Inveraray 56 13 N 5 05 W
  Furnace 56 09 N 5 11 W
  Ardrishaig 56 00 N 5 26 W
`[Y][G][B][ ][ ][ ][ ][ ][ ]`

  Crinan Canal (S. Entrance)
  Tarbert 55 52 N 5 26 W
Isle of Arran — 11B
  Brodick 55 34 N 5 06 W
  Lamlash 55 32 N 5 04 W
  Kildonan Point 55 27 N 5 06 W
Campbeltown 55 25 N 5 35 W
`[G][R][B][A][ ][ ][ ][ ][ ]`

Mull of Kintyre 55 18 N 5 48 W
Gigha Island 55 39 N 5 46 W
Islay Island
  Ardbeg 55 38 N 6 06 W
  Port Ellen 55 37 N 6 13 W
`[G][R][A][ ][ ][ ][ ][ ][ ]`

  Loch Indaal
    Bowmore 55 46 N 6 17 W
    Bruichladdich 55 46 N 6 22 W
  Kilchoman 55 47 N 6 28 W
  Bunnahabhainn Bay 55 53 N 6 07 W
  Port Askaig 55 51 N 6 06 W
`[G][R][B][A][ ][ ][ ][ ][ ]`

Jura Island — 11C
  Feolin 55 51 N 6 05 W
Oronsay Island 56 02 N 6 11 W
Colonsay Island 56 03 N 6 11 W
Loch Crinan 56 05 N 5 34 W
  Crinan Canal (N. Entrance)
Oban 56 25 N 5 29 W
`[G][R][B][A][ ][ ][ ][ ][ ]`

Loch Etive
  Bonawe 56 26 N 5 14 W
Lismore Island 56 27 N 5 36 W
Barcaldine 56 31 N 5 24 W
Loch Linnhe
  Glensanda 56 34 N 5 32 W
`[Y][ ][ ][ ][ ][ ][ ][ ][ ]`

Loch Leven
  Kinlochleven 56 43 N 4 59 W
Fort William 56 49 N 5 07 W
Corpach 56 50 N 5 07 W
`[G][B][A][ ][ ][ ][ ][ ][ ]`

  Caledonian Canal (S. Entrance)
Sound of Mull
  Loch Aline 56 32 N 5 47 W
`[Y][G][ ][ ][ ][ ][ ][ ][ ]`

Mull Island — 11D
  Tobermory 56 37 N 6 03 W
  Craignure 56 28 N 5 42 W
Dubh Artach 56 08 N 6 38 W
Skerryvore 56 19 N 7 07 W
Tiree Island 56 31 N 6 48 W
Coll Island 56 37 N 6 32 W
Kilchoan 56 41 N 6 07 W
Mallaig 57 00 N 5 50 W
`[G][R][B][ ][ ][ ][ ][ ][ ]`

Glenelg 57 13 N 5 38 W
Kyle of Lochalsh 57 16 N 5 43 W
`[G][B][T][A][ ][ ][ ][ ][ ]`

Isle of Skye
  Kyleakin 57 16 N 5 44 W
  Carbost 57 18 N 6 23 W

Column 3 — 12A

Dunvegan 57 27 N 6 35 W
Vaternish Point 57 36 N 6 38 W
Uig 57 35 N 6 21 W
Portree 57 24 N 6 11 W
`[P][G][B][A][ ][ ][ ][ ][ ]`

Loch Carron
  South Strome 57 21 N 5 34 W
Loch Kishorn
  Kishorn 57 23 N 5 36 W
  Applecross 57 26 N 5 49 W
  Loch Torridon 57 36 N 5 49 W
  Gairloch 57 43 N 5 41 W
Loch Ewe
  Aultbea 57 50 N 5 36 W
Ullapool 57 54 N 5 10 W
`[G][R][B][ ][ ][ ][ ][ ][ ]`

Lochinver 58 09 N 5 15 W
Kinlochbervie 58 27 N 5 02 W

OUTER HEBRIDES — 12B

Barra Island
  Castlebay 56 56 N 7 28 W
South Uist
  Lochboisdale 57 09 N 7 18 W
`[G][R][B][A][ ][ ][ ][ ][ ]`

  Loch Carnan 57 20 N 7 15 W
Benbecula 57 25 N 7 23 W
North Uist
  Loch Eport 57 33 N 7 08 W
  Lochmaddy 57 36 N 7 08 W
`[G][R][B][A][ ][ ][ ][ ][ ]`

St. Kilda 57 49 N 8 34 W
Lewis
  Butt of Lewis 58 31 N 6 16 W
  Tiumpan Head 58 16 N 6 08 W
  Stornoway 58 12 N 6 23 W
`[P][Q][G][R][B][T][A][L][ ][ ][ ]`

Sound of Harris
  Leverburgh 57 46 N 7 01 W
Scarp 58 01 N 7 10 W
Cape Wrath 58 37 N 5 00 W — 12C
Durness 58 34 N 4 44 W
Sule Skerry 59 05 N 4 24 W
Scrabster 58 37 N 3 32 W
`[P][G][R][B][A][ ][ ][ ][ ]`

Thurso 58 35 N 3 31 W
Pentland Firth
  Dunnet Head 58 40 N 3 22 W
  Canisbay 58 38 N 3 08 W
  Duncansby Head 58 39 N 3 01 W
  Pentland Skerries 58 41 N 2 55 W

ORKNEY ISLANDS

  Stroma 58 40 N 3 08 W
  Swona 58 44 N 3 04 W
South Ronaldsay
  St. Margaret's Hope 58 50 N 2 57 W
  Burray 58 51 N 2 54 W
Scapa Flow
`[P][Q][Y][G][R][B][T][A][ ][ ]`

  Flotta
    Flotta Terminal 58 49 N 3 07 W
South Walls 58 47 N 3 08 W
Hoy
  Longhope 58 49 N 3 11 W
  Lyness 58 50 N 3 11 W
Mainland Orkney — 12D
  Scapa 58 57 N 3 00 W
  Stromness 58 58 N 3 18 W
  Kirkwall 59 00 N 2 59 W
`[P][Y][G][C][R][B][A][L][ ][ ]`

Shapinsay 59 03 N 2 51 W
Stronsay
  Lamb Head 59 05 N 2 32 W
Sanday 59 13 N 2 30 W
Westray
  Pierowall Harbour 59 19 N 2 58 W
  Noup Head 59 20 N 3 04 W
North Ronaldsay
  Dennis Head 59 23 N 2 23 W

P Petroleum Q Other Liquid Bulk Y Dry Bulk G General Cargo
C Containers R Ro-Ro B Bunkers D Dry Dock T Towage
A Airport (within 100km) L Lloyd's Agent (not including sub-agents)

GEOGRAPHIC INDEX

SHETLAND ISLANDS · 13A

Fair Isle 59 31 N 1 39 W
Mainland Shetland
  Sumburgh Head 59 51 N 1 16 W
  Scalloway 60 08 N 1 16 W

Q	Y	G	B	A				

  Walls 60 14 N 1 34 W
  Sullom Voe 60 27 N 1 20 W

P	Q	Y	G	R	B	T	A	

  Vidlin Voe 60 23 N 1 08 W
  Lerwick 60 09 N 1 08 W

G	R	B	D	T	A	L		

  Sandwick 60 00 N 1 14 W
Bressay 60 08 N 1 05 W
Yell
  Tofts Voe 60 30 N 1 11 W
  Bay of Ulsta 60 30 N 1 10 W
  Mid Yell Voe 60 36 N 1 04 W
Unst
  Baltasound 60 45 N 0 50 W

G	A							

Muckle Flugga 60 51 N 0 53 W

NORTH SEA TERMINALS · 13B

Thistle 61 23 N 1 36 E
Statfjord (Norwegian) 61 15 N 1 51 E — p.19
Gullfaks (Norwegian) 61 12 N 2 12 E
Brent 61 05 N 1 43 E
Emerald 60 41 N 1 02 E
Oseberg (Norwegian) 60 30 N 2 50 E
Beryl 59 33 N 1 32 E
Maureen 58 08 N 1 42 E
Buchan 57 54 N 0 02 E
Kittiwake 57 28 N 0 31 E
Montrose 57 27 N 1 23 E
Ekofisk (Norwegian) 56 33 N 3 13 E
Fulmar 56 28 N 2 09 E
Auk 56 23 N 2 04 E
Argyll 56 09 N 2 48 E
Gorm (Danish) 55 35 N 4 46 E

SCOTLAND · 13C

Sinclair's Bay 58 29 N 3 03 W — p.16/17
Wick 58 26 N 3 05 W

P	Y	G	C	B	A			

Lybster 58 18 N 3 17 W
Dunbeath 58 15 N 3 25 W
Helmsdale 58 07 N 3 39 W
Dornoch Firth
  Portmahomack 57 50 N 3 49 W
Tarbat Ness Light 57 52 N 3 46 W
Moray Firth
  Donan Field 58 21 N 0 59 E
  Cromarty Firth

P	Y	G	T	A				

    Nigg Terminal 57 42 N 4 02 W
    Invergordon 57 41 N 4 10 W

P	Y	G	R	B				

    Dingwall 57 36 N 4 25 W
    Cromarty 57 41 N 4 02 W
  Inverness Firth
    Inverness 57 30 N 4 14 W · 13D

P	Y	G	B	A				

    Caledonian Canal (N. Entrance)
    Ardersier 57 34 N 4 02 W
Nairn 57 35 N 3 52 W
Findhorn 57 39 N 3 36 W
Burghead 57 42 N 3 30 W

G	A							

Lossiemouth 57 43 N 3 17 W

G	B	A						

Port Gordon 57 40 N 3 01 W
Buckie 57 41 N 2 57 W

Q	Y	G	B	A				

Findochty 57 42 N 2 54 W
Portknockie 57 42 N 2 52 W
Portsoy 57 41 N 2 41 W
Banff 57 40 N 2 31 W

Macduff 57 40 N 2 30 W · 14A

Y	G	B	A					

Gardenstown 57 40 N 2 20 W
Rosehearty 57 42 N 2 07 W
Kinnairds Head 57 42 N 2 00 W
Fraserburgh 57 41 N 2 00 W

Q	Y	G	C	R	B	D	T	A

Rattray Head 57 37 N 1 49 W
Peterhead 57 30 N 1 47 W

Y	G	C	B	D	A			

Buchan Ness 57 28 N 1 46 W
Port Erroll 57 25 N 1 50 W
Newburgh 57 19 N 2 00 W
River Dee
  Aberdeen 57 09 N 2 04 W

P	Q	Y	G	C	R	B	D	T	A	L

Portlethen 57 03 N 2 07 W
Stonehaven 56 58 N 2 12 W
Gourdon 56 50 N 2 17 W
Johnshaven 56 48 N 2 20 W
Montrose 56 42 N 2 28 W · 14B

Q	Y	G	C	R	B	T	A	L

Arbroath 56 33 N 2 35 W
Carnoustie 56 30 N 2 42 W
Firth of Tay
  Broughty Ferry 56 28 N 2 52 W
  Dundee 56 28 N 2 58 W

Y	G	C	R	B	T	A	L	

  River Tay
    Perth 56 24 N 3 26 W

Y	G	B	A					

  Newburgh 56 21 N 3 15 W
  Tayport 56 27 N 2 53 W
Firth of Forth
  Crail 56 15 N 2 38 W
  Isle of May 56 11 N 2 33 W
  Anstruther 56 12 N 2 42 W
  Pittenweem 56 13 N 2 44 W
  St. Monance 56 12 N 2 46 W
  Elie 56 11 N 2 49 W
  Largo Bay 56 13 N 2 56 W
  Leven 56 12 N 3 00 W
  Methil 56 11 N 3 00 W · 14C

Y	G	B	A					

  Buckhaven 56 10 N 3 02 W
  Kirkcaldy 56 07 N 3 09 W

Y	G	B	A					

  Kinghorn 56 04 N 3 10 W
  Inchkeith 56 02 N 3 09 W
  Burntisland 56 03 N 3 14 W

Q	Y	G	B	A				

  Aberdour 56 03 N 3 18 W
  Braefoot Bay 56 02 N 3 18 W

Q	T	A						

  St. Davids 56 02 N 3 22 W
  Inverkeithing 56 02 N 3 24 W
  River Forth
    North Queensferry 56 00 N 3 24 W
    St. Margaret's Hope 56 01 N 3 24 W
    Rosyth 56 01 N 3 27 W · 14D

P	G	B	T	A				

    Charlestown 56 02 N 3 30 W
    Crombie 56 02 N 3 34 W
    Longannet 56 03 N 3 41 W
    Alloa 56 06 N 3 48 W
    Stirling 56 07 N 3 56 W
    Grangemouth 56 02 N 3 41 W

P	Q	Y	G	C	R	B	D	T	A

    Forth and Clyde Canal (E. entrance)
    Bo'ness (Borrowstounness) 56 01 N 3 36 W
    South Queensferry 55 59 N 3 24 W
    Hound Point 56 00 N 3 22 W

P	T	A						

    Granton 55 59 N 3 13 W

G	R	B	A					

Leith 55 59 N 3 10 W · 15A

P	Q	Y	G	C	R	B	D	T	A	L

Fisherrow 55 57 N 3 04 W
Musselburgh 55 57 N 3 02 W
Morrison's Haven 55 57 N 3 00 W
Cockenzie 55 58 N 2 57 W
Aberlady Bay 56 01 N 2 51 W
North Berwick 56 04 N 1 43 W
Dunbar 56 00 N 2 31 W
St. Abb's Head 55 55 N 2 08 W
Eyemouth 55 52 N 2 05 W

ENGLAND

River Tweed
  Berwick-upon-Tweed 55 46 N 2 00 W

Y	G	B	A					

Holy Island 55 40 N 1 48 W
Farne Islands
  Longstone Light 55 39 N 1 36 W
North Sunderland (Seahouses) 55 35 N 1 39 W
Craster 55 28 N 1 35 W · 15B
Boulmer 55 25 N 1 35 W
Alnmouth 55 23 N 1 37 W
Warkworth (Amble) 55 20 N 1 34 W
Coquet Island 55 20 N 1 32 W
Blyth 55 07 N 1 29 W

Y	G	C	R	B	T	A		

Cullercoats 55 02 N 1 26 W
River Tyne
  Tyne

P	Q	Y	G	C	R	B	D	T	A	L

    Tynemouth 55 01 N 1 25 W
    North Shields 55 01 N 1 26 W
    Wallsend 54 59 N 1 30 W
    Newcastle 54 58 N 1 35 W
    Dunston 54 57 N 1 38 W
    Gateshead 54 58 N 1 36 W
    Hebburn 54 59 N 1 31 W
    Jarrow 54 59 N 1 28 W
    Tyne Dock 54 59 N 1 27 W
    South Shields 55 00 N 1 26 W
River Wear · 15C
  Sunderland 54 55 N 1 22 W

P	Y	G	C	R	B	D	T	A	

Seaham 54 50 N 1 19 W

Y	G	C	B	T	A			

Hartlepool 54 42 N 1 12 W

Y	G	R	B	T	A			

West Hartlepool 54 41 N 1 12 W
River Tees
  Tees

P	Q	Y	G	C	R	B	D	T	A	L

    Seal Sands 54 37 N 1 10 W
    North Tees 54 36 N 1 10 W
    Billingham 54 35 N 1 15 W
    Middlesbrough 54 35 N 1 13 W
    South Bank 54 35 N 1 11 W
    Teesport 54 36 N 1 09 W
Redcar 54 37 N 1 04 W · 15D
Saltburn-by-the-Sea 54 35 N 0 58 W
Skinningrove 54 34 N 0 54 W
Staithes 54 33 N 0 48 W
Whitby 54 29 N 0 37 W

Y	G	C	B	A				

Scarborough 54 17 N 0 23 W

G	B	T						

Filey 54 13 N 0 16 W
Flamborough Head 54 07 N 0 04 W
Bridlington 54 05 N 0 11 W
Spurn Head 53 35 N 0 07 E
River Humber
  Salt End 53 44 N 0 14 W
  Hull (Kingston upon Hull) 53 45 N 0 18 W

P	Q	Y	G	C	R	B	D	T	A	L

  Hessle 53 43 N 0 26 W
  Brough 53 43 N 0 35 W

ENGLAND *continued* 16A

River Ouse
  Goole 53 42 N 0 52 W

`Y G C R B D T A`

  Hook 53 43 N 0 51 W
  Howdendyke 53 45 N 0 52 W

`Y G B A`

  Drax 53 44 N 0 59 W
  Selby 53 47 N 1 04 W

`G B A`

River Trent

`Q Y G C B`

  Burton upon Stather 53 39 N 0 41 W
  Flixborough 53 37 N 0 41 W
  Neap House 53 37 N 0 40 W
  Grove Wharf 53 36 N 0 41 W
  Keadby 53 36 N 0 40 W
  Gunness Wharf 53 35 N 0 41 W
  Beckingham 53 24 N 0 50 W
  Gainsborough 53 24 N 0 46 W   **16B**

`Y G B T A`

  Whitton 53 43 N 0 38 W
  Barton on Humber 53 42 N 0 26 W
  Barrow on Humber 53 41 N 0 23 W
  New Holland 53 42 N 0 21 W

`Q Y G B`

  Killingholme 53 40 N 0 14 W

`P Q B`

  Immingham 53 38 N 0 11 W

`P Q Y G C R B T A`

  Grimsby 53 35 N 0 04 W

`Y G C R B A`

  Tetney Terminal 53 32 N 0 06 E

`P B T A`

River Witham   **16C**
  Boston 52 58 N 0 01 W

`Y G C R B T A L`

River Welland
  Fosdyke 52 52 N 0 02 W

`Y G T`

River Nene
  Sutton Bridge 52 46 N 0 12 E

`Y G C B T A`

  Wisbech 52 39 N 0 09 E

`Y G B T A`

River Ouse
  King's Lynn 52 45 N 0 24 E

`P Q Y G C R B T A`

  Snettisham 52 53 N 0 30 E
  Wells 52 58 N 0 51 E

`G B A`

  Cromer 52 56 N 1 18 E
River Yare   **16D**
  Great Yarmouth 52 36 N 1 44 E

`P Y G C R B D T A`

  Reedham 52 33 N 1 34 E
  Cantley 52 34 N 1 32 E
  Norwich 52 38 N 1 17 E
  Gorleston 52 35 N 1 44 E
River Waveney
  Lowestoft 52 28 N 1 45 E

`Y G C B D T A L`

  Oulton Broad 52 29 N 1 44 E
  Southwold 52 20 N 1 41 E
  Aldeburgh 52 09 N 1 36 E
River Alde
  Orford Haven 52 05 N 1 32 E
  Snape Bridge 52 09 N 1 30 E
River Deben
  Woodbridge 52 05 N 1 19 E
  Felixstowe 51 57 N 1 19 E

`P Q Y G C R B T A`

River Orwell
  Butterman's Bay 52 00 N 1 14 E

  Pinmill 52 00 N 1 13 E   **17A**
  Ipswich 52 03 N 1 10 E

`P Y G C R B T A L`

River Stour
  Manningtree 51 57 N 1 04 E
  Mistley 51 57 N 1 05 E

`Y G A`

  Parkeston Quay 51 57 N 1 15 E
  Harwich 51 57 N 1 17 E

`P G C R B A`

  Great Oakley 51 54 N 1 15 E
  The Naze 51 52 N 1 17 E
River Colne
  Brightlingsea 51 47 N 1 02 E

`Y G B T A`

  Wivenhoe 51 52 N 0 57 E
  Colchester 51 53 N 0 55 E

`Y G B T A L`

  Rowhedge 51 51 N 0 57 E
  Fingringhoe 51 50 N 0 58 E
  Mersea Island 51 46 N 0 54 E   **17B**
River Blackwater
  Tollesbury 51 45 N 0 51 E
  Heybridge 51 43 N 0 42 E
  Maldon 51 44 N 0 40 E

`G B A`

  Stansgate 51 43 N 0 47 E
  Bradwell 51 45 N 0 53 E
River Crouch
  Burnham on Crouch 51 37 N 0 49 E
  Creeksea 51 37 N 0 47 E

`Y G A`

  Battlesbridge 51 37 N 0 34 E
River Roach
  Rochford 51 35 N 0 44 E

`G A`

FAROE (FAEROE) ISLANDS (Danish)   **17C**

Suduroy   p.20/21
  Tvoroyri 61 33 N 6 48 W

`Q Y G`

  Trongisvagsfjordur 61 32 N 6 45 W
  Drelnaes 61 32 N 6 48 W
  Vagur 61 28 N 6 48 W

`G`

Sandoy
  Sandsfjordur (Sans Vaag) 61 49 N 6 48 W
  Skopunarfjordur 61 55 N 6 51 W
Vagar
  Midvaag 62 03 N 7 10 W
  Sorvagur 62 05 N 7 25 W
Streymoy
  Torshavn (Thorshavn) 62 00 N 6 45 W

`P Q Y G R B T A L`

  Vestmanna 62 09 N 7 10 W

`G`

Eysturoy   **17D**
  Skaalefjord
    Kongshavn 62 07 N 6 43 W
  Fuglafjordur 62 15 N 6 49 W

`G B`

Bordoy
  Klaksvik 62 14 N 6 35 W

`G B A`

ICELAND

Hornafjordur
  Hofn 64 16 N 15 13 W

`Q Y G C B D T A`

  Djupivogur 64 40 N 14 15 W

`G`

  Breidhdalsvik 64 44 N 13 59 W
  Stodhvarfjordur 64 50 N 13 50 W

`G B`

Faskrudhsfjordur   **18A**
  Budir 64 56 N 13 48 W

`P G B A`

Reydharfjordur
  Eskifjordur 65 05 N 13 59 W

`G A`

  Budareyri 65 02 N 14 12 W
Nordfjordur
  Neskaupstadur 65 09 N 13 41 W

`P G C B A`

  Seydhisfjordur 65 15 N 13 55 W

`P G C R B A`

  Njardhvik 65 35 N 13 51 W
  Vopnafjordur 65 45 N 14 49 W

`G`

  Bakkafjordur 66 03 N 14 45 W
  Thorshofn 66 12 N 15 20 W

`G`

  Raufarhofn 66 27 N 15 54 W   **18B**

`Q Y G B A`

  Kopasker 66 17 N 16 27 W
  Husavik 66 03 N 17 22 W

`P G C A`

Eyjafjordur
  Grenivik 65 58 N 18 12 W

`G`

  Svalbardhseyri 65 45 N 18 06 W
  Akureyri 65 41 N 18 03 W

`P Y G C B T A`

  Krossanes 65 42 N 18 07 W
  Hjalteyri 65 51 N 18 12 W
  Dalvik 65 58 N 18 31 W

`G A`

  Hrisey 66 02 N 18 25 W
  Olafsfjordur 66 05 N 18 38 W
  Siglufjordur 66 12 N 18 52 W   **18C**

`G B A`

  Hofsos 65 53 N 19 24 W
  Grafaros 65 33 N 19 24 W
  Saudarkrok 65 45 N 19 36 W
  Hofdhakaupstadur (Skagastrond) 65 50 N 20 19 W
  Blonduos 65 40 N 20 18 W
  Hvammstangi 65 24 N 20 57 W

`G`

  Bordeyri 65 13 N 21 09 W
  Holmavik 65 42 N 21 41 W
  Djupavik 65 57 N 21 34 W
  Hesteyri 66 21 N 22 51 W
  Isafjordur 66 05 N 23 06 W

`P G C B A`

  Bolungavik 66 10 N 23 14 W

`G`

Sugandafjordur   **18D**
  Sudureyri 66 08 N 23 32 W

`G`

  Flateyri 66 03 N 23 29 W
Dyrafjord
  Thingeyri 65 52 N 23 29 W
  Bildudal 65 41 N 23 36 W
  Talknafjordur 65 37 N 23 49 W
  Patrekshofn (Vatneyri) 65 35 N 23 59 W
  Flatey 65 22 N 22 55 W
  Reykholar 65 27 N 22 13 W
  Stykkisholmur 65 04 N 22 41 W
  Grundarfjordur 64 55 N 23 13 W

`G`

  Olafsvik 64 54 N 23 43 W
  Rifshofn 64 53 N 23 40 W
  Sandur 64 55 N 23 49 W
  Borgarnes 64 32 N 21 55 W
  Akranes 64 19 N 22 05 W

`Y G B T`

P Petroleum **Q** Other Liquid Bulk **Y** Dry Bulk **G** General Cargo
C Containers **R** Ro-Ro **B** Bunkers **D** Dry Dock **T** Towage
A Airport (within 100km) **L** Lloyd's Agent (not including sub-agents)

Column 19A–19D

Hvalfjordur — 19A
Grundartangi 64 21 N 21 47 W
`Y B`
Hvaleyri 64 20 N 21 44 W
Hrafneyri 64 23 N 21 32 W
Helguvik 64 23 N 21 28 W
Gufunes 64 09 N 21 49 W
Reykjavik 64 08 N 21 54 W
`P Q Y G C R B T A L`

Skerjafjordur
Korsnes 64 07 N 21 54 W
Hafnarfjordur 64 04 N 21 58 W
`P G B T A`

Straumsvik 64 03 N 22 03 W — 19B
`Q Y G B A`

Keflavik 64 00 N 22 33 W
`G T B A`

Sandgerdhi 64 03 N 22 43 W
Reykjanes 63 48 N 22 42 W
Grindavik 63 50 N 22 26 W
`G`

Thorlakshofn 63 51 N 21 20 W
`G`

Eyrarbakki 63 52 N 21 09 W
Stokkseyri 63 50 N 21 05 W
Vestmannaeyjar 63 26 N 20 16 W
`P Y G C B T A`

Dyrholaey 63 24 N 19 08 W

NORWAY — 19C

Varangerfjord
Vestre Jakobselv 70 06 N 29 20 E
Kirkenes 69 44 N 30 03 E
`P Y G B D T A L`

Vadso 70 04 N 29 44 E
`P G B T A`

Vardo 70 23 N 31 06 E
`G B A`

Batsfjord 70 38 N 29 44 E
Berlevaag 70 51 N 29 06 E
Mehamn 71 02 N 27 51 E
Nordkyn 71 08 N 27 39 E
Kjollefjord 70 57 N 27 21 E
Porsangerfjord
Leirpollen 70 23 N 25 31 E
Hamnbukt 70 06 N 25 07 E
Billefjord 70 22 N 25 06 E
Kistrand 70 26 N 25 12 E
Honningsvaag 70 59 N 25 59 E
North Cape (Nord Kapp) 71 10 N 25 46 E
Hjelmsoy 71 05 N 24 40 E
Hammerfest 70 40 N 23 40 E
`P Y G C R B T A`

Soroy — 19D
Finnfjord 70 49 N 23 05 E
Kobbevag 70 30 N 22 08 E
Stjernoy
Lillebukt 70 20 N 22 30 E
Komagfjord 70 16 N 23 23 E
Altafjord
Elvebakken 69 55 N 23 25 E
Bukta 69 59 N 23 18 E
Alta 69 58 N 23 15 E
Bossekop 69 59 N 23 15 E
Oksfjord 70 14 N 22 18 E
Skjervoy 70 02 N 21 00 E
Karlsoy 70 00 N 19 54 E
Lyngenfjord
Kaafjord 69 35 N 20 31 E
Kvesmenes 69 17 N 19 58 E
Lyngseidet 69 34 N 20 13 E
Jovik 69 36 N 19 50 E
Tromso 69 39 N 18 58 E
`P G C R B T A L`

Gjovik 69 27 N 18 21 E
Ramfjordnes 69 33 N 19 01 E
Balsfjord 69 19 N 19 21 E
Skaland 69 27 N 17 18 E
Gryllefjord 69 22 N 17 04 E

Column 20A–20D

Gibostad 69 21 N 18 05 E — 20A
Finnsnes 69 14 N 17 58 E
Oyjordneset 69 10 N 18 05 E
Sorreisa 69 08 N 18 08 E
Salangen 68 54 N 17 43 E
Sjovegan 68 53 N 17 50 E
Vesteraalen
Andenes 69 19 N 16 08 E
Sortland 68 42 N 15 26 E
Stokmarknes 68 34 N 14 55 E
Melbu 68 30 N 14 48 E
Lofoten Islands
Borkenes 68 46 N 16 11 E
Harstad 68 48 N 16 33 E
`P Y G C R B D A L`

Lodingen 68 25 N 16 00 E
`G R B A`

Trollfjord 68 22 N 14 59 E
Digermulen 68 18 N 15 01 E
Brettesnes 68 14 N 14 52 E
Svolvaer 68 14 N 14 34 E
`P Y G B A`

Kabelvaag 68 13 N 14 30 E
Henningsvaer 68 09 N 14 13 E
Stamsund 68 07 N 13 51 E
Gravdal 68 07 N 13 33 E
Ballstad 68 04 N 13 32 E
Nusfjord 68 02 N 13 21 E
Rost 67 30 N 12 00 E
Skomvaer 67 25 N 11 53 E
Ofotfjord
Bogen 68 31 N 17 00 E
Narvik 68 26 N 17 26 E
`P Y G C B T A L`

Heklestrand 68 24 N 16 50 E
Ballangen 68 22 N 16 56 E
Tysfjord
Kjopsvik 68 05 N 16 23 E
Drag 68 03 N 16 05 E
Korsnes 68 15 N 16 04 E
Tranoy 68 11 N 15 40 E
Sorfolla
Djupvik 67 22 N 15 34 E
Hammerfall 67 25 N 15 32 E — 20C
Saltfjord
Bodo 67 17 N 14 23 E
`P G C R B T A`

Kvalvaag 67 18 N 14 40 E
Fauske 67 15 N 15 23 E
Finneid 67 15 N 15 24 E
Saltdal 67 05 N 15 30 E
Gildeskal 67 04 N 14 03 E
Glomfjord 66 49 N 13 37 E
`Q Y G`

Meloyvaer 66 50 N 13 17 E
Halsa 66 45 N 13 34 E
Ranafjord
Vikholmen 66 12 N 12 58 E
Nesna 66 12 N 13 01 E
Utskarpen 66 08 N 13 27 E
Bosmo 66 20 N 14 07 E
Gullsmedvik 66 20 N 14 09 E
Mo i Rana 66 19 N 14 08 E
`Y G R B T A`

Andfiskaa 66 17 N 14 06 E
Hemnesberget 66 13 N 13 36 E
Sandnessjoen 66 01 N 12 38 E
Sovik 65 55 N 12 26 E
Alstahaug 65 54 N 12 23 E
Mosjoen 65 50 N 13 11 E
`P Y G B T A`

Hommelsto 65 32 N 12 20 E
Bronnoysund 65 28 N 12 13 E
Kolvereid 64 53 N 11 35 E
Rorvik 64 52 N 11 14 E
Kongsmoen 64 53 N 12 26 E
Foldenfjord
Abelvaer 64 44 N 11 10 E
Opploygfjord 64 48 N 11 52 E
Salsbruket 64 48 N 11 53 E
Namsenfjord
Vik 64 31 N 11 17 E
Namsos 64 28 N 11 30 E
`P Y G B T A`

Column 21A–21D

Bangsund 64 24 N 11 23 E — 21A
Statland 64 30 N 11 09 E
Lauvsnes 64 30 N 10 54 E
Haltenoy 64 10 N 9 25 E
Stokksund 64 02 N 10 02 E
Lysoysund 63 53 N 9 53 E
Uthaug 63 44 N 9 36 E
Bjugn 63 46 N 9 44 E
Brekstad 63 41 N 9 40 E

`p.24/25`

Trondheimsfjord
Follafoss 63 59 N 11 06 E
Malm 64 04 N 11 13 E
`Y G`

Eggebogen 64 00 N 11 28 E
Steinkjer 64 01 N 11 30 E
`P Y G B A`

Hylla 63 50 N 11 24 E
Trones 63 49 N 11 26 E
Verdal 63 47 N 11 26 E
Levanger 63 45 N 11 18 E
Fiborgtangen 63 43 N 11 10 E
Langstein 63 33 N 10 55 E
Stjordal 63 27 N 10 53 E
Muruvik 63 26 N 10 51 E
Hommelvik 63 25 N 10 48 E
Trondheim 63 26 N 10 24 E — 21B
`P Y G C R B D T A L`

Buvika 63 19 N 10 11 E
Thamshavn 63 20 N 9 52 E
Orkanger 63 20 N 9 52 E
`Y G B A`

Agdenes 63 39 N 9 45 E
Hitra Island
Hestvika 63 34 N 9 11 E
Forsnes 63 26 N 8 25 E
Hemnefjord
Kyrksaetrora 63 17 N 9 05 E
Holla 63 17 N 9 07 E
Averoy 63 07 N 7 40 E
Elnesvagen 62 51 N 7 09 E
Sunndalsora 62 41 N 8 36 E
`Q Y G B`

Kristiansund 63 07 N 7 44 E — 21C
`Y G C R B T A`

Raudsandnes 63 04 N 7 41 E
Aarnes 62 58 N 8 30 E
Tingvoll 62 55 N 8 12 E
Hustad 62 57 N 7 06 E
Bud 62 54 N 6 54 E
Aukra 62 47 N 6 58 E
Molde 62 44 N 7 10 E
`P Y G C R`

Romsdalsfjord
Aandalsnes 62 34 N 7 41 E
Vestnes 62 38 N 7 04 E
Spjelkavik 62 27 N 6 22 E
Humblen 62 26 N 6 18 E
More 62 28 N 6 09 E
Aalesund 62 28 N 6 10 E
`P G C R B T A`

Storfjord — 21D
Merok 62 06 N 7 13 E
Hellesylt 62 05 N 6 53 E
Oye 62 12 N 6 40 E
Geiranger 62 06 N 7 13 E
Norddal 62 15 N 7 15 E
Hjorungavaag 62 21 N 6 05 E
Hareid 62 22 N 6 02 E
Ulsteinvik 62 21 N 5 51 E
Fosnavaag 62 21 N 5 38 E
Eggesbones 62 19 N 5 39 E
Moltustranda 62 18 N 5 39 E
Larsnes 62 12 N 5 39 E
Volda 62 09 N 6 04 E
Haugsholmen 62 10 N 5 24 E
Aaheim 62 03 N 5 31 E
Selje 62 03 N 5 22 E
Vaagsoy
Maaloy 61 55 N 5 07 E
`G R B A`

Stryn 61 55 N 6 44 E
Nordfjord
Bryggja 61 56 N 5 25 E
Loen 61 52 N 6 51 E

P Petroleum **Q** Other Liquid Bulk **Y** Dry Bulk **G** General Cargo
C Containers **R** Ro-Ro **B** Bunkers **D** Dry Dock **T** Towage
A Airport (within 100km) **L** Lloyd's Agent (not including sub-agents)

NORWAY *continued* — 22A

Olden 61 50 N 6 49 E
Davika 61 53 N 5 33 E
Bremanger
Haugsvik 61 50 N 5 00 E
Svelgen 61 46 N 5 18 E

| G | A | | | | | | | |

Kalvaag 61 46 N 4 53 E
Floro 61 36 N 5 02 E

| P | Q | Y | G | C | R | B | T | A | | |

Askvoll 61 21 N 5 04 E
Dalsfjord
Holmedal 61 21 N 5 11 E
Bygstad 61 23 N 5 40 E
Risnes 61 09 N 5 10 E
Steinsund 61 05 N 4 49 E
Utvaer 61 02 N 4 31 E
Sognefjord
Vadheim 61 12 N 5 49 E
Hoyanger 61 13 N 6 04 E

22B

| Y | G | A | | | | | |

Balholm 61 13 N 6 32 E
Balestrand 61 14 N 6 33 E
Mundal 61 24 N 6 45 E
Sogndal 61 14 N 7 06 E
Ofredal 61 12 N 7 31 E
Skjolden 61 29 N 7 36 E
Aardal 61 14 N 7 41 E
Aardalstangen 61 14 N 7 42 E

| P | Y | G | B | A | | | |

Laerdalsoyri 61 06 N 7 29 E
Gudvangen 60 52 N 6 50 E
Dyrdal 60 57 N 6 56 E
Vik 61 05 N 6 35 E
Forde 61 02 N 5 49 E
Mongstad 60 49 N 5 02 E

| P | Q | Y | G | R | B | T | A | | |

Eikefet 60 42 N 5 33 E
Fedje 60 45 N 4 44 E
Sture 60 37 N 4 51 E

22C

| P | T | A | | | | | |

Vaksdal 60 29 N 5 45 E
Garnes 60 26 N 5 29 E
Sandvik 60 25 N 5 19 E
Bergen 60 24 N 5 19 E

| P | Q | Y | G | C | R | B | D | T | A | L |

Puddefjord
Laksevaag 60 23 N 5 18 E
Knarrevik 60 22 N 5 10 E
Hilleren 60 10 N 5 05 E
Store Sotra
Aagotnes 60 24 N 5 01 E

| G | B | A | | | | | |

Telavag 60 15 N 5 00 E
Austevoll 60 06 N 5 15 E
Bjornefjord
Saevareid 60 11 N 5 46 E
Stordoy
Stord 59 47 N 5 31 E
Leirvik 59 46 N 5 31 E

22D

| G | B | T | A | | | | |

Sagvaag 59 46 N 5 23 E
Hardangerfjord
Mundheim 60 10 N 5 55 E
Norheimsund 60 22 N 6 09 E
Oystese 60 23 N 6 13 E
Aalvik 60 26 N 6 24 E
Eide 60 31 N 6 43 E
Ulvik 60 34 N 6 55 E
Eidfjord 60 28 N 7 04 E
Tyssedal 60 07 N 6 34 E
Odda 60 04 N 6 33 E

| Q | Y | G | C | B | | | |

Eitrheim 60 06 N 6 32 E
Utne 60 25 N 6 38 E
Rosendal 59 59 N 6 01 E
Heroysund 59 55 N 5 47 E
Husnes 59 52 N 5 46 E

| Y | G | A | | | | | |

23A

Aakrafjord
Aakra 59 47 N 6 06 E
Skaanevik 59 45 N 5 56 E
Hoylandssundet 59 47 N 5 48 E
Fjelberg 59 44 N 5 43 E
Etne 59 40 N 5 57 E
Valevaag 59 42 N 5 30 E
Bomlo
Mosterhamn 59 42 N 5 24 E
Espevaer 59 35 N 5 09 E
Haugesund 59 25 N 5 16 E

| P | Y | G | R | B | D | T | A | | |

Borgoen 59 21 N 5 40 E
Utsira 59 18 N 4 53 E
Karmoy
Vigsnes 59 24 N 5 08 E
Aakrehamn 59 15 N 5 10 E
Avaldsnes 59 21 N 5 17 E
Haavik 59 19 N 5 19 E

| Y | G | C | R | B | A | | |

Kopervik 59 17 N 5 18 E

| P | G | R | T | A | | | |

Skudeneshavn 59 08 N 5 16 E

23B

| G | R | B | D | T | A | | |

Kaarsto 59 17 N 5 33 E

| Q | G | R | T | A | | | |

Sauda 59 39 N 6 21 E

| Y | G | C | R | A | | | |

Vanvik 59 33 N 6 23 E
Sand 59 29 N 6 15 E
Tau 59 04 N 5 56 E
Jorpeland 59 01 N 6 03 E
Sandnes 58 51 N 5 45 E

| Y | G | R | B | A | | | |

Fiskeneset 58 53 N 5 45 E
Stavanger 58 58 N 5 44 E

| P | Y | G | C | R | B | T | A | L |

Sola 58 55 N 5 34 E

23C

| P | Q | B | T | A | | | |

Hvidingso 59 04 N 5 24 E
Tananger 58 56 N 5 35 E
Obrestad 58 39 N 5 34 E
Egersund 58 27 N 6 00 E

| Y | G | C | R | B | T | A | | |

Rekefjord 58 20 N 6 16 E
Jossingfjord 58 19 N 6 20 E
Flekkefjord 58 18 N 6 40 E

| G | R | B | | | | | |

Kvinesdal 58 18 N 7 00 E
Leirvik 58 16 N 6 53 E
Feda 58 16 N 6 49 E
Abelsnes 58 14 N 6 39 E
Eidsfjord
Pollen 58 10 N 6 43 E
Farsund 58 06 N 6 49 E

23D

| Y | G | B | T | A | | | |

Rosfjord 58 03 N 6 59 E
Lyngdal 58 08 N 7 02 E
Helvig 58 06 N 6 45 E
Gronsfjord 58 01 N 7 02 E
Agnefest 58 07 N 7 03 E
Lindesnes 57 59 N 7 03 E
Lindesneshalvoya 58 03 N 7 09 E
Hattholmen 58 00 N 7 27 E
Mandal 58 02 N 7 28 E

| G | C | R | B | T | A | | |

Kleven 58 01 N 7 29 E
Ryvingen 57 58 N 7 30 E
Ny Hellesund 58 03 N 7 51 E
Flekkeroy 58 06 N 7 59 E
Fiskaa 58 07 N 7 58 E
Kristiansand 58 09 N 8 00 E

| Y | G | C | R | B | D | T | A | L |

Aalefjaer 58 14 N 8 02 E
Hoivaag 58 10 N 8 15 E
Fossbekk 58 14 N 8 23 E
Lillesand 58 15 N 8 23 E

| Y | G | B | A | | | | |

24A

Kalvild 58 16 N 8 26 E
Grimstad 58 20 N 8 36 E

| G | C | R | T | A | | | |

Fevik 58 22 N 8 41 E
Arendal 58 28 N 8 46 E

| G | B | T | A | | | |

Tromoy 58 28 N 8 54 E
Eydehamn 58 30 N 8 53 E
Kilsund 58 33 N 8 59 E
Tvedestrand 58 38 N 8 56 E

| G | | | | | | | |

Sandvik 58 34 N 9 01 E
Dybvaag 58 37 N 9 04 E
Lyngor 58 38 N 9 08 E
Gjevingstangholmen 58 39 N 9 08 E
Risor 58 43 N 9 14 E

| G | | | | | | | |

Krana 58 44 N 9 14 E
Sondeled 58 43 N 9 12 E
Portor 58 48 N 9 26 E
Rorvik 58 52 N 9 23 E
Kragero 58 52 N 9 25 E

24B

| G | B | T | | | | |

Fossing 58 56 N 9 29 E
Asvall 59 01 N 9 36 E
Langesundsfjord
Langesund 59 00 N 9 45 E
Brevikfjord
Stathelle 59 02 N 9 42 E
Frierfjord
Bamble 59 01 N 9 40 E
Rafnes 59 06 N 9 36 E
River Skien
Heroya 59 06 N 9 38 E
Porsgrunn 59 08 N 9 39 E

| P | Q | Y | G | R | B | D | T | A | | |

Borgestad 59 09 N 9 39 E
Menstad 59 10 N 9 39 E
Nenseth 59 10 N 9 38 E
Waterloo 59 10 N 9 37 E
Bole 59 11 N 9 38 E
Skien 59 12 N 9 37 E

24C

| G | C | R | B | T | A | | |

Brevik 59 03 N 9 43 E
Trosvik 59 03 N 9 42 E
Dalen 59 04 N 9 42 E
Nystrand 59 06 N 9 43 E
Langangen 59 05 N 9 48 E
Larvik 59 03 N 10 02 E

| P | Y | G | C | R | B | A | | |

Sandefjord 59 08 N 10 14 E

| P | Q | G | R | B | T | A | |

Oslofjord
Faerder 59 02 N 10 32 E
Tonsbergfjord
Tjome 59 06 N 10 23 E
Vrengen 59 10 N 10 24 E
Melsomvik 59 13 N 10 21 E
Tonsberg 59 16 N 10 25 E

24D

| Y | G | C | R | B | T | A | | |

Husoy 59 14 N 10 28 E
Valloy 59 16 N 10 30 E
Slagen 59 19 N 10 32 E

| P | Q | B | T | A | | | |

Horten 59 25 N 10 30 E

| G | C | R | B | D | T | A | |

Holmestrand 59 32 N 10 16 E

| G | B | T | A | | | | |

Sande 59 35 N 10 15 E
Dramsfjord
Svelvik 59 37 N 10 25 E

| G | B | A | | | | | |

Drammen 59 44 N 10 14 E

| P | Q | Y | G | C | R | B | D | T | A | |

Gilhus 59 45 N 10 16 E
Gullaug 59 44 N 10 17 E
Hurumlandet 59 37 N 10 27 E
Sagene 59 32 N 10 32 E

P Petroleum **Q** Other Liquid Bulk **Y** Dry Bulk **G** General Cargo
C Containers **R** Ro-Ro **B** Bunkers **D** Dry Dock **T** Towage
A Airport (within 100km) **L** Lloyd's Agent (not including sub-agents)

GEOGRAPHIC INDEX

25A

Tofte 59 33 N 10 35 E
Filtvet 59 34 N 10 37 E
Halvorshavn 59 35 N 10 37 E
Verpen 59 40 N 10 35 E
Engene 59 41 N 10 33 E
Saetrepollen 59 41 N 10 32 E
Naersnes 59 46 N 10 31 E
Slemmestad 59 47 N 10 30 E
Leangen 59 50 N 10 29 E
Sandvika 59 53 N 10 32 E
Lysaker 59 55 N 10 38 E

P G A

Oslo 59 54 N 10 43 E

P Y G C R B T A L

Steilene 59 49 N 10 37 E
Granerudstoa 59 47 N 10 36 E
Fagerstrand 59 44 N 10 36 E

P T A

Digerudgrunnen 59 43 N 10 35 E
Drobak 59 39 N 10 38 E
Son (Soon) 59 32 N 10 42 E
Kambo 59 29 N 10 42 E
Moss 59 26 N 10 40 E

25B

P Y G C R T A

Mellos 59 25 N 10 40 E
Larkollen 59 19 N 10 41 E
Glomma River
Borg Harbour

P Q Y G C R B T

Fredrikstad 59 12 N 10 57 E
Greaker 59 16 N 11 02 E
Sannesund 59 16 N 11 06 E
Sarpsborg 59 16 N 11 06 E
Selbak 59 13 N 11 00 E
Bolingshavn 59 03 N 11 01 E
Herfol 59 00 N 11 03 E
Torsokilen 59 10 N 11 05 E
Iddefjord
Slottet 59 07 N 11 23 E
Halden 59 07 N 11 22 E

25C

G C B T

Holm 59 06 N 11 23 E
Hov 59 05 N 11 24 E
Torp 59 04 N 11 25 E
Ystehedkilen 59 04 N 11 26 E
Fagerholt 59 03 N 11 26 E
Ostdalen 59 02 N 11 26 E
Liholt 59 02 N 11 27 E
Aarebakken 59 01 N 11 27 E

SWEDEN

Krokstrand 59 00 N 11 27 E
Dynekilen 59 00 N 11 14 E
Stromstad 58 56 N 11 10 E
Grebbestad 58 41 N 11 15 E
Fjallbacka 58 36 N 11 17 E
Hamburgsund 58 34 N 11 15 E
Heestrand 58 31 N 11 16 E
Bovallstrand 58 29 N 11 20 E
Ulebergshamn 58 28 N 11 18 E
Hunnebostrand 58 26 N 11 18 E

25D

Ramsvik 58 26 N 11 16 E
Smogen 58 21 N 11 14 E
Gravarne 58 22 N 11 15 E
Kungshamn 58 22 N 11 14 E
Rorvik 58 22 N 11 21 E
Stensjo 58 24 N 11 24 E
Fagelvik 58 22 N 11 23 E
Ryxo (Rixo) 58 22 N 11 26 E
Brofjorden 58 20 N 11 23 E

P Q B T

Lysekil 58 16 N 11 26 E

Y G C B T

Munkedalhamn 58 26 N 11 40 E
Saltkallan 58 27 N 11 41 E
Skredsvik 58 23 N 11 39 E
Fiskebackskil 58 15 N 11 28 E
Mollosund 58 04 N 11 29 E
Uddevalla 58 21 N 11 55 E

P Y G C R B T A

Gustavsberg 58 20 N 11 54 E

26A

Stenungsund 58 05 N 11 49 E

P Q Y B A

Tjorn Island
Wallhamn 58 00 N 11 42 E

Y G C R B T A

Ronnang 58 05 N 11 40 E
Mossholmen 57 57 N 11 34 E
Skarhamn 57 59 N 11 33 E
Marstrand 57 53 N 11 35 E
Kungalv 57 52 N 12 00 E
Vinga 57 38 N 11 37 E
Rivofjord 57 40 N 11 48 E
Hjartholmen 57 41 N 11 48 E
Gothenburg (Goteborg) 57 42 N 11 57 E

P Q Y G C R B D T A L

Gota Alv
Agnesberg 57 47 N 12 00 E
Surte 57 50 N 12 01 E
Bohus 57 51 N 12 02 E
Nol 57 56 N 12 08 E
Lodose 58 02 N 12 09 E
Gota 58 06 N 12 09 E
Trollhatte Canal
Trollhattan 58 17 N 12 17 E
Stallbacka 58 18 N 12 18 E
Vargon 58 21 N 12 23 E
Lake Vanern

26B

Vanersborg 58 23 N 12 20 E

Y G B A

Kopmannebro 58 46 N 12 31 E
Amal 59 03 N 12 43 E
Spesshult 59 04 N 12 55 E
Krokstad 59 06 N 12 55 E
Saffle 59 08 N 12 56 E
Arvika 59 40 N 12 35 E
Kyrkebyn 59 16 N 13 04 E
Slottsbron 59 20 N 13 06 E
Gruvon 59 20 N 13 07 E
Norsbron 59 25 N 13 14 E
Edsvalla 59 26 N 13 14 E
Hoglunda 59 25 N 13 15 E
Aelvenaes 59 22 N 13 11 E
Skoghall 59 19 N 13 27 E

26C

P Q Y G B T

Karlstad 59 23 N 13 31 E

P Y G C R B T A

Skattkarr 59 25 N 13 42 E
Kristinehamn 59 19 N 14 07 E

P Q Y G B T A

Otterbacken 58 57 N 14 03 E

P Y G B T A

Sjotorp 58 50 N 14 00 E
Mariestad 58 43 N 13 50 E

G B T

Hallekis 58 40 N 13 25 E
Honsater 58 38 N 13 27 E
Lidkoping 58 30 N 13 10 E

G B T A

26D

Gota Canal
Lake Vattern
Jonkoping 57 46 N 14 10 E
Motala 58 32 N 15 04 E
Askersund 58 52 N 14 55 E
Olshammar 58 45 N 14 50 E
Hjo 58 17 N 14 07 E
Saro 57 30 N 11 56 E
Onsala 57 25 N 12 00 E
Kungsbacka 57 29 N 12 05 E
Varberg 57 06 N 12 15 E

P Y G C R B T

Falkenberg 56 53 N 12 30 E

Y G C R B D A

Halmstad 56 40 N 12 51 E

P Y G C R B T A L

Torekov 56 25 N 12 37 E
Angelholm 56 15 N 12 52 E
Jonstorp 56 14 N 12 40 E
Arildslage 56 16 N 12 35 E
Molle 56 17 N 12 30 E

27A

Hoganas 56 12 N 12 33 E

P Y G A

Helsingborg 56 03 N 12 41 E

P Q Y G C R B D T A L

Kopparverkshamn 56 01 N 12 43 E
Raa 55 59 N 12 45 E
Ven Island
Backviken 55 54 N 12 43 E
Borstahusen 55 54 N 12 48 E
Landskrona 55 52 N 12 50 E

Q Y G B D T A

Barsebackshamn 55 45 N 12 54 E
Lomma 55 41 N 13 04 E
Malmo 55 37 N 13 00 E

P Q Y G C R B D T A L

Limhamn 55 35 N 12 56 E

P Y G B T A

Klagshamn 55 31 N 12 53 E
Falsterbo 55 25 N 12 50 E
Trelleborg 55 22 N 13 09 E

27B

P G R B T A

Smygehuk 55 20 N 13 21 E
Ystad 55 26 N 13 50 E

P Q G C R B T A

Kaaseberga 55 23 N 14 04 E
Sandhammaren 55 23 N 14 12 E
Skillinge 55 28 N 14 17 E
Brantevik 55 31 N 14 21 E
Simrishamn 55 33 N 14 22 E

G B A

Baskemolla 55 36 N 14 19 E
Kivik 55 41 N 14 14 E
Ahus 55 56 N 14 19 E

Y G B T A

Solvesborg 56 03 N 14 35 E

27C

P Q Y G C R B T A

Hallevik 56 01 N 14 43 E
Pukavik 56 09 N 14 41 E
Elleholm 56 10 N 14 44 E
Karlshall 56 09 N 14 40 E
Karlshamn 56 10 N 14 52 E

P Q Y G C R B T A L

Tarno 56 07 N 14 58 E
Jarnavik 56 11 N 15 05 E
Ronnebyhamn 56 10 N 15 18 E

G B A

Torko 56 09 N 15 24 E
Karlskrona 56 10 N 15 36 E

P G R B D T A

Sturko 56 05 N 15 42 E
Torhamn 56 06 N 15 49 E
Bergkvara 56 23 N 16 05 E
Kalmar 56 40 N 16 22 E

27D

P Q Y G C R B T A L

Pataholm 56 55 N 16 26 E
Timmernabben (Tillingenabben)
56 58 N 16 26 E
Monsteras 57 02 N 16 28 E
Paaskallavik 57 10 N 16 28 E
Vanevik 57 12 N 16 27 E
Oskarshamn 57 16 N 16 27 E

P G C R B D T A

Virbodraget 57 19 N 16 34 E
Figeholm 57 22 N 16 34 E
Oland Island
Sandviken 57 04 N 16 52 E
Borgholm 56 53 N 16 39 E

Y G

Farjestaden 56 39 N 16 28 E
Morbylanga 56 32 N 16 22 E
Degerhamn 56 21 N 16 25 E

Y G B A

Gronhogen 56 16 N 16 24 E
Nasby 56 35 N 16 41 E

P Petroleum	Q Other Liquid Bulk	Y Dry Bulk	G General Cargo
C Containers	R Ro-Ro	B Bunkers	D Dry Dock	T Towage
A Airport (within 100km)		L Lloyd's Agent (not including sub-agents)

SWEDEN *continued* — 28A

Boda 57 14 N 17 05 E
Grankullaviken 57 21 N 17 06 E
Gotland Island
Visby 57 39 N 18 17 E

`P Y G R B A L`

Klintehamn 57 23 N 18 12 E

`Y G B A`

Burgsvik 57 02 N 18 16 E
Ronehamn 57 10 N 18 32 E
Ljugarn 57 20 N 18 43 E
Slite 57 42 N 18 49 E

`Y G R B A`

Rutehamn 57 47 N 18 57 E
St. Olofsholm 57 43 N 18 55 E
Smojen 57 44 N 18 57 E
Kyllej 57 45 N 18 57 E
Furillen 57 46 N 19 00 E
Bungenas 57 49 N 19 05 E
Farosund 57 52 N 19 04 E
Straa 57 54 N 19 02 E
Ar 57 55 N 18 57 E
Blase 57 55 N 18 50 E
Storugns 57 50 N 18 48 E

`Y A`

Kappelshamn 57 51 N 18 47 E
Blankaholm 57 35 N 16 32 E — 28B
Gunnebo 57 43 N 16 33 E
Verkeback 57 44 N 16 32 E
Vastervik 57 45 N 16 39 E

`G R T`

Almvik 57 50 N 16 28 E
Gamleby 57 54 N 16 25 E
Kallvik 57 53 N 16 43 E
Helgenas 58 00 N 16 30 E
Valdemarsvik 58 12 N 16 36 E
Orrfjarden 58 16 N 16 42 E
Gota Canal
Soderkoping 58 29 N 16 20 E

`G D`

Mem 58 29 N 16 25 E
Arkosund 58 29 N 16 57 E
Braviken — 28C
Norrkoping 58 36 N 16 12 E

`P Y G C R B T A`

Djuron 58 38 N 16 20 E
Sandviken 58 40 N 16 24 E
Navekvarn 58 38 N 16 48 E
Marsviken 58 40 N 16 57 E
Oxelosund 58 40 N 17 07 E

`P Y G R T`

Nykoping 58 45 N 17 01 E

`G R B T`

Studsvik 58 45 N 17 17 E
Sodertalje 59 11 N 17 39 E

`P Q Y G C R A`

Igelstaviken 59 12 N 17 38 E
Lake Malaren — 28D
Strangnas 59 23 N 17 02 E

`G A`

Stallarholmen 59 20 N 17 15 E
Torshalla 59 26 N 16 29 E
Eskilstuna 58 22 N 16 01 E
Arboga 59 26 N 15 51 E
Kungsor 59 26 N 16 06 E

`G A`

Orebro 59 17 N 15 11 E
Koping 59 31 N 16 00 E

`P Q Y G C B T`

Vasteras 59 36 N 16 33 E

`P Y G C R B T A`

Enkoping 59 28 N 17 05 E
Balsta 59 33 N 17 33 E
Uppsala 59 52 N 17 39 E
Sigtuna 59 37 N 17 44 E
Kagghamra 59 06 N 17 47 E
Oaxen 58 58 N 17 43 E
Stora Vika 58 56 N 17 47 E

29A

Nynashamn 58 54 N 17 57 E

`P G R A`

Dalaro 59 08 N 18 25 E
Gustavsberg 59 20 N 18 23 E
Tollare 59 18 N 18 14 E
Gaddviken 59 19 N 18 08 E
Stockholm 59 19 N 18 03 E

`P Q Y G C R B T A L`

Maryvik 59 19 N 18 02 E
Arstadalshamnen 59 18 N 18 02 E
Liljeholmsviken 59 19 N 18 00 E
Loudden 59 20 N 18 08 E
Stocksund 59 23 N 18 03 E
Vartahamnen 59 21 N 18 11 E
Vaxholm 59 24 N 18 21 E
Ytterby 59 26 N 18 21 E
Flaxenvik 59 28 N 18 24 E — 29B
Idsatravik 59 29 N 18 24 E
Hogmarso 59 39 N 18 51 E
Furusund 59 39 N 18 54 E
Norrtalje 59 45 N 18 42 E
Arholma 59 51 N 19 06 E
Grisslehamn 60 06 N 18 49 E
Herrang 60 08 N 18 39 E
Hallstavik 60 03 N 18 36 E

`P G R B T A`

Hargshamn 60 10 N 18 29 E

`Y G R B T A`

Oregrund 60 20 N 18 27 E
Forsmark 60 25 N 18 12 E
Karlholm 60 31 N 17 38 E
Skutskar 60 39 N 17 24 E

`G B`

Karskar 60 41 N 17 17 E
Granudden 60 41 N 17 15 E
Gavle (Gefle) 60 40 N 17 10 E

`P Y G C R B T A L`

Norrsundet 60 56 N 17 09 E — 29C

`Y G B T`

Axmar 61 01 N 17 10 E
Axmarbruk 61 03 N 17 10 E
Vallvik 61 07 N 17 11 E
Stor Orrskar 61 12 N 17 10 E
Ljusne 61 13 N 17 08 E
Ala 61 13 N 17 10 E
Kallskar 61 15 N 17 12 E
Sandarne 61 16 N 17 11 E
Asbacka 61 17 N 17 09 E
Grundvik 61 18 N 17 08 E
Stugsund 61 18 N 17 07 E
Soderhamn 61 19 N 17 06 E

`P Q Y G B T`

Branthalls Redd 61 16 N 17 14 E
Ago 61 33 N 17 28 E
Iggesund 61 39 N 17 06 E

`P G C R B T A`

Hudiksvall 61 43 N 17 07 E

`P Q Y G C R B T A`

Arnoviken 61 43 N 17 24 E — 28D
Arno 61 42 N 17 24 E
Stocka 61 54 N 17 20 E
Gnarp 62 02 N 17 26 E
Essvik 62 19 N 17 24 E
Svartvik 62 19 N 17 22 E
Stockvik 62 20 N 17 22 E
Kubikenborg 62 23 N 17 20 E
Rosenborg 62 24 N 17 21 E
Sundsvall 62 25 N 17 20 E

`P Q Y G C R B T A L`

Alno Island
Ankarsvik 62 23 N 17 25 E
Gustavsberg 62 24 N 17 25 E
Ortviken 62 24 N 17 22 E
Tunadal 62 26 N 17 23 E
Johannedal 62 26 N 17 24 E
Sundsbruk 62 27 N 17 22 E
Skonvik 62 28 N 17 20 E
Ostrand 62 29 N 17 20 E
Vivstavarv 62 30 N 17 22 E
Fagervik 62 30 N 17 24 E
Soraker 62 30 N 17 30 E

30A

Harnosand (Hernosand) 62 38 N 17 56 E

`P G B D T A`

Utansjo 62 46 N 17 56 E
Ramvik 62 49 N 17 52 E
Gustafsvik 62 50 N 17 52 E
Sprangsviken 62 51 N 17 53 E
Stromnas 62 53 N 17 52 E
Frano 62 55 N 17 51 E
Bjorknas 62 55 N 17 50 E
Kramfors 62 56 N 17 47 E
Sandviken 62 58 N 17 47 E
Dynas 62 58 N 17 45 E
Vaja 62 59 N 17 43 E
Bollsta 63 00 N 17 41 E
Nas 63 00 N 17 42 E
Nyland 63 00 N 17 46 E
Marieberg 63 00 N 17 48 E
Koja 62 58 N 17 50 E
Hallstanas 62 55 N 17 54 E
Norrland 62 55 N 17 55 E
Lugnvik 62 55 N 17 56 E
Svanon 62 54 N 17 53 E — 30B
Sando 62 53 N 17 55 E
Dal 62 49 N 17 56 E
Norastrom 62 51 N 18 02 E
Bergkvistviken 62 49 N 18 06 E
Berghamn 62 49 N 18 15 E
Barstahamn 62 52 N 18 24 E
Salsaker 63 00 N 18 17 E
Ullanger 63 01 N 18 12 E
Askja 63 01 N 18 13 E
Docksta 63 03 N 18 20 E
Ulvohamn 63 01 N 18 39 E
Kopmanholmen 63 11 N 18 38 E
Hornskaten 63 13 N 18 53 E
Arnas 63 15 N 18 46 E
Domsjo 63 16 N 18 44 E
Horneborg 63 17 N 18 43 E
Ornskoldsvik 63 16 N 18 43 E

`Q G C R B T A L`

Alne 63 16 N 18 46 E
Skagenshamn 63 13 N 19 02 E
Husum 63 20 N 19 09 E
Rundvik 63 32 N 19 27 E
Nordmaling (Notholmen) 63 34 N 19 29 E
Norrbyskar 63 33 N 19 53 E
Hornefors 63 37 N 19 54 E — 30C

`G A`

Bredskar 63 40 N 20 19 E
Bredvik 63 41 N 20 18 E
Obbola 63 42 N 20 20 E
Umea 63 50 N 20 16 E

`P Y G R B A`

Sandvik 63 43 N 20 23 E
Djupvik 63 43 N 20 22 E
Holmsund 63 42 N 20 21 E
Ratan 64 00 N 20 54 E   `p.26`
Sikea 64 08 N 20 59 E
Robertsfors 64 12 N 20 55 E
Gumbodahamn 64 13 N 21 05 E
Krakanger 64 13 N 21 15 E
Kallviken 64 20 N 21 22 E
Bjuroklubb 64 29 N 21 35 E
Backfors 64 30 N 21 25 E
Burea 64 37 N 21 15 E — 29D
Orviken 64 40 N 21 13 E
Skelleftea 64 44 N 20 57 E

`P Q Y G B T A`

Ursviken 64 42 N 21 11 E
Savenas 64 41 N 21 13 E
Skelleftehamn 64 41 N 21 15 E
Ronnskar 64 40 N 21 17 E
Kagefjarden
Kage 64 50 N 21 02 E
Storkage 64 50 N 21 01 E
Frostkage 64 52 N 21 02 E
Furuogrund 64 55 N 21 14 E
Byske 64 57 N 21 11 E
Batvik 64 57 N 21 18 E
Brannfors 65 01 N 21 24 E
Storfors 65 18 N 21 23 E
Bergsviken 65 19 N 21 23 E
Pitea 65 19 N 21 30 E

`P Y G R B T A`

Haraholmen 65 14 N 21 38 E — 30D
Lovholmen 65 18 N 21 29 E
Munksund 65 17 N 21 29 E

GEOGRAPHIC INDEX

Petroleum **Q** Other Liquid Bulk **Y** Dry Bulk **G** General Cargo
C Containers **R** Ro-Ro **B** Bunkers **D** Dry Dock **T** Towage
A Airport (within 100km) **L** Lloyd's Agent (not including sub-agents)

ESTONIA continued — 34A

Paldiski 59 21 N 24 03 E
Osmusaar Island 59 18 N 23 22 E
Vormsi Island
   Forby 59 00 N 23 10 E
Hiiumaa Island
   Heltermaa 58 52 N 23 04 E
   Dagerort 58 55 N 22 12 E
Muhu Island
   Kuivastu 58 35 N 23 24 E
Saaremaa Island
   Triigi 58 36 N 22 45 E
   Orissaare 58 34 N 23 05 E
   Roomassaar 58 13 N 22 31 E
   Kingissepp 58 15 N 22 30 E
   Taga Bay 58 28 N 22 05 E
   Kihelkonna 58 23 N 22 00 E
Haapsalu 58 57 N 23 32 E
Parnu 58 23 N 24 29 E
`G B T`

LATVIA — 34B

Ainazi 57 52 N 24 22 E
Salacgriva 57 45 N 24 22 E
River Daugava
   Milgravis 57 02 N 24 07 E
   Bolderaya 57 02 N 24 03 E
   Riga 56 58 N 24 06 E
`P Q Y G C R B D T A`

Engure 57 10 N 23 14 E
Mersrags 57 22 N 23 08 E
Kaltene 57 27 N 22 53 E
Rojas Osta 57 30 N 22 50 E
Gipka 57 34 N 22 40 E
Kolka 57 48 N 22 39 E
Lielirbe 57 37 N 22 05 E
Ventspils 57 24 N 21 33 E
`P Q Y G R B T`

Uzava 57 12 N 21 25 E
Labrags 56 59 N 21 22 E
Pavilosta 56 54 N 21 11 E
Liepaja 56 32 N 21 01 E

LITHUANIA — 34C

Palanga 55 55 N 21 05 E
Klaipeda 55 43 N 21 07 E
`P Y G R B T A`

RUSSIA

Baltiysk 54 39 N 19 54 E
Peyse 54 39 N 20 06 E
Svetlyy 54 38 N 20 09 E
Kaliningrad 54 43 N 20 31 E
`P Q Y G R B D T A`

POLAND — 34D

Elblag 54 10 N 19 24 E
River Wisla
   Port Polnocny 54 24 N 18 43 E
   Nowy Port 54 24 N 18 40 E   `p.24/25`
   Tczew 54 05 N 18 46 E
   Martwa Wisla
      Gdansk 54 21 N 18 39 E
`P Q Y G C R B D T A`

Sopot 54 27 N 18 34 E
Gdynia 54 32 N 18 33 E
`P Q Y G C R B D T A L`

Wladyslawowo 54 48 N 18 25 E
`G B A`

Hel 54 36 N 18 48 E
Rozewie 54 50 N 18 20 E
Ustka 54 35 N 16 52 E
`Y G B T A`

Darlowo 54 26 N 16 23 E
`Y G T A`

(column 2) — 35A

Kolobrzeg 54 11 N 15 34 E
`Y G R B A`

Niechorze 54 06 N 15 04 E
Kamien Pomorski 53 58 N 14 46 E
Swinoujscie 53 55 N 14 15 E
`Y G T A`

Lubin 53 52 N 14 26 E
Wolin 53 51 N 14 37 E
River Oder
   Stepnica 53 39 N 14 38 E
   Szczecin 53 25 N 14 33 E
`Q Y G C R B D T A L`

Zelechowa 53 27 N 14 35 E
Goclaw 53 29 N 14 36 E
Krasnica 53 30 N 14 37 E
Glinki 53 30 N 14 36 E
Skolwin 53 32 N 14 37 E
Police 53 33 N 14 36 E
`Q Y G`

Nowe Warpno 53 44 N 14 17 E

GERMANY — 35B

Ueckermunde 53 44 N 14 03 E
River Peene
   Anklam 53 52 N 13 41 E
   Jarmen 53 47 N 13 10 E
   Demmin 53 54 N 13 01 E
   Malchin 53 45 N 12 45 E
Wolgast 54 03 N 13 47 E
Kroslin 54 08 N 13 45 E
Greifswald 54 06 N 13 23 E
Rugen Island
   Lauterbach 54 20 N 13 31 E
   Mukran 54 29 N 13 35 E
   Sassnitz 54 31 N 13 38 E
   Cap Arkona 54 41 N 13 26 E
Stralsund 54 19 N 13 06 E
`Y G B D T A`

Barhoft 54 26 N 13 02 E
Barth 54 22 N 12 44 E
Zingst 54 27 N 12 40 E
Ribnitz 54 15 N 12 26 E
River Warnow
   Rostock 54 09 N 12 06 E
`P Q Y G C R B D T`

   Warnemunde 54 11 N 12 05 E
Wismar 53 54 N 11 28 E
`P Q Y G R B D T`

River Trave
   Schlutup 53 53 N 10 47 E
   Siems 53 53 N 10 45 E
   Lubeck 53 52 N 10 40 E
`Y G C R B D T A L`

   Danischburg 53 55 N 10 44 E
   Herrenwyk 53 54 N 10 48 E
   Travemunde 53 58 N 10 54 E
`G C R B A`

Neustadt 54 06 N 10 49 E
Gromitz 54 09 N 10 59 E
Fehmarn Island
   Burgstaaken 54 25 N 11 12 E
   Orth 54 27 N 11 03 E
   Puttgarden 54 30 N 11 14 E
Heiligenhafen 54 22 N 10 59 E
`Y G B`

Laboe 54 24 N 10 13 E
`Y G B`

Kiel 54 19 N 10 08 E
`P Q Y G C R B D T A L`

Kiel Canal (Nord-Ostsee Kanal)
   Holtenau 54 22 N 10 09 E
`G B T`

   Flemhude 54 19 N 9 58 E
   Audorf 54 19 N 9 43 E
   Rendsburg 54 19 N 9 40 E
`Y G B D T A`

   River Eider
      Breiholz 54 12 N 9 32 E

(column 3) — 36A

      Fischerhutte 54 09 N 9 22 E
      Dukerswisch 54 03 N 9 19 E
      Hochdonn 54 01 N 9 18 E
      Burg 53 59 N 9 17 E
      Ostermoor 53 55 N 9 11 E
Eckernforde 54 29 N 9 51 E
`Y G B A`

Schleswig 54 31 N 9 34 E
Kappeln 54 40 N 9 56 E
`Y G B A`

Gelting 54 44 N 9 54 E
Murwik 54 49 N 9 28 E
Flensburg 54 48 N 9 26 E
`P Y G B`

DENMARK — 36B

BORNHOLM

Ronne 55 06 N 14 42 E
`P Y G C R B T A`

Nekso (Nexo) 55 04 N 15 09 E
`G B D A`

Svaneke 55 08 N 15 09 E
`G`

Gudhjem 55 13 N 14 58 E
Allinge 55 17 N 14 48 E
`G B A`

Hammeren 55 17 N 14 45 E
Hammerhavn 55 16 N 14 45 E
`G B A`

Vang 55 15 N 14 44 E
Hasle 55 11 N 14 42 E
`Y G A`

MON — 36C

Stege 54 59 N 12 17 E
Klintholm 54 57 N 12 28 E

SJAELLAND

Kalvehave 54 59 N 12 10 E
Praesto 55 07 N 12 02 E
Fakse Ladeplads 55 13 N 12 10 E
`Y G B T A`

Rodvig 55 15 N 12 23 E
Stevns Pier 55 19 N 12 27 E
`G`

Holtug 55 21 N 12 27 E
Stroby 55 24 N 12 18 E
Koge 55 27 N 12 12 E
`P Q Y G C R B T A`

Mosede 55 34 N 12 17 E
Drogden Light 55 32 N 12 43 E
Amager Island
   Dragor 55 35 N 12 41 E
   Kastrup 55 38 N 12 39 E
   Valby 55 40 N 12 33 E
Copenhagen (Kobenhavn)
55 42 N 12 37 E — 36D
`P Q Y G C R B D T A L`

Tuborg Havn 55 43 N 12 35 E
Hellerup 55 44 N 12 35 E
Taarbaek 55 47 N 12 36 E
Nivaa 55 56 N 12 31 E
Snekkersten 56 01 N 12 36 E
Elsinore (Helsingor) 56 02 N 12 37 E
`G B D A`

Gilleleje 56 08 N 12 19 E
Hundested 55 58 N 11 51 E
Frederiksvaerk 55 58 N 12 01 E
`Y G B A`

Frederikssund 55 50 N 12 03 E
`Y G T`

Roskilde 55 39 N 12 05 E
Lyngby 55 40 N 11 56 E

P Petroleum **Q** Other Liquid Bulk **Y** Dry Bulk **G** General Cargo
C Containers **R** Ro-Ro **B** Bunkers **D** Dry Dock **T** Towage
A Airport (within 100km) **L** Lloyd's Agent (not including sub-agents)

GEOGRAPHIC INDEX

Kyndby 55 49 N 11 53 E   **37A**
[P | Y | G | B | T]

Holbaek 55 43 N 11 43 E
[Q | Y | G | B | T | A]

Nykobing 55 55 N 11 41 E
Rorvig 55 57 N 11 46 E
Odden 55 58 N 11 22 E
Sejero 55 53 N 11 09 E
Kalundborg 55 41 N 11 05 E
[P | Y | G | R | B | T | A]

Asnaesvaerkets Havn 55 40 N 11 05 E
[Q | Y | G | B | T | A]

Mullerup 55 30 N 11 11 E
Halsskov 55 20 N 11 06 E
Korsor 55 20 N 11 08 E
[P | Y | G | R | B | T]

Skaelskor 55 15 N 11 17 E   **37B**
[G]

Stigsnaesvaerkets Havn 55 13 N 11 15 E
[P | Y | B]

Gulfhavn 55 12 N 11 15 E
[P | Q | B]

Karrebaeksminde 55 10 N 11 38 E
Naestved 55 14 N 11 45 E
[P | Y | G | B | T | A]

Masnedsund 55 00 N 11 54 E
[Y | G | B | T | A]

Masnedovaerkets Havn 54 58 N 11 53 E
[Q | Y | B | T | A]

Vordingborg 55 00 N 11 54 E

FALSTER   **37C**

Orehoved 54 57 N 11 51 E
[Y | G | B | T | A]

Stubbekobing 54 53 N 12 02 E
[G | B]

Gedser 54 34 N 11 56 E
Nykobing 54 46 N 11 52 E
[P | G | B | T]

LOLLAND

Vigsnaes 54 53 N 11 39 E
Sakskobing 54 48 N 11 38 E
[Q | Y | G | B | D]

Bandholm 54 50 N 11 30 E
[P | Y | G | B | A]

Nakskov 54 50 N 11 08 E
[P | Y | G | R | B | D | A]

Rodbyhavn 54 39 N 11 21 E
[P | Y | G | B | A]

Nysted 54 40 N 11 44 E   **37D**
Guldborg 54 52 N 11 45 E

LANGELAND

Bagenkop 54 45 N 10 40 E
Rudkobing 54 56 N 10 43 E
[Y | G | B | T | A]

Dagelokke 55 04 N 10 52 E
Lohals 55 08 N 10 54 E

AERO

Marstal 54 51 N 10 31 E
Aeroskobing 54 53 N 10 25 E
[Y | G | B | T | A]

Soby 54 57 N 10 16 E

TAASINGE

Troense 55 02 N 10 39 E

THURO   **38A**

Thuro 55 02 N 10 41 E

FUNEN

Svendborg 55 03 N 10 37 E
[Y | G | C | R | B | D | T | A]

Nyborg 55 18 N 10 47 E
[P | Y | G | R | B | D | T | A]

Kerteminde 55 27 N 10 40 E
[Y | G | B | T | A]

Lindo 55 28 N 10 32 E
Odense 55 25 N 10 23 E
[P | Y | G | C | R | B | T | A | L]

Aebelo 55 39 N 10 10 E
Bogense 55 34 N 10 05 E
Strib 55 32 N 9 46 E
Middelfart 55 30 N 9 44 E
[P | Q | Y | G | C | R | B | T | A]

Assens 55 16 N 9 54 E   **38B**
[Y | G | B | D | T | A]

Faaborg 55 06 N 10 14 E
[G | B | A]

Avernako 55 02 N 10 15 E
Fjellebroen 55 04 N 10 23 E

SAMSO

Kolby Kaas 55 48 N 10 32 E
Maarup 55 56 N 10 33 E
Ballen 55 49 N 10 39 E

ALS

Sonderborg 54 55 N 9 47 E
[P | Y | G | C | B | T | A]

Mommark 54 56 N 10 03 E
Augustenborg 54 57 N 9 52 E
Katholm 54 56 N 9 50 E

JUTLAND   **38C**

Egernsund 54 54 N 9 36 E
Graasten 54 55 N 9 37 E
[G | B | A]

Enstedvaerkets Havn 55 01 N 9 26 E
[P | Y | B | A]

Aabenraa 55 02 N 9 26 E
[P | Q | Y | G | B | D | T | A]

Aarosund 55 16 N 9 43 E
Haderslev 55 15 N 9 30 E
[Y | G | B | T | A]

Kolding 55 30 N 9 30 E
[Q | Y | G | R | B | T | A]

Skaerbaek 55 31 N 9 37 E   **38D**
[P | G | B | T | A]

Snoghoj 55 32 N 9 42 E
Lyngs Odde 55 31 N 9 45 E
[Q | B | A]

Fredericia 55 34 N 9 45 E
[P | Q | Y | G | C | R | B | D | T | A]

Vejle 55 43 N 9 33 E
[P | Q | Y | G | R | B | T | A]

Juelsminde 55 43 N 10 01 E
Horsens 55 51 N 9 52 E
[P | Q | Y | G | B | T | A]

Hov 55 55 N 10 15 E
Aarhus 56 09 N 10 13 E
[P | Q | Y | G | C | R | B | D | T | A | L]

Studstrup 56 15 N 10 21 E
[Y | G | B | T | A]

Nappedam 56 17 N 10 30 E

Knebel 56 13 N 10 30 E   **39A**
Sletterhage 56 06 N 10 31 E
Lyngsbaek Bridge 56 14 N 10 37 E
Ebeltoft 56 12 N 10 40 E
Glatved 56 18 N 10 51 E
Grenaa 56 25 N 10 56 E
[P | Q | Y | G | C | R | B | T | A]

Fornaes 56 27 N 10 58 E
Gerrild 56 32 N 10 50 E
Anholt 56 43 N 11 31 E
Udbyhoj 56 37 N 10 19 E
Voer 56 31 N 10 14 E
Mellerup 56 31 N 10 16 E
Randers 56 28 N 10 03 E
[Q | Y | G | B | T | A]

Mariager Fjord
  Kongsdal 56 40 N 10 03 E
  [Y | G | R | B | T | A]

  Mariager 56 39 N 9 59 E
  Hobro 56 38 N 9 48 E
  [G | B | T | A]

  Hadsund 56 43 N 10 07 E
  [G | A]

Als 56 45 N 10 18 E   **39B**
Rordal 57 04 N 9 58 E
Limfjord
  Aalborg 57 03 N 9 57E
  [P | Q | Y | G | C | R | B | D | T | A | L]

  Lindholm Pier 57 04 N 9 51 E
  Norresundby 57 04 N 9 55 E
  Hals 56 59 N 10 19 E
Laeso 57 13 N 10 42 E
Saeby 57 20 N 10 31 E
Understed 57 23 N 10 30 E
Frederikshavn 57 26 N 10 33 E
[P | Y | G | R | B | D | T | A]

Strandby 57 29 N 10 31 E
Skagen 57 43 N 10 36 E   **39C**
[G | B | T | A]

Skaw 57 44 N 10 38 E
Hirtshals 57 36 N 9 58 E
[P | Y | G | B | T | A]

Hanstholm 57 07 N 8 35 E
[Y | G | R | B | D | T | A]

Klitmoller 57 02N 8 30 E
Lodbjerg 56 49 N 8 16 E
Limfjord
  Krik 56 46 N 8 16 E
  Mors Island
    Vilsund 56 56 N 8 39 E
    Sundby 56 53 N 8 41 E
    Nykobing 56 48 N 8 52 E
  [P | Y | G | B | A]

  Ejerslev 56 55 N 8 55 E
  Skarrehage 56 57 N 8 52 E

JUTLAND   **39D**

Thisted 56 57 N 8 42 E
[Y | G | B | T | A]

Aggersund 57 01 N 9 17 E
Nibe 56 59 N 9 38 E
Logstor 56 58 N 9 15 E
Skive 56 34 N 9 02 E
Fur Island
  Fur Molervaerk 56 50 N 8 58 E
  Fur 56 50 N 9 00 E
  Faerker Vig 56 50 N 9 04 E
Struer 56 30 N 8 36 E
[P | Q | Y | G | C | R | B | T | A]

Lemvig 56 33 N 8 18 E
[G | B | T | A]

Thyboron 56 42 N 8 13 E
Ringkobing 56 05 N 8 14 E
Blaavand 55 33 N 8 05 E
Fano Island
  Nordby 55 27 N 8 24 E
  Esbjerg 55 28 N 8 26 E
[P | Q | Y | G | C | R | B | T | A | L]

GEOGRAPHIC INDEX

Column 40A

DENMARK *continued*

Ribe 55 20 N 8 46 E
Hojer 54 57 N 8 41 E

GERMANY

Sylt Island   p.22/23
  Ellenbogen 55 03 N 8 25 E
  List 55 01 N 8 26 E
  Munkmarsch 54 55 N 8 22 E
  Hornum 54 45 N 8 18 E
Fohr Island
  Wyk 54 42 N 8 35 E
Amrum Island 54 38 N 8 21 E
Nordstrand Island 54 29 N 8 55 E
Husum 54 29 N 9 03 E

Y	G	B	D	T					

Tonning 54 19 N 8 57 E

G	B								

Friedrichstadt 54 23 N 9 05 E
Busum 54 08 N 8 52 E

G	R	B	D	T	A				

Meldorf 54 05 N 9 04 E
River Elbe
  Brunsbuttel 53 54 N 9 08 E

Column 40B

P	Q	Y	G	C	B	T	A		

  Kiel Canal (Nord-Ostsee Kanal)
  (*see Col. 35D*)
  River Stor
    Wewelsfleth 53 51 N 9 24 E
    Beidenfleth 53 52 N 9 26 E
    Itzehoe 53 55 N 9 31 E

Y	G	B	A						

  Gluckstadt 53 47 N 9 25 E

G	B	A							

  River Kruckau
    Elmshorn 53 45 N 9 39 E

Column 40C

  River Pinnau
    Utersen 53 40 N 9 39 E
  Schulau 53 34 N 9 42 E

G	B	A							

  Blankenese 53 33 N 9 49 E
  Altona 53 33 N 9 56 E
  Hamburg 53 33 N 9 58 E

P	Q	Y	G	C	R	B	D	T	A	L

  Wilhelmsburg 53 27 N 9 57 E
  Harburg 53 29 N 9 58 E
  Lauenburg 53 23 N 10 33 E
  Boizenburg 53 23 N 10 44 E
  Finkenwerder 53 32 N 9 52 E
  River Schwinge
    Stade 53 36 N 9 29 E
    Stadersand 53 37 N 9 32 E
    Brunshausen 53 38 N 9 32 E
    Butzfleth 53 39 N 9 31 E

Q	Y	G	B	T	A				

  Abbenfleth 53 41 N 9 30 E

Column 40D

  Ruthenstrom 53 44 N 9 24 E
  Krautsand 53 46 N 9 23 E
  Wischhafen 53 47 N 9 20 E
  Freiburg 53 49 N 9 18 E
  River Oste
    Neuhaus 53 48 N 9 02 E
    Hemmoor 53 42 N 9 08 E
    Schwarzenhutten 53 42 N 9 10 E
  Altenbruch Roads 53 51 N 8 49 E
  Cuxhaven 53 52 N 8 42 E

G	C	R	B	D	T				

River Weser
  Bremerhaven 53 33 N 8 35 E

P	Y	G	C	R	B	D	T	A		

  Wesermunde 53 32 N 8 35 E
  Farge 53 12 N 8 31 E
  Blumenthal 53 11 N 8 34 E
  Vegesack 53 10 N 8 38 E
  Oslebshausen 53 08 N 8 44 E
  Bremen 53 05 N 8 47 E

P	Q	Y	G	C	R	B	D	T	A	L

Column 41A

Hoya 52 48 N 9 08 E
Minden 52 18 N 8 54 E
River Hunte
  Oldenburg 53 09 N 8 14 E

P	Y	G	D	A					

Elsfleth 53 14 N 8 28 E

Y	G	B	A						

Brake 53 20 N 8 29 E

P	Q	Y	G	C	B	D	T	A		

Nordenham 53 29 N 8 29 E

Q	Y	G	C	B	T	A			

Einswarden 53 31 N 8 31 E
Blexen 53 32 N 8 32 E
Hohe Weg Light 53 43 N 8 15 E
Jade Bay
  Varel 53 24 N 8 10 E
  Wilhelmshaven 53 31 N 8 09 E

P	Q	Y	G	R	B	D	T		

Helgoland 54 09 N 7 53 E

Column 41B

East Frisian Islands
  Wangerooge 53 47 N 7 54 E
  Spiekeroog 53 46 N 7 41 E
  Langeoog 53 45 N 7 32 E
  Baltrum 53 44 N 7 24 E
  Norderney 53 42 N 7 10 E
  Juist 53 41 N 7 00 E
  Memmert 53 38 N 6 53 E
  Borkum 53 35 N 6 40 E
Norrdeich 53 38 N 7 10 E
River Ems
  Emden 53 21 N 7 11 E

P	Q	Y	G	C	R	B	D	T	A	

  Oldersum 53 19 N 7 20 E
  Leer 53 13 N 7 27 E

Y	G	B	T	A					

  Papenburg 53 05 N 7 23 E

P	Y	G	B	D	T				

Column 41C

NETHERLANDS

Farmsum 53 19 N 6 56 E
Delfzijl (Delfzyl) 53 20 N 6 54 E

Q	Y	G	C	B	D	T	A		

Eems Canal
  Appingedam 53 19 N 6 51 E
  Ten Post 53 18 N 6 44 E
  Groningen 53 14 N 6 32 E

Y	G	C	B	T	A				

Winschoter Diep
  Winschoten 53 09 N 7 02 E
Eemshaven 53 27 N 6 50 E

Y	G	C	R	T	A				

Lauwersmeer
  Oostmahorn 53 23 N 6 10 E
  Zoutkamp 53 20 N 6 18 E
West Frisian Islands
  Rottum 53 33 N 6 33 E
  Schiermonnikoog 53 29 N 6 09 E
  Ameland 53 27 N 5 38 E
  Terschelling

Column 41D

    West Terschelling 53 22 N 5 13 E
  Vlieland 53 18 N 5 05 E
  Texel 53 11 N 4 51 E
Harlingen 53 11 N 5 25 E

Q	Y	G	C	B	D	T			

Van Harinxma Canal
  Franeker 53 11 N 5 33 E
  Leeuwarden 53 12 N 5 47 E
  Dokkumer Ee Canal
    Dokkum 53 20 N 6 00 E
IJsselmeer
  Makkum 53 04 N 5 24 E
  Lemmer 52 51 N 5 41 E
  Prinses Margriet Canal
    Sneek 53 02 N 5 40 E
    Grouw 53 06 N 5 51 E
    Bergum 53 12 N 5 59 E
  Urk 52 40 N 5 36 E
  Zwartsluis 52 38 N 6 04 E
  Steenwijk 52 47 N 6 07 E
  Meppel 52 42 N 6 12 E

Column 42A

Hasselt 52 35 N 6 05 E
River IJssel
  Kampen 52 35 N 5 48 E
  Zwolle 52 31 N 6 07 E
  Deventer 52 15 N 6 09 E
  Berkel Twente Canal
    Twente Canal
      Almelo 52 22 N 6 38 E
    Hengelo 52 16 N 6 46 E
  Zutphen 52 08 N 6 12 E
Lelystad 52 30 N 5 26 E
Enkhuizen 52 42 N 5 18 E
Den Helder 52 58 N 4 47 E

G	B	D	T	A					

North Holland Canal
  Alkmaar 52 38 N 4 43 E

G	T	A							

Egmond aan Zee 52 37 N 4 37 E
Wijk aan Zee 52 30 N 4 35 E
North Sea Canal

Column 42B

  Ymuiden (IJmuiden) 52 27 N 4 35 E

Q	Y	G	B	D	T	A			

  Velsen 52 28 N 4 38 E
  Beverwijk 52 29 N 4 38 E

Y	G	R	B	T	A				

  Buitenhuizen 52 26 N 4 43 E
  Spaarndam 52 25 N 4 41 E
  Haarlem 52 23 N 4 39 E
  Halfweg 52 23 N 4 45 E
  Westzaan 52 27 N 4 47 E
  Zaan Canal
    Zaandam 52 26 N 4 49 E

P	Y	G	C	R	D	T	A		

    Koog aan de Zaan 52 27 N 4 49 E
    Wormerveer 52 28 N 4 47 E
  Amsterdam 52 22 N 4 54 E

P	Q	Y	G	C	R	B	D	T	A	L

  Amsterdam-Rhine Canal
    Utrecht 52 05 N 5 07 E
Zandvoort 52 22 N 4 32 E
Katwijk aan Zee 52 12 N 4 24 E
Old Rhine (Oude Rijn)

Column 42C

  Leiden 52 09 N 4 28 E
  Alphen aan den Rijn 52 08 N 4 38 E
  Woerden 52 06 N 4 54 E
Scheveningen 52 06 N 4 16 E

G	C	R	B	T	A				

'sGravenhage (Den Haag, The Hague)
52 05 N 4 18 E
  Schie Canal
    Voorburg 52 04 N 4 18 E
    Delft 52 01 N 4 22 E
    Overschie 51 56 N 4 25 E
New Rotterdam Waterway (Nieuwe Waterweg)
  Maasvlakte 51 58 N 4 04 E
  Hook of Holland 51 59 N 4 07 E

R	A								

  Europoort 51 57 N 4 05 E
  Poortershaven 51 56 N 4 12 E
  Maassluis 51 55 N 4 15 E

G	A								

Column 42D

  Rozenburg 51 54 N 4 15 E
  Vondelingen Plaat 51 53 N 4 20 E
  Vlaardingen 51 54 N 4 21 E

Q	Y	G	B	D	T	A			

  Pernis 51 54 N 4 23 E
  Schiedam 51 54 N 4 24 E

G	D	T	A						

  Rotterdam 51 54 N 4 29 E

P	Q	Y	G	C	R	B	D	T	A	L

New Maas (Nieuwe Maas)
  Kralingscheveer 51 54 N 4 32 E
  IJsselmonde 51 54 N 4 31 E
  River Hollandsch IJssel
    Krimpen aan den IJssel
    51 54 N 4 35 E
    Capelle aan den IJssel 51 55 N 4 34 E
    Ouderkerk 51 56 N 4 36 E
    Nieuwerkerk aan den IJssel
    51 58 N 4 35 E
    Gouda 52 01 N 4 42 E

P Petroleum **Q** Other Liquid Bulk **Y** Dry Bulk **G** General Cargo
C Containers **R** Ro-Ro **B** Bunkers **D** Dry Dock **T** Towage
A Airport (within 100km) **L** Lloyd's Agent (not including sub-agents)

Bolnes 51 54 N 4 34 E — 43A
River Lek
  Krimpen aan den Lek 51 53 N 4 37 E
  Lekkerkerk 51 55 N 4 38 E
  Nieuw Lekkerland 51 53 N 4 38 E
  Groot-Ammers 51 55 N 4 50 E
  Vianen 51 59 N 5 02 E
  Lower Rhine (Neder Rijn)
    Wageningen 51 58 N 5 40 E
    Arnhem 51 58 N 5 53 E
De Noord
  Slikkerveer 51 53 N 4 36 E
  Alblasserdam 51 52 N 4 37 E
  Hendrik Ido Ambacht 51 51 N 4 37 E
  Papendrecht 51 50 N 4 38 E
Old Maas (Oude Maas)
  Oud Beijerland 51 50 N 4 24 E
  Puttershoek 51 48 N 4 34 E
  Dordrecht 51 49 N 4 40 E

| P | Q | Y | G | B | T | A | | | |

River Merwede — 43B
  Sliedrecht 51 50 N 4 45 E
  Hardinxveld 51 49 N 4 51 E
  Gorinchem 51 49 N 4 59 E
  Spijk 51 52 N 5 03 E
River Waal
  Haaften 51 49 N 5 11 E
  Zaltbommel 51 48 N 5 12 E
  Tiel 51 53 N 5 27 E
  Wamel 51 52 N 5 27 E
  Druten 51 53 N 5 37 E
  Maas-Waal Canal
  Nijmegen (Nymegen) 51 50 N 5 50 E

| P | G | C | R | B | T | | | | |

River Rhine (Rijn)
  Lobith 51 52 N 6 08 E

GERMANY

River Rhine (Rhein)
  Spoy Canal
    Kleve 51 47 N 6 09 E
  Emmerich 51 51 N 6 15 E
  Wesel 51 39 N 6 36 E
  Walsum 51 33 N 6 41 E
  Orsoy 51 32 N 6 41 E
  Homberg 51 27 N 6 43 E
  Ruhrort 51 27 N 6 44 E
  Duisburg 51 26 N 6 45 E — 43C

| P | Q | Y | G | C | R | B | A | L | |

  Rheinhausen 51 25 N 6 44 E
  Urdingen 51 21 N 6 40 E
  Krefeld 51 20 N 6 34 E

| P | Q | Y | G | B | A | | | | |

  Dusseldorf 51 15 N 6 46 E

| G | C | A | | | | | | | |

  Neuss 51 12 N 6 42 E

| Y | G | T | A | | | | | | |

  Monheim 51 07 N 6 49 E
  Leverkusen 51 01 N 7 02 E
  Mulheim 50 57 N 7 03 E
  Cologne (Koln) 50 56 N 7 00 E

| Y | G | C | B | T | A | | | | |

  Porz 50 53 N 7 03 E — 43D
  Wesseling 50 50 N 7 00 E
  Bonn 50 43 N 7 05 E
  Remagen 50 34 N 7 13 E — p.20/21
  Brohl 50 25 N 7 18 E
  Andernach 50 25 N 7 23 E
  Neuwied 50 26 N 7 29 E
  Weissenthurm 50 25 N 7 29 E
  Bendorf 50 25 N 7 35 E
  Vallendar 50 24 N 7 37 E
  Koblenz 50 20 N 7 35 E
  River Mosel
    Trier 49 45 N 6 39 E
    River Saar
      Saarlouis 49 19 N 6 45 E
      Saarbrucken 49 15 N 6 58 E
    Thionville (French) 49 22 N 6 11 E
    Metz (French) 49 07 N 6 11 E
  Lahnstein 50 18 N 7 37 E
  Bingen 49 57 N 7 54 E
  Mainz 50 00 N 8 17 E

River Main — 44A
  Frankfurt 50 07 N 8 40 E

| Q | Y | G | C | B | A | | | | |

    Aschaffenburg 49 57 N 9 10 E
  Gernsheim 49 45 N 8 28 E
  Worms 49 38 N 8 21 E
  Mannheim 49 29 N 8 28 E

| P | Q | Y | G | C | R | B | A | L | |

  Ludwigshafen 49 28 N 8 27 E

| Q | Y | G | C | | | | | | |

  Speyer 49 18 N 8 26 E
  Karlsruhe 49 03 N 8 20 E

| P | Q | G | C | R | | | | | |

  Kehl 48 35 N 7 50 E

| P | Y | G | C | R | A | | | | |

  Strasbourg (French) 48 34 N 7 42 E

| P | Y | G | C | B | T | A | | | |

  Basle (Swiss) 47 33 N 7 34 E

| P | Q | Y | G | C | R | B | T | A | L |

NETHERLANDS — 44B

River Maas — p.22/23
  Nederhemert 51 46 N 5 10 E
  Zuid-Willemsvaart Canal
    'sHertogenbosch 51 42 N 5 18 E
    Helmond 51 29 N 5 39 E
  Lithoijen 51 49 N 5 26 E
  Grave 51 45 N 5 44 E
  Maashees 51 34 N 6 02 E
  Venlo 51 22 N 6 10 E
  Belfeld 51 18 N 6 04 E
  Swalmen 51 13 N 6 01 E
  Roermond 51 12 N 5 59 E
  Maastricht 50 51 N 5 41 E
  Brielle 51 54 N 4 11 E
  Hellevoetsluis 51 49 N 4 08 E — 44C

| G | A | | | | | | | | |

  Middelharnis 51 47 N 4 12 E
  Den Bommel 51 43 N 4 17 E
  Willemstad 51 42 N 4 26 E
  Numansdorp 51 43 N 4 25 E
  Moerdijk 51 42 N 4 37 E
  Wilhelmina Canal
    Oosterhout 51 37 N 4 52 E
    Tilburg 51 33 N 5 04 E
  Galathesche 51 40 N 4 19 E
  Ouddorp 51 48 N 3 56 E
  Scheldt-Rhine Canal 51 38 N 4 14 E
  Schouwen
    Brouwershaven 51 44 N 3 55 E
    Bruinisse 51 40 N 4 06 E
    Zijpe 51 39 N 4 06 E
    Zierikzee 51 38 N 3 53 E

| G | B | A | | | | | | | |

  Eastern Scheldt (Oosterschelde) — 44D
    St. Annaland 51 37 N 4 06 E
    Tholen 51 32 N 4 13 E
    Bergen-op-Zoom 51 30 N 4 16 E
    Yerseke (Ierseke) 51 30 N 4 03 E
    Wemeldinge 51 31 N 4 00 E
    Sas van Goes 51 32 N 3 56 E
    Wolphaartsdijk 51 32 N 3 49 E
    Colijnsplaat 51 36 N 3 51 E
  West Kapelle 51 32 N 3 27 E
  Western Scheldt (Westerschelde)
    Flushing (Vlissingen) 51 27 N 3 35 E

| P | Q | Y | G | C | R | B | D | T | A |

  Walcheren Canal
    Middelburg 51 30 N 3 37 E

| Q | Y | G | | | | | | | |

  Flushing East (Sloehaven)
  51 27 N 3 40 E
  Borssele 51 25 N 3 44 E
  Hansweert 51 27 N 4 00 E

| G | B | T | A | | | | | | |

  Bath 51 24 N 4 13 E

BELGIUM — 45A

River Scheldt (Schelde)
  Zandvliet 51 21 N 4 17 E
  Doel 51 19 N 4 16 E
  Lillo 51 18 N 4 18 E
  Liefkenshoek 51 18 N 4 17 E
  Antwerp (Antwerpen) 51 14 N 4 25 E

| P | Q | Y | G | C | R | B | D | T | A | L |

  Albert Canal
    Merksem 51 14 N 4 29 E
    Schoten 51 15 N 4 30 E
    Olen 51 09 N 4 52 E
    Tessenderlo 51 04 N 5 05 E
    Kwaadmechelen 51 06 N 5 09 E
    Lixhe 50 44 N 5 42 E
    Liege 50 40 N 5 34 E

| P | Y | G | C | R | A | | | | |

  Kallo 51 15 N 4 17 E
  Zwijndrecht 51 13 N 4 20 E
  Burcht 51 12 N 4 20 E
  Hoboken 51 10 N 4 20 E
  Kruibeke 51 10 N 4 19 E
  Hemiksem 51 09 N 4 20 E
  Schelle 51 08 N 4 19 E
  River Rupel — 45B
    Niel 51 07 N 4 20 E
  Brussels Maritime Canal
    Willebroek 51 03 N 4 21 E
    Tisselt 51 02 N 4 22 E
    Kapelle op den Bos 51 01 N 4 22 E
    Humbeek 50 58 N 4 23 E
    Verbrande Brug 50 57 N 4 23 E
    Vilvoorde 50 57 N 4 25 E
    Haren 50 54 N 4 23 E
    Marly 50 53 N 4 23 E
    Brussels (Bruxelles) 50 52 N 4 21 E

| G | B | A | | | | | | | |

  Ruisbroek 50 47 N 4 17 E
  River Rupel — 45C
    Boom 51 05 N 4 22 E
    Terhagen 51 05 N 4 23 E
    Rumst 51 04 N 4 25 E
    Mechelen 51 02 N 4 28 E
    Rupelmonde 51 08 N 4 17 E
    Temse 51 08 N 4 13 E
    Tielrode 51 07 N 4 13 E
    Baasrode 51 03 N 4 10 E
    Dendermonde 51 02 N 4 07 E
    Melle 51 00 N 3 48 E

NETHERLANDS

Western Scheldt (Westerschelde)
  Paal 51 21 N 4 07 E
  Waalsoorden 51 27 N 4 02 E
  Terneuzen 51 20 N 3 49 E

| Q | Y | G | C | R | B | T | | | |

  Ghent-Terneuzen Canal
    Sluiskil 51 18 N 3 50 E
    Axel Sassing 51 17 N 3 52 E
    Sas van Ghent 51 14 N 3 48 E

BELGIUM — 45D

    Zelzate 51 12 N 3 48 E
    Ertvelde 51 12 N 3 47 E
    Rieme 51 10 N 3 46 E
    Terdonk 51 09 N 3 47 E
    Langerbrugge 51 07 N 3 45 E
    Wondelgem 51 05 N 3 43 E
    Ghent (Gent) 51 04 N 3 43 E

| P | Q | Y | G | C | R | B | D | T | A | L |

NETHERLANDS

Breskens 51 24 N 3 34 E
Wielingen 51 23 N 3 23 E

BELGIUM

Zeebrugge 51 20 N 3 12 E

| P | Q | Y | G | C | R | B | T | A | |

Baudouin Canal
  Bruges (Brugge) 51 14 N 3 13 E

| P | G | B | A | | | | | | |

GEOGRAPHIC INDEX

P Petroleum Q Other Liquid Bulk Y Dry Bulk G General Cargo
C Containers R Ro-Ro B Bunkers D Dry Dock T Towage
A Airport (within 100km) L Lloyd's Agent (not including sub-agents)

BELGIUM *continued* 46A

Blankenberge 51 19 N 3 08 E
Ostend (Oostende) 51 14 N 2 55 E

| Y | G | C | R | B | T | A | | | |

Ostend-Bruges Canal
   Zandvoorde 51 13 N 2 58 E
Nieuwpoort 51 09 N 2 43 E

| G | B | A | | | | | | | |

FRANCE

Dunkirk (Dunkerque) 51 03 N 2 21 E   p.18

| P | Q | Y | G | C | R | B | D | T | A | L |

Gravelines 50 59 N 2 08 E

| G | A | | | | | | | | |

Sandettie Light Vessel 51 09 N 1 47 E
Calais 50 58 N 1 51 E   46B

| Q | Y | G | C | R | B | D | T | A | | |

Cap Gris Nez 50 52 N 1 35 E
Wimereux 50 46 N 1 36 E
Boulogne 50 44 N 1 37 E

| P | Y | G | C | R | B | T | A | L | | |

Etaples 50 31 N 1 38 E
Montreuil 50 28 N 1 46 E
River Somme
   Le Hourdel 50 13 N 1 34 E
   Le Crotoy 50 13 N 1 38 E
   Noyelles 50 11 N 1 43 E
   Abbeville 50 06 N 1 51 E
   St. Valery sur Somme 50 11 N 1 39 E
Le Treport 50 04 N 1 22 E

| Y | G | R | B | T | A | | | | |

Eu 50 03 N 1 25 E
Dieppe 49 56 N 1 05 E

| Y | G | C | R | B | D | T | A | | |

St. Valery en Caux 49 52 N 0 43 E
Fecamp 49 46 N 0 22 E   46C

| G | B | A | | | | | | | |

Cap d'Antifer 49 41 N 0 10 E
Antifer 49 40 N 0 10 E
River Seine
   Le Havre 49 29 N 0 07 E

| P | Q | Y | G | C | R | B | D | T | A | L |

   Harfleur 49 30 N 0 12 E
   Gonfreville L'Orcher 49 29 N 0 14 E
   Tancarville 49 29 N 0 28 E
   Radicatel 49 25 N 0 29 E
   Lillebonne 49 31 N 0 32 E
   Port Jerome 49 28 N 0 32 E
   Villequier 49 30 N 0 40 E
   Caudebec 49 32 N 0 44 E
   St. Wandrille 49 32 N 0 45 E
   Le Trait 49 28 N 0 48 E
   Yainville 49 27 N 0 49 E
   Duclair 49 27 N 0 52 E
   Dieppedalle 49 25 N 1 01 E
   Rouen 49 29 N 1 05 E   46D

| P | Q | Y | G | C | R | B | D | T | A | |

   Limay 48 58 N 1 47 E
   Paris 48 52 N 2 20 E

| P | Y | G | C | R | B | D | A | L | |

   Bonnieres 49 02 N 1 35 E
River Marne
    Bonneuil 48 47 N 2 29 E
   Gennevilliers 48 57 N 2 16 E
   Nanterre 48 54 N 2 12 E
   Elbeuf 49 17 N 1 07 E
   Petit Quevilly 49 26 N 1 03 E
   Le Grand Quevilly 49 25 N 1 00 E
   Petit Couronne 49 22 N 1 00 E
   Grand Couronne 49 22 N 0 59 E
   La Mailleraye 49 29 N 0 46 E
   Quillebeuf 49 28 N 0 31 E
River Risle
    Pont Audemer 49 20 N 0 23 E
   Berville sur Mer 49 26 N 0 22 E
   Honfleur 49 25 N 0 14 E

| P | Q | Y | G | B | T | A | | | |

Trouville 49 22 N 0 05 E   47A
Deauville 49 21 N 0 04 E
Ouistreham 49 17 N 0 15 E
Caen 49 11 N 0 21 E

| P | Y | G | C | R | B | T | A | | |

Courseulles sur Mer 49 20 N 0 27 E
Port en Bessin 49 21 N 0 46 W
Isigny 49 20 N 1 07 W
Carentan 49 19 N 1 15 W
St. Vaast la Hougue 49 35 N 1 16 W
Barfleur 49 40 N 1 15 W
Cherbourg 49 38 N 1 38 W

| P | Q | G | C | R | B | D | T | A | L |

Cap de la Hague 49 44 N 1 56 W
Dielette 49 33 N 1 51 W
Carteret 49 22 N 1 48 W
Portbail 49 20 N 1 43 W
Regneville 49 00 N 1 34 W
Granville 48 50 N 1 36 W

| P | Y | G | | | | | | | |

Avranches 48 42 N 1 21 W   47B
Pontaubault 48 38 N 1 22 W
Le Vivier sur Mer 48 36 N 1 46 W
Cancale 48 40 N 1 51 W

| G | B | A | | | | | | | |

St. Malo 48 39 N 2 01 W

| P | Q | Y | G | C | R | B | D | T | A | L |

St. Servan 48 38 N 2 01 W
Dinard 48 38 N 2 03 W
Le Guildo 48 38 N 2 14 W

| G | B | A | | | | | | | |

Port Barrier 48 38 N 2 25 W
Erquy 48 38 N 2 28 W
Dahouet 48 35 N 2 34 W
St. Brieuc (Le Legue) 48 32 N 2 43 W

| G | B | A | | | | | | | |

Binic 48 36 N 2 49 W
Saint Quay Portrieux 48 39 N 2 50 W
Paimpol 48 47 N 3 03 W

| G | B | A | | | | | | | |

Pontrieux 48 42 N 3 10 W   47C
Lezardrieux 48 47 N 3 06 W
Pleubian 48 51 N 3 10 W
Treguier 48 47 3 14 W

| G | B | | | | | | | | |

Port Blanc 48 50 N 3 19 W
Perros Guirec 48 48 N 3 26 W
Lannion 48 44 N 3 27 W
Locquirec 48 42 N 3 39 W
Morlaix 48 38 N 3 53 W
Roscoff 48 43 N 3 59 W

| G | R | B | A | | | | | | |

Plouescat 48 39 N 4 13 W
Brignogan 48 40 N 4 19 W
L'Aber Wrach 48 35 N 4 33 W
Paluden 48 35 N 4 31 W
L'Aberildut 48 28 N 4 45 W
Ushant Island (Ile d'Ouessant)
   Creac'h Point 48 28 N 5 08 W   47D
Ile Molene 48 24 N 4 58 W
Corsen Point 48 25 N 4 48 W
Le Conquet 48 22 N 4 47 W
Blanc-Sablons 48 22 N 4 46 W
Pointe St. Mathieu 48 20 N 4 46 W
Brest 48 23 N 4 29 W

| P | Y | G | B | D | T | A | L | | |

Landerneau 48 26 N 4 15 W
Plougastel 48 23 N 4 24 W
Faou 48 18 N 4 10 W
Port Launay 48 18 N 4 15 W
Roscanvel 48 19 N 4 33 W
Camaret 48 17 N 4 36 W

| G | B | A | | | | | | | |

Douarnenez 48 06 N 4 20 W
Audierne 48 01 N 4 32 W
Penmarc'h Point 47 48 N 4 23 W
Guilvinec 47 48 N 4 17 W
Loctudy 47 50 N 4 10 W
Pont l'Abbe 47 52 N 4 13 W

River Odet   48A
   Quimper 47 58 N 4 07 W

| P | G | B | A | | | | | | |

   Corniguel 47 57 N 4 07 W
   Benodet 47 53 N 4 07 W
Concarneau 47 52 N 3 55 W

| P | Q | G | B | T | A | | | | |

Iles de Glenan 47 47 N 4 02 W
Le Pouldu 47 46 N 3 32 W
Lorient 47 45 N 3 22 W

| P | Y | G | R | B | T | A | L | | |

Hennebont 47 48 N 3 16 W
Port Louis 47 42 N 3 22 W
Ile de Groix
   Port Tudy 47 39 N 3 27 W
Etel 47 39 N 3 12 W
Quiberon 47 30 N 3 07 W
Belle Ile
   Le Palais 47 21 N 3 10 W
La Trinite sur Mer 47 35 N 3 02 W
Morbihan   48B
   Locmariaquer 47 34 N 3 00 W
   Auray 47 40 N 3 00 W
   Vannes 47 39 N 2 45 W

| G | A | | | | | | | | |

River Vilaine
   La Roche Bernard 47 31 N 2 18 W
   Redon 47 39 N 2 04 W
Mesquer 47 25 N 2 28 W
Piriac 47 23 N 2 33 W   p.30
Le Croisic 47 18 N 2 31 W
Le Pouliguen 47 16 N 2 25 W
River Loire   48C
   St. Nazaire 47 16 N 2 12 W

| P | Y | G | C | R | B | D | T | A | |

   Montoir 47 20 N 2 08 W

| Q | G | C | R | B | T | A | | | |

   Donges 47 18 N 2 04 W

| P | Q | B | T | A | | | | | |

   Cordemais 47 16 N 1 53 W
   Coueron 47 12 N 1 42 W
   Basse Indre 47 12 N 1 41 W
   Ile Chevire 47 11 N 1 36 W
   Chantenay 47 12 N 1 36 W
   Nantes 47 14 N 1 34 W

| P | Q | Y | G | C | B | T | A | L | |

   Paimboeuf 47 17 N 2 02 W

| P | Q | G | | | | | | | |

Pornic 47 07 N 2 07 W
Ile de Noirmoutier 47 02 N 2 18 W
Ile d'Yeu
   Port Joinville 46 44 N 2 21 W
Sables d'Olonne 46 30 N 1 48 W

| Q | Y | G | B | A | | | | | |

Marans 46 19 N 1 02 W   48D
Ile de Re
   Ars 46 12 N 1 32 W
   St. Martin de Re 46 12 N 1 22 W
   La Flotte 46 11 N 1 19 W
Port du Plomb 46 12 N 1 12 W
La Pallice 46 10 N 1 14 W

| P | Y | G | C | R | B | D | T | A | L |

La Rochelle 46 09 N 1 09 W
River Charente
   Rochefort 45 56 N 0 58 W

| Y | G | B | A | | | | | | |

   Tonnay Charente 45 57 N 0 53 W

| Y | G | B | | | | | | | |

Ile d'Oleron
   Chateau d'Oleron 45 53 N 1 12 W
   La Perotine 45 58 N 1 14 W
Marennes 45 49 N 1 07 W
Pointe aux Herbes 45 48 N 1 09 W
La Tremblade 45 46 N 1 08 W
River Gironde
   La Coubre 45 42 N 1 14 W
   St. Palais sur Mer 45 38 N 1 05 W
   Royan 45 37 N 1 02 W
   Mortagne sur Gironde 45 29 N 0 47 W

P Petroleum **Q** Other Liquid Bulk **Y** Dry Bulk **G** General Cargo
C Containers **R** Ro-Ro **B** Bunkers **D** Dry Dock **T** Towage
A Airport (within 100km) **L** Lloyd's Agent (not including sub-agents)

49A

Blaye 45 07 N 0 40 W

| Q | Y | G | B | T | A | | | | |

Roque de Thau 45 05 N 0 38 W
River Dordogne
   Izon 44 57 N 0 22 W
   Libourne 44 55 N 0 14 W
   Bec d'Ambes 45 02 N 0 36 W

| P | Q | B | T | | | | | | |

River Garonne
   Bassens 44 54N 0 32 W
   Bordeaux 44 50 N 0 34 W

| Q | Y | G | C | R | B | D | T | A | L |

Pauillac 45 12 N 0 45 W

| P | B | T | A | | | | | | |

Trompeloup 45 14 N 0 45 W
Le Verdon 45 33 N 1 05 W

| Y | C | R | T | | | | | | |

Pointe de Grave 45 34 N 1 04 W
Cap Ferret 44 37 N 1 15 W
Arcachon 44 40 N 1 10 W
Boucau 43 31 N 1 29 W
Bayonne 43 30 N 1 29 W

49B

| P | Q | Y | G | B | D | T | A | | |

Biarritz 43 30 N 1 34 W
St. Jean de Luz 43 24 N 1 40 W

SPAIN

Fuenterrabia 43 22 N 1 48 W
Pasajes 43 20 N 1 56 W

| P | Q | Y | G | C | R | B | D | T | A |

Renteria 43 20 N 1 53 W
San Sebastian 43 19 N 1 59 W
Guetaria 43 18 N 2 12 W
Zumaya 43 18 N 2 15 W
Ondarroa 43 19 N 2 25 W
Lequeitio 43 22 N 2 29 W
Bermeo 43 25 N 2 43 W

| Y | G | B | A | | | | | | |

Nervion River **49C**
   Santurce 43 20 N 3 02 W
   Las Arenas 43 19 N 3 00 W
   Portugalete 43 19 N 3 02 W
   Bilbao 43 17 N 2 55 W

| P | Q | Y | G | C | R | B | D | T | A | L |

Povena 43 20 N 3 07 W
Onton 43 22 N 3 11 W
Punta Saltacaballo 43 22 N 3 11 W
Dicido 43 22 N 3 12 W
Castro Urdiales 43 24 N 3 14 W
Sanovia 43 24 N 3 20 W
Santona 43 28 N 3 28 W
Santander 43 28 N 3 46 W

| P | Q | Y | G | C | R | B | D | T | A |

Astillero 43 24 N 3 49 W
Suances 43 25 N 4 02 W **49D**
Requejada 43 20 N 4 05 W
Ribadesella 43 28 N 5 04 W
Villaviciosa 43 32 N 5 23 W
Gijon 43 33 N 5 40 W

| P | Q | Y | G | C | R | B | D | T | A | L |

Musel 43 34 N 5 41 W
Cabo de Penas 43 39 N 5 51 W
San Juan de Nieva 43 35 N 5 56 W
Aviles 43 35 N 5 56 W

| P | Q | Y | G | C | R | B | T | A | |

San Esteban de Pravia 43 34 N 6 05 W
Luarca 43 32 N 6 31 W
Navia 43 33 N 6 43 W
Tapia de Casariego 43 34 N 6 56 W
Ribadeo 43 32 N 7 02 W

| Y | G | B | | | | | | | |

Burela 43 39 N 7 20 W

| Y | G | B | | | | | | | |

San Ciprian 43 42 N 7 27 W

| P | Q | Y | G | T | | | | | |

Cillero 43 41 N 7 36 W

50A

Vivero 43 43 N 7 36 W

| Y | G | | | | | | | | |

Punta de la Estaca 43 47 N 7 41 W
Ortigueira 43 41 N 7 50 W
Carino 43 44 N 7 51 W
Cedeira 43 39 N 8 04 W
Ferrol 43 28 N 8 16W

| Y | G | B | D | T | A | L | | | |

Corunna 43 23 N 8 22 W

| P | Q | Y | G | C | R | B | T | A | L |

Corme 43 16 N 8 58 W
Lage 43 13 N 9 00 W
Cabo Villano 43 10 N 9 13 W
Camarinas 43 07 N 9 11 W
Cape Finisterre 42 53 N 9 16 W
Corcubion 42 57 N 9 11 W

| Y | G | A | | | | | | | |

Muros 42 45 N 9 01 W **50B**
Arosa Bay
   Santa Eugenia de Riveira
   42 33 N 8 59 W
   Caraminal 42 36 N 8 56 W
   Carril 42 37 N 8 46 W
   Villagarcia 42 36 N 8 46 W

| Q | Y | G | R | B | T | A | | | |

Sangenjo 42 24 N 8 48 W
Marin 42 24 N 8 42 W

| Y | G | C | B | D | A | | | | |

Rande 42 17 N 8 40 W
Vigo 42 14 N 8 40 W

| P | Q | Y | G | C | R | B | D | T | A | L |

La Guardia 41 54 N 8 53 W

p.28/29

PORTUGAL **50C**

Caminha 41 52 N 8 50 W
Viana do Castelo 41 41 N 8 50 W

| Q | Y | G | C | R | B | D | T | A | |

Esposende 41 32 N 8 48 W
Leixoes 41 11 N 8 43 W

| P | Q | Y | G | C | R | B | T | A | L |

Matosinhos 41 11 N 8 41 W
River Douro
   Oporto 41 09 N 8 37 W

| Q | Y | G | B | A | L | | | | |

Aveiro 40 39 N 8 45 W

| P | Q | Y | G | C | R | B | D | T | A |

Figueira da Foz 40 09 N 8 52 W

| Y | G | C | B | D | T | | | | |

Nazare 39 36 N 9 05 W
San Martinho 39 31 N 9 09 W
Farilhoes Islands 39 29 N 9 32 W
Berlenga Island 39 25 N 9 30 W
Cabo Carvoeiro 39 22 N 9 24 W
Peniche 39 22 N 9 23 W
Cabo da Roca 38 46 N 9 30 W
Oitavos 38 41 N 9 28 W
Cascais 38 41 N 9 25 W
River Tagus (Rio Tejo)
   Belem 38 41 N 9 13 W
   Lisbon 38 44 N 9 07 W

| P | Q | Y | G | C | R | B | D | T | A | L |

Barreiro 38 39 N 9 05 W
Cabo Espichel 38 25 N 9 14 W
Setubal 38 30 N 8 55 W

| Y | G | C | R | B | D | T | A | | |

Sines 37 57 N 8 52 W

p.30

| P | Q | Y | G | C | R | B | T | | |

Cabo de Sao Vicente 37 01 N 9 00 W
Sagres 36 59 N 8 56 W
Lagos 37 05 N 8 40 W
Portimao 37 08 N 8 32 W

| Y | G | C | R | T | A | | | | |

Albufeira 37 05 N 8 15 W
Faro 37 01 N 7 55 W

| P | Q | G | B | T | A | | | | |

51A

Olhao 37 01 N 7 50 W
Tavira 37 08 N 7 39 W
River Guadiana
   Vila Real de Santo Antonio
   37 11 N 7 25 W
   Pomarao 37 34 N 7 30 W

SPAIN

La Laja 37 30 N 7 28 W
Sanlucar de Guadiana 37 27 N 7 28 W
Ayamonte 37 13 N 7 24 W
Isla Cristina 37 12 N 7 20 W
Huelva 37 16 N 6 55 W

| P | Q | Y | G | C | R | B | D | T | |

River Guadalquivir
   Sanlucar de Barrameda 36 46 N 6 21 W
   Bonanza 36 48 N 6 20 W
   San Juan de Aznalfarache
   37 21 N 6 02 W
   Seville 37 22 N 6 00 W

| Y | G | C | R | B | D | T | A | | |

Chipiona 36 44 N 6 26 W **51B**
Rota 36 37 N 6 22 W
Puerto de Santa Maria 36 36 N 6 14 W

| P | Q | Y | G | C | B | A | | | |

Puerto Real 36 32 N 6 11 W
San Fernando 36 28 N 6 12 W
Cadiz 36 30 N 6 20 W

| P | Q | Y | G | C | R | B | D | T | A | L |

Cape Trafalgar 36 11 N 6 02 W
Barbate 36 10 N 5 59 W
Punta Camarinal 36 05 N 5 48 W
Tarifa 36 00 N 5 36 W
Getares 36 05 N 5 26 W
Algeciras 36 07 N 5 26 W

| P | Q | Y | G | C | R | B | T | | |

San Roque 36 11 N 5 24 W
Puente Mayorga 36 10 N 5 23 W
La Linea 36 10 N 5 21 W

GIBRALTAR (British) **51C**

Gibraltar 36 09 N 5 20 W

| P | Y | G | C | R | B | D | T | A | L |

Europa Point 36 06 N 5 21 W

MEDITERRANEAN SEA

SPAIN

Estepona 36 25 N 5 09 W
Marbella 36 30 N 4 53 W
Malaga 36 41 N 4 26 W

| P | Q | Y | G | C | R | B | D | T | A | L |

Nerja 36 44 N 3 53 W
Almunecar 36 44 N 3 41 W
Salobrena 36 45 N 3 35 W
Motril 36 43 N 3 31 W

| P | Y | G | R | B | T | A | | | |

Adra 36 43 N 3 02 W **51D**
Roquetas 36 45 N 2 37 W
Almeria 36 50 N 2 30 W

| P | Y | G | R | T | A | | | | |

Cabo de Gata 36 43 N 2 11 W
Agua Amarga 36 56 N 1 56 W
Carboneras 37 00 N 1 53 W

| Y | B | A | | | | | | | |

Garrucha 37 10 N 1 50 W

| G | B | T | A | | | | | | |

Villaricos 37 15 N 1 47 W
Aguilas 37 24 N 1 34 W

| Y | G | | | | | | | | |

Hornillo 37 25 N 1 34 W
Mazarron 37 34 N 1 15 W
La Calera 37 34 N 1 12 W
Cartagena 37 35 N 0 58 W

p.28/29

| P | Q | Y | G | C | B | D | T | A | |

Escombreras 37 33 N 0 58 W
Portman 37 35 N 0 51 W

GEOGRAPHIC INDEX

SPAIN continued — 52A

Cabo de Palos 37 38 N 0 41 W
San Pedro del Pinatar 37 49 N 0 45 W
Torrevieja 37 58 N 0 41 W

| Y | G | B | A | | | | | | |

Santa Pola 38 12 N 0 34 W
Alicante 38 20 N 0 29 W

| P | Q | Y | G | C | R | B | T | A | |

Cabo de las Huertas 38 21 N 0 24 W
Villajoyosa 38 30 N 0 14 W
Altea 38 36 N 0 03 W
Cabo de la Nao 38 44 N 0 14 E
Javea 38 48 N 0 11 E
Denia 38 50 N 0 07 E

BALEARIC ISLANDS — 52B

Ibiza Island
  Ibiza 38 54 N 1 28 E

| P | Q | G | R | B | T | A | | | |

  La Canal 38 50 N 1 23 E
Formentera Island 38 39 N 1 35 E
Cabrera Island 39 08 N 2 55 E
Majorca (Mallorca) Island
  Palma (Palma de Mallorca)
  39 33 N 2 38 E

| P | Y | G | C | R | B | T | A | L | |

  Porto Pi 39 33 N 2 37 E
Soller 39 48 N 2 41 E
Alcudia 39 50 N 3 08 E

| P | Q | G | C | R | B | T | A | | |

Dragonera Island 39 34 N 2 18 E
Minorca (Menorca) Island
  Mahon 39 52 N 4 18 E

| Q | G | R | B | T | A | | | | |

  Ciudadela 40 00 N 3 50 E

Gandia 39 00 N 0 09 W — 52C

| Y | G | C | R | B | T | A | | | |

Cullera 39 11 N 0 13 W
Valencia 39 27 N 0 18 W

| P | Q | Y | G | C | R | B | D | T | A | L |

Grao de Murviedro 39 38 N 0 15 W
Sagunto 39 39 N 0 13 W

| Y | G | C | R | T | A | | | | |

Burriana 39 52 N 0 04 W

| G | B | A | | | | | | | |

Castellon 39 58 N 0 01 E

| P | Q | Y | G | C | R | B | T | A | |

Benicarlo 40 25 N 0 26 E
Vinaroz 40 28 N 0 28 E
Alcanar 40 33 N 0 28 E
San Carlos de la Rapita 40 35 N 0 36 E

| Y | G | B | A | | | | | | |

Alfaques 40 36 N 0 40 E
Cabo de Tortosa 40 43 N 0 55 E
Tarragona 41 06 N 1 14 E — 52D

| P | Q | Y | G | C | R | B | T | A | L |

Villanueva y Geltru 41 13 N 1 44 E
Vallcarca 41 14 N 1 52 E
Barcelona 41 21 N 2 10 E   p.31

| P | Q | Y | G | C | R | B | C | T | A | L |

Badalona 41 27 N 2 15 E
Blanes 41 40 N 2 48 E
San Feliu de Guixols 41 46 N 3 01 E

| Y | G | B | A | | | | | | |

Palamos 41 50 N 3 08 E

| G | C | R | B | A | | | | | |

Rosas 42 15 N 3 11 E

| G | B | A | | | | | | | |

Port Selva 42 20 N 3 12 E
Portbou 42 25 N 3 09 E

FRANCE — 53A

Port Vendres 42 31 N 3 07 E

| Q | G | R | B | A | | | | | |

Barcares de Saint Laurent 42 47 N 3 02 E
La Nouvelle 43 01 N 3 04 E

| P | Q | G | R | B | T | A | | | |

Sete 43 24 N 3 42 E

| P | Q | Y | G | C | R | B | A | | |

Balaruc 43 28 N 3 41 E
Salin de Giraud 43 24 N 4 44 E
River Rhone
  Arles 43 41 N 4 38 E
Golfe de Fos
  St. Louis du Rhone 43 23 N 4 49 E

| P | Q | G | R | B | T | A | | | |

  Fos 43 23 N 4 51 E

| P | Q | Y | G | C | R | B | A | | |

Port de Bouc 43 24 N 4 59 E

| Q | Y | G | T | A | | | | | |

Lavera 43 23 N 5 00 E — 53B

| P | Q | B | T | A | | | | | |

Caronte 43 24 N 5 02 E
Etang de Berre 43 27 N 5 07 E

| P | Q | B | T | A | | | | | |

  Martigues 43 24 N 5 03 E
  Berre 43 29 N 5 10 E
  La Mede 43 24 N 5 06 E
Port de la Lave 43 22 N 5 18 E
L'Estaque 43 22 N 5 19 E
Marseilles (Marseille) 43 20 N 5 21 E

| P | Q | Y | G | C | R | B | D | T | A | L |

Cassis 43 13 N 5 32 E
La Ciotat 43 10 N 5 36 E — 53C
La Seyne 43 06 N 5 53 E
Toulon 43 07 N 5 55 E

| Y | G | C | R | B | D | T | A | | |

Hyeres-Plage 43 05 N 6 09 E
Porquerolles Island 43 00 N 6 12 E
St. Tropez 43 16 N 6 38 E
Ste. Maxime 43 18 N 6 38 E
St. Raphael 43 24 N 6 47 E
Cannes 43 33 N 7 01 E
Antibes 43 35 N 7 09 E
Nice 43 42 N 7 17 E

| G | B | A | L | | | | | | |

Villefranche 43 42 N 7 19 E
Beaulieu 43 42 N 7 20 E

MONACO

Monte Carlo 43 44 N 7 25 E

| G | A | | | | | | | | |

FRANCE — 53D

Menton 43 47 N 7 30 E

CORSICA (CORSE)

Cap Corse 43 00 N 9 22 E
Bastia 42 42 N 9 27 E

| P | G | R | A | | | | | | |

Lucciana Terminal 42 32 N 9 33 E
Solenzara 41 52 N 9 24 E
Porto Vecchio 41 36 N 9 17 E

| G | R | A | | | | | | | |

Cap Pertusato 41 22 N 9 11 E
Bonifacio 41 23 N 9 06 E

| G | R | A | | | | | | | |

Propriano 41 40 N 8 54 E

| G | R | B | A | | | | | | |

Ajaccio 41 55 N 8 44 E

| G | R | B | A | L | | | | | |

Calvi 42 35 N 8 48 E — 54A

| G | R | B | A | | | | | | |

Ile Rousse 42 39 N 8 56 E

| G | R | A | | | | | | | |

St. Florent 42 41 N 9 18 E

ITALY

SARDINIA (SARDEGNA)

Cape Testa 41 14 N 9 08 E
Maddalena Island
  La Maddalena 41 13 N 9 24 E

| G | B | D | T | | | | | | |

Palau 41 11 N 9 23 E
Golfo Aranci 41 00 N 9 37 E
Olbia 40 55 N 9 34 E

| G | T | A | | | | | | | |

Arbatax 39 56 N 9 42 E   p.28/29

| G | R | B | T | | | | | | |

Cape Carbonara 39 06 N 9 31 E
Cagliari 39 12 N 9 05 E — 54B

| P | Q | Y | G | C | R | B | T | A | |

Sarroch 39 05 N 9 02 E

| P | Q | G | T | A | | | | | |

Cape Spartivento 38 53 N 8 51 E
Sant' Antioco Island 39 02 N 8 26 E

| Y | G | B | | | | | | | |

San Pietro Island
  Carloforte 39 09 N 8 19 E

| G | A | | | | | | | | |

Porto Vesme 39 12 N 8 24 E

| P | Y | G | B | T | A | | | | |

Portoscuso 39 13 N 8 22 E — 54C
Porto Flavia 39 20 N 8 26 E
Gulf of Oristano
  Oristano 39 52 N 8 33 E

| P | Q | Y | G | C | R | B | T | A | |

Alghero 40 34 N 8 19 E   p.31

| G | B | A | | | | | | | |

Cape Argentiera 40 44 N 8 08 E
Asinara Island 41 06 N 8 18 E
Porto Torres 40 50 N 8 24 E

| P | Q | Y | G | C | R | B | T | A | |

Cape Mortola 43 47 N 7 33 E
Ventimiglia 43 47 N 7 36 E
Bordighera 43 47 N 7 40 E
San Remo 43 49 N 7 47 E

| G | B | A | | | | | | | |

Riva Ligure 43 50 N 7 53 E
Imperia 43 53 N 8 02 E

| Q | G | C | B | A | | | | | |

Pietra Ligure 44 09 N 8 17 E — 54D
Vado Ligure 44 16 N 8 26 E
Savona 44 18 N 8 29 E

| P | Q | Y | G | C | R | B | T | A | |

Voltri 44 26 N 8 45 E
Multedo 44 25 N 8 50 E
Sestri Ponente 44 25 N 8 51 E
Genoa (Genova) 44 25 N 8 55 E

| P | Q | Y | G | C | R | B | D | T | A | L |

Recco 44 22 N 9 09 E
Camogli 44 21 N 9 09 E
Portofino 44 18 N 9 14 E
Santa Margherita 44 20 N 9 13 E
Rapallo 44 21 N 9 14 E
Sestri Levante 44 16 N 9 23 E
Portovenere 44 02 N 9 51 E
La Spezia 44 07 N 9 50 E

| P | Q | Y | G | C | R | B | D | T | A | |

Pertusola 44 05 N 9 53 E
Marina di Carrara 44 02 N 10 03 E

| G | B | T | A | | | | | | |

Viareggio 43 52 N 10 15 E

P Petroleum **Q** Other Liquid Bulk **Y** Dry Bulk **G** General Cargo
C Containers **R** Ro-Ro **B** Bunkers **D** Dry Dock **T** Towage
A Airport (within 100km) **L** Lloyd's Agent (not including sub-agents)

GEOGRAPHIC INDEX

Navicelli Canal — **55A**
   Pisa 43 43 N 10 24 E
Leghorn (Livorno) 43 33 N 10 19 E
`P Y G C B D T A L`

Porto Baratti 43 00 N 10 30 E
Vada 43 21 N 10 27 E
`P G`

Piombino 42 56 N 10 33 E
`P Y G C R B T A`

Elba Island
   Portoferraio 42 49 N 10 20 E
`Y G B A`

   Rio Marina 42 49 N 10 26 E
`G`

   Porto Azzurro 42 46 N 10 24 E
   Calamita 42 43 N 10 24 E
   Vallone 42 42 N 10 24 E
Follonica 42 55 N 10 45 E
`P Q Y G A`

Portiglione 42 53 N 10 46 E
Talamone 42 33 N 11 08 E — **55B**
`G`

Santa Liberata 42 25 N 11 09 E
Porto Santo Stefano 42 27 N 11 07 E
`P Y G B`

Giglio Island 42 22 N 10 55 E
Civitavecchia 42 06 N 11 48 E
`P Y G B T A`

Fiumicino 41 46 N 12 14 E — p.28/29
`P G B T A`

Ostia 41 43 N 12 18 E
Anzio 41 27 N 12 38 E
`G A`

Terracina 41 17 N 13 15 E
Ponza Island — **55C**
   Ponza 40 54 N 12 58 E
Gaeta 41 13 N 13 35 E
`P Y G R B D T A`

Formia 41 15 N 13 36 E
`Y G B`

Procida Island — p.31
   Procida 40 47 N 14 02 E
Ischia Island
   Porto d'Ischia 40 44 N 13 57 E
Miseno 40 47 N 14 05 E
Baia 40 49 N 14 05 E
`G B`

Pozzuoli 40 49 N 14 07 E
`P G B A`

Bagnoli 40 48 N 14 10 E
`Y G B A`

Naples (Napoli) 40 51 N 14 16 E — **55D**
`P Q Y G C R B D T A L`

Portici 40 49 N 14 20 E
`G B A`

Torre del Greco 40 47 N 14 22 E
Torre Annunziata 40 45 N 14 27 E
`Y G A`

Castellammare di Stabia 40 42 N 14 29 E
`G B A`

Sorrento 40 38 N 14 23 E
Massalubrense 40 36 N 14 20 E
Punta Campanella 40 34 N 14 20 E
Capri Island
   Marina Grande 40 33 N 14 15 E
Amalfi 40 38 N 14 36 E
Minori 40 39 N 14 38 E
Maiori 40 39 N 14 39 E
Salerno 40 41 N 14 46 E
`G C B T A`

Scario 40 03 N 15 30 E — p.28/29
Paola 39 22 N 16 02 E

Vibo Valentia 38 43 N 16 08 E — **56A**
Lipari Islands
   Stromboli Island 38 48 N 15 15 E
   Panarea Island 38 38 N 15 04 E
   Salina Island
      Salina 38 34 N 14 52 E
      Rinella 38 33 N 14 50 E
   Lipari Island
      Lipari 38 28 N 14 57 E
`G B`

      Canneto 38 30 N 14 58 E
Vulcano Island
   La Fabbrica 38 24 N 14 58 E
Ustica Island
   Ustica 38 42 N 13 11 E
Gioia Tauro 38 26 N 15 54 E
Bagnara Calabra 38 17 N 15 48 E
Scilla 38 15 N 15 43 E

SICILY (SICILIA) — **56B**

Messina 38 12 N 15 34 E
`G B D T A L`

Forte Spuria 38 16 N 15 37 E
Milazzo 38 13 N 15 15 E
`P Q G B T`

Termini Imerese 37 59 N 13 42 E
Porticello 38 05 N 13 32 E
Palermo 38 07 N 13 22 E
`P Q Y G C R B D T A L`

Castellammare del Golfo 38 02 N 12 53 E
Trapani 38 02 N 12 31 E
`G B D T A`

Favignana Island
   Favignana 37 56 N 12 20 E
Marsala 37 48 N 12 26 E
`P Q Y G B A`

Mazara del Vallo 37 39 N 12 35 E
`Q G B A`

Sciacca 37 30 N 13 05 E
Porto Empedocle 37 17 N 13 32 E — **56C**
`Y G B T`

Licata 37 06 N 13 56 E
`G B`

Gela 37 04 N 14 15 E
`P Q Y G B T A`

Scoglitti 36 53 N 14 26 E
Pozzallo 36 43 N 14 51 E
Cape Passero 36 41 N 15 09 E
Pantelleria Island 36 47 N 12 00 E
Lampedusa Island 35 30 N 12 36 E
`Q G B A`

Avola 36 54 N 15 09 E
`G A`

Siracusa (Syracuse) 37 03 N 15 18 E — **56D**
`Y G B T A`

Santa Panagia (Melilli) 37 07 N 15 16 E
`P Q B T A`

Priolo 37 09 N 15 12 E
Magnisi 37 09 N 15 15 E
Augusta 37 12 N 15 13 E
`P Q Y G C R B D T A`

Catania 37 31 N 15 06 E
`P Y G C R B T A`

Acireale 37 36 N 15 11 E
Riposto 37 44 N 15 13 E
Giardini 37 50 N 15 17 E
Taormina 37 51 N 15 18 E

MALTA

Valletta 35 54 N 14 31 E
`P Q Y G C R B D T A L`

Marsaxlokk 35 49 N 14 34 E
`P Q G C R A`

Gozo (Ghawdex) Island — **57A**
   Mgarr 36 01 N 14 18 E

ITALY

Reggio di Calabria 38 07 N 15 39 E
`G R B A`

Cape Armi 37 57 N 15 41 E
Cape Spartivento 37 55 N 16 04 E
Soverato 38 41 N 16 33 E
Catanzaro 38 49 N 16 37 E
Cape Colonne 39 02 N 17 12 E
Crotone 39 05 N 17 08 E
`P Q Y G B T`

Ciro Marina 39 22 N 17 08 E
`Y`

Trebisacci 39 52 N 16 32 E
Taranto 40 27 N 17 12 E
`P Y G B T A L`

Gallipoli 40 03 N 18 00 E
`G B A`

Otranto 40 09 N 18 30 E — **57B**
`G B A`

Brindisi 40 39 N 17 59 E
`P G B T A L`

Monopoli 40 57 N 17 18 E
`P Y G B A`

Bari 41 08 N 16 53 E
`P Y G C B T A L`

Molfetta 41 13 N 16 38 E
`Y G B A`

Barletta 41 19 N 16 16 E
`Y G B T A`

Margherita di Savoia 41 23 N 16 09 E
Manfredonia 41 37 N 15 55 E — **57C**
`P Q G B T A`

Termoli 42 00 N 15 00 E
Vasto 42 06 N 14 43 E
`G B`

Ortona 42 21 N 14 25 E
`P Y G B A`

Pescara 42 28 N 14 14 E
`G B`

San Benedetto del Tronto 42 57 N 13 53 E
`P G`

Porto Recanati 43 25 N 13 40 E — p.31
Ancona 43 36 N 13 31 E
`P Y G C R B T A L`

Falconara 43 40 N 13 24 E
Fano 43 51 N 13 01 E
Pesaro 43 55 N 12 54 E — **57D**
`P Y G B A`

Cattolica 43 58 N 12 46 E
Rimini 44 04 N 12 35 E
Porto Corsini 44 29 N 12 17 E
Ravenna 44 25 N 12 27 E
`P Q Y G C R B D T A`

River Po
   Cremona 45 08 N 10 01 E
Porto di Levante 45 04 N 12 22 E
Chioggia 45 13 N 12 17 E
`Y G R B T A`

Pellestrina 45 16 N 12 18 E
Lido 45 25 N 12 26 E
Venice (Venezia) 45 26 N 12 20 E
`P Q Y G C R B D T A L`

Porto Marghera 45 28 N 12 17 E
Santa Margherita 45 35 N 12 52 E
Porto Nogaro 45 49 N 13 14 E
`G C A`

Porto Buso 45 43 N 13 15 E

GEOGRAPHIC INDEX

Column 1 — 58A

ITALY continued

Torviscosa 45 50 N 13 17 E
Monfalcone 45 47 N 13 33 E

`P Y G B T A`

Sistiana 45 46 N 13 38 E
Trieste 45 39 N 13 48 E

`P Q Y G C R B D T A L`

Servola 45 38 N 13 47 E
Zaule 45 36 N 13 47 E

SLOVENIA

Koper (Capodistria) 45 33 N 13 44 E

`P Q Y G C R B T A`

Izola 45 33 N 13 40 E

`G D`

Piran 45 32 N 13 34 E

`G A`

Portoroz 45 31 N 13 35 E

CROATIA 58B

Umag 45 26 N 13 31 E
Novigrad (Cittanuova) 45 19 N 13 34 E
Luka Mirna (Port Quito) 45 18 N 13 34 E
Tar (Val di Torre) 45 19 N 13 36 E
Porec (Parenzo) 45 14 N 13 36 E
Vrsar (Orsera) 45 09 N 13 36 E
Limski Canal (Canal di Leme)
45 07 N 13 36 E
Rovinj (Rovigno) 45 05 N 13 38 E

`G A`

Brijuni Island 58C
   Brijuni 44 54 N 13 47 E
Pula (Pola) 44 53 N 13 50 E

`Y G R B T A`

Budava (Port Bado) 44 54 N 13 59 E
Rasa (Arsa) 45 02 N 14 04 E

`G A`

Gradac (Porto Gradaz) 44 58 N 14 06 E
Koromacna Bay (Valmazzinghi)
44 58 N 14 07 E
Prtlog (Porto Longo) 45 03 N 14 09 E
Rabac (Port Albona) 45 04 N 14 10 E
Plomin (Fianona) 45 07 N 14 13 E
Opatija (Abbazia) 45 20 N 14 19 E
Rijeka (Fiume) 45 19 N 14 26 E

`P Q Y G C R B D T A L`

Bakar (Buccari) 45 18 N 14 32 E
Kraljevica (Porto Re) 45 17 N 14 34 E
Urinj 45 16 N 14 34 E
Novi (Porto Novi) 45 07 N 14 48 E
Senj (Segna) 45 00 N 14 53 E

`G`

Jurievo (San Giorgio) 44 56 N 14 55 E 58D
Krk (Veglia) Island
   Krk (Veglia) 45 01 N 14 35 E
   Port Dina 45 12 N 14 32 E
   Omisalj 45 13 N 14 32 E

`P Q B A`

Cres (Cherso) Island
   Beli (Caisole) 45 06 N 14 22 E
   Mali Losinj (Lussinpiccolo)
   44 32 N 14 28 E
Rab (Arbe) Island
   Rab (Arbe) 44 45 N 14 46 E
Velika Stinica 44 43 N 14 52 E
Jablanac 44 42 N 14 52 E
Karlobag (Carlopago) 44 30 N 15 07 E
Pag (Pago) Island
   Pag (Pago) 44 27 N 15 03 E
Maslenica 44 13 N 15 32 E

`Y T A`

Zadar (Zara) 44 07 N 15 14 E

`P Q Y G D T A`

Dugi Island
   Veli Rat (Punte Bianche)
   44 09 N 14 49 E
Sali 43 55 N 15 10 E

Column 2 — 59A

Sibenik (Sebenico) 43 44 N 15 54 E

`Q Y G B T A`

Trogir (Trau) 43 31 N 16 15 E
Kastel Sucurac (Castel San Giorgio)
43 33 N 16 25 E   p.28/29
Solin (Salona) 43 32 N 16 28 E
Supaval Bay 43 30 N 16 23 E
Vranjic (Vragnizza) 43 30 N 16 27 E
Split (Spalato) 43 30 N 16 27 E

`P Q Y G B D T A`

Solta Island 43 24 N 16 12 E
Brac (Brazza) Island
   Supetar (San Pietro) 43 23 N 16 33 E
   Milna 43 19 N 16 27 E
Dugi Rat (Punta Lunga) 43 27 N 16 39 E

`Y G A`

Omis (Almissa) 43 26 N 16 42 E
Ravnice 43 25 N 16 42 E
Makarska (Macarsca) 43 17 N 17 01 E
Hvar (Lesina) Island
   Hvar (Lesina) 43 16 N 16 27 E

`G`

Korcula (Curzola) Island 59B
   Korcula (Curzola) 42 48 N 17 08 E

`G`

   Vela Luka (Vallegrande)
   42 59 N 16 37 E
   Brna (Berna) 42 54 N 16 51 E
Ploce (Kardeljevo) 43 02 N 17 25 E

`P Q Y G C B T A`

Metkovic 43 03 N 17 39 E
Gruz (Gravosa) 42 40 N 18 05 E
Dubrovnik (Ragusa) 42 38 N 18 07 E

`P Y G C R A`

YUGOSLAVIA 59C

Hercegnovi (Castelnuovo)
42 27 N 18 32 E
Zelenika 42 27 N 18 35 E
Bijela 42 27 N 18 40 E
Risan (Risano) 42 31 N 18 42 E
Kotor (Cattaro) 42 25 N 18 46 E

`P G T A`

Tivat (Teodo) 42 26 N 18 42 E
Budva (Budua) 42 17 N 18 51 E
Petrovac (Castellastua) 42 12 N 18 55 E
Bar (Antivari) 42 05 N 19 05 E

`P Q Y G C R B T A`

Ulcinj (Dulcigno) 41 55 N 19 12 E

ALBANIA

Shengjin (San Giovanni di Medua)
41 49 N 19 36 E

`G T`

Durres (Durazzo) 41 19 N 19 27 E 59D

`P Y G B T A`

Vlore (Valona) 40 29 N 19 29 E

`P Y G`

Sarande (Santi Quaranta) 39 53 N 20 00 E

`G`

GREECE

Corfu (Kerkira) Island
   Corfu (Kerkira) 39 37 N 19 57 E

`P Q Y G B T A`

Igoumenitsa 39 32 N 20 13 E

`P Y G R B T A`

Gulf of Arta
   Preveza 38 57 N 20 45 N

`G B A`

   Cape Kopraina 39 02 N 21 06 E
   Amfilochia 38 52 N 21 10 E
Levkas Island
   Drepanon 38 47 N 20 44 E

Column 3 — 60A

Astakos 38 32 N 21 05 E

`G B`

Ithaka Island
   Vathi 38 22 N 20 44 E

`G R B`

Cephalonia (Kefallinia) Island

`Y G A`

   Lixuri 38 12 N 20 28 E
   Argostoli 38 12 N 20 29 E
   Samos 38 15 N 20 40 E
Zante (Zakinthos) Island
   Zante (Zakinthos) 37 47 N 20 54 E

`G A`

Mesolongion (Mesolongi)
38 19 N 21 22 E

`G`

Krioneri 38 21 N 21 35 E
Navpaktos 38 24 N 21 49 E
Eratini 38 21 N 22 14 E
Itea 38 26 N 22 25 E

`Y G R B`

Aspra Spitia 38 22 N 22 38 E
Andikiron Bay 38 21 N 22 40 E
Corinth Canal 60B
   Corinth (Korinthos) 37 57 N 22 56 E
   Poseidonia 37 57 N 22 57 E
   Isthmia 37 55 N 23 00 E
Kiato 38 01 N 22 44 E
Valimitika 38 14 N 22 08 E
Aegion 38 15 N 22 06 E
Rion 38 18 N 21 48 E
Patras 38 15 N 21 44 E

`P Q Y G C R B T`

Alyssos 38 09 N 21 35 E
Kyllini 37 57 N 21 09 E
Katakolon 37 39 N 21 20 E

`Y G B T`

Pyrgos 37 40 N 21 27 E
Kyparissia 37 15 N 21 41 E
Proti Island 37 03 N 21 33 E
Navarino Bay 60C
   Pylos (Pilos) 36 55 N 21 42 E

`G B T A`

   Sfaktiria Island 36 57 N 21 40 E
Methoni 36 50 N 21 43 E
Kalamata 37 00 N 22 07 E

`Y G C B A`

Cape Tainaron (Cape Matapan)   p.32
36 23 N 22 29 E
Gythion (Yithion) 36 45 N 22 34 E

`G`

Plytra 36 41 N 22 50 E
Kelendhi Point 36 33 N 22 56 E
Vatika Bay 36 31 N 23 00 E
Cape Maleas 36 26 N 23 12 E
Kithira Island 60D
   Kithira 36 08 N 23 00 E
Monemvasia 36 41 N 23 03 E
Nauplia (Navplion) 37 34 N 22 48 E

`G`

Kheli 37 19 N 23 09 E
Spetsai Island 37 16 N 23 10 E
Hydra (Idhra) Island 37 21 N 23 28 E
Poros 37 30 N 23 28 E
Epidaurus (Epidhavros) 37 38 N 23 10 E
Aegina (Aiyina) Island
   Aegina (Aiyina) 37 44 N 23 25 E
   Ayia Marina 37 44 N 23 32 E
Metokhi 37 42 N 23 23 E
Kalamaki Bay
   Kalamaki 37 55 N 23 01 E

`Y B`

Sousaki 37 55 N 23 07 E
Agioi Theodoroi 37 55 N 23 05 E

`P B T`

Pachi (Pakhi) 37 58 N 23 23 E

`P A`

P Petroleum **Q** Other Liquid Bulk **Y** Dry Bulk **G** General Cargo
C Containers **R** Ro-Ro **B** Bunkers **D** Dry Dock **T** Towage
A Airport (within 100km) **L** Lloyd's Agent (not including sub-agents)

GEOGRAPHIC INDEX

61A

Megara 37 58 N 23 24 E
P A
Salamis Island
Ambelaki Bay
Ambelaki 37 57 N 23 32 E
Cape Kynosoura 37 57 N 23 35 E
Eleusis 38 02 N 23 30 E
P Q Y G B T A
Skaramanga 38 00 N 23 35 E
Aspropyrgos 38 01 N 23 35 E
P Q B A
Perama 37 57 N 23 35 E
Keratsini Bay
St. George Harbour (Irakleous Harbour) 37 57 N 23 36 E
Drapetzona 37 56 N 23 37 E
Piraeus 37 56 N 23 38 E
P Q Y G C R B D T A L
Phaleron Bay 37 56 N 23 41 E
Fleves Island 37 46 N 23 46 E
Kythnos Island 37 24 N 24 28 E
Serifos Island
G B
Serifos 37 07 N 24 32 E
Koutala 37 08 N 24 27 E
Livadhi 37 08 N 24 32 E

61B

Sifnos Island 36 58 N 24 43 E
Kimolos Island
Kimolos 36 47 N 24 34 E
Milos Island
Y G R
Kastro 36 45 N 24 26 E
Voudia Bay 36 45 N 24 32 E
Adhamas 36 43 N 24 27 E
Kanaba 36 42 N 24 28 E
Folegandros Island
Karavostassi 36 37 N 24 58 E

61C

Crete (Kriti) Island
Iraklion (Heraklion) 35 16 N 25 09 E
P Q Y G C R B T A
Spinalonga 35 18 N 25 45 E
Ayios Nikolaos 35 11 N 25 43 E
Y G B A
Mokhlos 35 06 N 25 49 E
Pachia Ammos 35 07 N 25 50 E
Altsi 35 10 N 25 53 E
Sitia 35 13 N 26 07 E
Ierapetra 35 00 N 25 45 E
Kali Limenes 34 55 N 24 48 E
B T A
Ayia Galini 35 06 N 24 41 E
Sfakia 35 12 N 24 09 E
Paleochora 35 12 N 23 41 E
Gavdo (Gavados) Island 34 50 N 24 04 E
Canea (Khania) 35 31 N 24 01 E

61D

Suda Bay 35 29 N 24 03 E
Q G A
Georgioupoli 35 21 N 24 16 E
Rethimnon 35 22 N 24 28 E
G A
Panormos Bay 35 25 N 24 42 E
Thira (Santorini) Island
Thira 36 25 N 25 27 E
Amorgos Island
Krikelo 36 54 N 26 03 E
Aigialli 36 54 N 25 59 E
Katapola Bay 36 50 N 25 52 E
Naxos Island
Matsuna 37 05 N 25 37 E
Naxos 37 06 N 25 23 E
Paros Island
Paros 37 05 N 25 19 E
Delos (Dhilos) Island 37 24 N 25 17 E
Mykonos Island
Y G A
Mykonos 37 27 N 25 20 E
Ayias Annas 37 26 N 25 25 E

62A

Syros Island
Syros 37 26 N 24 57 E
G B D T A
Tinos Island
Tinos 37 32 N 25 10 E
Panormos 37 39 N 25 04 E
Andros Island
Gavrion 37 53 N 24 45 E
Kea Island
Ayios Nikolaos 37 40 N 24 19 E
Makronisi Island 37 43 N 24 08 E
Laurium (Lavrion) 37 42 N 24 04 E
P Q Y G T A
Oropos 38 19 N 23 48 E
Euboea (Evvoia) Island
Chalkis (Khalkis) 38 27 N 23 36 E
Q Y G B T A
Psakhna 38 33 N 23 36 E
Limni 38 46 N 23 19 E
Kymassi 38 49 N 23 31 E
P Y G
Mandoudhi 38 49 N 23 32 E
Pyli 38 46 N 23 35 E
Kimi 38 38 N 24 06 E
Karistos 38 01 N 24 25 E

62B

Skyros Island
Lithari Point 38 47 N 24 41 E
Euboea (Evvoia) Island
Milaki 38 22 N 24 04 E
Aliveri 38 23 N 24 03 E
P Y G T
Levkandi 38 25 N 23 41 E
Larimna 38 34 N 23 18 E
Atalantis Bay
Ayios Ioannis Theologos 38 39 N 23 12 E
Tragana 38 40 N 23 06 E
Ayios Konstantinos 38 45 N 22 52 E
Ayia Marina 38 53 N 22 35 E
Y

62C

Stylis 38 54 N 22 37 E
G B
Achladi (Akhladhi) 38 53 N 22 49 E
Y G B
Volos 39 21 N 22 57 E
P Y G R B T
Skiathos Island
Skiathos 39 10 N 23 29 E
Skopelos Island
Skopelos 39 07 N 23 45 E
Thessaloniki (Salonica) 40 38 N 22 56 E
P Q Y G C R B D T A
Nea Playia 40 16 N 23 13 E
Nea Moudhania 40 14 N 23 17 E
Kalyvia 40 16 N 23 24 E
Yerakini 40 16 N 23 26 E
Y B A
Ormilia 40 15 N 23 34 E

62D

Psahoudia 40 13 N 23 36 E
Stratoni 40 31 N 23 51 E
Y
Nea Peramos 40 49 N 24 18 E
Elevtherai 40 50 N 24 19 E
Kavala 40 55 N 24 25 E
P Q Y G B T A
Nea Karvali 40 57 N 24 29 E
Prinos Terminal 40 56 N 24 31 E
Thasos Island
Limenaria 40 38 N 24 35 E
Lagos 41 00 N 25 07 E
Lemnos Island
Kastro 39 53 N 25 04 E
Myrina 39 52 N 25 03 E
Samothraki Island
Kamariotissa Bay 40 28 N 25 29 E
Cape Akrotiri 40 28 N 25 27 E
Alexandroupolis 40 51 N 25 57 E
P Y G B A

63A

TURKEY

SEA OF MARMARA

Kabatepe 40 12 N 26 16 E
Dardanelles (Canakkale Bogazi)
Gelibolu (Gallipoli) 40 25 N 26 41 E
G
Cape Mehmetcik 40 02 N 26 11 E
Tekirdag 40 57 N 27 31 E
Q Y G T
Eregli 40 58 N 27 58 E
Silivri 41 03 N 28 16 E
Buyuk Cekmece 40 59 N 28 33 E
Ambarli 40 58 N 28 42 E
Bosporus
Istanbul 41 00 N 28 58 E
Y G C R T A
Beyolgu 41 02 N 28 59 E
Rumelikavagi 41 11 N 29 04 E
Buyukdere 41 11 N 29 03 E

BLACK SEA

Podima 41 29 N 28 17 E
Kiyikoy (Midye) 41 38 N 28 07 E

63B

BULGARIA

Michurin 42 10 N 27 54 E
Druzba 42 27 N 27 32 E
Bourgas (Burgas) 42 30 N 27 29 E
P Y G C R B D T A
Pomorie 42 32 N 27 39 E
Nessebar 42 40 N 27 44 E p.28/29
Varna 43 12 N 27 55 E
P Q Y G C R B D T A
Balchik 43 23 N 28 11 E
Kavarna 43 27 N 28 21 E
Cape Kaliakra 43 22 N 28 30 E

63C

ROMANIA

Mangalia 43 49 N 28 35 E
G B D T A
Constantza 44 10 N 28 39 E
P Q Y G C R B D T A
River Danube
Sulina 45 09 N 29 39 E
Y G C B T A
Tulcea 45 10 N 28 49 E
Y G B T A
Vilkovo **(Ukrainian)** 45 24 N 29 36 E
Kiliya **(Ukrainian)** 45 26 N 29 16 E
Y G

63D

Caslita **(Ukrainian)** 45 24 N 29 02 E
Izmail (Ismail) **(Ukrainian)** 45 20 N 28 51 E
Y G C R B T
Isaccea 45 15 N 28 28 E
Reni **(Ukrainian)** 45 26 N 28 18 E
P Y G C B T A
Galatz (Galati) 45 25 N 28 05 E
Y G B D T
Braila 45 15 N 27 59 E
Y G B D T
Tutrakan **(Bulgarian)** 44 02 N 26 40 E
Giurgiu 43 54 N 25 58 E
Rousse **(Bulgarian)** 43 50 N 25 58 E
Turnu Severin 44 38 N 22 40 E
Kladovo **(Yugoslavian)** 44 36 N 22 33 E
Orsova 44 42 N 22 25 E
Pancevo **(Yugoslavian)** 44 52 N 20 40 E
Belgrade (Beograd) **(Yugoslavian)** 44 50 N 20 31 E
Novi Sad **(Yugoslavian)** 45 16 N 19 50 E
Mohacs **(Hungarian)** 46 00 N 18 41 E
Budapest **(Hungarian)** 47 30 N 19 02 E
Komarno **(Slovakian)** 47 46 N 18 05 E

P Petroleum   **Q** Other Liquid Bulk   **Y** Dry Bulk   **G** General Cargo
C Containers   **R** Ro-Ro   **B** Bunkers   **D** Dry Dock   **T** Towage
A Airport (within 100km)   **L** Lloyd's Agent (not including sub-agents)

ROMANIA *continued*   64A

Gyor **(Hungary)** 47 41 N 17 40 E
Korneuburg **(Austrian)** 48 22 N 16 20 E
Linz **(Austrian)** 48 19 N 14 18 E
Straubing **(German)** 48 53 N 12 35 E
Deggendorf **(German)** 48 50 N 12 58 E
Regensburg **(German)** 49 01 N 12 07 E

UKRAINE

Ust-Dunaysk 45 28 N 29 50 E
`Y G B`

River Dnestr
Bugaz 46 04 N 30 28 E
Belgorod-Dnestrovskiy 46 11 N 30 21 E
`G C B T`

Cetatea Alba 46 11 N 30 20 E
Ilichevsk 46 18 N 30 39 E   64B
`P Q Y G C R B D T A`

Odessa 46 29 N 30 45 E
`P Q Y G C R B T A`

Yuzhnyy 46 36 N 31 01 E
`P Q Y G C B T`

Ochakov 46 36 N 31 33 E
Nikolayev 46 58 N 31 58 E
`Y G`

River Dnepr
Kherson 46 37 N 32 36 E
`P Q Y G B T`

Zaporozhye 47 50 N 35 10 E
Dnepropetrovsk 48 29 N 35 00 E
Dneprodzerzhinsk 48 30 N 34 37 E
Kremenchug 49 03 N 33 25 E
Skadovsk 46 06 N 32 55 E   64C
Khorly 46 05 N 33 18 E
Yevpatoriya 45 11 N 33 23 E
Sevastopol 44 37 N 33 22 E
Yalta 44 30 N 34 10 E
`Y G C T`

Theodosia (Feodosiya) 45 02 N 35 24 E
`P G`

Kertch 45 21 N 36 28 E
`P Y G C R T`

Yenikale 45 21 N 36 36 E

SEA OF AZOV

Ghenichesk 46 10 N 34 48 E
Berdiansk 46 45 N 36 47 E
`Y G B T A`

Mariupol 47 03 N 37 30 E
`P Q Y G C R B T A`

RUSSIA   64D

Taganrog 47 12 N 38 57 E
`Y G C B T`

River Don
Azov 47 08 N 39 25 E
Rostov 47 10 N 39 42 E
Ust Donets 47 40 N 40 57 E
River Volga   p.27
Astrakhan 46 22 N 48 04 E
Akhtubinsk 48 20 N 46 10 E
Volgograd 48 45 N 44 30 E
Saratov 51 30 N 45 55 E
Balakovo 52 04 N 47 46 E
Syzran 53 10 N 48 29 E
Samara (Kuybyshev) 53 10 N 50 10 E
Tolyatti 53 32 N 49 24 E
Nizhnekamsk 55 25 N 51 53 E
Nizhniy Novgorod (Gorkiy) 56 20 N 44 00 E
River Oka
Navashino 55 33 N 42 11 E
Yaroslavl 57 34 N 39 52 E
Rybinsk (Andropov) 58 01 N 38 52 E
Cherepovets 59 09 N 37 50 E

CASPIAN SEA   65A

KAZAKHSTAN

Bautino 44 34 N 50 14 E
Aktau 44 25 N 50 09 E

TURKMENISTAN

Bekdash 41 32 N 52 36 E
Turkmenbashi (Krasnovodsk) 40 01 N 53 00 E
`P Y G`

IRAN

Bandar Torkeman 36 55 N 54 05 E
Bandar Gaz 36 45 N 53 58 E
River Neka
Neka 36 36 N 53 19 E
Babol Sar 36 41 N 52 39 E
Now Shahr 36 38 N 51 30 E
`Q Y G B T`

Bandar Anzali 37 26 N 49 29 E
`G B T A`

AZERBAIJAN   65B

Lenkoran 38 46 N 48 50 E
Baku 40 22 N 49 53 E

RUSSIA

Derbent 42 03 N 48 18 E
Makhachkala 42 59 N 47 30 E

SEA OF AZOV

Yeisk 46 44 N 38 16 E
Akhtari 46 02 N 38 09 E   p.28/29
Temryuk 45 17 N 37 22 E

BLACK SEA

Kavkaz 45 20 N 36 39 E
Anapa 44 53 N 37 18 E
Novorossisk 44 44 N 37 47 E
`P Y G C R B D T A`

Jubska 44 19 N 38 43 E
Tuapse 44 05 N 39 04 E
`P Y G B D T`

Sochi 43 35 N 39 44 E
`Y G R T A`

GEORGIA   65C

Gagry 43 19 N 40 16 E
Cape Pitsunda 43 09 N 40 20 E
Sukhumi (Sukhum) 43 10 N 41 02 E
`P G B`

Ochamchire 42 44 N 41 26 E
Poti 42 09 N 41 39 E
`P Y G C B T`

Batumi (Batum) 41 39 N 41 39 E
`P Q Y G B T`

TURKEY   65D

Hopa 41 25 N 41 24 E
`P Y G C R B T`

Pazar 41 12 N 40 52 E
Rize 41 03 N 40 32 E
`P Y G B A`

Of 40 57 N 40 20 E
Surmene 40 56 N 40 10 E
Trabzon 41 00 N 39 45 E
`P Y G C R B T A`

Akcaabat 41 02 N 39 35 E
Vakfikebir 41 05 N 39 21 E
Gorele 41 04 N 39 05 E
Tirebolu 41 01 N 38 49 E

Giresun 40 55 N 38 23 E   66A
`P Y G C B T`

Ordu 41 00 N 37 54 E
`Y G B`

Fatsa 41 02 N 37 23 E
`Y G B`

Unye 41 08 N 37 18 E
Azot 41 16 N 36 26 E
Samsun 41 18 N 36 20 E
`P Y G C R B T A`

Bafra 41 44 N 35 58 E
Gerze 41 49 N 35 14 E
Sinop 42 00 N 35 09 E
`G B`

Ayancik 41 55 N 34 22 E   66B
Inebolu 41 59 N 33 45 E
`Y G B T`

Cide 41 53 N 32 55 E
Kurucasile 41 50 N 32 42 E
Amasra 41 45 N 32 23 E
Bartin 41 38 N 32 20 E
Hisaronu (Filyos) 41 35 N 32 05 E
Kilimli 41 32 N 31 56 E
Catalagzi 41 32 N 31 54 E
Zonguldak 41 27 N 31 47 E
`Y G T`

Kozlu 41 27 N 31 46 E
Camli 41 19 N 31 28 E
Eregli 41 18 N 31 27 E
`Y G B T`

SEA OF MARMARA

Bosporus   p.32
Anadolukavagi 41 10 N 29 04 E
Kandilli 41 04 N 29 03 E
Uskudar 41 01 N 29 01 E
Haydarpasa 41 00 N 29 01 E
`Y G C R T A`

Maltepe 40 54 N 29 09 E
Kartal 40 53 N 29 11 E
Tuzla 40 49 N 29 18 E
Darica 40 45 N 29 23 E
`Y`

Gebze 40 46 N 29 26 E
Diliskelesi 40 46 N 29 32 E   66C
Hereke 40 42 N 29 37 E
`Y T A`

Yarimca 40 44 N 29 46 E
`Y G T`

Tutunciftlik 40 45 N 29 47 E
`P Q B T`

Zeytinburnu 40 45 N 29 46 E
Derince 40 44 N 29 49 E
`Y G R B T`

Izmit 40 46 N 29 55 E   66D
`Y G T`

Basiskele 40 43 N 29 55 E
Seimen 40 43 N 29 54 E
Batak Burnu 40 44 N 29 52 E
Kazuklu Iskelessi 40 43 N 29 50 E
Golcuk 40 43 N 29 48 E
Yalova 40 40 N 29 15 E
Gemlik 40 25 N 29 07 E
`Y G C R B T A`

Mudanya 40 27 N 28 52 E
`Y G A`

Bandirma 40 21 N 27 58 E
`Q Y G B T A`

Edincik 40 21 N 27 52 E
Karabiga 40 24 N 27 18 E
Dardanelles (Canakkale Bogazi)
Canakkale 40 09 N 26 25 E
`Y G`

P Petroleum **Q** Other Liquid Bulk **Y** Dry Bulk **G** General Cargo
C Containers **R** Ro-Ro **B** Bunkers **D** Dry Dock **T** Towage
A Airport (within 100km) **L** Lloyd's Agent (not including sub-agents)

GEOGRAPHIC INDEX

MEDITERRANEAN SEA · 67A

Gokceada (Imroz Island)
  Kalekoy 40 13 N 25 52 E
  Kuzu 40 14 N 25 57 E
Bozcaada (Tenedos Island)
  Tenedos 39 50 N 26 04 E
Odunluk 39 47 N 26 10 E
Akcay 39 35 N 26 54 E
Burhaniye 39 35 N 26 57 E
Altinoluk 39 33 N 26 42 E
Edremit 39 35 N 26 57 E
Ayvalik 39 19 N 26 43 E
Lesvos Island (Greek)
  Sigri 39 12 N 25 52 E
  Mytilene (Mitilini) 39 06 N 26 35 E
`Q G B A L`

  Port Hiera 39 00 N 26 35 E
  Plomarion 38 58 N 26 23 E
  Kallonis 39 07 N 26 08 E
Dikili 39 05 N 26 53 E · 67B
`Q Y G B`

Candarli 38 56 N 26 58 E
Rema Bay
  Resadiye 38 55 N 27 03 E
Aliaga 38 48 N 26 59 E
`P Y G B T A`

Foca 38 45 N 26 56 E
Nemrut Bay 38 45 N 26 55 E
`Q Y G R T A`

Tcham Bay
  Camalti 38 30 N 26 53 E
Izmir 38 26 N 27 08 E
`Y G C R B T A L`

Urla 38 22 N 26 47 E
Psara Island (Greek)
  Psaron 38 32 N 25 34 E
Chios (Khios) Island (Greek)
  Chios (Khios) 38 23 N 26 09 E
`G B A`

Oinousa Island (Greek)
  Fourkero Bay 38 31 N 26 15 E
Cesme 38 19 N 26 18 E
`G R A`

Kusadasi 37 52 N 27 14 E
`P B T A`

Samos Island (Greek) · 67C
`G A L`

  Karlovassi 37 48 N 26 41 E
  Samos 37 45 N 26 58 E
  Pythagorion 37 41 N 26 56 E
Gulluk 37 15 N 27 38 E
`Y G B A`

Gumusluk 37 03 N 27 15 E
Patmos Island (Greek)
  Patmos 37 18 N 26 35 E
`G`

Leros Island (Greek)
`G A`

  Ayia Marina 37 09 N 26 51 E
  Port Lakki 37 07 N 26 51 E
Kalymnos Island (Greek) · 67D
  Kalymnos 36 57 N 26 59 E
`G B`

Kos Island (Greek)
  Kos 36 53 N 27 19 E
`G A`

Yali Island (Greek) 36 39 N 27 07 E
`Y T A`

Nisiros Island (Greek) 36 37 N 27 08 E
Bodrum 37 02 N 27 25 E
Gokova 37 03 N 28 22 E
Karpathos Island (Greek)
  Cape Vronti 35 32 N 27 14 E
Rhodes Island (Greek)
  Rhodes 36 27 N 28 14 E
`G T A L`

(column 2) · 68A

Simi Island (Greek)
  Port Simi 36 37 N 27 50 E
Kizilyer 36 39 N 28 08 E
Kargi 36 46 N 28 19 E
Marmaris 36 51 N 28 16 E
`G B A`

Karagace 36 51 N 28 28 E
Gocek 36 45 N 28 59 E
`G B A`

Fethiye 36 38 N 29 06 E
`G B A`

Megisti (Kastellorizon) Island (Greek)
36 09 N 29 36 E
Andifli 36 12 N 29 41 E
Finike 36 18 N 30 09 E · `p.33`
`G B`

Adrazan 36 18 N 30 32 E · 68B
Atbuku 36 25 N 30 33 E
Tekirova 36 31 N 30 34 E
Agva 36 35 N 30 38 E
Antalya 36 50 N 30 37 E
`Y G R B T A`

Alanya 36 32 N 32 01 E
`G`

Anamur 36 01 N 32 49 E
Aydincik 36 09 N 33 21 E
Ovacik 36 08 N 33 43 E
Tasucu 36 14 N 33 59 E
Silifke 36 20 N 33 59 E
Mersin 36 48 N 34 37 E
`P Q Y G C R B T A L`

Yumurtalik Bay
  Yumurtalik 36 46 N 35 45 E
  Ayas 36 46 N 35 47 E
Ceyhan 36 53 N 35 56 E
`P Q Y T A`

Toros 36 55 N 35 59 E
Dortyol 36 50 N 36 14 E
Payas 36 45 N 36 11 E
Isdemir 36 44 N 36 11 E
Sariseki 36 40 N 36 13 E
Iskenderun 36 36 N 36 10 E
`P Q Y G C R B T L`

Arsuz 36 25 N 35 53 E

CYPRUS · 68C

Kyrenia 35 20 N 33 19 E
`G R B T A`

Morphou Bay
`Y G A`

  Xeros Pier 35 08 N 32 50 E
  Karavostassi 35 08 N 32 49 E
Khrysokhu Bay
  Latchi 35 02 N 32 24 E
Paphos 34 45 N 32 25 E
Akrotiri 34 34 N 33 02 E
Limassol 34 40 N 33 03 E
`P Y G C R B D T A L`

Moni 34 42 N 33 12 E
`P`

Vassiliko Bay 34 42 N 33 20 E · 68D
`P Q Y G R B T A`

Zyyi 34 43 N 33 20 E
Larnaca 34 55 N 33 38 E
`P Q Y G C R B T A`

Dhekelia 34 59 N 33 44 E
`P T A`

Famagusta 35 07 N 33 56 E
`P Q Y G C R B T A`

Bogaz 35 19 N 33 57 E
Gastria Bay
  Kalecik 35 19 N 33 59 E
`P Y G A`

SYRIA · 69A

Borj Islam 35 40 N 35 48 E
Minet el Beida 35 37 N 35 46 E
Lattakia (Latakia) 35 31 N 35 46 E
`P Y G C R B T A L`

Banias (Baniyas) 35 14 N 35 56 E
`P A`

Tartous (Tartus) 34 54 N 35 52 E
`P Y G C R B T A`

Arwad (Rouad) Island 34 51 N 35 51 E

LEBANON

Tripoli 34 28 N 35 50 E
`P G B T A`

Chekka 34 20 N 35 44 E
Selaata 34 16 N 35 39 E
`Q Y G B T A`

Jounieh 33 59 N 35 39 E · 69B
Zouk 33 58 N 35 35 E
Dbayeh 33 56 N 35 35 E
Beirut (Beyrouth) 33 54 N 35 31 E
`P Q Y G C R B A L`

Jieh 33 40 N 35 24 E
Sidon (Saida) 33 34 N 35 22 E
`G A`

Zahrani Terminal 33 32 N 35 19 E
`P B A`

Sour (Tyr) 33 16 N 35 12 E
`G`

ISRAEL · 69C

Akko (Acre) 32 55 N 35 04 E
Kishon 32 49 N 35 01 E
Haifa 32 49 N 35 00 E
`P Q Y G C R B D T L`

Hadera 32 27 N 34 55 E
`P Y B T A`

Tel Aviv 32 06 N 34 47 E
Yafo (Jaffa) 32 03 N 34 45 E
Ashdod 31 49 N 34 38 E
`Y G C R B T A`

Ashkelon 31 40 N 34 33 E
`P`

Gaza 31 30 N 34 27 E
Rafah 31 19 N 34 12 E

EGYPT · 69D

El Arish 31 07 N 33 48 E
Suez Canal · `p.28/29`
  Port Said 31 15 N 32 18 E
`P Y G C R B D T A L`

  Port Fouad 31 14 N 32 20 E
  El Qantara 30 51 N 32 19 E
  Ismailia 30 35 N 32 17 E
  Nifisha 30 34 N 32 15 E
  Lake Timsah 30 34 N 32 18 E
  Bitter Lakes
    Abu Sultan 30 25 N 32 18 E
    Fayid 30 20 N 32 18 E
    Fanara 30 17 N 32 21 E
  Marakib 29 55 N 32 34 E
  Port Tewfik 29 56 N 32 34 E
  Port Ibrahim 29 56 N 32 33 E
  Suez 29 58 N 32 33 E
`P G B D T`

  El Mina El Gedida 29 57 N 32 32 E
Damietta 31 23 N 31 48 E
`Y G C R B T A`

Abu Kir 31 19 N 30 04 E · `p.33`
`Y G`

P Petroleum Q Other Liquid Bulk Y Dry Bulk G General Cargo
C Containers R Ro-Ro B Bunkers D Dry Dock T Towage
A Airport (within 100km) L Lloyd's Agent (not including sub-agents)

EGYPT *continued* 70A

Alexandria 31 11 N 29 52 E
| P | Q | Y | G | C | R | B | D | T | A | L |

El Dekheila 31 09 N 29 48 E
| Y | G | C | R | T | A |

El Agami Island 31 09 N 29 47 E
Sidi Kerir Terminal 31 06 N 29 37 E
| P | T |

Mersa El Hamra Terminal (El Alamein)
30 59 N 28 52 E
| P |

Mersa Matruh 31 22 N 27 14 E   p.28/29
| G | C | R |

Salum 31 34 N 25 11 E

LIBYA 70B

Bardia 31 45 N 25 07 E
Marsa El Hariga 32 04 N 24 00 E
| P | T |

Tobruk 32 05 N 23 59 E
| G | B | T | A |

Derna 32 46 N 22 39 E
| G | R | T |

Ras el-Hilal 32 55 N 22 11 E
| G |

Apollonia 32 54 N 21 58 E
Tolmeta 32 43 N 20 57 E
Benghazi 32 07 N 20 03 E
| P | Y | G | C | R | B | T | A | L |

Zuetina Terminal 30 51 N 20 03 E
| P | Q |

Marsa el Brega 30 25 N 19 35 E
| P | Q | Y | G | R | T | A |

Ras Lanuf 30 31 N 18 34 E
| P | A |

Es Sider Terminal 30 38 N 18 21 E
| P | A |

Sirte 31 13 N 16 35 E 70C
Misurata (Qasr Ahmed) 32 22 N 15 13 E
| Y | G | C | R | T |

Zliten 32 30 N 14 34 E
Homs 32 39 N 14 16 E
| G |

Tripoli (Tarabulus) 32 54 N 13 11 E
| Q | G | C | R | B | T | A |

Az Zawiyah 32 49 N 12 43 E
Zawia Terminal 32 49 N 12 41 E
| P |

Bouri Terminal 33 54 N 12 39 E
Zuara 32 55 N 12 07 E
| G | T |

Abu Kammash 33 04 N 11 49 E
| G |

TUNISIA 70D

Zarzis 33 30 N 11 07 E
Djerba Island 33 53 N 10 52 E
Bou Grara 33 30 N 10 40 E
Gabes 33 55 N 10 06 E
| P | Q | Y | G | R | B | T |

Ashtart Terminal 34 17 N 11 24 E
| P | T |

La Skhira 34 14 N 10 04 E
| P | T | A |

Ras Tina 34 39 N 10 41 E
Sfax 34 44 N 10 46 E
| P | Q | Y | G | C | R | B | T | A |

Kerkennah Islands 34 41 N 10 58 E 71A
Mahdia 35 31 N 11 05 E
Ras Dimasse 35 35 N 11 01 E
Monastir 35 47 N 10 50 E
Sousse (Susa) 35 50 N 10 39 E
| Q | Y | G | C | R | T | A |

Tazerka Terminal 36 36 N 11 41 E
Cap Bon 37 05 N 11 03 E
Tunis 36 48 N 10 12 E
| G | C | R | B | T | A | L |

Rades 36 48 N 10 14 E
| G | C | R | B | T | A |

La Goulette 36 49 N 10 18 E
| P | Y | G | C | R | B | T | A |

Cap Farina 37 11 N 10 17 E 71B
Menzel Bourguiba 37 09 N 9 48 E
| Y | G | D | T | A |

Bizerta 37 16 N 9 53 E
| P | Q | Y | G | B | T | A |

Cap Serrat 37 15 N 9 13 E   p.28/29
Galita Island 37 32 N 8 56 E
Tabarka 36 58 N 8 46 E

ALGERIA

La Calle 36 54 N 8 26 E
Annaba 36 54 N 7 45 E
| P | Q | Y | G | R | B | D | T | A |

Mersa Takouch 37 04 N 7 23 E
Port Methanier 36 53 N 6 57 E
Skikda 36 53 N 6 54 E
| P | Q | Y | G | T | A |

Collo 37 00 N 6 34 E
| G |

Cap Bougaroni 37 05 N 6 28 E
Jijel 36 50 N 5 47 E
| Y | G | R | T | A |

Les Falaises 36 39 N 5 25 E
Bejaia 36 45 N 5 06 E
| P | Q | Y | G | B | T | A |

Azzeffoun 36 54 N 4 25 E 71C
Dellys 36 55 N 3 55 E
| G | A |

Algiers (Alger) 36 47 N 3 04 E
| P | Q | Y | G | C | R | B | D | T | A | L |

Cherchell 36 37 N 2 11 E
| G |

Sidi Ghiles 36 32 N 2 07 E
Gouraya 36 34 N 1 53 E
Port Breira 36 32 N 1 35 E
Tenes 36 31 N 1 19 E
| G |

Mostaganem 35 56 N 0 04 E
| Y | G | T |

Bethioua 35 48 N 0 12 E 71D
| Q | T |

Arzew 35 52 N 0 18 W
| P | Q | Y | G | B | T | A |

Oran 35 43 N 0 39 W
| P | Y | G | C | R | B | T | A |

Mers el Kebir 35 44 N 0 42 W
Beni Saf 35 18 N 1 23 W
| Y | G | D | A |

Honian 35 11 N 1 40 W
Ghazaouet 35 06 N 1 52 W   p.30
| Y | G | T | A |

Port Kelah 35 06 N 2 09 W
Port Say 35 05 N 2 12 W

MOROCCO

Chafarinas Islands 35 11 N 2 26 W

Nador 35 17 N 2 56 W 72A
| Y | G | T |

Melilla (**Spanish**) 35 18 N 2 56 W
| P | Y | G | C | B | T | A |

Cabo Tres Forcas 35 26 N 2 58 W
Afrau 35 12 N 3 30 W
Al Hoceima (Alhucemas) 35 15 N 3 54 W
Puerto Capaz 35 13 N 4 41 W
Al Mediq 35 41 N 5 19 W
Ceuta (**Spanish**) 35 53 N 5 19 W
| P | Q | G | C | R | B | T | A | L |

Tangier (Tanger) 35 47 N 5 48 W
| G | C | R | T | A |

Cape Spartel 35 47 N 5 56 W 72B
Larache (El Aaraich) 35 12 N 6 09 W
Oued Sebou
  Mehdia 34 18 N 6 39 W
  Kenitra 34 16 N 6 35 W
| Y | G | B | T | A |

Rabat 34 02 N 6 50 W   p.34/35
Mohammedia (Fedala) 33 43 N 7 22 W
| P | Y | B | T | A |

Casablanca 33 37 N 7 36 W
| P | Q | Y | G | C | R | B | D | T | A | L |

El Jadida 33 16 N 8 31 W
| Y | G | T | A |

Jorf Lasfar 33 07 N 8 38 W
| P | Q | Y | G | R |

Safi 32 18 N 9 15 W
| Q | Y | G | B | T |

Essaouira 31 30 N 9 47 W
Anza 30 26 N 9 39 W
Agadir 30 25 N 9 38 W
| P | Q | Y | G | R | B | T | A | L |

Sidi Ifni 29 22 N 10 12 W
Tan Tan 28 30 N 11 21 W
Cape Juby 27 57 N 12 55 W
Tarfaya 27 56 N 12 56 W

AZORES (Portuguese) 72C

Corvo Island 39 40 N 31 07 W
Flores Island
  Santa Cruz 39 27 N 31 07 W
Fayal Island
  Horta 38 32 N 28 38 W
| P | Q | G | C | B | T | A |

Pico Island
  Lajes 38 23 N 28 16 W
San Jorge Island
  Velas 38 40 N 28 13 W
Graciosa Island
  Santa Cruz 39 05 N 28 01 W
  Praia da Graciosa 39 03 N 27 58 W
| G | A |

Terceira Island 72D
  Angra do Heroismo 38 39 N 27 13 W
| Q | G | B | A |

  Praia da Vitoria 38 44 N 27 03 W
| P | Y | G | C | T | A | L |

St. Michael's (San Miguel) Island
  Ponta Delgada 37 44 N 25 40 W
| P | Q | G | C | R | B | T | A | L |

  Ponta do Arnel 37 49 N 25 08 W
Santa Maria Island
  Vila do Porto 36 56 N 25 09W

MADEIRA ISLANDS (Portuguese)

Madeira Island
  Funchal 32 38 N 16 54 W
| P | Q | Y | G | C | B | T | A | L |

  Praia Formosa 32 38 N 16 57 W
  Pargo Point 32 49 N 17 16 W

p.31
p.28/29
p.30
p.34/35

P Petroleum   **Q** Other Liquid Bulk   **Y** Dry Bulk   **G** General Cargo
C Containers   **R** Ro-Ro   **B** Bunkers   **D** Dry Dock   **T** Towage
A Airport (within 100km)   **L** Lloyd's Agent (not including sub-agents)

Jebel Dhanna (Jabal az Zannah) Terminal
24 13 N 52 40 E   **85A**

P	G	A							

QATAR

Mesaieed (Umm Said) 24 55 N 51 35 E

P	Q	Y	G	C	D	T	A		

Wakrah 25 10 N 51 38 E
Doha (Ad Dawhah) 25 17 N 51 32 E

G	C	T	A	L					

Halul Island Terminal 25 40 N 52 25 E

P									

Ras Laffan 25 56 N 51 32 E

BAHRAIN   **85B**

Sitra Island
   Sitra 26 10 N 50 40 E

P	Q	B	T	A					

Bahrain Island
   Mina Sulman 26 14 N 50 35 E

G	C	R	B	D	T	A			

SAUDI ARABIA

Quarrayah 26 02 N 50 08 E
Al Khobar 26 17 N 50 13 E
Dammam (King Abdul Aziz Port)
26 27 N 50 06 E

Y	G	C	R	B	D	T	A	L	

Ras Tanura 26 38 N 50 10 E

P	Q	B	T	A					

Juaymah Terminal 26 55 N 50 01 E

P	Q	B	T	A					

Ras al Ghar 26 53 N 49 52 E
Jubail 27 01 N 49 39 E

P	Q	Y	G	C	R	B	T		

Ras as Saffaniya 28 00 N 48 48 E
Ras Mishab 28 06 N 48 37 E

Y	G	R	T						

Ras al Khafji 28 24 N 48 31 E

P	G	B	T						

KUWAIT   **85C**

Khor al Mufatta 28 39 N 48 23 E

G	A								

Khor al Ami 28 40 N 48 23 E
Mina Saud Terminal 28 45 N 48 26 E

P	B	A							

Mina Abdulla Terminal 29 01 N 48 10 E

P	B	A							

Shuaiba 29 02 N 48 10 E   **85D**

P	Y	G	C	R	B	T	A		

Mina al Ahmadi 29 04 N 48 09 E

P	Q	T	A						

Kubbar Island 29 04 N 48 34 E
Sea Island Terminal 29 07 N 48 17 E
Kuwait (Al Kuwayt) 29 21 N 47 56 E

Y	G	C	R	B	D	T	A	L	

Shuwaikh 29 21 N 47 55 E

IRAQ

Umm Qasr 30 02 N 47 57 E

Y	G	C	T						

Khor al Zubair 30 11 N 47 54 E

Q	Y	G							

Mina al Bakr Terminal (Khor al Kafka)
29 41 N 48 48 E

P	T								

Khor al Amaya Terminal 29 47 N 48 48 E   **86A**

P	T								

Shatt al Arab
   Fao (Al Faw) 29 59 N 48 28 E

P	T								

Kabda 30 11 N 48 25 E
Abu al Fulus 30 27 N 48 02 E
Basrah 30 30 N 47 49 E

P	Y	G	B	T					

IRAN

Khorramshahr 30 20 N 48 10 E

Y	G	A							

River Karun
   Ahvaz 31 29 N 48 43 E
   Hartah Point 30 23 N 48 11 E
   Abadan 30 20 N 48 17 E

P	G	B	T	A					

Bavardeh 30 19 N 48 18 E
Khor Musa
   Bandar Khomeini (Bandar Shahpour)
   30 25 N 49 04 E

Y	G	C	R	B	T				

   Bandar Mahshahr 30 28 N 49 11 E

P	Q	Y	G	C	R	B	T		

Ras Bahregan Terminal 29 47 N 50 11 E

P	T								

Imam Hasan 29 48 N 50 11 E
Ganaveh 29 34 N 50 31 E
Kharg Island 29 14 N 50 19 E

P	Q	T	A						

   Darius Terminal 29 12 N 50 20 E
   Sea Island Terminal 29 14 N 50 17 E
Cyrus (Souroush) Terminal
29 02 N 49 28 E

P	T								

Bushire (Bushehr) 28 59 N 50 50 E

G	B	T	A						

Lavan Island 26 47 N 53 20 E

P	B	T							

Sirri Island 25 57 N 54 32 E   **86C**

P	T	A							

Abu Musa 25 33 N 55 02 E
Bandar Lengeh (Lingah) 26 33 N 54 53 E
Qeshm Island
   Qeshm 26 58 N 56 16 E
Henjam (Hangam) Island 26 39 N 55 54 E
Bandar Shahid Rejaie 27 06 N 56 04 E

P	Q	Y	G	C	R	B	T	A	

Bandar Abbas 27 08 N 56 12 E

P	Q	Y	G	C	B	D	T	A	

Hormuz Island 27 04 N 56 28 E
Hormuz Terminal 26 50 N 56 44 E
Jask 25 39 N 57 46 E
Ras Maidani 25 24 N 59 06 E
Chah Bahar 25 20 N 60 32 E

Y	G	C	B	T	A				

PAKISTAN   **86D**

p.40

Gwadar 25 06 N 62 24 E
Pasni 25 15 N 63 28 E
Sonmiani Bay
   Sonmiani 25 25 N 66 40 E
Ormara 25 06 N 64 38 E
Gadani Beach 25 06 N 66 43 E
Karachi 24 50 N 67 00 E

P	Q	Y	G	C	R	B	D	T	A	L

Korangi 24 48 N 67 08 E
Phitti Creek
   Port Muhammad Bin Qasim
   24 46 N 67 21 E

Y	G	C	B	T	A				

INDIA   **87A**

Jakhau 23 14 N 68 35 E
Mandvi 22 49 N 69 21 E

Y	A								

Mundra 22 45 N 69 42 E

Y	G	A							

Kandla 23 02 N 70 13 E

P	Q	Y	G	C	B	D	T	A	

Navlakhi 22 58 N 70 27 E

Y	G								

Bedi 22 31 N 70 02 E

Y	G	B	T	A					

Rozi Island 22 32 N 70 03 E
Sachana 22 32 N 69 57 E
Sikka 22 26 N 69 50 E   **87B**

P	Q	Y	B	A					

Vadinar Terminal 22 30 N 69 42 E

P	B	T	A						

Salaya 22 25 N 69 34 E
Port Okha 22 28 N 69 05 E

P	Y	G	B	T					

Dwarka 22 15 N 68 58 E
Porbandar 21 38 N 69 37 E

Y	G	B	T	A					

Mangrol 21 06 N 70 06 E
Veraval 20 54 N 70 22 E

Y	G	T	A						

Diu 20 43 N 70 59 E
Jafarabad 20 52 N 71 22 E
Rajula 20 57 N 71 32 E
Pipavav 20 59 N 71 34 E
Alang 21 24 N 72 09 E
Bhavnagar 21 45 N 72 14 E

Y	G	B	T	A					

Dholera 22 14 N 72 17 E
Khambat 22 19 N 72 37 E
Hazira Anchorage 21 05 N 72 40 E
Tapti River
   Magdalla 21 08 N 72 43 E
   Surat 21 10 N 72 54 E
Daman 20 25 N 72 49 E   **87C**
Bombay 18 54 N 72 49 E

P	Q	Y	G	C	R	B	D	T	A	L

Jawaharlal Nehru (Nhava Sheva)
18 56 N 72 51 E

Y	C	R	B	T	A				

Alibag 18 38 N 72 52 E
Revadanda Port 18 33 N 72 54 E
Janjira 18 18 N 72 58 E
Srivardhan Bay 18 01 N 73 00 E
Bankot 17 59 N 73 02 E
Port Dabhol 17 35 N 73 09 E
Jaigarh 17 18 N 73 12 E
Mirya Bay
   Bhagwati Bunder 17 00 N 73 16 E
Ratnagiri 16 59 N 73 17 E
Malvan 16 05 N 73 30 E
Vengurla 15 50 N 73 37 E   **87D**

G									

Redi 15 45 N 73 40 E

Y									

Panaji 15 29 N 73 49 E

G	A								

Aguada 15 29 N 73 47 E
Mormugao 15 25 N 73 48 E

P	Q	Y	G	C	R	B	T	A	

Betul 15 08 N 73 56 E
Karwar 14 49 N 74 06 E

Y	G	B	T	A					

Belekeri 14 42 N 74 15 E

Y	G								

Tadri 14 31 N 74 21 E
Kumta 14 25 N 74 23 E

P Petroleum **Q** Other Liquid Bulk **Y** Dry Bulk **G** General Cargo
C Containers **R** Ro-Ro **B** Bunkers **D** Dry Dock **T** Towage
A Airport (within 100km) **L** Lloyd's Agent (not including sub-agents)

INDIA *continued* 88A

Honavar 14 16 N 74 25 E
Coondapoor 13 37 N 74 40 E
`G B T`

Malpe 13 21 N 74 42 E
`G A`

New Mangalore 12 55 N 74 48 E
`P Q Y G C R B T A`

Mangalore 12 50 N 74 49 E
`G D T A L`

Kasaragod 12 30 N 75 00 E
Azhikal 11 57 N 75 18 E
Cannanore 11 52 N 75 22 E
`G T`

Tellicherry 11 45 N 75 28 E 88B
`G`

Mahe 11 42 N 75 31 E
Badagara 11 36 N 75 35 E
Calicut 11 16 N 75 46 E
`G A`

Beypore 11 10 N 75 48 E
`G A`

Tanur 10 59 N 75 52 E
Ponnani 10 47 N 75 54 E
Cochin 9 58 N 76 14 E
`P Q Y G C R B D T A L`

Alleppey 9 30 N 76 19 E
`G T A`

Neendakara 8 56 N 76 33 E
`G B T A`

Quilon 8 52 N 76 35 E
`G A`

Vizhinjam (Trivandrum) 8 29 N 76 57 E
Colachel 8 10 N 77 15 E
Cape Comorin 8 05 N 77 33 E
Lakshadweep (Laccadive Islands)
  Kiltan Island 11 29 N 73 00 E
  Androth Island 10 49 N 73 40 E
  Kavaratti Island 10 34 N 72 38 E
  Kalpeni Island 10 06 N 73 39 E
  Minicoy Island 8 17 N 73 04 E p.34/35

MALDIVES 88C

Kelaa 6 58 N 73 12 E
Male Island
  Male 4 10 N 73 30 E
`G T A`

Addu Atoll 0 40 S 73 10 E
Gan Island 0 41 S 73 10 E

BRITISH INDIAN OCEAN TERRITORY (British)

Chagos Archipelago
  Diego Garcia 7 17 S 72 25 E

INDIA 88D

Tiruchchendur Point 8 30 N 78 08 E p.40
New Tuticorin 8 45 N 78 13 E
`P Y G C B A`

Tuticorin 8 48 N 78 11 E
`G T`

Kilakkaria 9 14 N 78 47 E
Pamban 9 17 N 79 12 E
Mandapam 9 16 N 79 09 E
Tondi 9 45 N 79 00 E
Attirampattinam (Adirampatnam) 10 20 N 79 23 E
Point Calimere 10 17 N 79 53 E

SRI LANKA

Point Pedro 9 50 N 80 15 E
Point Palmyra 9 50 N 80 17 E
Mullaittivu 9 16 N 80 49 E
Kokkilai 8 59 N 80 57 E

Pulmoddai 8 56 N 80 59 E 89A
Trincomalee 8 34 N 81 13 E
`P Y G B T A`

Batticaloa 7 45 N 81 41 E
Okanda 6 39 N 81 46 E
Pottuvil 6 53 N 81 49 E
Hambantota 6 07 N 81 08 E
Matara 5 57 N 80 32 E
Galle 6 01 N 80 13 E
`Y G B L`

Kalutara 6 35 N 79 59 E
Colombo 6 57 N 79 51 E
`P Q Y G C B D T A L`

Negombo 7 12 N 79 50 E
Puttalam 8 02 N 79 50 E
Kayts 9 42 N 79 52 E
Jaffna 9 40 N 79 59 E 89B
`G`

Kankesanturai 9 49 N 80 03 E
`G`

INDIA

Nagapattinam 10 46 N 79 51 E
`G`

Nagore 10 49 N 79 51 E
Karikal 10 55 N 79 51 E
Tirumullaivasal 11 15 N 79 50 E
Porto Novo 11 29 N 79 45 E
Cuddalore 11 42 N 79 46 E
`Y G`

Pondicherry 11 56 N 79 50 E
`Y G`

Marakkanam 12 15 N 79 59 E
Madras 13 05 N 80 17 E
`P Y G C R B D T A L`

Ennore 13 14 N 80 20 E
Pulicat 13 25 N 80 19 E
Krishnapatnam 14 18 N 80 05 E
Muttukuru 14 21 N 80 09 E
Nizimpatnam 15 56 N 80 44 E
Machilipatnam 16 10 N 81 12 E
`G T A`

Narasapur Point 16 18 N 81 43 E
Kakinada 17 00 N 82 17 E
`Y G C B A`

Visakhapatnam 17 42 N 83 18 E
`P Q Y G C B D T A L`

Bheemunipatnam 17 54 N 83 27 E
`G A`

Calingapatnam 18 20 N 84 08 E
`G`

Baruva 18 53 N 84 36 E
Gopalpur 19 15 N 84 54 E
Puri 19 48 N 85 50 E
Mahanadi River
  Paradip 20 16 N 86 41 E 89D
`Y G C B T`

False Point 20 20 N 86 44 E
Palmyras Point 20 46 N 86 59 E
Digha 21 40 N 87 39 E
River Hooghly
  Sandheads 20 54 N 88 14 E
  Haldia 22 02 N 88 05 E
`P Q Y G B T`

  Kulpi 22 06 N 88 13 E
  Ulubaria 22 28 N 88 07 E
  Calcutta 22 35 N 88 21 E
`P Y G C B D T A L`

  Garden Reach 22 33 N 88 18 E
  Budge Budge 22 29 N 88 11 E
  Achipur 22 28 N 88 08 E
  Hooghly Point 22 13 N 88 04 E
  Diamond Harbour 22 11 N 88 11 E
  Mud Point 21 55 N 88 07 E
  Saugor Island 21 39 N 88 03 E

Port Canning 22 15 N 88 38 E 90A

BANGLADESH

Pussur River
  Mongla 22 27 N 89 35 E
`Y G C B T`

  Chalna 22 36 N 89 31 E
  Khulna 22 48 N 89 35 E
Fouzderhat Beach 22 23 N 91 45 E
Chittagong 22 20 N 91 50 E
`P Q Y G C R B D T A L`

Kutubdia Island 21 52 N 91 51 E
Cox's Bazar 21 26 N 91 58 E
Elephant Point 21 11 N 92 03 E

MYANMAR 90B

Maungdaw 20 49 N 92 22 E
River Kaladan
  Sittwe 20 08 N 92 55 E
`G`

Kyaukpyu 19 28 N 93 29 E p.41
Cheduba Island 18 55 N 93 37 E
Sandoway 18 28 N 94 21 E
Diamond Island 15 22 N 94 17 E
Ayeyarwady River
  Pathein River
    Pathein 16 46 N 94 43 E
`G`

  Yangon River
    Elephant Point 16 28 N 96 20 E
    Yangon 16 46 N 96 10 E
`P Y G C B D T L`

Mawlamyine 16 30 N 97 38 E
`G T`

Amherst 16 06 N 97 33 E
Heinze Creek 14 43 N 97 55 E
Dawei River
  Dawei 14 04 N 98 11 E
Mergui 12 26 N 98 36 E
Tanintharyi River
  Tanintharyi 12 17 N 98 50 E
Karathuri 10 53 N 98 35 E
Victoria Point 9 58 N 98 33 E
Coco Islands 14 11 N 93 23 E p.40

ANDAMAN and NICOBAR ISLANDS (Indian) 90C

Andaman Islands
  North Andaman Island
    Stewart Sound
      Mayabunder 12 56 N 92 54 E
  Middle Andaman Island
    Elphinstone Harbour 12 19 N 92 54 E
  South Andaman Island
    Port Meadows 12 01 N 92 47 E
    Port Blair 11 40 N 92 43 E
`P Y G C R B D A`

  Little Andaman Island
    Tambeibui 10 32 N 92 30 E
    Toibalewe 10 26 N 93 34 E
Nicobar Islands 90D
  Car Nicobar 9 10 N 92 45 E
  Nancowry Harbour 8 01 N 93 31 E
  Little Nicobar Island
    Patua 7 17 N 93 40 E
  Great Nicobar Island
    Kanalla 6 52 N 93 43 E

THAILAND

Takua Pa 9 16 N 98 19 E p.41
Phuket 7 50 N 98 25 E
`P Y G C B T A`

Krabi 8 04 N 98 52 E
Kantang 7 24 N 99 31 E

MALAYSIA

PENINSULAR MALAYSIA

Langkawi Island
  Teluk Ewa 6 26 N 99 45 E

P Petroleum	Q Other Liquid Bulk	Y Dry Bulk	G General Cargo
C Containers	R Ro-Ro	B Bunkers	D Dry Dock	T Towage
A Airport (within 100km)	L Lloyd's Agent (not including sub-agents)		

91A

Kuala Perlis 6 24 N 100 07 E
Kedah River
　Alor Setar 6 07 N 100 23 E
Tanjong Dawai 5 41 N 100 22 E
Penang (Pinang)

`P Q Y G C R B D T A L`

　Georgetown 5 25 N 100 20 E
Butterworth 5 24 N 100 22 E
Perai 5 23 N 100 22 E
Port Weld 4 50 N 100 38 E
Lumut 4 16 N 100 39 E

`P Y B A`

Pulau Pangkhor 4 13 N 100 35 E
Sitiawan 4 11 N 100 42 E
Sembilan Islands 4 03 N 100 33 E
Teluk Intan (Telok Anson)
4 01 N 101 01 E
Bagan Datoh 4 00 N 100 45 E
Kuala Selangor 3 21 N 101 15 E
Port Kelang 3 00 N 101 24 E

91B

`P Q Y G C R B T A L`

Port Dickson 2 31 N 101 47 E

`P Q G B T A`

Sungai Udang 2 15 N 102 08 E
Tanjong Bruas 2 13 N 102 09 E
Melaka (Malacca) 2 11 N 102 15 E

`G A`

Muar 2 00 N 102 24 E
Batu Pahat 1 47 N 102 53 E
Pulau Pisang 1 28 N 103 15 E
Johore Bahru 1 28 N 103 50 E
Pasir Gudang 1 26 N 103 54 E

p.42/43

`P Q Y G C R B D T A`

SINGAPORE

Seletar 1 25 N 103 50 E
Sembawang 1 28 N 103 50 E
Woodlands 1 27 N 103 47 E
Changi 1 22 N 103 58 E
Jurong Port 1 18 N 103 43 E
Tanjong Penjuru 1 18 N 103 45 E
Pulau Merlimau 1 17 N 103 43 E
Pulau Ayer Chawan 1 17 N 103 42 E
Selat Sinki 1 13 N 103 40 E
Pulau Sebarok 1 12 N 103 48 E
Pulau Bukom 1 14 N 103 46 E

`P Q B`

Pasir Panjang 1 16 N 103 47 E
Singapore 1 16 N 103 50 E

91C

`P Q Y G C R B D T A L`

Tanjong Pagar 1 16 N 103 51 E
Tanjong Rhu 1 18 N 103 52 E

MALAYSIA

PENINSULAR MALAYSIA

Telok Ramunia 1 21 N 104 14 E
Endau 2 40 N 103 38 E
Kuala Rompin 2 45 N 103 36 E
Nenasi 3 08 N 103 27 E
Pekan 3 29 N 103 24 E
Kuala Pahang 3 32 N 103 27 E
Kuantan 3 58 N 103 26 E

p.41

91D

`P Q Y G C R B T A`

Udang Terminal 4 02 N 106 30 E
Belida Terminal 4 08 N 105 08 E
Tanjong Gelang 4 10 N 103 26 E
Kemaman 4 11 N 103 30 E

`P Q Y G B T A`

Tanjong Berhala 4 15 N 103 28 E
Kerteh Terminal 4 28 N 103 24 E

`P T`

Dungun 4 47 N 103 26 E

`G`

Kakap Terminal 5 01 N 105 57 E
Anoa Terminal 5 13 N 105 36 E
Kuala Trengganu 5 20 N 103 09 E
Tapis Terminal 5 31 N 105 01 E

`P T`

92A

Dulang Terminal 5 49 N 104 10 E
Kelantan River
　Kota Baharu 6 08 N 102 14 E
Tumpat 6 13 N 102 11 E

SARAWAK

Sematan Anchorage 1 53 N 109 49 E
Lundu 1 40 N 109 52 E
Sarawak River
　Sijingkat 1 35 N 110 26 E
　Tanjong Pending 1 33 N 110 24 E
　Biawak 1 34 N 110 23 E
　Kuching 1 34 N 110 24 E

p.42/43

`P Y G C R B D T A L`

Lingga 1 21 N 111 10 E

92B

Sungei Rajang
　Rajang 2 09 N 111 12 E
　Tanjong Mani 2 09 N 111 21 E

`G B`

　Sarikei 2 08 N 111 31 E

`G B A`

　Binatang 2 10 N 111 38 E

`G B A`

　Sibu 2 17 N 111 49 E

`P G C B A`

Bintulu 3 10 N 113 02 E

`P G A`

Tanjong Kidurong 3 16 N 113 03 E

`Q Y G C R T A`

Niah 3 54 N 113 46 E
Miri 4 23 N 113 59 E

`P Q Y G T A`

Lutong Terminal 4 28 N 113 56 E
Baram 4 36 N 113 58 E

BRUNEI

92C

Kuala Belait 4 35 N 114 11 E

`P Q G B D`

Seria Terminal 4 43 N 114 19 E

`P`

Lumut 4 40 N 114 27 E

`Q`

Brunei Bay
　Muara Port 5 02 N 115 05 E

`P G C R B T A`

　Bandar Seri Begawan 4 54 N 114 56 E

MALAYSIA

SARAWAK

92D

　Limbang 4 45 N 115 00 E

BRUNEI

Tanjong Salirong 4 54 N 115 06 E

`G`

MALAYSIA

SARAWAK

　Lawas 4 56 N 115 23 E

SABAH

　Sipitang 5 05 N 115 33 E
　Weston 5 13 N 115 36 E
Labuan Island

`P Q Y G B D T A`

　Victoria 5 17 N 115 14 E
　Labuan Terminal 5 16 N 115 07 E
Kota Kinabalu 6 00 N 116 04 E

`P Q G C R B T A L`

Sapangar Bay 6 05 N 116 07 E
Usukan Bay 6 23 N 116 20 E

93A

Tembungo Terminal 6 38 N 115 47 E
Kudat 6 52 N 116 50 E

`G C B A`

Jambongan Island 6 40 N 117 30 E
Sandakan 5 50 N 118 08 E

`P Q Y G C B T A L`

Tambisan Island 5 29 N 119 08 E
Darvel Bay
　Bakapit 4 57 N 118 35 E
　Kennedy Bay 4 55 N 118 28 E
　Lahad Datu 5 02 N 118 20 E

`Q G B A`

　Silam 4 57 N 118 14 E
Bohayan Island 4 48 N 118 19 E

93B

Kunak 4 41 N 118 15 E

`Q G`

Semporna 4 29 N 118 37 E
Port Elphinstone 4 22 N 118 35 E
Tawau 4 15 N 117 53 E

`P Q Y G C R B T A`

Tanjong Batu 4 15 N 117 52 E
Sebatik Island (Malaysian Sector)
　Wallace Bay 4 15 N 117 40 E

INDONESIA

KALIMANTAN

Sebatik Island (Indonesian Sector)
4 14 N 117 39 E
Nunukan 4 05 N 117 37 E
Sebuku Terminal 3 52 N 118 05 E
Pulau Bunyu
　Bunyu Terminal 3 27 N 117 49 E

`P`

Sessayap 3 34 N 117 01 E
Tarakan Island

93C

　Tarakan 3 17 N 117 36 E

`G A`

River Berau
　Tanjungredeb 2 10 N 117 29 E
Sangkulirang 1 00 N 118 00 E
Tanjung Bara 0 32 N 117 37 E

`Y G T A`

Sangatta Terminal 0 25 N 117 35 E

`P`

Bontang 0 06 N 117 29 E

`Q Y G T A`

Santan Terminal 0 07 S 117 32 E

`P`

Samarinda 0 30 S 117 09 E

93D

`G`

Bekapai Terminal 1 00 S 117 30 E

`P`

Senipah Terminal 1 03 S 117 13 E

`P T A`

Balikpapan 1 16 S 116 49 E

`P G B T A`

Lawe-Lawe Terminal 1 27 S 116 45 E

`P`

Teluk Adang
　Tanahgrogot 1 49 S 116 13 E
Tanjung Berlayar 3 01 S 116 16 E
Pulau Laut
　Kota Baru 3 14 S 116 14 E
　Setagin 3 17 S 116 09 E
Batu Licin 3 27 S 116 00 E
Satui 3 49 S 115 29 E
Taboneo 3 47 S 114 39 E
Banjarmasin 3 20 S 114 35 E

`P G T A`

River Murung
　Kuala Kapuas 3 00 S 114 22 E

`G`

GEOGRAPHIC INDEX

P Petroleum	Q Other Liquid Bulk	Y Dry Bulk	G General Cargo
C Containers	R Ro-Ro	B Bunkers	D Dry Dock	T Towage
A Airport (within 100km)	L Lloyd's Agent (not including sub-agents)

INDONESIA *continued* — 94A

KALIMANTAN

River Kahayan
  Pulang Pisau 2 45 S 114 15 E
  [G]

Sabangan Bay 3 17 S 113 23 E
Sampit 2 59 S 113 03 E
  [G]

River Arut
Pangkalan Bun 2 57 S 111 24 E
Ketapang 1 50 S 109 59 E
  [G | A]

Telok Ayer 0 44 S 109 34 E — 94B
Pontianak 0 01 S 109 21 E
  [G | C | A]

Singkawang 0 55 N 108 58 E
  [G]

River Sambas
  Pemangkat 1 08 N 108 55 E
  [G]

  Sintete 1 13 N 109 03 E
  Sambas 1 22 N 109 18 E
  [G]

SUMATERA

Sunda Strait
  Lampung Bay
    Tarahan 5 40 S 105 28 E
    Panjang 5 28 S 105 20 E
    [P | Y | G | C | B | D | T | A]

    Telukbetung 5 27 S 105 16 E
  Semangka Bay
    Kota Agung 5 30 S 104 37 E
    Semangka Bay Terminal 5 35 S 104 37 E
    [P | B | T | A]

Kru 5 11 S 103 56 E
Bintuhan 4 49 S 103 22 E
Enggano Island 5 25 S 102 15 E — 94C
Pulau Baai 3 55 S 102 17 E
Bengkulu 3 47 S 102 15 E
  [Y | G | B | T | A]

Pagai Utara Island 2 15 S 100 05 E
Pagai Selatan Island 3 00 S 100 20 E
Sipura Island 2 10 S 99 40 E
Teluk Bayur 1 00 S 100 22 E
  [Y | G | B | T | A]

Padang 0 56 S 100 22 E
Siberut Island 1 36 S 99 13 E
Batu Island 0 05 S 98 21 E
Nias Island
  Gunung Sitoli 1 17 N 97 37 E
  [G | A]

Sibolga 1 44 N 98 46 E — 94D
  [P | G | A]

Barus 2 05 N 98 23 E
Singkel 2 16 N 97 48 E
Simeulue Island
  Sinabang 2 29 N 96 23 E
Tapaktuan 3 16 N 97 12 E
  [G | A]

Meulaboh 4 08 N 96 08 E
Calang 4 37 N 95 35 E
Lhoknga 5 27 N 95 14 E
  [G | B]

Uleelheue 5 33 N 95 17 E
Kruengraya 5 36 N 95 30 E
Weh Island
  Sabang 5 53 N 95 19 E
  [G | A]

Sigli 5 24 N 95 59 E
Kruenggeukueh 5 14 N 97 03 E

95A

Blang Lancang Terminal (Arun)
5 15 N 97 04 E
  [P | Q | G | T | A]

Blang Lancang 5 13 N 97 06 E
  [P | Q | G | T | A]

Lhokseumawe 5 10 N 97 09 E
  [Y | G | T | A]

Kuala Beukah Terminal 4 53 N 97 57 E
Kualalangsa 4 31 N 97 59 E
Aru Bay
  Sembilan Island 4 08 N 98 15 E
  Pangkalan Susu 4 07 N 98 12 E
  [P | Q | G | B | T | A]

  Pangkalan Brandan 4 02 N 98 17 E
Belawan 3 48 N 98 43 E
  [G | C | B | D | T | A]

Kuala Tanjung 3 21 N 99 29 E — 95B
River Asahan
  Telok Nibung 3 00 N 99 49 E
  [G | A]

  Tanjung Balai 2 58 N 99 48 E
Sungei Bila
  Labuhan Bilik 2 31 N 100 10 E
Bagan Si Api Api 2 09 N 100 48 E
Dumai 1 41 N 101 27 E
  [P | G | B | T | A]

Siak River
  Siak 0 45 N 102 05 E
  Buatan 0 43 N 101 50 E
  Kuala Mandau 0 47 N 101 47 E
  Perawang 0 39 N 101 37 E
  Rumbai 0 33 N 101 30 E
  Pekanbaru 0 33 N 101 27 E
  [P | G | A]

Bengkalis 1 28 N 102 06 E
  [G]

Sungei Pakning 1 22 N 102 11 E
  [P | G | T | A]

Lalang Terminal 1 11 N 102 13 E
  [P | T]

Batu Ampar 1 10 N 104 00 E — 95C
Pulau Sambu 1 09 N 103 54 E
  [P | G | B | T]

Pulau Batam 1 08 N 103 55 E
Bintan Island
  Tanjung Uban 1 04 N 104 13 E
  [P | Q | G | B | A]

  Tanjung Pinang 0 56 N 104 27 E
  Kijang Strait
    Kijang 0 51 N 104 37 E
  [Y | G | A]

Tembilahan 0 20 S 103 10 E
Selajar Island
  Penuba 0 20 S 104 28 E
  [G]

Singkep Island — 95D
  Dabo 0 30 S 104 34 E
  [G | B | T | A]

  Kuala Enok 00 32 S 103 24 E
River Jambi
  Jambi (Telanaipura) 1 35 S 103 37 E
  [P | Y | G | A]

River Banyu Asin
  Tanjung Apiapi 2 17 S 104 51 E
  Lalang River 2 22 S 104 38 E
Musi River
  Sungei Gerong 2 59 S 104 51 E
  Plaju 2 59 S 104 50 E
  Pusri 2 59 S 104 47 E
  Palembang 2 59 S 104 46 E
  [P | Q | Y | G | C | B | D | T | A | L]

Bangka Island
  Muntok 2 04 S 105 10 E
  Belinyu 1 39 S 105 47 E
  Sungei Liat 1 51 S 106 08 E

96A

Pangkalbalam 2 06 S 106 10 E
  [P | G | B | T | A]

Pangkalpinang 2 08 S 106 09 E
Toboali 3 01 S 106 27 E
Belitung Island
  Tanjung Pandan 2 45 S 107 38 E
  [G | T | A]

  Manggar 2 50 S 108 10 E

JAWA

Anyer 6 02 S 105 56 E
Cigading 6 01 S 105 57 E
  [Y | G]

Banten 6 01 S 105 58 E
  [Y | G]

Prointal 5 57 S 106 00 E — 96B
  [Q | G]

Merak 5 56 S 105 58 E
  [P | G]

Tanjung Sekong 5 55 S 106 00 E
  [P | Q | G | B]

Suralaya 5 53 S 106 01 E
Serang 6 07 S 106 09 E
Cinta Terminal 5 27 S 106 14 E
  [P | T | A]

Intan Terminal 4 35 S 106 39 E
Widuri Terminal 4 40 S 106 39 E
Jakarta 6 06 S 106 52 E
  [P | Q | Y | G | C | B | D | T | A | L]

Tanjung Priok 6 05 S 106 53 E
Bima Terminal 5 45 S 107 05 E
  [P | T]

Arjuna Terminal 5 53 S 107 45 E
  [P | Q]

Pamanukan 6 12 S 107 46 E
Balongan Terminal 6 16 S 108 27 E
  [P | T]

Cirebon 6 41 S 108 33 E
  [Y | G | B | D | T | A]

Tegal 6 51 S 109 08 E — 96C
  [G | C | B | T]

Pekalongan 6 52 S 109 41 E
Semarang 6 58 S 110 25 E
  [P | Q | Y | G | C | B | T | A | L]

Jepara 6 35 S 110 39 E
Taju 6 32 S 111 03 E
Rembang 6 41 S 111 20 E
Lasem 6 41 S 111 26 E
Kampung Bantjar 6 48 S 111 45 E
Tuban 6 54 S 112 04 E
  [G]

Bawean Island
  Sangkapura 5 52 S 112 41 E
Madura Island — 96D
  Sumenep Bay
    Kalianget 7 04 S 113 57 E
    [G | R | A]

  Camplong 7 12 S 113 42 E
Gresik 7 09 S 112 39 E
  [P | Q | Y | G | A]

Tanjung Perak 7 12 S 112 43 E
Surabaya 7 12 S 112 44 E
  [P | Q | Y | G | C | B | T | A | L]

Pasuruan 7 37 S 112 53 E
  [G | T | A]

Probolinggo 7 43 S 113 13 E
  [P | Q | G | T | A]

Panarukan 7 42 S 113 56 E
  [G | T]

Jangkar 7 40 S 114 10 E

P Petroleum **Q** Other Liquid Bulk **Y** Dry Bulk **G** General Cargo
C Containers **R** Ro-Ro **B** Bunkers **D** Dry Dock **T** Towage
A Airport (within 100km) **L** Lloyd's Agent (not including sub-agents)

Meneng 8 07 S 114 23 E

| P | G | T | | | | | | | |

97A

Banyuwangi 8 12 S 114 23 E

| G | | | | | | | | | |

Cilacap 7 44 S 109 00 E

| P | Q | Y | G | B | T | A | | | |

Jawa Head 6 46 S 105 12 E
Christmas Island **(Australian)**
  Flying Fish Cove 10 25 S 105 43 E

| P | Y | G | B | A | L | | | | |

Cocos (Keeling) Islands **(Australian)**
  Port Refuge 12 06 S 96 52 E p.12/13
Bali Island p.42/43
  Gilimanuk 8 10 S 114 26 E

| G | R | | | | | | | | |

Celukan Bawang 8 11 S 114 50 E **97B**

| G | | | | | | | | | |

  Buleleng 8 06 S 115 06 E
  Labuan Amuk 8 33 S 115 33 E
  Benoa 8 45 S 115 15 E

| P | G | A | | | | | | | |

Lombok Island
  Lembar (Ampenan) 8 34 S 116 04 E

| P | Y | G | B | A | | | | | |

  Labuan Haji 8 42 S 116 34 E
Sumbawa Island
  Kempo 8 40 S 118 11 E

| G | | | | | | | | | |

  Bima 8 25 S 118 43 E

| G | A | | | | | | | | |

  Badas 8 30 S 117 26 E
Sumba Island
  Waingapu 9 37 S 120 13 E
Flores Island
  Ende 8 51 S 121 39 E
  Larantuka 8 20 S 123 00 E
  Maumere 8 36 S 122 13 E

| G | B | A | | | | | | | |

Timor Island
  Kupang 10 10 S 123 34 E

| P | Y | G | B | T | A | | | | |

  Atapupu 9 02 S 124 53 E
  Dili 8 32 S 125 34 E
  Aliambata 8 48 S 126 35 E
Tanimbar Islands **97C**
  Yandema
    Saumlaki 8 00 S 131 17 E
Aru Islands
  Dobo 5 46 S 134 13 E

IRIAN JAYA

Merauke 8 28 S 140 23 E
Amamapare 4 49 S 136 58 E

| Y | B | T | A | | | | | | |

Adi Island
  Mangawitoe 4 13 S 133 29 E
Fak Fak 2 56 S 132 18 E
Babo 2 33 S 133 26 E
Sungei Muturi **97D**
  Muturi 2 12 S 133 42 E
Steenkool 2 07 S 133 31 E
Salawati 1 21 S 130 59 E
Kasim 1 18 S 131 01 E

| P | T | A | | | | | | | |

Sorong 0 53 S 131 14 E

| P | G | C | B | T | | | | | |

Manokwari 0 52 S 134 05 E

| P | G | B | A | | | | | | |

Nabire 3 23 S 135 31 E
Biak Island
  Biak 1 10 S 136 04 E

| P | Y | G | C | B | T | A | | | |

Humboldt Bay 2 35 S 140 47 E
Jayapura 2 32 S 140 43 E

| P | G | B | A | | | | | | |

MALUKU (MOLUCCAS) **98A**

Halmahera Island
  Tobelo 1 44 N 128 00 E
  Jailolo 1 06 N 127 27 E
  Payahe 0 22 N 127 42 E
Gebe Island
  Tanjung Sofa 0 03 N 129 17 E
  Tanjung Ubulie 0 03 S 129 23 E
Geser Island 3 52 S 130 53 E
Banda Island
  Naira 4 33 S 129 54 E
Seram Island
  Waisarissa 3 12 S 128 16 E
  Wahai Bay 2 47 S 129 30 E
  Bula 3 05 S 130 29 E
  Masohi 3 19 S 128 59 E
Ambon Island
  Ambon 3 42 S 128 10 E

| P | G | C | B | T | A | | | | |

Buru Island 3 06 S 126 06 E **98B**
Sula Islands
  Taliabu Island 0 02 S 125 00 E
Mangole Island
  Mangole 1 56 S 125 50 E
Obi Island 1 30 S 127 40 E
Bacan Island
  Labuha 0 38 S 127 28 E
Ternate Island
  Ternate 0 47 N 127 23 E

| P | G | B | A | | | | | | |

Talaud Island 4 14 N 126 47 E
Sangihe Island
  Tahuna 3 35 N 125 30 E

SULAWESI

Bitung 1 26 N 125 11 E

| P | G | B | T | A | | | | | |

Belang 0 55 N 124 48 E
Gorontalo 0 30 N 123 03 E

| P | G | B | A | | | | | | |

Bumbulan 0 28 N 122 04 E
Marisa 0 27 N 121 56 E
Moutong 0 27 N 121 13 E
Tomini 0 30 N 120 33 E
Parigi 0 50 S 120 13 E
Poso 1 23 S 120 45 E
Luwuk 0 56 S 122 47 E
Batui 1 15 S 122 34 E
Kendari 3 58 S 122 35 E **98C**
Baubau (Buton) 5 27 S 122 36 E
Pomalaa 4 10 S 121 35 E
Mangkasa Terminal 2 44 S 121 04 E
Malili 2 38 S 120 59 E
Palopo 2 59 S 120 13 E
Kajang 5 20 S 120 22 E
Bonthain 5 33 S 119 57 E
Ujung Pandang 5 08 S 119 24 E

| P | Q | Y | G | C | B | T | A | L | |

Biringkassi 4 49 S 119 30 E
Pare Pare 4 00 S 119 37 E

| G | | | | | | | | | |

Majene 3 33 S 118 58 E

| G | | | | | | | | | |

Mamuju 2 41 S 118 55 E **98D**
Sampaga 2 18 S 119 09 E
Karosa 1 46 S 119 21 E
Pantoloan 0 42 S 119 51 E

| P | G | B | T | A | | | | | |

Palu 0 52 S 119 51 E
Tanjung Ogogili 0 48 N 120 30 E
Tolitoli 1 05 N 120 48 E
Buol 1 10 N 121 27 E
Kuandang 0 51 N 122 55 E
Inobonto 0 55 N 124 06 E
Amurang 1 12 N 124 34 E
Manado (Menado) 1 30 N 124 50 E

| G | A | | | | | | | | |

PHILIPPINES

Palawan Island
  Honda Bay p.44

Babuyan 9 59 N 118 54 E **99A**
Matinloc Terminal 11 29 N 119 01 E
Cadlao Terminal 11 20 N 118 59 E
Nido Terminal 11 03 N 118 49 E
Boayan Island 10 33 N 119 07 E
Port Barton 10 29 N 119 15 E
Ulugan Bay 10 10 N 118 48 E
Rio Tuba 8 30 N 117 25 E
Puerto Princesa 9 45 N 118 44 E

| P | Y | G | B | A | | | | | |

West Linapacan Terminal
11 49 N 119 07 E
Calamian Islands
  Busuanga Island
    Port Calton 12 11 N 120 06 E
    Coron 12 00 N 120 12 E
  Coron Island 11 56 N 120 15 E
Semirara Island
  Dapdap 12 03 N 121 22 E
Mindoro Island **99B**
  San Jose 12 25 N 121 03 E
  Mangarin 12 20 N 121 04 E
  Bongabong 12 45 N 121 29 E
  Quinabigan 12 58 N 121 28 E
  Naujan 13 20 N 121 18 E
  Calapan 13 23 N 121 10 E
  San Teodoro 13 26 N 121 01 E
Luzon Island
  Lokanin Point 14 29 N 120 37 E
  Lamao 14 31 N 120 36 E
  Bataan 14 32 N 120 37 E

| P | Q | G | B | | | | | | |

  Quitang Point 14 33 N 120 36 E
  Limay 14 34 N 120 36 E

| P | Y | G | B | | | | | | |

  Manila 14 35 N 120 58 E

| P | Q | Y | G | C | R | B | D | T | A | L |

  Cavite 14 30 N 120 55 E
  Rosario 14 25 N 120 51 E
  Nasugbu 14 05 N 120 38 E
  Calaca 13 55 N 120 48 E
  Batangas 13 45 N 121 03 E

| P | Q | G | B | D | | | | | |

  Tabangao 13 43 N 121 03 E
  Castanas 13 53 N 121 33 E
Marinduque Island **99C**
  Gasan 13 20 N 121 51 E
  Pangi 13 20 N 121 50 E
  Port Balanacan 13 32 N 121 52 E
  Balogo 13 31 N 122 03 E
  Santa Cruz 13 30 N 122 03 E

| Y | G | B | T | | | | | | |

  Masagasai Bay 13 25 N 122 06 E
Luzon Island
  Catanauan 13 35 N 122 19 E
  Pasacao 13 29 N 123 02 E
  Sorsogon 12 58 N 124 00 E
  Magallanes 12 50 N 123 51 E
  Bulan 12 40 N 123 52 E
  Legaspi 13 09 N 123 45 E

| P | Q | Y | G | B | T | A | | | |

  Tabaco 13 22 N 123 44 E

| Y | G | B | A | | | | | | |

  Nato 13 36 N 123 34 E **99D**
  Sabang 13 43 N 123 35 E
Catanduanes Island
  Virac 13 44 N 124 14 E
  Lamit Bay 13 58 N 123 32 E
  Tandoc 14 03 N 123 18 E

| G | | | | | | | | | |

Daet River
  Mercedes 14 07 N 123 00 E
  Paracale 14 17 N 122 47 E
  Jose Panganiban 14 19 N 122 40 E

| P | G | B | | | | | | | |

Larap Bay 14 18 N 122 38 E
Dahikan Islands
  Dahikan Bay 14 19 N 122 36 E
Capalonga 14 21 N 122 31 E
Lamon Bay
  Hondagua 13 57 N 122 14 E
  Siain 13 57 N 122 01 E
  Atimonan 14 00 N 121 55 E

P Petroleum	Q Other Liquid Bulk	Y Dry Bulk	G General Cargo
C Containers	R Ro-Ro	B Bunkers	D Dry Dock	T Towage
A Airport (within 100km)	L Lloyd's Agent (not including sub-agents)		

PHILIPPINES *continued*   100A

Mauban 14 11 N 121 44 E
Puerto Real 14 45 N 121 36 E
Polillo Island
    Polillo 14 45 N 121 54 E
Dingalan Bay 15 15 N 121 26 E
Baler 15 45 N 121 34 E
Casiguran 16 17 N 122 07 E
Diapitan Bay 16 25 N 122 14 E
San Vicente 18 30 N 122 08 E
Batan Island
    Basco 20 27 N 121 58 E
`G A`

Irene 18 23 N 122 06 E
`G A`

Cagayan River
    Aparri 18 21 N 121 38 E
`P G B A`

    Lallo 18 12 N 121 39 E
Pamplona 18 30 N 121 22 E
Abulug 18 27 N 121 27 E
Claveria 18 37 N 121 05 E   100B
`Y G A`

Laoag 18 12 N 120 36 E
Currimao 17 59 N 120 29 E
`G A`

Tagudin 16 57 N 120 26 E
Carlatan 16 38 N 120 19 E
San Fernando Harbour
`P Y G B T A`

    Poro 16 37 N 120 19 E
Lingayen 16 01 N 120 13 E
Port Sual 16 04 N 120 06 E
Bolinao 16 24 N 119 54 E
Santa Cruz 15 44 N 119 52 E
`Y A`

Masinloc 15 32 N 119 57 E
`Y B`

Port Matalvi 15 29 N 119 55 E
Subic Bay
`G D T`

    Olongapo 14 48 N 120 16 E
Mariveles 14 25 N 120 30 E
`Q G B D`

Romblon Island
    Romblon 12 35 N 122 16 E
Masbate Island
    Colorada Point 12 33 N 123 23 E
    Port Barrera 12 33 N 123 24 E
    Masbate 12 12 N 123 37 E
Santo Nino Island   100C
    Santo Nino 11 55 N 124 26 E
Samar Island
    Catbalogan 11 47 N 124 53 E
    Calbayog 12 04 N 124 36 E
    Pambuhan 12 33 N 124 55 E
    Laoang 12 34 N 125 01 E
    Port Libas 11 46 N 125 28 E
    Borongan 11 37 N 125 28 E
    Hernani 11 19 N 125 37 E
    Port General MacArthur
    11 15 N 125 33 E
Leyte Island
    Tacloban 11 15 N 125 00 E
`P Y G A`

Tanauan 11 07 N 125 01 E   100D
Tolosa 11 04 N 125 02 E
Maasin 10 08 N 124 50 E
Baybay 10 41 N 124 48 E
Ormoc 11 00 N 124 36 E
Isabel 10 55 N 124 25 E
`Q Y B`

Palompon 11 04 N 124 22 E
Poro Island
    Poro 10 38 N 124 25 E
Panay Island
    Banate 11 01 N 122 52 E
    Bayang Point 11 02 N 122 55 E
    Estancia 11 27 N 123 09 E
    Roxas (Capiz) 11 37 N 122 42 E

Port Batan 11 36 N 122 30 E   101A
Buson 11 03 N 122 03 E
San Jose de Buenavista 10 45 N 121 55 E
Iloilo 10 42 N 122 34 E
`Q Y G C R B D T A`

Guimaras Island 10 40 N 122 35 E
`Q Y G B T A`

Inampulugan Island 10 28 N 122 43 E
Nalunga Island 10 30 N 122 43 E
Negros Island
    Hinigaran 10 16 N 122 50 E
    Bulata 9 51 N 122 24 E
    Cartagena 9 48 N 122 23 E
    Hinobaan 9 34 N 122 30 E
    Asia 9 32 N 122 30 E
    Bacong 9 14 N 123 17 E
    Dumaguete 9 18 N 123 18 E
`Q Y G A`

Bais 9 35 N 123 07 E
`P Y`

Ayungon 9 52 N 123 19 E   101B
San Carlos 10 29 N 123 25 E
Escalante 10 52 N 123 31 E
Vito Point 10 54 N 123 31 E
Sagay 10 57 N 123 25 E
Cadiz 10 58 N 123 19 E
Victorias 10 54 N 123 04 E
Mambagid 10 51 N 122 57 E
Bacolod 10 40 N 122 57 E
Pulupandan 10 31 N 122 48 E
Cebu Island
    Cebu 10 18 N 123 54 E
`P Q Y G C B T A`

Naga 10 13 N 123 45 E
Alcoy 9 43 N 123 30 E
Mambagi 9 41 N 123 30 E
Toledo 10 22 N 123 38 E
Sangi 10 23 N 123 38 E
`Y G B A`

Hagnaya Bay 11 07 N 123 56 E
Bogo 11 03 N 124 00 E
Mactan Island 10 19 N 123 57 E
Bohol Island
    Talibon 10 09 N 124 20 E
    Jagna 9 39 N 124 22 E
    Tagbilaran 9 39 N 123 51 E
    Maribojoc 9 44 N 123 50 E
Camiguin Island
    Mambajao 9 15 N 124 43 E
Dinagat Island
    Dinagat 9 58 N 125 36 E
    Osmena 10 10 N 125 30 E
Nonoc Island
    Port Nonoc 9 49 N 125 37 E
Mindanao Island   101C
    Placer 9 39 N 125 36 E
    Surigao 9 47 N 125 30 E
    Cabadbaran 9 07 N 125 32 E
    Masao 9 01 N 125 33 E
    Butuan 8 57 N 125 33 E
    Nasipit 8 59 N 125 20 E
    Anakan 8 51 N 125 09 E
    Gingoog 8 50 N 125 06 E
    Medina 8 55 N 125 02 E
Macajalar Bay
    Villanueva 8 35 N 124 45 E
`Y B T A`

    Tagoloan 8 32 N 124 45 E
Bugo 8 31 N 124 45 E
Cagayan de Oro 8 29 N 124 39 E
`P Y G C B A`

Quinalang Cove 8 17 N 124 16 E   101D
Kiwalan 8 16 N 124 16 E
Iligan 8 14 N 124 14 E
`Q Y G C B A`

Kolambugan 8 07 N 123 53 E
Ozamiz (Misamis) 8 09 N 123 51 E
Jimenez 8 20 N 123 51 E
Oroquieta 8 29 N 123 48 E
Plaridel 8 37 N 123 42 E
Dapitan 8 39 N 123 25 E
Dipolog 8 35 N 123 20 E
Roxas 8 31 N 123 15 E
Port Santa Maria 7 46 N 122 06 E

Panabutan 7 35 N 122 07 E   102A
Caldera Bay 6 57 N 121 58 E
Zamboanga 6 54 N 122 04 E
`P Y G C B A`

Vitali Point 7 23 N 122 23 E
Kabasalan 7 48 N 122 46 E
Olutanga Island
    Suba Nipa 7 18 N 122 51 E
Malangas 7 38 N 123 02 E
Margosatubig 7 35 N 123 01 E
Polloc 7 21 N 124 13 E
`G C A`

Cotabato 7 14 N 124 15 E
Linek 7 10 N 124 08 E
Lebak 6 33 N 124 02 E
Milbuk 6 09 N 124 16 E
Sarangani Bay
    Makar 6 05 N 125 10 E
    General Santos (Dadiangas) 6 06 N 125 10 E
`G B A`

Malalag Bay 6 37 N 125 24 E   102B
Tagabuli Bay 6 48 N 125 24 E
Davao 7 04 N 125 37 E
`P Q Y G C R B D T A`

Sasa 7 07 N 125 39 E
Tibungeo (Tibungko) 7 12 N 125 39 E
Tambongon (Tambungon) 7 15 N 125 40 E
Panabo 7 18 N 125 41 E
La Paz 7 19 N 125 44 E
Maco 7 21 N 125 51 E
La Union 6 42 N 126 05 E
Mati 6 57 N 126 13 E
Bislig Bay
    Bislig 8 13 N 126 19 E
`G B A`

Lianga 8 38 N 126 06 E
Tandag 9 04 N 126 12 E
Adlay 9 25 N 125 54 E
Gigaquit 9 36 N 125 41 E
Basilan Island
    Isabela 6 42 N 121 58 E
`G A`

Lamitan 6 40 N 122 08 E
Maluso Bay
    Port Holland 6 33 N 121 52 E
Jolo Island
    Jolo 6 03 N 121 00 E
`P Q G B T A`

Siasi Island
    Siasi 5 33 N 120 49 E
Tawitawi Island
    Batu Batu 5 04 N 119 53 E

THAILAND   102C

`p.41`

Takbai 6 16 N 102 03 E
Narathiwat 6 28 N 101 51 E
Pattani 6 57 N 101 18 E
`Y G A`

Songkhla 7 14 N 100 35 E
`Y G C T A`

Lakon 8 23 N 99 59 E
Thasala 8 40 N 99 58 E
Erawan Terminal 9 02 N 101 17 E
Khanom 9 16 N 99 53 E
Surat Thani 9 09 N 99 20 E
Thap Sakae 11 30 N 99 35 E   102D
Prachuap Khiri Khan 11 47 N 99 49 E
Chao Phraya River
    Paknam 13 36 N 100 34 E
    Bangkok 13 42 N 100 34 E
`P Y G C R B D T A L`

Sriracha 13 07 N 100 53 E
`P Y G B T`

Ko Sichang 13 09 N 100 48 E
Laem Chabang 13 05 N 100 53 E
`Y G C B T A`

Pattaya 12 57 N 100 53 E
Sattahip 12 39 N 100 51 E
`G B T`

Legend:
P Petroleum Q Other Liquid Bulk Y Dry Bulk G General Cargo
C Containers R Ro-Ro B Bunkers D Dry Dock T Towage
A Airport (within 100km) L Lloyd's Agent (not including sub-agents)

Column 1 (103A–103D)

103A

Map Ta Phut 12 40 N 101 08 E
Rayong 12 38 N 101 17 E
Chanthaburi 12 28 N 102 04 E

CAMBODIA (KAMPUCHEA)

Pointe du Depart 10 43 N 103 32 E
Sihanoukville (Kompong Som)
10 38 N 103 30 E
`P G B T A`

Kampot 10 34 N 104 09 E

VIETNAM

Phu Quoc Island 10 00 N 104 03 E
River Mekong
Can Tho 10 03 N 105 46 E
`G C T A`

Phnom Penh (Cambodian) 11 36 N 104 54 E
`G B T A`

River Saigon
My Tho 10 21 N 106 22 E
`Y G C A`

Nha Be 10 41 N 106 46 E
Ho Chi Minh City (Saigon) 10 46 N 106 43 E
`P Q Y G C B D T A`

103B

Vung Tau (Cap St. Jacques)
10 21 N 107 04 E
`P B T`

Ca Na 11 20 N 108 54 E
Cam-Ranh Bay
Ba Ngoi 11 52 N 109 07 E
Nha Trang 12 16 N 109 11 E
`Y G B T A`

Hon Khoi 12 34 N 109 14 E
Vung Ro 12 51 N 109 24 E
Tuy Hoa 13 03 N 109 20 E
Qui Nhon 13 46 N 109 14 E
`P G C B T A`

Paracel Islands (Disputed)
Triton Island 15 47 N 111 12 E
Ky Ha 15 18 N 108 41 E
Da Nang 16 06 N 108 18 E
`P Y G C R B D T A`

103C

Lien Chieu Bay 16 08 N 108 07 E
Hue 16 29 N 107 33 E
Vinh 18 30 N 106 00 E
Nghe Tinh 18 39 N 105 42 E
Sam Son 19 45 N 105 54 E
Thanh Hoa 19 49 N 105 48 E
Diemdien 20 33 N 106 43 E
Hanoi 21 02 N 105 50 E
Haiphong 20 52 N 106 40 E
`P Y G C R B D T`

Quang Yen 20 56 N 106 48 E
Port Redon 20 59 N 106 46 E
Parseval Bay 20 49 N 107 03 E
Ha Long Bay
Port Courbet 20 58 N 106 59 E
Hongay 20 57 N 107 03 E
`P Q Y G B T A`

Pak Ha Mun 20 58 N 107 32 E
Campha 21 04 N 107 21 E
`Y G B T`

Port Wallut 21 12 N 107 37 E

CHINA

103D

Fangcheng 21 45 N 108 21 E
`Y G B T`

Beihai 21 27 N 109 03 E
`Y G B T A`

Hainan Island
Haikou 20 01 N 110 16 E
`P Y G C R B T A`

Yangpu 19 42 N 109 20 E
`Y G C`

Column 2 (104A–104D)

104A

Basuo (Dongfang) 19 06 N 108 37 E
`Y G T`

Sanya (Ya Xian) 18 11 N 109 28 E
`Y G T A`

Yulin 18 13 N 109 32 E
Qinglan 19 35 N 110 53 E
Kwangchow Bay
Zhanjiang 21 12 N 110 25 E
`P Y G C R B T A`

Tinpak 21 30 N 111 15 E
Xi Jiang
Jiangmen 22 40 N 113 05 E
Wuzhou 23 29 N 111 16 E
Lasawei 22 08 N 113 49 E
Macau (Portuguese) 22 12 N 113 33 E
`P Q G C A`

p.38/39

Zhu Jiang (Pearl River)
Jiuzhou 22 14 113 35 E
Zhuhai 22 17 N 113 35 E
`G B`

Zhongshan 23 03 N 113 31 E
`G`

Huangpu 23 05 N 113 25 E
`P Y G C R B T A`

Guangzhou (Canton) 23 06 N 113 14 E
`G B D T A L`

Shenzhen 22 31 N 114 08 E
Chiwan 22 28 N 113 53 E
`P Y G C T`

Shekou 22 29 N 113 54 E

104B

HONG KONG (British)
`P Q Y G C R B D T A L`

Tap Shek Kok 22 23 N 113 55 E
Tsing Yi Island 22 21 N 114 06 E
Kwai Chung 22 21 N 114 07 E
Kowloon 22 18 N 114 10 E
Victoria 22 17 N 114 10 E
Ap Lei Chau 22 14 N 114 09 E
Lamma Island 22 13 N 114 07 E

CHINA

104C

Yantian 22 36 N 114 16 E
`Y G C R`

Aotou 22 43 N 114 31 E
Bias Bay 22 35 N 114 35 E
Pinghai 22 34 N 114 53 E
Shanwei 22 48 N 115 20 E
`P Y G`

Shantou 23 20 N 116 45 E
`P Y G C A`

Xiamen 24 27 N 118 04 E
`P Y G C B A`

TAIWAN

104D

Jinmen Island (Quemoy) 24 27 N 118 23 E
Pescadores Islands
Makung 23 33 N 119 33 E
An-Ping 22 59 N 120 08 E
`G`

Tainan 23 06 N 120 05 E
Kaohsiung 22 37 N 120 15 E
`P Q Y G C R B D T A`

Hualien 23 59 N 121 38 E
`P Y G B T A`

Suao 24 36 N 121 52 E
`Y G C B T`

Shenao 25 07 N 121 49 E
Keelung (Chilung) 25 09 N 121 44 E
`P Y G C B D T A`

Tamsui 25 10 N 121 25 E

Column 3 (105A–105D)

105A

Sha Lung 25 09 N 121 11 E
Taichung 24 17 N 120 30 E
`P Q Y G C B T`

CHINA

Quanzhou 24 54 N 118 35 E
`P G B T`

Hunghwa 25 30 N 119 20 E
Min Jiang
Mawei 25 59 N 119 27 E
Nantai 26 03 N 119 19 E
Fuzhou 26 03 N 119 18 E
`P Q Y G C A`

Sharp Peak Island 26 08 N 119 40 E
Matsu Island 26 09 N 119 56 E
Sanduao 26 38 N 119 39 E
Wenzhou 28 02 N 120 39 E
`Y G T A`

Haimen 28 41 N 121 26 E
`G`

Beilun 29 56 N 121 53 E
Zhenhai 29 58 N 121 42 E
Ningbo 29 52 N 121 33 E
`P Q Y G C B T A`

Hangzhou 30 15 N 120 10 E
Jinshan 30 43 N 121 19 E
`P Q`

105B

Yangtze River (Chang Jiang)
Baoshan 31 25 N 121 29 E
Wusong 31 24 N 121 32 E
Shanghai 31 15 N 121 30 E
`P Y G C R B D T A L`

Nantong 32 00 N 120 49 E
`P Y G C B D T A`

Zhangjiagang 31 58 N 120 24 E
`Y G C T`

Jingjiang 32 01 N 120 18 E
Jiangyin 31 55 N 120 15 E
Zhenjiang 32 13 N 119 26 E
`Y G B T`

105C

Yangzhou 32 22 N 119 22 E
Yizheng 32 12 N 119 12 E
Nanjing 32 03 N 118 47 E
`P Y G C T A`

Pukou 32 02 N 118 40 E
Ma-An-Shan 31 49 N 118 32 E
Wuhu 31 20 N 118 22 E
`Y G T`

Tongling 30 57 N 117 40 E
Anqing 30 31 N 117 02 E
`P Y G T`

Jiujiang 29 38 N 115 56 E
`Y G B T`

Huangshi 30 13 N 115 05 E
`Y G B T`

Wuhan 30 35 N 114 19 E
`G B T`

Hankou 30 35 N 114 17 E
Chenglingji 29 26 N 113 09 E
`G`

105D

Xiang Jiang
Changsha 28 12 N 112 59 E
Shashi 30 19 N 112 16 E
Zhicheng 30 19 N 111 30 E
`Y G`

Yichang 30 42 N 111 18 E
Badong 31 03 N 110 24 E
Chongqing 29 34 N 106 35 E
`Y G T A`

Lianyungang 34 44 N 119 27 E
`Y G C D T`

GEOGRAPHIC INDEX

CHINA *continued* — 106A

Lanshan 35 05 N 119 21 E
`Y G T`

Shijiugang 35 23 N 119 34 E
`P Y G T`

Rizhao 35 29 N 119 29 E
Jiaozhou Bay
   Qingdao 36 05 N 120 18 E
`. P Y G C B D T A L`

   Huangdao 36 03 N 120 13 E
Shidao 36 53 N 122 28 E
Weihai 37 30 N 122 09 E
`P Y G T`

Yantai 37 32 N 121 23 E
`P Y G T A`

Longkou 37 39 N 120 20 E
`P Y G T`

Huanghua 38 26 N 117 23 E — 106B
Hai He River
   Xingang 38 59 N 117 45 E
`P Y G C B D T A`

   Dagu 38 58 N 117 40 E
   Tianjin 39 06 N 117 10 E
Qinhuangdao 39 54 N 119 36 E
`P Y G C B D T`

Huludao 40 43 N 120 59 E
Jinzhou 40 45 N 121 06 E
`P Y G`

Yingkou 40 41 N 122 14 E
`Y G T`

Bayuquan 40 17 N 121 58 E
Pulandian 39 18 N 121 40 E
Lushun 38 48 N 121 15 E
Dalian 38 55 N 121 41 E
`P Y G C R B D T A L`

Yalu River
   Dandong 40 08 N 124 24 E
`Y G T`

NORTH KOREA — 106C

Tasado 39 48 N 124 25 E
Nampo (Chinnampo) 38 44 N 125 25 E `p.45`
`Y G B D T A`

Taedong River
   Kyomipo 38 45 N 125 38 E
   Pyongyang 39 00 N 125 45 E
Haeju 38 00 N 125 42 E
`Y G B`

SOUTH KOREA — 106D

Yeonpyung 37 36 N 125 43 E
Inchon 37 28 N 126 36 E
`P Q Y G C R B T A`

Daesan 37 01 N 126 25 E
`P B T`

Pyongtaek 37 00 N 126 47 E
Gojeong 36 18 N 126 27 E
Changhang 36 01 N 126 41 E
`Y G B`

Kunsan 36 00 N 126 43 E
`P Q Y G C R B T`

Mokpo 34 47 N 126 23 E
`P Y G B T A`

Cheju (Quelpart) Island
   Cheju 33 31 N 126 33 E
`P G T A`

Yosu 34 45 N 127 47 E
`P Y G B T A`

Samil 34 52 N 127 47 E — 107A
`P Q Y G B A`

Kwangyang 34 54 N 127 42 E
`Y G`

Samchonpo 34 55 N 128 04 E
Chungmu 34 50 N 128 25 E
Koje Island
   Okpo 34 53 N 128 43 E
   Jangseungpo 34 51 N 128 51 E
Chinhae (Jinhae) 35 08 N 128 39 E
`Y G B T A`

Masan 35 11 N 128 36 E
`Y G B T A`

Busan (Pusan) 35 06 N 129 04 E
`P Q Y G C R B D T A L`

Suyong 35 09 N 129 09 E
Onsan 35 27 N 129 22 E
Ulsan 35 29 N 129 24 E
`P Q Y G C B D T A`

Mipo 35 31 N 129 27 E
Pohang 36 02 N 129 26 E — 107B
`P Y G B T`

Samchok 37 26 N 129 12 E
`Y G B T`

Donghae (Bukpyung) 37 29 N 129 09 E
`Y G B T`

Mukho 37 33 N 129 07 E
`Y G B T`

Daepo 38 10 N 128 37 E

NORTH KOREA

Wonsan 39 10 N 127 26 E
`P G B T A`

Songjon 39 20 N 127 30 E
Rempo 39 47 N 127 32 E
Sohojin Harbour
   Hungnam 39 48 N 127 40 E
`G A`

Songjin 40 40 N 129 12 E — 107C
`G`

Chongjin 41 46 N 129 49 E
`Y G C B T`

Najin (Rajin) 42 11 N 130 19 E
Unggi 42 20 N 130 25 E

JAPAN

HOKKAIDO

Nemuro 43 20 N 145 35 E
Abashiri 44 01 N 144 17 E
`G B T`

Monbetsu 44 21 N 143 22 E
`G B T`

Esashi (Kitami-Esashi) 44 56 N 142 36 E
Wakkanai 45 25 N 141 42 E
`G B D T A`

Rumoi 43 57 N 141 38 E
`P Y G C B T`

Mashike 43 52 N 141 31 E
Ishikariwan Shinko 43 13 N 141 18 E — 107D
`G T`

Otaru 43 12 N 141 01 E
`Y G B T A`

Yoichi 43 13 N 140 47 E
Iwanai 42 59 N 140 31 E
Fukushima 41 28 N 140 16 E
Hakodate 41 47 N 140 43 E
`P Y G C R B D T A`

Uchiura Bay
   Mori 42 07 N 140 35 E
   Wanishi 42 20 N 141 00 E

Muroran 42 21 N 140 57 E — 108A
`P Y G B D T A`

Tomakomai 42 38 N 141 38 E
`P Q Y G C B T A`

Urakawa 42 10 N 142 46 E
Samani 42 07 N 142 55 E
Erimo 42 01 N 143 09 E
Tokachi 42 18 N 143 20 E
`G`

Kushiro 42 59 N 144 22 E
`P Y G C R B D T A`

Akkeshi 43 03 N 144 51 E

HONSHU

Shiriya 41 24 N 141 28 E
Sekinehama 41 22 N 141 13 E
Kawauchi 41 10 N 141 00 E
Ominato 41 14 N 141 11 E — 108B
Noheji 40 52 N 141 07 E
Aomori 40 49 N 140 45 E
`P Q Y G R B D T A`

Noshiro 40 13 N 140 00 E
`G`

Funakawa 39 53 N 139 52 E
`P Y G B T A`

Akita 39 46 N 140 04 E
`P Y G B T A`

Sakata 38 56 N 139 49 E
`P Y G B T A`

Ebisu 38 05 N 139 26 E
Niigata-Higashi 38 00 N 139 14 E
`Q G C B`

Niigata 37 57 N 139 04 E
`P Y G B D T A`

Sadoshima
   Ryotsu 38 05 N 138 27 E
   Ogi 37 49 N 138 17 E
Kashiwazaki 37 22 N 138 33 E
`Y G B T`

Naoetsu 37 11 N 138 15 E
`P Y G B T`

Himekawa 37 02 N 137 51 E — 108C
`Y G B`

Toyama 36 45 N 137 14 E
`P Y G B D T A`

Toyama Shinko (Shinminato) 36 46 N 137 07 E
`P Y G B T A`

Fushiki 36 47 N 137 03 E
`P Y G B T A`

Nanao 37 06 N 137 02 E
`P Q Y B T`

Kanazawa 36 37 N 136 36 E
`P G B T A`

Fukui 36 13 N 136 08 E
`G B T`

Tsuruga 35 40 N 136 05 E — 108D
`P Q Y G B T A`

Takahama 35 30 N 135 32 E
Uchiura 35 32 N 135 30 E
`G T`

Maizuru 35 29 N 135 22 E
`P Y G B D T A`

Oppama 35 34 N 135 15 E
Miyazu 35 35 N 135 13 E
`Y G B T`

Sakaiminato 35 32 N 133 15 E
`P G B T A`

P Petroleum	**Q** Other Liquid Bulk	**Y** Dry Bulk **G** General Cargo
C Containers	**R** Ro-Ro	**B** Bunkers **D** Dry Dock **T** Towage
A Airport (within 100km)	**L** Lloyd's Agent (not including sub-agents)	

GEOGRAPHIC INDEX

109A

Nishinoshima
  Urago 36 05 N 133 00 E
Hamada 34 53 N 132 02 E

`Y G B T`

Esaki 34 39 N 131 39 E
Senzaki 34 24 N 131 12 E
Mutsure 33 58 N 130 52 E
Shimonoseki 33 56 N 130 56 E

`P Y G B D T A`

Onoda 34 00 N 131 11 E

`G B`

Ube 33 56 N 131 12 E

`P Y G B T A`

Ajisu 34 00 N 131 22 E
Nakanoseki 34 00 N 131 34 E
Mitajiri 34 01 N 131 36 E

`P Y G B`

109B

Tonda 34 02 N 131 44 E
Tokuyama 34 00 N 131 48 E

`P Q Y G B T`

Kudamatsu 34 00 N 131 51 E
Kasado 33 57 N 131 47 E
Hikari 33 57 N 131 56 E
Hirao 33 54 N 132 03 E

`G T A`

Yanai 33 57 N 132 08 E
Hiroshima Bay
  Iwakuni 34 10 N 132 15 E

`P G B A`

  Kanokawa 34 10 N 132 26 E

`P Q B T A`

  Hiroshima 34 20 N 132 27 E

`Y G C R B T A`

  Ujina 34 21 N 132 28 E
  Etajima 34 11 N 132 29 E
Kure 34 14 N 132 33 E

`P Y G B D T A`

109C

Mitsukoshima 34 11 N 132 31 E
Akitsu 34 19 N 132 49 E
Takehara 34 19 N 132 55 E
Omishima 34 15 N 133 00 E
Hakatashima
  Kinoura 34 12 N 133 08 E
Ikuchishima
  Setoda 34 18 N 133 06 E
Saizaki 34 20 N 133 02 E
Mihara 34 23 N 133 06 E
Itozaki 34 23 N 133 06 E
Innoshima
  Habu 34 17 N 133 11 E
Mukaishima 34 23 N 133 12 E
Onomichi 34 24 N 133 11 E

`G D T A`

Matsunaga 34 25 N 133 15 E
Tsuneishi 34 22 N 133 17 E
Fukuyama 34 26 N 133 27 E

`Y G B T`

Kasaoka 34 30 N 133 30 E
Mizushima 34 30 N 133 45 E

`P Q Y G B D T A`

Hibi 34 27 N 133 56 E
Naoshima 34 27 N 134 00 E

`Y B A`

Uno 34 29 N 133 57 E

109D

`P Q Y G B D A`

Okayama 34 36 N 133 59 E
Shodoshima 34 30 N 134 15 E
Katagami 34 43 N 134 13 E
Aioi 34 47 N 134 28 E

`G B D T A`

Aboshi 34 46 N 134 36 E
Hirohata 34 46 N 134 38 E
Himeji 34 46 N 134 38 E

`P Q Y G B T A`

Shikama 34 47 N 134 40 E

110A

Mega 34 46 N 134 42 E
Takasago 34 44 N 134 48 E
Higashi-Harima 34 43 N 134 50 E

`Q Y G B T A`

Kakogawa 34 42 N 134 50 E
Befu 34 43 N 134 51 E
Kobe 34 40 N 135 12 E

`P Q Y G C R B D T A L`

Nishinomiya 34 43 N 135 21 E
Amagasaki 34 41 N 135 23 E

`P Q G T A`

Osaka 34 39 N 135 24 E

`P Q Y G C R B D T A`

Sakai 34 34 N 135 24 E

`P Q Y G B D T A`

Kishiwada 34 28 N 135 22 E
Hannan 34 28 N 135 21 E

`P Q Y G B A`

Izumisano 34 23 N 135 18 E
Wakayama 34 12 N 135 08 E

`P Q Y G B T A`

Kainan 34 09 N 135 11 E
Shimotsu 34 07 N 135 08 E
Yura 33 57 N 135 06 E
Tanabe 33 43 N 135 21 E

`G B A`

Katsuura 33 37 N 135 57 E
Owase 34 04 N 136 13 E

`P G B`

Shingu 33 42 N 136 00 E

`Y G B T`

110B

Tsu 34 41 N 136 33 E
Yokkaichi 34 57 N 136 38 E

`P Q Y G C R B T A`

Nagoya 35 03 N 136 51 E

`P Q Y G C R B D T A`

Handa 34 53 N 136 56 E
Hekinan 34 56 N 136 57 E
Kinuura 34 51 N 136 57 E

`P Q Y G R B T A`

Gamagori 34 48 N 137 13 E

`P Y G B T A`

Toyohashi 34 43 N 137 19 E

`G R B T A`

Tahara 34 40 N 137 18 E
Atsumi 34 40 N 137 04 E

`P B`

Hamaoka 34 37 N 138 08 E
Omaezaki 34 36 N 138 14 E

`G B T`

110C

Yaizu 34 52 N 138 20 E
Shimizu 35 01 N 138 32 E

`P Q Y G C B D T`

Tagonoura 35 08 N 138 42 E

`P Y G B T`

Numazu 35 04 N 138 51 E

`G B`

Shimoda 34 40 N 138 57 E
Usami 35 00 N 139 06 E
Kurihama 35 13 N 139 44 E
Uraga 35 14 N 139 44 E
Yokosuka 35 17 N 139 41 E

`G R B D T A`

Taura 35 18 N 139 38 E
Negishi 35 24 N 139 38 E
Yokohama 35 27 N 139 40 E

`P Q Y G C R B D T A L`

Tsurumi 35 30 N 139 41 E
Kawasaki 35 30 N 139 45 E

`P Q Y G B D T A`

111A

Ogishima 35 30 N 139 46 E
Shibaura 35 37 N 139 45 E
Tokyo 35 41 N 139 44 E

`P Q Y G C R B D T A`

Izu-Oshima 35 39 N 139 54 E
Funabashi 35 40 N 139 58 E
Chiba 35 34 N 140 03 E

`P Q Y G R B D T A`

Goi 35 30 N 140 06 E
Kisarazu (Kimitsu) 35 22 N 139 53 E

`P Y G R B T A`

Futtsu 35 18 N 139 49 E
Tateyama 35 00 N 139 52 E
Choshi 35 44 N 140 41 E
Kashima 35 56 N 140 42 E

`P Q Y G B T A`

Hitachi 36 29 N 140 38 E

`P Y G C B T`

Tokai 36 42 N 140 46 E
Onahama 36 56 N 140 55 E

111B

`P G B T`

Hirono 37 14 N 141 01 E
Soma 37 50 N 140 58 E

`Y G T`

Sendai 38 16 N 141 03 E

`P Q G B A`

Shiogama 38 19 N 141 02 E

`P Y G B D T A`

Ishinomaki 38 25 N 141 18 E

`Y G B D T A`

Oginohama 38 23 N 141 22 E
Onagawa 38 27 N 141 28 E
Kesennuma 38 52 N 141 36 E

`P G B T`

Ofunato 38 59 N 141 45 E

`P Y G B T A`

Kamaishi 39 16 N 141 54 E

111C

`Y G B T A`

Miyako 39 38 N 141 58 E

`Y G B T`

Tamagawa 40 05 N 141 50 E
Hachinohe 40 32 N 141 32 E

`P Q Y G B D T A`

Mutsu-Ogawara 40 57 N 141 25 E

SHIKOKU

Kikuma 34 02 N 132 50 E

`P B T A`

Namikata 34 07 N 132 58 E

`P Q T`

Hashihama 34 06 N 132 58 E
Imabari 34 04 N 133 01 E

`Y G B D T A`

Niihama 33 59 N 133 17 E

`P Y G B T A`

Mishima-Kawanoe 34 01 N 133 34 E

`Y G B`

Takuma 34 15 N 133 42 E

111D

`Y G B`

Tadotsu 34 17 N 133 44 E
Marugame 34 18 N 133 47 E
Sakaide 34 20 N 133 51 E

`P Q Y G B D T A`

Takamatsu 34 21 N 134 03 E

`P Y G B A`

Naruto 34 11 N 134 37 E
Tokushima 34 03 N 134 36 E
Komatsushima 34 00 N 134 36 E

`P Y G B T A`

110D

GEOGRAPHIC INDEX

P Petroleum   Q Other Liquid Bulk   Y Dry Bulk   G General Cargo
C Containers   R Ro-Ro   B Bunkers   D Dry Dock   T Towage
A Airport (within 100km)   L Lloyd's Agent (not including sub-agents)

JAPAN *continued*   112A

Tomioka 33 55 N 134 42 E
`G B`

Anan 33 54 N 134 40 E
Tachibana 33 53 N 134 43 E
`Y G B`

Kannoura 33 35 N 134 18 E
Kochi 33 31 N 133 34 E
`P Y G B T A`

Urado 33 30 N 133 35 E
Susaki 33 23 N 133 18 E
`Y G T A`

Uwajima 33 13 N 132 33 E
Yoshida 33 16 N 132 32 E
Ikata 33 27 N 132 21 E
Yawatahama 33 27 N 132 24 E
Nagahama 33 37 N 132 29 E
Matsuyama 33 51 N 132 42 E
`P G B T A`

KYUSHU   112B

Kanda 33 48 N 131 00 E
`Y G B T A`

Tanoura 33 58 N 130 59 E
Moji 33 57 N 130 58 E
`P Y G C R B D T A L`

Kokura 33 54 N 130 54 E
`P G B`

Tobata 33 55 N 130 51 E
`Q Y G B T A`

Yawata 33 52 N 130 48 E
`Y G B T A`

Wakamatsu 33 55 N 130 49 E   112C
`Y G B T A`

Makiyama 33 53 N 130 49 E
Hakata 33 37 N 130 23 E
`Y G C B T A`

Fukuoka 33 39 N 130 21 E
Tsushima
   Shimoshima
      Izuhara 34 11 N 129 18 E
Kunisaki 33 35 N 131 43 E
Karatsu 33 28 N 129 58 E
`Q Y G B A`

Imari 33 16 N 129 49 E
`Q Y G B D A`

Matsuura 33 21 N 129 44 E
Usunoura 33 12 N 129 35 E
Ainoura 33 11 N 129 39 E
Sasebo 33 08 N 129 43 E
`P Y G B D T A`

Sakito 33 01 N 129 33 E
Matsushima 32 56 N 129 36 E
`Y G B T A`

Nagasaki 32 43 N 129 50 E
`P Y G B`

Kuchinotsu 32 36 N 130 12 E   112D
Suminoye 33 11 N 130 14 E
Miike 33 00 N 130 25 E
`P Q Y G B T A`

Omuta 33 02 N 130 26 E
Misumi 32 37 N 130 28 E
`G B T A`

Yatsushiro 32 31 N 130 32 E
`P Q G B T A`

Minamata 32 13 N 130 20 E
`Q G B T`

Kiire 31 23 N 130 33 E
`P B T A`

Taniyama 31 29 N 130 32 E   113A
Kagoshima 31 35 N 130 34 E
`P Q Y G B T A`

Shibushi 31 28 N 131 07 E
`Y G T A`

Aburatsu 31 34 N 131 24 E
Miyazaki 31 53 N 131 27 E
Hososhima 32 27 N 131 40 E
`P Q Y G B T A`

Nobeoka 32 35 N 131 43 E
Saiki 32 58 N 131 55 E
`Y G T`

Tsukumi 33 05 N 131 52 E
`Y G T`

Usuki 33 08 N 131 49 E
Seki Saki 33 16 N 131 54 E
Saganoseki 33 15 N 131 52 E
`Q Y G B T A`

Tsurusaki 33 15 N 131 41 E   113B
Oita 33 16 N 131 40 E
`P Q Y G B T A`

Beppu 33 18 N 131 31 E
Nagasu 33 35 N 131 22 E
Satsunan Islands
   Amami Island
      Naze 28 23 N 129 30 E
         Koniya 28 09 N 129 19 E
Ryukyu Islands
   Okinawa Island
      Naha 26 13 N 127 40 E
`G T A L`

      Nakagusuku Bay (Buckner Bay)
      Nakagusuku 26 13 N 127 51 E
      Kin Bay
         Heianza 26 21 N 127 57 E
`P Q Y T`

      Ishikawa 26 25 N 127 51 E   113C
   Miyako Island   p.38/39
      Hirara 24 48 N 125 17 E
   Ishigaki Island
      Ishigaki 24 20 N 124 10 E
Kazan Islands
   Iwojima 24 48 N 141 18 E
Ogasawara Islands
   Chichijima 27 05 N 142 12 E

PACIFIC ISLANDS

GUAM (American)

`P G C R B D T A L`

Apra 13 27 N 144 37 E
Agana 13 29 N 144 45 E

TRUST TERRITORY OF THE PACIFIC ISLANDS

NORTHERN MARIANA ISLANDS

Saipan Island 15 12 N 145 43 E
`G B A`

Tinian Island 14 58 N 145 37 E
`P G C R B A`

Rota Island
   Rota 14 10 N 145 10 E

PALAU (BELAU)   113D

Koror 7 20 N 134 29 E
`P G C B A`

Angaur 6 54 N 134 09 E

FEDERATED STATES OF MICRONESIA

Yap Island 9 30 N 138 08 E
`G C R B A`

Truk Islands
   Eten Anchorage 7 21 N 151 53 E

Truk 7 27 N 151 52 E   114A
`P G C B A`

Pohnpei (Ponape) Island 6 59 N 158 13 E
`Q G C B A`

Kosrae Island 5 20 N 163 00 E   p.48/49

MARSHALL ISLANDS

Jaluit 5 55 N 169 39 E
Lae Island 8 55 N 166 16 E
Kwajalein Atoll
   Kwajalein 8 43 N 167 44 E
Enewetak Atoll 11 21 N 162 21 E
Wotje Atoll 9 28 N 170 15 E
Maloelap Atoll
   Taroa 8 43 N 171 14 E
Majuro Atoll
`P G C B A`

   Djarrit 7 08 N 171 22 E
Milli Atoll 6 05 N 171 44 E

SOLOMON ISLANDS   114B

Santa Cruz Islands   p.46/47
   Vanikolo Island
      Paeu 11 41 S 116 50 E
San Cristobal (Makira) Island
   Cape Surville 10 50 S 162 23 E
   Pakera Point 10 24 S 161 48 E
Malaita Island
   Su'u Harbour 9 10 S 160 55 E
   Auki 8 45 S 160 44 E
Florida Islands
   Florida Island
      Tulagi 9 05 S 160 10 E
`G`

   Ghavutu Island 9 07 S 160 12 E
   Makambo Island 9 06 S 160 10 E
Guadalcanal Island   114C
   Aola Bay 9 31 S 160 30 E
`G A`

   Tetere 9 25 S 160 14 E
   Koli Point 9 24 S 160 09 E
   Lungga 9 25 S 160 02 E
   Kokum Beach 9 25 S 160 01 E
   Honiara 9 25 S 159 58 E
`P Q Y G C R B T A L`

   Kokumbona Beach 9 25 S 159 55 E
Santa Isabel Island
   Allardyce Harbour 7 49 S 158 39 E
Russell Islands
   Mbanika Island
      Lingatu Cove 9 07 S 159 11 E
      Renard Sound 9 04 S 159 14 E
      Yandina 9 04 S 159 13 E
`G A`

New Georgia Islands
   New Georgia Island
      Noro 8 13 N 157 12 E
`P G C B A`

   Barora 8 01 S 157 35 E   114D
   Lever Harbour 8 02 S 157 35 E
   Seghe Point 8 36 S 157 53 E
   Viru Harbour 8 30 S 157 43 E
`G A`

   Munda Point 8 20 S 157 15 E
Rendova Island
   Rendova Harbour 8 25 S 157 19 E
   Kenelo 8 28 S 157 16 E
Gizo Island
   Gizo 8 05 S 156 52 E
`P G A`

Kolombangara Island
   Ringi Cove 8 07 S 157 07 E
Vella Lavella Island
   Malloco Bay 7 35 S 156 36 E
`G A`

Choiseul Island
   Choiseul Bay 6 42 S 156 25 E
Treasury Island
   Blanche Harbour 7 24 S 155 35 E

P Petroleum   Q Other Liquid Bulk   Y Dry Bulk   G General Cargo
C Containers   R Ro-Ro   B Bunkers   D Dry Dock   T Towage
A Airport (within 100km)   L Lloyd's Agent (not including sub-agents)

Shortland Island — 115A
  Shortland Harbour 7 07 S 155 51 E
  Lofung 7 04 S 155 52 E
Faisi Island 7 05 S 155 53 E

PAPUA NEW GUINEA

Bougainville Island
  Anewa Bay 6 12 S 155 33 E   [p.48/49]
  `P Q Y G C B T A`
  Kieta 6 13 S 155 38 E
  `G B T A`
  Tonolei 6 47 S 155 53 E
  Empress Augusta Bay 6 30 S 155 05 E
  Soraken 5 34 S 154 43 E
Buka Island
  Buka 5 26 S 154 40 E

BISMARCK ARCHIPELAGO — 115B

New Britain
  Timbuer 4 20 S 152 17 E
  Kokopo 4 20 S 152 15 E
  Rabaul 4 12 S 152 11 E
  `P G C B T A L`
  Cape Hoskins 5 25 S 150 30 E
  Kimbe Bay
    Kimbe 5 32 S 150 09 E
    `P Q G`
  Cape Gloucester 5 25 S 148 25 E
  Arawe Harbour 6 11 S 149 04 E
  Wasum 6 03 S 149 20 E
  Mowe Harbour 6 14 S 149 35 E
  Gasmata Island 6 20 S 150 20 E
  Linden Harbour 6 15 S 150 30 E
    Fulleborn 6 10 S 150 40 E
New Ireland
  Kavieng 2 34 S 150 48 E
  `G C B A`
  Nabuto Bay
    Namatanai 3 40 S 152 26 E
  Emirau Island 1 35 S 149 58 E
  Mussau Island
    Melle Channel 1 32 S 149 35 E
Admiralty Islands — 115C
  Los Negros Island
    Hyane Harbour 2 03 S 147 26 E
  Manus Island
    Kelaua Harbour 2 05 S 147 20 E
    Seeadler Harbour
      Lombrum 2 02 S 147 24 E
      Lorengau 2 00 S 147 15 E
      `P G B A`
    Rengau 2 00 S 147 16 E
    Nares Harbour 1 57 S 146 40 E
Mainland Papua New Guinea
  Vanimo 2 40 S 141 20 E
  Aitape 3 08 S 142 21 E
  Wewak 3 35 S 143 40 E
  `G C B A`
  Sarang 4 45 S 145 40 E
  Alexishafen 5 05 S 145 50 E
  Madang 5 15 S 145 50 E
  `P Y G C B A`
  Astrolabe Bay
    Konstantin Harbour 5 28 S 145 38 E
  Saidor 5 40 S 146 30 E
  Finschafen 6 33 S 147 53 E
  Langemak Bay 6 35 S 147 52 E
  Dreger Harbour 6 39 S 147 53 E
  Cape Cretin 6 40 S 147 50 E
  Lae 6 44 S 146 59 E — 115D
  `P Q G C B T A L`
  Salamaua 7 00 S 147 05 E
  Morobe 7 45 S 147 35 E
  Buna 8 40 S 148 25 E
  Cape Sudest 8 45 S 148 28 E
Oro Bay 8 50 S 148 30 E
  `G A`
  Port Harvey 8 54 S 148 36 E
  Porlock Harbour 9 02 S 149 04 E
  Goodenough Island
    Cape Varieta 9 24 S 150 08 E
    Beli Beli 9 22 S 150 22 E

Kiriwina Island — 116A
  Muiao 8 30 S 151 08 E
Woodlark Island 9 20 S 152 48 E
Misima Island
  Maika Harbour 10 42 S 152 48 E
Tagula Island
  Cape Siri 11 37 S 153 47 E
Milne Bay
  Ahioma 10 20 S 150 31 E
  Alotau 10 19 S 150 27 E
  `G A`
  Gili Gili 10 19 S 150 23 E
  Gamadodo 10 24 S 150 24 E
  Vatavaila 10 25 S 150 25 E
Samarai Island
  Samarai 10 37 S 150 40 E
  Marshall Lagoon 10 06 S 148 05 E
  Port Moresby 9 26 S 147 06 E
  `P G C R B T A L`
  Kumul Terminal 8 06 S 144 33 E
  Fly River
    Kiunga 6 07 S 141 17 E
  Umuda Terminal 8 28 S 143 52 E
  Daru 9 04 S 143 12 E

AUSTRALIA — 116B

QUEENSLAND

Torres Strait   [p.46/47]
  Thursday Island 10 35 S 142 13 E
  `P Q G B A`
  Good's Island 10 34 S 142 09 E
Cape York 10 41 S 142 32 E
Weipa 12 40 S 141 55 E
  `Y G B T A`
  Archer River 13 55 S 142 00 E
  Nassau River 15 55 S 141 35 E
  Karumba 17 28 S 140 51 E
  Normanton 17 37 S 141 10 E
  Mornington Island
    Timber Point 16 45 S 139 15 E

NORTHERN TERRITORY — 116C

Groote Eylandt
  Milner Bay 13 52 S 136 25 E
  `P Y G R B T A`
Gove 12 12 S 136 40 E
  `P Q Y G C T A`
Cape Wessel 11 00 S 136 45 E
Cape Van Diemen 11 10 S 130 23 E
Darwin 12 28 S 130 51 E
  `P Q Y G C R B D T A L`

WESTERN AUSTRALIA

Wyndham 15 27 S 128 06 E
  `G C B A`
Cape Londonderry 13 45 S 126 57 E
Cape Bougainville 13 54 S 126 05 E
Challis Terminal 12 07 S 125 01 E
  `P`
Jabiru Terminal 11 55 S 125 00 E
  `P`
Skua Terminal 12 30 S 124 25 E
  `P`
Yampi Sound 16 08 S 123 38 E
Derby 17 17 S 123 37 E
Broome 18 00 S 122 15 E
  `P Y G C B A`
Port Hedland 20 20 S 118 37 E
  `Y G B T A`
Balla Balla 20 38 S 117 47 E
Port Walcott 20 36 S 117 11 E
  `P Y G T A`
Cape Lambert 20 35 S 117 11 E
Talisman Terminal 19 40 S 116 56 E
Wandoo Terminal 20 08 S 116 28 E

Dampier 20 39 S 116 43 E — 117A
  `P Q Y G R B T A`
Varanus Island Terminal 20 38 S 115 36 E
  `P`
Barrow Island 20 40 S 115 27 E
  Barrow Island Terminal
  20 48 S 115 33 E
  `P`
Beadon 21 38 S 115 07 E
Airlie Island
  Airlie Island Terminal 21 19 S 115 10 E
Griffin Terminal 21 13 S 114 38 E
Saladin Terminal 21 24 S 115 03 E
  `P`
Exmouth Gulf
  Learmonth 22 13 S 114 05 E
  Exmouth 21 54 S 114 11 E
  Port Exmouth (Point Murat)
  21 49 S 114 11 E
North West Cape 21 47 S 114 10 E — 117B
Point Cloates 22 43 S 113 40 E
Maud Landing 23 03 S 113 46 E
Cape Cuvier 24 13 S 113 24 E
  `Y T A`
Carnarvon 24 53 S 113 40 E
Shark Bay
  Denham 25 54 S 113 32 E
  Useless Loop 26 05 S 113 25 E
  `Y A`
Geraldton 28 47 S 114 36 E
  `P Y G C B T A`
Point Moore 28 47 S 114 35 E
Dongarra 29 19 S 114 56 E
Perth 31 57 S 115 52 E
Fremantle 32 00 S 115 45 E
  `P Y G C R B T A L`
Rottnest Island 32 00 S 115 30 E
Kwinana 32 13 S 115 45 E
Bunbury 33 19 S 115 38 E
  `P Q Y G R B T A`
Busselton 33 38 S 115 20 E — 117C
Cape Naturaliste 33 32 S 115 01 E
Cape Leeuwin 34 22 S 115 08 E
D'Entrecasteaux Point 34 50 S 116 00 E
Albany 35 02 S 117 55 E
  `P Y G C R B T A`
Breaksea Island 35 07 S 118 01 E
Esperance 33 52 S 121 53 E
  `P Y G R B T A`

SOUTH AUSTRALIA

Thevenard 32 09 S 133 39 E
  `Y G B T A`
Ceduna 32 08 S 133 41 E
Elliston 33 39 S 134 53 E
Spencer Gulf
  Port Lincoln 34 45 S 135 53 E
  `P Y G R B T A`
  Tumby Bay 34 25 S 136 08 E — 117D
  Lipson Cove 34 16 S 136 16 E
  Whyalla 33 02 S 137 36 E
  `P Y G T A`
  Port Bonython 33 01 S 137 45 E
  `P Q T A`
  Port Augusta 32 30 S 137 47 E
  Port Germein 33 02 S 138 01 E
  Port Pirie 33 11 S 138 01 E
  `P Q Y G B T A`
  Port Broughton 33 34 S 137 53 E
  Wallaroo 33 56 S 137 37 E
  `Y G B T`
  Port Victoria 34 30 S 137 28 E
  Port Rickaby 34 40 S 137 29 E
  Cape Spencer 35 18 S 136 52 E
  Stenhouse Bay 35 17 S 136 56 E

GEOGRAPHIC INDEX

Symbol	Meaning	Symbol	Meaning
P	Petroleum	Q	Other Liquid Bulk
Y	Dry Bulk	G	General Cargo
C	Containers	R	Ro-Ro
B	Bunkers	D	Dry Dock
T	Towage	A	Airport (within 100km)
L	Lloyd's Agent (not including sub-agents)		

AUSTRALIA *continued*   118A

SOUTH AUSTRALIA

Kangaroo Island
    Cape Borda 35 45 S 136 35 E
    Nepean Bay
        Kingscote 35 39 S 137 37 E
    Ballast Head 35 46 S 137 48 E
    Cape Willoughby 35 51 S 138 08 E
Gulf of St. Vincent
    Edithburgh 35 05 S 137 45 E
    Port Giles 35 02 S 137 45 E

`Y G T A`

Port Vincent 34 57 S 137 52 E
Port Alfred 34 37 S 137 54 E
Ardrossan 34 26 S 137 55 E

`Y T`

Port Wakefield 34 11 S 138 09 E
Adelaide (Port Adelaide) 34 47 S 138 30 E

`P Q Y G C R B T A L`

Glenelg 34 59 S 138 31 E   **118B**
Port Stanvac 35 07 S 138 28 E

`P B A`

Rapid Bay 35 31 S 138 11 E
Cape Jervis 35 36 S 138 06 E
Port Elliot 35 34 S 138 40 E
Port Caroline 36 50 S 139 50 E
Kingston 36 50 S 139 51 E
Cape Jaffa 36 58 S 139 39 E
Robe 37 10 S 139 45 E
Beachport 37 30 S 140 01 E
Cape Northumberland 38 04 S 140 40 E

VICTORIA

Cape Nelson 38 26 S 141 32 E
Portland 38 20 S 141 36 E

`P Q Y G C B T A`

Port Fairy 38 23 S 142 14 E
Warrnambool 38 24 S 142 29 E
Cape Otway 38 51 S 143 31 E

TASMANIA   118C

King Island 39 50 S 144 00 E
    Grassy 40 04 S 144 09 E
River Tamar
    Inspection Head 41 09 S 146 49 E
    Beauty Point 41 10 S 146 49 E
    Bell Bay 41 08 S 146 52 E
    Launceston 41 26 S 147 08 E

`P Y G C R B D T A L`

Devonport 41 11 S 146 22 E

`P Q Y G C R B T A`

Ulverstone 41 14 S 146 10 E
Burnie 41 03 S 145 55 E

`P Q Y G C R B T A`

Port Latta 40 51 S 145 23 E

`Q Y T A`

Stanley 40 46 S 145 18 E
Macquarie Harbour
    Strahan 42 10 S 145 20 E
Huon River
    Port Huon 43 10 S 147 00 E
Electrona 43 05 S 147 17 E
River Derwent   **118D**
    Hobart 42 52 S 147 20 E

`P Q Y G C R B T A L`

Risdon 42 49 S 147 19 E
Spring Bay 42 33 S 147 56 E
Eddystone Point 41 00 S 148 21 E
Flinders Island 40 00 S 148 00 E

VICTORIA

Port Phillip Bay
    Port Phillip 38 18 S 144 38 E
    Queenscliff 38 16 S 144 40 E
    Geelong 38 07 S 144 23 E

`P Q Y G C R B T A L`

Point Wilson 38 06 S 144 30 E   **119A**
Williamstown 37 52 S 144 55 E
Yarraville 37 49 S 144 54 E
Melbourne 37 50 S 144 55 E

`P Q Y G C R B D T A L`

Portsea 38 19 S 144 43 E
Hastings (Westernport) 38 20 S 145 15 E

`P Q G R T A`

Wilson's Promontory 39 08 S 146 22 E
Barry Beach 38 43 S 146 23 E
Port Welshpool 38 42 S 146 27 E
Gippsland Lakes 37 53 S 147 58 E

NEW SOUTH WALES

Twofold Bay
    Eden 37 04 S 149 55 E

`P Y G C B T A`

Jervis Bay 35 06 S 150 47 E
Port Kembla 34 28 S 150 54 E

`Q Y G R B T A`

Bulli 34 20 S 150 55 E   **119B**
Botany Bay 34 00 S 151 14 E

`P Q G C R B T A`

    Port Botany 33 58 S 151 13 E
    Kurnell 34 00 S 151 14 E
Port Jackson 33 50 S 151 17 E
Sydney 33 50 S 151 15 E

`P Q Y G C R B D T A L`

Catherine Hill Bay 33 10 S 151 38 E

`Y A`

Newcastle 32 56 S 151 47 E

`P Q Y G C R D T A`

Lord Howe Island 31 32 S 159 05 E
Port Stephens 32 42 S 152 12 E
Port Macquarie 31 25 S 152 55 E
Trial Bay
    South West Rocks 30 53 S 153 02 E
Coffs Harbour 30 18 S 153 09 E
Clarence River   **119C**

`G B D T A`

    Yamba 29 26 S 153 21 E
    Grafton 29 42 S 152 57 E
    Ballina 28 52 S 153 37 E

QUEENSLAND

Brisbane 27 19 S 153 10 E

`P Q Y G C R B T A L`

Pumice Stone Strait 26 49 S 153 10 E
Cape Moreton 27 02 S 153 28 E
Caloundra Head 26 48 S 153 09 E
Maryborough 25 25 S 152 45 E
Urangan 25 17 S 152 55 E
Bundaberg 24 46 S 152 23 E

`P Q Y B T A`

Gladstone 23 50 S 151 15 E

`P Q Y G B T A`

Port Alma 23 35 S 150 52 E

`P Q Y G C B A`

Rockhampton 23 24 S 150 33 E
Hay Point 21 16 S 149 18 E

`Y T A`

Flat Top Island 21 10 S 149 13 E   **119D**
Mackay 21 06 S 149 13 E

`P Q Y G C B T A L`

Hayman Island 20 04 S 148 52 E
Port Denison
    Bowen 20 01 S 148 15 E
Abbot Point 19 51 S 148 04 E

`Y T`

Townsville 19 15 S 146 50 E

`P Q Y G C R B T A L`

Great Palm Island
    Challenger Bay 18 44 S 146 34 E

Lucinda 18 31 S 146 20 E   **120A**

`Y A`

Mourilyan 17 36 S 146 07 E

`Y T`

Innisfail 17 31 S 146 05 E
Cairns 16 56 S 145 47 E

`P Q Y G C B D T A`

Archer Point 15 36 S 145 20 E
Cooktown 15 28 S 145 10 E
Cape Flattery 14 58 S 145 22 E

`Y`

NEW ZEALAND

NORTH ISLAND

North Cape 35 24 S 173 03 E
Kaipara 36 25 S 174 04 E
Onehunga 36 56 S 174 46 E

`G C B T A`

Raglan 37 46 S 174 54 E
Taharoa Terminal 38 10 S 174 40 E   **120B**

`Y`

Waitara 39 00 S 174 14 E
Port Taranaki
    New Plymouth 39 04 S 174 05 E

`P Q Y G C B T A`

Patea 39 47 S 174 29 E
Waverley Terminal 39 51 S 174 35 E
Wanganui 39 57 S 175 00 E

`Y G C B T A`

Port Nicholson 41 19 S 174 51 E
Wellington 41 17 S 174 46 E

`P Q Y G C R B T A L`

Hawke Bay
    Napier 39 29 S 176 55 E

`P Q Y G C R B T A`

Gisborne 38 41 S 178 02 E   **120C**

`P Y G B T A`

Tokomaru 38 06 S 178 21 E
East Cape 37 41 S 178 33 E
Whakatane 37 57 S 177 00 E
Tauranga Harbour
    Mount Maunganui 37 41 S 176 14 E
    Tauranga 37 39 S 176 10 E

`P Q Y G C R B T A`

Thames 37 08 S 175 32 E
Auckland 36 51 S 174 48 E

`P Y G C R B D T A L`

Whangarei Harbour
    Marsden Point 35 50 S 174 31 E
    Portland 35 48 S 174 20 E
    Whangarei 35 44 S 174 21 E

`P Y G C B T A`

Cape Brett 35 10 S 174 19 E
Port Russell 35 15 S 174 07 E
Opua 35 18 S 174 08 E

`G B T A`

Whangaroa 35 03 S 173 48 E

SOUTH ISLAND   120D

Wairau 41 30 S 174 03 E
Picton 41 16 S 174 00 E

`Y G C R B A`

Nelson 41 16 S 173 19 E

`P G C R B T A`

Tarakohe 40 51 S 172 54 E

`B A`

Cape Farewell 40 30 S 172 41 E
Westport 41 44 S 171 35 E

`Y G B T A`

Greymouth 42 26 S 171 13 E

`Y G C R B A`

GEOGRAPHIC INDEX

121A

Hokitika 42 43 S 170 58 E
Doubtful Sound
    Deep Cove 45 17 S 166 51 E
Cape Providence 46 01 S 166 29 E
Invercargill 46 26 S 168 21 E
Bluff Harbour
    Bluff 46 37 S 168 22 E
`[P][Q][Y][G][C][R][B][T][A][L][ ][ ]`
    Tiwai Point 46 36 S 168 23 E
Stewart Island
    Oban 46 54 S 168 08 E
Otago Harbour
`[P][Q][Y][G][C][R][B][T][A][L][ ][ ]`
    Ravensbourne 45 52 S 170 32 E
    Dunedin 45 53 S 170 31 E
    Port Chalmers 45 49 S 170 37 E
Oamaru 45 07 S 170 59 E
Timaru 44 23 S 171 15 E
`[P][Q][Y][G][C][R][B][T][A][ ][ ][ ]`
Akaroa 43 51 S 172 56 E
Lyttelton 43 37 S 172 43 E

121B

`[P][Q][Y][G][C][R][B][D][T][A][L][ ]`
Macquarie Island (**Australian**)   `p.12/13`
54 35 S 158 58 E
Campbell Island 50 32 S 166 14 E
Auckland Islands 50 31 S 166 08 E
Antipodes Islands 49 30 S 178 50 E
Bounty Islands 47 42 S 179 03 E   `p.46/47`
Chatham Islands 44 00 S 176 30 W
Kermadec Islands 29 17 S 177 53 W
Norfolk Island (**Australian**)
`[P][Q][Y][G][A][L][ ][ ][ ][ ][ ][ ]`
    Cascade Bay 29 01 S 167 59 E

PACIFIC ISLANDS

NEW CALEDONIA (French)   **121C**

Noumea 22 17 S 166 26 E
`[P][Q][Y][G][C][B][T][A][L][ ][ ][ ]`
Ducos 22 15 S 166 25 E
Ouinne 22 17 S 166 30 E
Boulari 22 17 S 166 32 E
Ngoe 22 20 S 166 42 E
Prony 22 22 S 166 52 E
Port Boise 22 21 S 166 58 E
Goro 22 20 S 167 02 E
Ounia 22 02 S 166 51 E
Thio 21 37 S 166 15 E
`[P][Y][ ][ ][ ][ ][ ][ ][ ][ ][ ][ ]`
Nakety (Nekete) 21 30 S 166 05 E
Canala 21 29 S 165 59 E
Kouaoua 21 23 S 165 50 E
`[Y][ ][ ][ ][ ][ ][ ][ ][ ][ ][ ][ ]`
Houailou 21 18 S 165 44 E
Poro 21 18 S 165 43 E
`[P][Y][ ][ ][ ][ ][ ][ ][ ][ ][ ][ ]`
Baie Ugue 21 09 S 165 33 E
`[Y][ ][ ][ ][ ][ ][ ][ ][ ][ ][ ][ ]`
Baie de Pam 20 14 S 164 18 E
Poume 20 15 S 163 53 E
Nehoue 20 20 S 164 07 E
Babouillat 20 23 S 164 08 E
Paagoumene 20 30 S 164 11 E
Tangadiou 20 30 S 164 15 E
Karembe 20 38 S 164 19 E
Teoudie 20 44 S 164 25 E   **121D**
Gomen 20 44 S 164 23 E
Gatope 20 58 S 164 38 E
Vouavoutou 20 58 S 164 39 E
Pouembout 21 09 S 164 53 E
Moueo 21 24 S 164 56 E
Poya 21 23 S 165 05 E
Bourail 21 37 S 165 26 E
Tomo 21 57 S 166 10 E
Tontouta 22 00 S 166 10 E
Paita 22 11 S 166 18 E

VANUATU

Aneityum Island
    Port Aneityum 20 15 S 169 45 E

122A

Tanna Island
    Lenakel 19 33 S 169 15 E
Erromango Island
    Port Narevin 18 45 S 169 12 E
Efate Island
    Port Vila 17 45 S 168 18 E
`[P][Q][G][C][R][B][T][A][L][ ][ ][ ]`
    Havannah Harbour 17 35 S 168 14 E
    Undine Bay 17 30 S 168 20 E
    Metensa Bay
        Forari 17 41 S 168 33 E
Malakula Island
    Port Sandwich 16 25 S 167 48 E
Espiritu Santo Island
    Luganville Bay 15 31 S 167 09 E
    Santo 15 31 S 167 10 E
`[P][Q][Y][G][C][R][B][A][ ][ ][ ][ ]`
    Palikulo Bay 15 29 S 167 14 E

FIJI   **122B**

Viti Levu Island
    Suva 18 08 S 178 25 E
`[P][Q][Y][G][C][R][B][T][A][L][ ][ ]`
    Navua 18 16 S 178 12 E
    Navuloa 17 53 S 177 16 E
    Nandi (Nadi) Waters 17 41 S 177 15 E
    Vuda Point Terminal 17 41 S 177 23 E
    Lautoka 17 36 S 177 26 E
`[P][Q][Y][G][C][R][B][T][A][ ][ ][ ]`
    Vatia 17 24 S 177 46 E
    Ellington 17 20 S 178 13 E
Ovalau Island
    Levuka 17 41 S 178 51 E
`[G][B][T][ ][ ][ ][ ][ ][ ][ ][ ][ ]`
Vanua Levu Island
    Savusavu Bay
        Savusavu 16 46 S 179 20 E
`[P][G][T][A][ ][ ][ ][ ][ ][ ][ ][ ]`
    Nandi Bay 16 58 S 178 46 E   **122C**
    Labasa 16 26 S 179 23 E
`[P][Q][Y][G][A][ ][ ][ ][ ][ ][ ][ ]`
    Malau 16 21 S 179 22 E
Rotuma Island 12 30 S 177 05 E

WALLIS and FUTUNA ISLANDS (French)

Uvea Island
    Mua 13 21 S 176 10 W
    Port Halalo 13 20 S 176 11 W
    Matu Uta 13 17 S 176 08 W

TONGA

Tongatapu Island   `p.48/49`
    Nukualofa 21 08 S 175 11 W
`[P][Q][G][B][A][L][ ][ ][ ][ ][ ][ ]`
Nomuka Island 20 15 S 174 45 W
Lifuka Island
    Pangai 19 48 S 174 21 W
`[G][A][ ][ ][ ][ ][ ][ ][ ][ ][ ][ ]`
Vavau Island
    Neiafu 18 39 S 173 59 W
`[G][A][ ][ ][ ][ ][ ][ ][ ][ ][ ][ ]`
Niuafoo Island 15 36 S 175 38 W
Niuatoputapu Island 15 58 S 173 46 W

WESTERN SAMOA   **122D**

Savaii Island
    Asau 13 30 S 172 38 W
Upolu Island
    Apia 13 49 S 171 46 W
`[P][Y][G][C][R][T][A][L][ ][ ][ ][ ]`

AMERICAN SAMOA (American)

Tutuila Island
    Pago Pago 14 17 S 170 40 W
`[P][G][C][R][B][T][A][L][ ][ ][ ][ ]`
Tau Island 14 15 S 169 27 W

NIUE (New Zealand)   **123A**

Niue
    Alofi 19 03 S 169 55 W

COOK ISLANDS (New Zealand)

Aitutaki Island
    Arutunga 18 52 S 159 48 W
Rarotonga Island
    Avarua 21 12 S 159 46 W
    Avatiu 21 12 S 159 47 W
`[P][Q][G][C][B][R][T][A][L][ ][ ][ ]`

FRENCH POLYNESIA (French)

Society Islands
    Bora Bora
`[G][A][ ][ ][ ][ ][ ][ ][ ][ ][ ][ ]`
        Vaitape 16 30 S 151 45 W   **123B**
    Raiatea Island
        Uturoa 16 44 S 151 26 W
    Tahiti Island
        Papeete 17 32 S 149 35 W
`[P][Q][G][C][B][D][T][A][L][ ][ ][ ]`
Australes (Tubuai) Islands
    Tubuai Island
        Mataura 23 22 S 149 28 W
    Raivavae Island
        Rairua 23 52 S 147 41 W
    Rapa Island
        Ahurei 27 37 S 144 20 W
Tuamotu Archipelago
    Mangareva Island
        Rikitea 23 07 S 134 58 W
    Mururoa 21 50 S 138 55 W
    Hao Island 18 15 S 140 55 W
    Makatea 15 51 S 148 15 W
    Manihi 14 28 S 146 04 W
    Takaroa 14 29 S 145 03 W
Marquesas Islands   **123C**
    Nuku-Hiva Island
        Taiohae 8 56 S 140 06 W

PITCAIRN ISLANDS (British)

Oeno Island 23 56 S 130 44 W
Pitcairn Island 25 04 S 130 06 W
Henderson Island 24 22 S 128 19 W
Ducie Island 24 40 S 124 48 W

TOKELAU ISLANDS (New Zealand)

Atafu Island 8 32 S 172 31 W

TUVALU

Funafuti Island
    Funafuti 8 31 S 179 12 E
`[G][B][A][ ][ ][ ][ ][ ][ ][ ][ ][ ]`
Nukufetau Atoll 8 00 S 178 20 E
Nanumea Island 5 40 S 176 07 E

NAURU

Nauru Island 0 31 S 166 56 E
`[P][Y][G][C][A][L][ ][ ][ ][ ][ ][ ]`

KIRIBATI   **123D**

Banaba (Ocean Island) 0 53 S 169 32 E
Gilbert Islands
    Little Makin Island 3 20 N 172 58 E
    Butaritari Island 3 04 N 172 47 E
    Abaiang Island 1 49 N 173 01 E
    Tarawa Atoll
        Betio 1 21 N 172 55 E
`[P][G][C][B][T][A][ ][ ][ ][ ][ ][ ]`
    Abemama Island 0 24 N 173 56 E
    Nonouti Island 0 40 S 174 28 E
    Beru Island 1 21 S 175 59 E
Phoenix Islands
    Canton (Kanton) Island 2 47 S 171 40 W
    Enderbury Island 3 08 S 171 06 W
    Gardner Island (Nikumaroro Atoll)
    4 40 S 174 32 W

P Petroleum	Q Other Liquid Bulk	Y Dry Bulk	G General Cargo
C Containers	R Ro-Ro	B Bunkers	D Dry Dock	T Towage
A Airport (within 100km)	L Lloyd's Agent (not including sub-agents)		

Column 1 — 127A, 127B, 127C, 127D

Murmansk 68 58 N 33 05 E — **127A**

P	Y	G	C	R	B	D	T				

Rosta 69 00 N 33 05 E
Kola 68 53 N 33 02 E
Saida Bay 69 15 N 33 15 E
Polyarnyy 69 13 N 33 26 E
Port Vladimir 69 25 N 33 09 E
Trifona 69 36 N 31 16 E
Pechenga 69 33 N 31 10 E
Linakhamari 69 39 N 31 22 E

NORWAY

Svalbard
  Bear Island (Bjornoya) — p.14
    Austervag 74 30 N 19 12 E
  Barents Island
    Cape Bessels 78 35 N 21 50 E
  Spitsbergen
    Sveagruva 77 50 N 16 51 E
    Braganza Bay 77 55 N 16 59 E — **127B**
    Gronfjord
      Barentsburg 78 05 N 14 13 E
    Coles Bay
      Grumantbyen 78 10 N 15 10 E
    Advent Bay
      Longyearbyen 78 15 N 15 35 E
    Templefjord 78 23 N 16 50 E
    Kongsfjord
      Ny Aalesund 78 55 N 11 56 E
    Magdalenefjord 79 34 N 11 00 E
    Smeerenburgfjord 79 44 N 11 01 E
Jan Mayen Island
  Cape Fishburn 71 00 N 8 10 W

GREENLAND (Danish)

Danmarkshavn 76 46 N 18 45 W
Daneborg 74 18 N 20 15 W
Zackenberg 74 28 N 20 38 W
Ella Island 72 52 N 24 55 W
Mesters Vig 72 09 N 23 45 W
Ittoqqortoormiit (Scoresby Sound) — **127C**
  Uunarteq (Kap Tobin) 7030 N 21 50 W
  Cape Brewster 70 09 N 22 03 W
Aputiteq 67 48 N 32 13 W
Kuummiut 65 52 N 37 00 W
Kulusuk 65 32 N 37 15 W
Ammassalik Island
  Ammassalik 65 35 N 37 30 W

G	B	A							

Ikkatseq 65 38 N 37 57 W
Umivik 64 15 N 40 50 W
Skjoldungen 63 14 N 41 27 W
Qutdleq 62 31 N 42 13 W
Tingmiarmiut Fjord 62 30 N 42 12 W
Ikerasassuaq (Prins Christians Sound)
  Natsek Cove 60 03 N 43 07 W
Cape Farewell 59 46 N 43 54 W
Narsaq Kujalleq (Frederiksdal)
60 00 N 44 40 W
Nanortalik 60 08 N 45 15 W

P	G	C	B	A					

Alluitsup Paa (Sydproven)
60 28 N 45 34 W
Qaqortoq (Julianehaab) 60 43 N 46 02 W

G	C	B	A						

Narsarsuaq 61 09 N 45 26 W

P	G	A							

Narsaq 60 54 N 45 59 W — **127D**

P	G	C	B	A					

Ivittuut 61 12 N 48 10 W
Kangilinnguit (Gronnedal)
61 12 N 48 06 W

G	B	A							

Paamiut (Frederikshaab) 62 00 N 49 40 W

P	G	C	B	A					

Fiskenaesset 63 05 N 50 41 W
Kangerluarsoruseq (Faeringehavn)
63 42 N 51 33 W

P	G	B	A						

Nuuk (Godthaab) 64 10 N 51 44 W

P	Q	G	C	A					

Column 2 — 128A, 128B, 128C, 128D

Tovqussaq 64 52 N 52 12 W — **128A**
Maniitsoq (Sukkertoppen)
65 25 N 52 54 W

G	C	B	A						

Kangaamiut 65 49 N 53 18 W
Sondre Stromfjord
  Kangerlussuaq 66 58 N 50 57 W

P	G	B	A						

Sisimiut (Holsteinsborg) 66 57 N 53 41 W

P	Y	G	C	B	A				

Nordre Stromfjord 67 45 N 52 20 W
Aasiaat (Egedesminde) 68 43 N 52 53 W

G	C	B	A						

Qasigiannguit (Christianshaab)
68 49 N 51 11 W

P	G	C	A						

Ilulissat (Jakobshavn) 69 13 N 51 06 W — **128B**

G	C	B	A						

Disko Island
  Qeqertarsuaq (Godhavn)
  69 15 N 53 33 W

G	B	A							

  Qutdligssat 70 04 N 52 50 W
Uummannaq (Umanak) 70 41 N 52 08 W

G	A								

Marmorilik 71 08 N 51 17 W
Upernavik 72 47 N 56 09 W

P	G	A							

Savissivik 76 02 N 64 51 W
North Star Bay 76 33 N 68 52 W
Uummannaq (Dundas) 76 33 N 68 49 W
Qaanaaq (Thule) 77 28 N 69 13 W

G	A								

Siorapaluk 77 47 N 70 42 W

CANADA — **128C**

QUEBEC

Ungava Bay — p.50/51
  Port Burwell 60 25 N 64 51 W
  Port Nouveau Quebec 58 41 N 65 56 W
  Fort Chimo 58 09 N 68 18 W
Hudson Strait
  Diana Bay 60 55 N 70 00 W
  Douglas Harbour 61 55 N 72 37 W
  Deception Bay 62 14 N 74 45 W
Hudson Bay
  Great Whale River 55 18 N 77 45 W

ONTARIO

James Bay
  Moosonee 51 16 N 80 39 W
Winisk 55 17 N 85 14 W

MANITOBA

York Factory 57 00 N 92 16 W
Port Nelson 57 00 N 92 56 W
Churchill 58 47 N 94 13 W

P	Y	G	B	T	A				

NORTH WEST TERRITORIES — **128D**

Rankin Inlet 62 49 N 92 05 W
Chesterfield Anchorage
63 20 N 90 41 W
Chesterfield Inlet
  Baker Lake 64 18 N 96 06 W
Roes Welcome Sound
  Cape Fullerton 63 59 N 88 44 W
Southampton Island
  Coral Harbour 64 07 N 83 05 W
  Seahorse Point 63 47 N 80 09 W
Foxe Basin
  Prince Charles Island 67 12 N 76 41 W
Baffin Island
  Cape Dorset 64 10 N 76 29 W
  Resolution Island 61 30 N 65 00 W
  Frobisher 63 45 N 68 32 W

Column 3 — 129A, 129B, 129C, 129D

Cumberland Sound — **129A**
  Pangnirtung 66 13 N 65 45 W
Cape Mercy 64 53 N 63 32 W
Padloping Island 67 00 N 62 50 W
Admiralty Inlet — p.14
  Strathcona Sound
    Nanisivik 73 04 N 84 33 W

Y	G	A							

Devon Island 75 00 N 85 00 W
Cornwallis Island
  Resolute 74 41 N 94 52 W
Little Cornwallis Island 75 23 N 96 57 W
Bathurst Island 76 00 N 100 00 W
Melville Island
  Winter Harbour 74 47 N 110 48 W
Wise Bay 70 06 N 124 45 W — p.50/51
McKinley Bay 69 57 N 131 27 W
Tuktoyaktuk 69 26 N 133 03 W

P	G	C	B	D	T	A			

U.S.A. — **129B**

ALASKA (AK)

Prudhoe Bay 70 20 N 148 20 W
Point Barrow 71 17 N 156 40 W
Cape Lisburne 68 52 N 166 09 W
Kivalina 67 45 N 164 40 W
Nome 64 31 N 165 25 W

P	Y	G	C	B	T	A			

St. Lawrence Island 63 00 N 169 30 W
Bethel 60 48 N 161 30 W
Bristol Bay
  Togiak 59 05 N 160 30 W
  Clarks Point 58 50 N 158 33 W
  Naknek 58 44 N 157 02 W
  Port Heiden 56 57 N 158 50 W
Amak Island
  Amak Bight 55 25 N 163 00 W
Aleutian Islands
  Unimak Island — p.14
    Cape Lazaref 54 37 N 163 36 W
    West Anchor Cove 54 41 N 163 09 W
  Akun Island
    Lost Harbour 54 13 N 165 39 W
  Akutan Island
    Akutan 54 08 N 165 45 W
  Unalaska Island — **129C**
    Iliuliuk Harbour 53 53 N 166 32 W
    Dutch Harbour 53 54 N 166 32 W

P	G	C	R	B	T	A			

    Anderson Bay 53 41 N 166 51 W
    Chernofski Harbour 53 24 N 167 31 W
  Umnak Island
    Cape Tanak 53 35 N 168 00 W
  Atka Island
    Nazan Bay 52 09 N 174 07 W
    Atka 52 12 N 174 12 W
  Great Sitkin Island
    Sand Bay 51 59 N 176 06 W
    Yoke Bay 52 01 N 176 02 W
  Adak Island
    Adak 51 51 N 176 39 W
    Kuluk Bay 51 52 N 176 35 W
    Chapel Roads 51 37 N 176 48 W
    Shagak Bay 51 52 N 176 45 W
  Tanaga Island
    Tanaga Bay 51 45 N 178 05 W
  Amchitka Island — **129D**
    Constantine Harbour
    51 24 N 179 16 E
  Kiska Island
    Kiska Harbour 51 59 N 177 34 E
    Gertrude Cove 51 56 N 177 27 E
  Shemya Island 52 43 N 174 06 E
  Attu Island
    Massacre Bay 52 49 N 173 18 E
    Chichagof Harbour 52 56 N 173 15 E
Cold Bay — p.50/51
  Lenard Harbour 55 07 N 162 31 W
Balboa Bay 55 35 N 160 35 W
Chignik 56 18 N 158 24 W
Puale Bay 57 44 N 155 32 W
Kodiak Island
  Kodiak 57 47 N 152 24 W

P	G	C	R	B	T	A			

  Womens Bay
    St. Paul Harbour 57 44 N 152 26 W

GEOGRAPHIC INDEX

Column 1 — 130A

U.S.A. *continued*

ALASKA (AK)

Afognak Island
  Afognak 58 00 N 152 50 W
Cook Inlet
  Drift River Terminal 60 33 N 152 08 W
  West Foreland 60 43 N 151 44 W
  Tyonek 61 04 N 151 09 W
  Susitna 61 28 N 150 30 W
  Anchorage 61 13 N 149 53 W

`P Y G C R B T A L`

Nikishka 60 44 N 151 18 W
East Foreland 60 43 N 151 25 W
Nikiski 60 41 N 151 23 W
Kenai 60 33 N 151 16 W

`P Q Y G B A`

Homer 59 38 N 151 30 W

`G B T A`

Jakolof Bay 59 27 N 151 40 W
Seldovia 59 26 N 151 43 W
Seward 60 07 N 149 26 W

130B

`P Y G C B T A`

Prince William Sound
  Whittier 60 47 N 148 40 W

`P G R B T`

Valdez 61 08 N 146 21 W

`P Y G C R B T A`

Orca 60 35 N 145 43 W
Cordova 60 33 N 145 46 W

`G C R B A`

Yakutat 59 33 N 139 45 W
Cape Spencer 58 13 N 136 40 W
Glacier Bay 58 30 N 136 00 W
Pleasant Island 58 23 N 135 45 W
Excursion Inlet 58 26 N 135 28 W
Haines 59 14 N 135 27 W

`P Y G R T A`

Skagway 59 27 N 135 19 W

130C

`P Y G C R B T A`

Juneau 58 18 N 134 25 W

`G R A`

Admiralty Island
  Hawk Inlet 58 06 N 134 44 W
  Tyee 57 03 N 134 33 W
Chichagof Island
  Hoonah 58 07 N 135 26 W
  Chichagof 57 40 N 136 06 W
  Chatham 57 31 N 134 57 W
Baranof Island
  Sitka 57 03 N 135 20 W

`P Q Y G C B A`

Silver Bay 57 02 N 135 14 W
Port Conclusion 56 16 N 134 39 W
Kupreanof Island
  Kake 56 55 N 133 52 W
  Castle Island 56 39 N 133 10 W

`Y A`

Mitkof Island
  Petersburg 56 49 N 132 57 W
Wrangell Island

130D

  Wrangell 56 28 N 132 22 W

`G T A`

Prince of Wales Island
  Kasaan 55 32 N 132 24 W
  Klawock 55 33 N 133 06 W

`G B T A`

Craig 55 28 N 133 09 W
Hydaburg 55 12 N 132 49 W
Dall Island
  Waterfall Bay 55 16 N 133 16 W
Ward Cove 55 25 N 131 44 W
Ketchikan 55 21 N 131 39 W

`G C R D T A`

Column 2 — 131A

Annette Island
  Metlakatla 55 08 N 131 34 W

`Y G R T A`

CANADA

BRITISH COLUMBIA

Stewart 55 55 N 130 00 W

`Y G B A`

Anyox 55 25 N 129 48 W
Port Simpson 54 35 N 130 28 W
Prince Rupert 54 19 N 130 22 W

`P Q Y G R B T A`

Porpoise Harbour
  Watson Island 54 14 N 130 17 W
  Port Edward 54 14 N 130 18 W
Queen Charlotte Islands
  Harriet Harbour
    Jedway 52 18 N 131 13 W
  Tasu Bay 52 46 N 132 03 W
Kitimat 54 00 N 128 42 W

131B

`Q Y G C R B T A`

Ocean Falls 52 21 N 127 42 W
Bella Coola 52 23 N 126 46 W

`P G B A`

Vancouver Island
  Port Hardy 50 43 N 127 29 W

`P G B A`

Quatsino Sound
  Rupert Inlet 50 33 N 127 34 W
  Port Alice 50 23 N 127 27 W

`P Y G B T A`

Zeballos 49 59 N 126 51 W
Nootka 49 35 N 126 37 W
Tahsis 49 55 N 126 40 W
Gold River 49 41 N 126 07 W

131C

`G B T`

Estevan Point 49 23 N 126 32 W
Ucluelet 48 56 N 125 32 W
Toquart Bay
  Lake Kennedy 49 02 N 125 20 W
Port Alberni 49 14 N 125 00 W

`G B T A`

William Head 48 20 N 123 32 W
Esquimalt 48 26 N 123 26 W

`G B D T A`

Victoria 48 25 N 123 23 W

`G C B T A`

James Island 48 36 N 123 21 W
Sidney 48 39 N 123 24 W
Senanus Island 48 35 N 123 29 W
Bamberton 48 35 N 123 31 W
Plumper Sound 48 46 N 123 12 W
Hatch Point 48 41 N 123 32 W
Cowichan Bay 48 45 N 123 36 W

`G B T`

Crofton 48 52 N 123 38 W

`G T A`

Chemainus 48 55 N 123 42 W

131D

`G B T A`

Ladysmith 48 59 N 123 47 W

`G B T A`

Harmac 49 08 N 123 51 W
Duke Point 49 09 N 123 52 W
Nanaimo 49 10 N 123 56 W

`P G C R B T A`

Nanoose 49 15 N 124 09 W
Texada Island 49 42 N 124 33 W
Union Bay 49 35 N 124 52 W

`G A`

Comox 49 40 N 124 55 W

`P B A`

Campbell River 50 02 N 125 14 W

[p.52]

Column 3 — 132A

Duncan Bay 50 05 N 125 17 W

`P Q Y G A`

Menzies Bay 50 07 N 125 22 W
Beaver Cove 50 32 N 126 51 W
Englewood 50 32 N 126 52 W
River Nimpkish 50 34 N 126 58 W
Port McNeill 50 36 N 127 05 W
Powell River 49 52 N 124 33 W

`P Q G B T A`

Westview 49 50 N 124 32 W
Port Mellon 49 31 N 123 29 W

`Y G T A`

Woodfibre 49 40 N 123 15 W

`G`

Squamish 49 43 N 123 07 W

`Q Y G B T A`

Britannia Beach 49 37 N 123 12 W
Dollarton 49 18 N 122 57 W
Ioco 49 18 N 122 53 W
Port Moody 49 17 N 122 51 W
Shellburn 49 17 N 122 56 W
Vancouver 49 17 N 123 07 W

`P Q Y G C R B D T A L`

132B

Fraser River
  New Westminster 49 12 N 122 55 W

`Q Y G C R B T A`

Fraser Mills 49 12 N 122 52 W
Port Mann 49 11 N 122 50 W
Ladner 49 05 N 123 05 W
Roberts Bank 49 01 N 123 08 W

U.S.A.

WASHINGTON (WA)

Blaine 49 00 N 122 50 W
Cherry Point 48 52 N 122 45 W
Ferndale 48 50 N 122 43 W

`P B T A`

Bellingham 48 45 N 122 30 W

`P G C R B T A`

Vendovi Island 48 37 N 122 37 W
San Juan Island
  Friday Harbour 48 32 N 123 00 W
March Point 48 30 N 122 34 W
Anacortes 48 31 N 122 37 W

`P Y G B D T A`

Holmes Harbour 48 05 N 122 34 W
Everett 47 59 N 122 13 W

132C

`Y G R B T A`

Mukilteo 47 57 N 122 18 W
Puget Sound
  Edmonds 47 49 N 122 22 W
  Point Wells 47 47 N 122 24 W
  Seattle 47 38 N 122 20 W

`P Y G C R B D T A L`

Tacoma 47 15 N 122 25 W

`P Q Y G C R B T A`

Olympia 47 03 N 122 54 W

`Y G C R B A`

132D

Manchester 47 33 N 122 32 W
Port Orchard 47 32 N 122 38 W
Bremerton 47 34 N 122 37 W
Port Blakely 47 36 N 122 31 W
Eagle Harbour 47 37 N 122 30 W
Winslow 47 37 N 122 31 W
Port Madison 47 42 N 122 34 W
Port Gamble 47 52 N 122 35 W
Bangor Wharf 47 45 N 122 43 W
Port Ludlow 47 55 N 122 41 W
Hadlock 48 02 N 122 45 W
Port Townsend 48 07 N 122 45 W

`P G B A`

Port Angeles 48 08 N 123 25 W

`G B T A`

Crescent Bay 48 10 N 123 43 W
Clallam Bay 48 16 N 124 16 W

Key: P Petroleum Q Other Liquid Bulk Y Dry Bulk G General Cargo
C Containers R Ro-Ro B Bunkers D Dry Dock T Towage
A Airport (within 100km) L Lloyd's Agent (not including sub-agents)

133A

Neah Bay 48 23 N 124 36 W
Cape Flattery 48 23 N 124 43 W
Tatoosh Island 48 23 N 124 44 W
Grays Harbour 46 56 N 123 51 W

| G | C | R | B | T | A | | | | |

Hoquiam 46 58 N 123 54 W
Aberdeen 46 58 N 123 51 W
Willapa River
South Bend 46 40 N 123 48 W
Raymond 46 41 N 123 44 W
Willapa Harbour 46 44 N 124 04 W
Cape Disappointment 46 17 N 124 03 W
Columbia River
Knappton 46 17 N 123 49 W
Longview 46 08 N 122 56 W

| Y | G | C | R | B | T | A | | | |

Kelso 46 09 N 122 55 W
Kalama 46 01 N 122 50 W

| Y | | | | | | | | | |

Vancouver 45 38 N 122 40 W

| P | Q | Y | G | C | R | B | T | A | |

OREGON (OR) **133B**

Willamette River
Portland 45 34 N 122 44 W

| P | Q | Y | G | C | R | B | D | T | A | L |

Willbridge 45 34 N 122 45 W
Linnton 45 36 N 122 47 W
St. Helens 45 52 N 122 48 W
Prescott 46 03 N 122 53 W
Rainier 46 05 N 122 56 W
Wesport Range 46 08 N 123 24 W
Wauna Range 46 09 N 123 25 W
Bradwood 46 12 N 123 27 W
Astoria 46 11 N 123 50 W

| Y | G | C | R | B | T | A | | | |

Warrenton 46 10 N 123 55 W
Yaquina Bay
Newport 44 38 N 124 03 W   [p.50/51]

| G | C | R | B | T | A | | | | |

Umpqua River
Gardiner 43 44 N 124 07 W
Reedsport 43 42 N 124 06 W
Coos River   **133C**
Empire 43 24 N 124 16 W
North Bend 43 24 N 124 13 W
Coos Bay 43 22 N 124 22 W

| P | Y | G | B | T | A | | | | |

Bandon 43 07 N 124 25 W
Cape Blanco 42 50 N 124 34 W
Port Orford 42 45 N 124 30 W
Brookings 42 02 N 124 17 W

CALIFORNIA (CA)

Crescent City 41 45 N 124 12 W
Humboldt Bay

| P | Y | G | B | T | A | | | | |

Fairhaven 40 47 N 124 12 W
Samoa 40 49 N 124 11 W
Eureka 40 48 N 124 10 W
Cape Mendocino 40 26 N 124 25 W   **133D**
Westport 39 38 N 123 47 W
Fort Bragg 39 26 N 123 49 W
Noyo 39 26 N 123 49 W
Bodega Harbour 38 20 N 123 03 W   [p.53]
Point Reyes 38 00 N 123 02 W
Golden Gate
Sausalito 37 52 N 122 31 W
San Pablo Bay
Mare Island 38 04 N 122 15 W
Vallejo 38 06 N 122 15 W
Benicia 38 02 N 122 09 W
Sacramento River
Sacramento 38 32 N 121 30 W

| Y | G | C | B | T | A | | | | |

San Joaquin River
Stockton 37 57 N 121 19 W

| P | Q | Y | G | C | B | T | A | | |

Suisun Bay
Antioch 38 01 N 121 49 W

134A

Pittsburg 38 01 N 121 52 W
Port Chicago 38 03 N 122 01 W
Avon 38 03 N 122 05 W
Martinez 38 01 N 122 08 W
Port Costa 38 03 N 122 11 W
Crockett 38 04 N 122 14 W
Selby 38 03 N 122 15 W
Oleum 38 03 N 122 16 W
Point Orient 37 57 N 122 26 W
Molate Point 37 57 N 122 25 W
Richmond 37 55 N 122 23 W

| P | Q | Y | G | C | R | B | D | T | A |

Berkeley 37 52 N 122 19 W
San Francisco Bay
Oakland 37 48 N 122 17 W

| Y | G | C | R | B | D | T | A | | |

Alameda 37 46 N 122 19 W
Redwood City 37 30 N 122 13 W
San Francisco 37 48 N 122 25 W

| Q | Y | G | C | R | B | D | T | A | L |

Davenport 37 01 N 122 12 W
Santa Cruz 36 57 N 122 02 W
Moss Landing 36 48 N 121 47 W
Seaside 36 36 N 121 52 W
Monterey 36 36 N 121 53 W
Estero Bay 35 24 N 120 53 W
Morro Bay 35 22 N 120 51 W
San Luis Obispo Bay   **134B**
Port San Luis 35 10 N 120 45 W

| P | Q | G | D | T | A | | | | |

Avila 35 10 N 120 44 W
Port Petrol 34 51 N 120 37 W
Point Conception 34 27 N 120 28 W
Gaviota 34 28 N 120 14 W
Capitan 34 28 N 120 02 W
Elwood 34 26 N 119 53 W
Santa Barbara 34 24 N 119 41 W
Carpinteria 34 26 N 119 37 W
Ventura 34 16 N 119 18 W
Port Hueneme 34 09 N 119 13 W

| P | Y | G | C | R | B | T | A | | |

Santa Monica 34 01 N 118 30 W
El Segundo Terminal 33 55 N 118 26 W

| P | A | | | | | | | | |

Redondo Beach 33 51 N 118 24 W
Los Angeles 33 43 N 118 16 W

| P | Q | Y | G | C | R | B | D | T | A | L |

San Pedro 33 43 N 118 15 W   **134C**
Wilmington 33 46 N 118 16 W
Terminal Island 33 45 N 118 15 W
Long Beach 33 45 N 118 13 W

| P | Q | Y | G | C | R | B | T | A | |

Seal Beach 33 44 N 118 06 W
Huntington Beach Terminal 33 40 N 118 00 W
San Clemente 33 26 N 117 36 W
Santa Catalina Island 33 22 N 118 25 W
Oceanside 33 12 N 117 23 W
San Diego 32 43 N 117 14 W

| Q | Y | G | C | B | T | A | | | |

MEXICO   **134D**

Rosarito Terminal 32 21 N 117 05 W

| P | Q | | | | | | | | |

Bahia de Todos Santos
Ensenada 31 51 N 116 38 W

| G | C | T | A | L | | | | | |

Black Warrior Lagoon
Venustiano Carranza 28 02 N 114 07 W   [p.59]
Cedros Island
Morro Redondo 28 03 N 115 11 W

| Y | T | A | | | | | | | |

San Carlos 24 47 N 112 07 W

| Y | G | A | | | | | | | |

Puerto Magdalena 24 38 N 112 09 W
Cabo San Lucas 22 50 N 109 55 W
Punta Prieta 24 13 N 110 18 W
La Paz 24 10 N 110 19 W

| P | G | B | A | | | | | | |

San Juan de la Costa 24 23 N 110 42 W   **135A**

| Y | | | | | | | | | |

Loreto 26 01 N 111 21 W
San Marcos Island 27 11 N 112 06 W

| Y | | | | | | | | | |

Santa Rosalia 27 20 N 112 16 W

| G | B | A | | | | | | | |

Port Isabel 31 48 N 114 43 W
Puerto Libertad 29 54 N 112 41 W
Guaymas 27 54 N 110 52 W

| P | Y | G | C | B | T | A | | | |

Yavaros 26 42 N 109 31 W
Navojoa 27 06 N 109 26 W
Topolobampo 25 35 N 109 03 W

| P | Y | G | C | B | T | A | | | |

Mazatlan 23 11 N 106 26 W

| P | Y | G | C | R | B | T | A | L | |

San Blas 21 32 N 105 19 W
Puerto Vallarta 20 37 N 105 16 W   **135B**

| G | R | A | | | | | | | |

Cape Corrientes 20 24 N 105 43 W
Manzanillo 19 03 N 104 20 W

| P | Q | G | C | B | D | T | A | L | |

Lazaro Cardenas 17 55 N 102 11 W

| P | Q | Y | G | C | B | T | A | | |

Zihuatanejo 17 39 N 101 33 W
Acapulco 16 50 N 99 55 W

| P | G | C | B | D | A | L | | | |

Escondido 15 50 W 97 05 W
Puerto Angel 15 39 N 96 31 W
Salina Cruz 16 10 N 95 11 W

| P | Q | Y | G | C | B | D | T | A | L |

Ventosa Bay 16 10 N 95 10 W
Puerto Madero 14 42 N 92 27 W

| G | T | A | | | | | | | |

GUATEMALA

Ocos 14 30 N 92 12 W
Champerico 14 18 N 91 56 W

| G | T | A | | | | | | | |

San Jose 13 55 N 90 50 W

| P | Q | A | | | | | | | |

Puerto Quetzal 13 55 N 90 47 W

| Q | Y | G | C | R | B | T | A | | |

EL SALVADOR   **135C**

Acajutla 13 36 N 89 50 W

| P | Q | Y | G | C | R | B | T | | |

La Libertad 13 29 N 89 19 W   [p.60/61]
La Union 13 20 N 87 50 W
Cutuco 13 19 N 87 49 W

| P | Q | Y | G | | | | | | |

HONDURAS   **135D**

Amapala 13 18 N 87 39 W
Bahia San Lorenzo
San Lorenzo 13 25 N 87 27 W

| Q | Y | G | C | R | T | | | | |

Henecan 13 24 N 87 25 W
Salamar 13 24 N 87 26 W

NICARAGUA

Corinto 12 28 N 87 11 W

| P | Q | G | C | R | T | | | | |

Puerto Sandino 12 11 N 86 47 W

| P | Y | G | B | A | | | | | |

Masachapa 11 46 N 86 32 W
San Juan del Sur 11 15 N 85 53 W

| G | | | | | | | | | |

GEOGRAPHIC INDEX

P Petroleum Q Other Liquid Bulk Y Dry Bulk G General Cargo
C Containers R Ro-Ro B Bunkers D Dry Dock T Towage
A Airport (within 100km) L Lloyd's Agent (not including sub-agents)

COSTA RICA — 136A

Golfo de Nicoya
  Punta Morales 10 00 N 84 58 W
  Puntarenas 9 59 N 84 51 W
`P G B A`

Caldera 9 55 N 84 43 W
`P Y G C R T A`

Quepos 9 24 N 84 10 W
`G B`

Punta Dominical 9 15 N 83 51 W
Golfo Dulce
  Bahia del Rincon 8 43 N 83 29 W
  Golfito 8 38 N 83 11 W
`P G A`

Cocos Island
  Wafer Bay 5 33 N 87 03 W

PANAMA — 136B

Puerto Armuelles 8 16 N 82 52 W
`G A`

Charco Azul Terminal 8 13 N 82 52 W
`P T`

Pedregal 8 21 N 82 26 W
`G B A`

Parida Island 8 06 N 82 22 W
Coiba Island 7 19 N 81 35 W
Parita Bay
  Aguadulce 8 14 N 80 30 W
`Q Y G B A`

Vacamonte 8 53 N 79 41 W
`G B T`

Panama Canal (see Col. 153B)
Panama 8 59 N 79 32 W
Taboguilla Island 8 49 N 79 31 W
Taboga Island
  Taboga 8 47 N 79 33 W
La Palma 8 24 N 78 08 W
Darien 8 22 N 78 03 W

COLOMBIA — 136C

Punta Charambira 4 17 N 77 29 W
Buenaventura 3 54 N 77 05 W
`Y G C B T A`

Tumaco 1 51 N 78 44 W
`P G C B T A`

ECUADOR

San Lorenzo 1 14 N 78 50 W
Rio Verde 1 01 N 79 32 W
Balao Terminal 1 02 N 79 44 W
`P B T A`

Tepre 1 01 N 79 40 W
`P Q B A`

Esmeraldas 0 58 N 79 41 W
`Y G C R B T A`

Atacames 0 53 N 79 52 W — 136D
Galapagos Islands
  Caleta Tagus 0 16 S 91 22 W p.12/13
Bahia de Caraquez 0 40 S 80 30 W
Manta 0 56 S 80 43 W p.62/63
`Y G C R B T A`

Machalilla 1 28 S 80 46 W
La Libertad 2 13 S 80 55 W
`P B T`

Salinas 2 10 S 80 57 W
Guayaquil 2 17 S 79 55 W
`P Q Y G C B D T A L`

Duran 2 12 S 79 54 W
Puna Island
  Puna 2 45 S 79 54 W

Puerto Bolivar 3 16 S 80 01 W — 137A
`G C T A`

PERU

Zorritos 3 40 S 80 39 W
Mancora 4 05 S 81 05 W
Los Organos 4 10 S 81 08 W
Cabo Blanco 4 16 S 81 15 W
Lobitos 4 27 S 81 17 W
Talara 4 34 S 81 17 W
`P Y G B T A`

Negritos 4 39 S 81 19 W
Paita 5 05 S 81 07 W
`P Y G C T A`

Puerto Bayovar 5 47 S 81 03 W
`P T`

Lobos de Tierra Island 6 28 S 80 50 W
Pimentel 6 49 S 79 56 W
Eten 6 56 S 79 52 W
Pacasmayo 7 24 S 79 36 W
Chicama 7 42 S 79 25 W
Huanchaco 8 02 S 79 10 W
Trujillo 8 08 S 79 05 W
Salaverry 8 14 S 79 00 W
`P Q Y G T A`

Guanape Islands 8 35 S 78 56 W
Coisco 9 01 S 78 37 W
Chimbote 9 05 S 78 38 W
`Y G D T A`

Samanco Bay
  Vesique 9 13 S 78 29 W
Casma 9 28 S 78 23 W
Huarmey 10 05 S 78 09 W
Paramonga 10 42 S 77 50 W
Supe 10 50 S 77 44 W
`G`

Huacho 11 08 S 77 37 W
Mazorca Island 11 24 S 77 44 W
Chancay 11 36 S 77 17 W
Ancon 11 47 S 77 11 W — 137B
Pescadores Islands 11 47 S 77 15 W
La Pampilla 11 56 S 77 11 W
`P`

Callao 12 03 S 77 09 W
`P Y G C R B D T A`

Conchan 12 10 S 77 00 W
`P`

Mala 12 44 S 76 39 W
Cerro Azul 13 03 S 76 31 W
Tambo de Mora 13 29 S 76 12 W
Chincha Islands 13 42 S 76 32 W
Pisco 13 43 S 76 15 W
General San Martin 13 50 S 76 16 W — 137C
`Y G T A`

San Nicolas 15 14 S 75 14 W
`P Y G B T A`

San Juan 15 21 S 75 11 W
Acari 15 25 S 74 37 W
Lomas 15 33 S 74 51 W
Chala 15 51 S 74 15 W
Atico 16 13 S 73 43 W
Matarani 16 59 S 72 07 W
`P Q Y G C R B T`

Mollendo 17 01 S 72 02 W
Ilo 17 38 S 71 21 W — 137D
`P Y G R B T A`

CHILE

Arica 18 29 S 70 20 W
`P G C A L`

Pisagua 19 33 S 70 14 W
Junin 19 36 S 70 14 W
Iquique 20 12 S 70 10 W
`P Q Y C B T A L`

Caleta Toyos 20 28 S 70 12 W — 138A
Caleta Patillos 20 45 S 70 12 W
`Y A`

Punta Patache 20 51 S 70 14 W
Pabellon de Pica 20 58 S 70 10 W
Lobos 21 05 S 70 13 W
Guanillo 21 18 S 70 09 W
Tocopilla 22 05 S 70 14 W
`P Y G T`

Gatico 22 30 S 70 16 W
Michilla Bay 22 43 S 70 19 W
Mejillones 23 06 S 70 28 W
`G A`

Antofagasta 23 38 S 70 26 W
`P Q Y G C R B T A`

Taltal 25 24 S 70 29 W
Chanaral 26 21 S 70 38 W
`P Y G C T A`

Caleta Barquito 26 21 S 70 39 W — 138B
Caldera 27 04 S 70 53 W
`P Y G T A`

Calderilla 27 05 S 70 52 W
Easter Island (Isla de Pascua)
  Vinapu Terminal 27 11 S 109 24 W p.48/49
Carrizal Bajo 28 04 S 71 11 W
Huasco 28 27 S 71 14 W p.62/63
`P Q Y B T A`

Cruz Grande 29 27 S 71 20 W
La Serena 29 50 S 71 15 W
Coquimbo 29 57 S 71 21 W
`Y G C R T A`

Guayacan 29 58 S 71 22 W
`P Q Y B A`

Los Vilos 31 55 S 71 31 W
Puerto Ventanas 32 45 S 71 30 W — 138C
Quintero 32 46 S 71 30 W
`P Q Y G B`

Las Salinas 33 01 S 71 34 W
Valparaiso 33 01 S 71 38 W
`P Q Y G C R B D T A`

San Antonio 33 36 S 71 37 W
`P Q Y G C R B T`

Matanzas 33 59 S 71 54 W
Tome 36 37 S 72 57 W
Lirquen 36 43 S 72 59 W
`Y G C B T A`

Penco 36 43 S 73 00 W
Talcahuano 36 41 S 73 06 W
`Y G C R B D T A`

San Vicente 36 44 S 73 09 W — 138D
`P Q Y G B A`

Coronel 37 02 S 73 10 W
`Y A`

Lota 37 06 S 73 10 W
`Y G A`

Lebu 37 37 S 73 40 W
Corral 39 52 S 73 25 W
Valdivia 39 48 S 73 14 W
`G T A`

Bahia Mansa 40 34 S 73 45 W
Puerto Montt 41 28 S 72 57 W
`P Y G C R B T A`

Chiloe Island
  Ancud 41 52 S 73 50 W
  Puerto Quemchi 42 08 S 73 28 W
  Castro 42 29 S 73 46 W
`G A`

  Leutepo 42 57 S 73 35 W
  Puerto Quellon 43 09 S 73 37 W
  Puerto Carmen 43 09 S 73 46 W

P Petroleum   **Q** Other Liquid Bulk   **Y** Dry Bulk   **G** General Cargo
C Containers   **R** Ro-Ro   **B** Bunkers   **D** Dry Dock   **T** Towage
A Airport (within 100km)   **L** Lloyd's Agent (not including sub-agents)

GEOGRAPHIC INDEX

139A

Ascension Island
  Puerto Melinka 43 54 S 73 44 W
Chacabuco 45 28 S 72 50 W
`P Y G R`

Puerto Eden 49 09 S 74 27 W
Guarello 50 21 S 75 20 W
`Y`

Puerto Bories 51 41 S 72 31 W
Puerto Natales 51 43 S 72 31 W
`G R A`

Strait of Magellan
  Desolation Island
    Cape Pilar 52 43 S 74 41 W
  Punta Arenas 53 10 S 70 54 W
`P Q Y G C R B T A L`

139B

Rio Seco 53 04 S 70 51 W
Cabo Negro 52 57 S 70 47 W
`Q`

Puerto Percy 52 55 S 70 17 W
`Q B`

Caleta Clarencia 52 54 S 70 09 W
`P T`

Gregorio Bay
  Gregorio 52 38 S 70 11 W
`P`

  Punta Dungeness 52 24 S 68 26 W
Stewart Island 54 50 S 71 30 W
Navarino Island
  Puerto Williams 54 55 S 67 37 W
`P B A`

Cape Horn 55 59 S 67 16 W

ANTARCTICA   **139C**

Commonwealth Bay 67 00 S 142 00 E   `p.15`
Dumont d'Urville (**French**)
66 40 S 140 01 E
Casey (**Australian**) 66 17 S 110 32 E
Bowman Island 65 30 S 103 25 E
Davis (**Australian**) 68 35 S 77 58 E
Mawson (**Australian**) 67 36 S 62 52 E
Casey Bay 67 30 S 46 00 E

FRENCH ANTARCTIC TERRITORY

St. Paul Island 38 43 S 77 31 E   `p.10/11`
Amsterdam Island 37 51 S 77 32 E
Kerguelen Island
  Port aux Francais 49 21 S 70 12 E
Crozet Islands 46 20 S 51 30 E

BRITISH ANTARCTIC TERRITORY   **139D**

South Orkney Islands   `p.15`
  Laurie Island
    Scotia Bay 60 43 S 44 38 W
South Shetland Islands
  Deception Island
    Port Foster 63 00 S 60 34 W

FALKLAND ISLANDS and Dependencies (British)

South Georgia
  Leith Harbour 54 08 S 36 41 W
  King Edward Cove
    Grytviken 54 17 S 36 30 W
Falkland Islands   `p.62/63`
  Port Stanley 51 39 S 57 43 W
`G C R B A L`

Port William 51 41 S 57 45 W
East Cove 51 52 N 58 10 W
Mare Harbour 51 55 S 58 28 W
Darwin 51 50 S 58 56 W
Ajax Bay 51 33 S 59 06 W

ARGENTINA   **140A**

Ushuaia 54 49 S 68 17 W
`P Y G C B T A`

Rio Grande 53 48 S 67 40 W
San Sebastian Bay 53 14 S 68 15 W
`P G`

Cape Virgenes 52 20 S 68 21 W
Punta Loyola 51 36 S 69 01 W
Rio Gallegos 51 36 S 68 58 W
`P Y G B A`

Punta Quilla 50 08 S 68 22 W
`P G B A`

Santa Cruz 50 08 S 68 23 W
San Julian 49 15 S 67 40 W
`G`

Puerto Deseado 47 45 S 65 54 W   **140B**
`G B A`

Caleta Olivia 46 26 S 67 31 W
Comodoro Rivadavia 45 52 S 67 28 W
`P G B T A`

Caleta Olivares 45 46 S 67 22 W
Caleta Cordova 45 43 S 67 21 W
Golfo Nuevo
  Puerto Madryn 42 46 S 65 03 W
`Y G C B A`

Golfo San Matias
  Punta Colorada 41 42 S 65 02 W
`Y G`

  San Antonio Este 40 49 S 64 54 W
`G B T A`

Bahia Blanca 39 03 S 61 50 W
`P Q Y G B D T A`

  Galvan 38 47 S 62 18 W
  Ingeniero White 38 48 S 62 16 W
  Puerto Belgrano 38 54 S 62 06 W
  Puerto Rosales 38 55 S 62 04 W
  Punta Ciguena 38 57 S 62 03 W
  Punta Ancla 38 57 S 62 02 W
Recalada 39 00 S 61 16 W
Necochea 38 34 S 58 42 W   **140C**
`P Q Y G T A`

Quequen 38 34 S 58 44 W
Mar del Plata 38 01 S 57 32 W
`Q Y G B T A`

Cape San Antonio 36 19 S 56 46 W
River Plate
  Puerto Santiago 34 51 S 57 53 W
  Ensenada 34 52 S 57 54 W
  La Plata 34 50 S 57 52 W   `p.64`
`P Q G B T`

Buenos Aires 34 36 S 58 22 W
`P Q Y G C R B D T A L`

San Fernando 34 27 S 58 32 W   **140D**
River Parana
  Campana 34 15 S 58 58 W
`P Y G B T`

Zarate 34 05 S 59 01 W
`P Q`

Atucha 33 59 S 59 17 W
`G`

San Pedro 33 42 S 59 39 W
`Y G B`

Puerto Obligado 33 38 S 59 48 W
Ramallo 33 32 S 59 59 W
`P Y G`

San Nicolas 33 20 S 60 13 W
`Y G B T A`

Puerto Acevedo 33 18 S 60 15 W
Villa Constitucion 33 15 S 60 17 W
`Y G B T A`

Arroyo Seco 33 08 S 60 26 W   **141A**
Rosario 32 57 S 60 38 W
`P Q Y G B A L`

Puerto Borghi 32 48 S 60 37 W
San Lorenzo 32 45 S 60 38 W
`P Q Y G B A`

San Martin 32 43 S 60 38 W
River Carcarana
  Gaboto 32 26 S 60 49 W
Diamante 32 04 S 60 39 W
`Q Y G T A`

Bajada Grande 31 43 S 60 29 W
Parana 31 44 S 60 27 W
Santa Fe 31 39 S 60 42 W
`P Q Y G B T A`

River Colastine   **141B**
  Colastine 31 37 S 60 28 W
La Paz 30 45 S 59 39 W
Puerto Barranqueras 27 29 S 58 54 W
Corrientes 27 29 S 58 50 W

PARAGUAY

River Paraguay
  Villa Oliva 26 00 S 57 43 W
  Puerto Villeta 25 30 S 57 36 W
`Y G`

  Villa Elisa (Medin) 25 26 S 57 36 W
  Guyrati Pass 25 26 S 57 38 W
  San Antonio 25 25 S 57 34 W
`Y G A`

  Asuncion 25 16 S 57 41 W
`P Q Y G C B D T A L`

  Concepcion 23 20 S 57 35 W
  Ladario (**Brazilian**) 19 03 S 57 44 W
`Y G`

  Porto Peixinho (**Brazilian**) 19 01 S 57 45 W
`Y`

  Corumba (**Brazilian**) 19 00 S 57 45 W
`Y G`

ARGENTINA   **141C**

River Ibicuy
  Ibicuy 33 45 S 59 11 W
River Uruguay
  Gualeguaychu 33 00 S 58 30 W
  Concepcion del Uruguay
  32 29 S 58 14 W
`P Y G B T A`

  Colon 32 13 S 58 07 W
  Concordia 31 24 S 57 57 W

URUGUAY   **141D**

Salto 31 21 S 57 56 W
Paysandu 32 18 S 58 02 W
`Y G T`

Fray Bentos 33 06 S 58 19 W
`Y G A`

Nueva Palmira 33 53 S 58 25 W
`Y G A`

Puerto de Carmelo 34 01 S 58 18 W
River Plate
  Martin Garcia 34 11 S 58 15 W
  Colonia 34 28 S 57 51 W
`G`

Sauce 34 27 S 57 26 W
Montevideo 34 54 S 56 16 W
`P Q Y G C B D T A L`

Maldonado 34 57 S 54 57 W
Jose Ignacio Terminal 34 57 S 54 42 W
`P`

GEOGRAPHIC INDEX

P Petroleum   **Q** Other Liquid Bulk   **Y** Dry Bulk   **G** General Cargo
C Containers   **R** Ro-Ro   **B** Bunkers   **D** Dry Dock   **T** Towage
A Airport (within 100km)   **L** Lloyd's Agent (not including sub-agents)

URURUAY *continued*   142A

Punta del Este 34 58 S 54 57 W
`G B A`

La Paloma 34 39 S 54 09 W

BRAZIL

Rio Grande 32 10 S 52 05 W
`P Q Y G C B T L`

Lagoa dos Patos
Rio Sao Goncalo
Pelotas 31 45 S 52 15 W
`G A`

River Guaiba   142B
Porto Alegre 30 02 S 51 13 W
`P Q Y G C B T A L`

River Jacui
Santa Clara 29 54 S 51 22 W
`Q Y B A`

Tramandai 30 00 S 50 08 W
`P T`

Porto Laguna 28 30 S 48 45 W
Imbituba 28 17 S 48 40 W
`P Q Y G C R B T A`

Florianopolis 27 36 S 48 34 W
Itajai 26 54 S 48 39 W
`P Q G C B T A`

Sao Francisco do Sul 26 14 S 48 38 W
`P Y G B T A`

Paranagua 25 30 S 48 31 W
`P Q Y G C R B T A`

Barao de Teffe (Antonina)
25 26 S 48 32 W
Santos 23 56 S 46 20 W
`P Q Y G C R B D T A L`

Barnabe Island 23 55 S 46 20 W   142C
Guaruja 24 00 S 46 22 W
Sao Sebastiao 23 48 S 45 23 W
`P Q G R B T`

Ilha Grande Bay
Angra dos Reis 23 01 S 44 19 W
`Y G R T`

Gebig 23 03 S 44 14 W
`P B T`

Mangaratiba 22 54 S 44 03 W
Sepetiba Bay
Guaiba Island 23 01 S 44 02 W
Sepetiba 22 56 S 43 50 W
`Y G T A`

Rio de Janeiro 22 55 S 43 12 W   142D
`P Q Y G C B D T L`

Niteroi 22 53 S 43 07 W
Forno 22 58 S 42 01 W
`Q Y G`

Cabo Frio 23 01 S 42 00 W
Campos 21 42 S 41 20 W
Ponta do Ubu 20 47 S 40 35 W
`Y G T A`

Vitoria 20 18 S 40 20 W
`P Y G C R B T A`

Tubarao 20 17 S 40 15 W
`P Y G A`

Praia Mole 20 17 S 40 14 W
`Y G`

Portocel (Barra do Riacho)
19 51 S 40 03 W
`Y G T A`

Abrolhos Islands 17 58 S 38 41 W
Caravellas 17 41 S 39 08 W

Cumuruxatiba 17 06 S 39 11 W
Porto Seguro 16 27 S 39 04 W
Ilheus 14 47 S 39 02 W
`P Q G C R B T A`

Camamu 13 57 S 39 07 W
Bay of Todos os Santos
Campinho 12 53 S 39 00 W
Sao Roque 12 51 S 38 51 W
Madre de Deus 12 45 S 38 37 W
Aratu 12 47 S 38 29 W
`P Q Y B D A`

Salvador 12 58 S 38 30 W
`P Q Y G C R B D T A L`

Aracaju 10 55 S 37 03 W
`P G B A`

Carmopolis 11 02 S 37 00 W
Sao Francisco do Norte River
Neopolis 10 19 S 36 34 W
Maceio 9 40 S 35 44 W
`P Q Y G B T A`

Suape 8 24 S 34 57 W
`P Q G C R T`

Recife 8 04 S 34 52 W
`P Q Y G C R B T A L`

Cabedelo 6 58 S 34 51 W
`G C R T`

Natal 5 47 S 35 11 W
`P Q Y G B D`

Fernando Noronha Island 3 48 S 32 23 W
Macau 5 06 S 36 38 W
Termisa Terminal 4 49 S 37 02 W
`Y`

Areia Branca 4 57 S 37 09 W
Aracati 4 25 S 37 45 W
Mucuripe 3 42 S 38 28 W
Fortaleza 3 41 S 38 29 W
`P Q Y G C R B T A`

Camocim 2 51 S 40 53 W
Luiz Correia 2 53 S 41 39 W
Parnaiba 2 56 S 41 47 W
Tutoia Bay   143C
Tutoia 2 46 S 42 16 W
Sao Luiz de Maranhao 2 30 S 44 18 W
Ponta da Madeira 2 34 S 44 23 W
Itaqui 2 34 S 44 21 W
`P Q Y G B T A`

Salinopolis 0 37 S 47 21 W
River Para
Icoraci 1 18 S 48 30 W
Belem 1 27 S 48 30 W
`P Q Y G C B D T A L`

River Moju
Moju 1 52 S 48 45 W
Vila do Conde 1 33 S 48 45 W
`Y A`

Capim Island 1 33 S 48 52 W
Os Estreitos
Breves 1 41 S 50 30 W
Portel 1 58 S 50 45 W
River Amazon   143D
Afua 0 10 S 50 22 W
Macapa 0 02 N 51 03 W
Santana 0 03 N 51 11 W
`P Y G R A`

River Jari
Munguba 1 05 S 52 23 W
`Y G A`

Santarem 2 25 S 54 42 W
`G A`

River Tapajos
Itaituba 4 15 S 55 56 W
Obidos 1 45 S 55 30 W
River Trombetas
Trombetas 1 28 S 56 23 W
`Y G T A`

143A
p.62/63

143B

Itacoatiara 3 09 S 58 27 W   144A
River Madeira
Porto Velho 8 37 S 63 43 W
Xiborena 3 10 S 59 55 W
Manaus 3 09 S 60 01 W
`P Q Y G C R B T A`

Coari 4 08 S 63 07 W
Leticia (**Colombian**) 4 09 S 69 57 W
Iquitos (**Peruvian**) 3 43 S 73 11 W
`Y G C R B D A`

River Ucayali
Pucallpa (**Peruvian**) 8 22 S 74 32 W

FRENCH GUIANA (French)

River Mahury
Degrad des Cannes 4 51 N 52 16 W
`P Q Y G C R B A`

Fourgassie 4 35 N 52 21 W
Cayenne 4 56 N 52 20 W   144B
`P L`

Larivot 4 54 N 52 22 W
Iles du Salut 5 17 N 52 36 W
Kourou 5 09 N 52 40 W
Maroni River
St. Laurent 5 30 N 54 02 W

SURINAME

Cottica River
Moengo 5 38 N 54 24 W
`P Y G B T A`

Suriname River
Belwaarde 5 51 N 55 05 W
Paramaribo 5 50 N 55 10 W
`P Q Y G C B D A L`

Smalkalden 5 37 N 55 05 W
Paranam 5 36 N 55 05 W
`Y G B T A`

Nickerie River
Nieuw Nickerie 5 57 N 57 00 W
`P G B A`

Wageningen 5 46 N 56 41 W
`P G`

Corentyn River
Apoera 5 11 N 57 11 W

GUYANA   144C

River Berbice
New Amsterdam 6 15 N 57 31 W
`P Y G`

Everton 6 11 N 57 31 W
Demerara River
Georgetown 6 49 N 58 11 W
`P Y G C B D A L`

Linden 6 01 N 58 18 W
Adventure 7 05 N 58 29 W
Essequibo River
Bartica 6 24 N 58 38 W
Pomeroon River
Charity 7 24 N 58 35 W
Pickersgill 7 16 N 58 42 W
River Kaituma
Port Kaituma 8 28 N 59 52 W

VENEZUELA   144D

River Orinoco   p.60/61
Punta Barima 8 36 N 60 25 W
Paradero 8 24 N 62 38 W
`P`

San Felix 8 22 N 62 40 W
`Y G C B`

Palua 8 22 N 62 42 W
`Y G B T A`

Puerto Ordaz 8 21 N 62 43 W
`Y G B T A`

P Petroleum   **Q** Other Liquid Bulk   **Y** Dry Bulk   **G** General Cargo
C Containers   **R** Ro-Ro   **B** Bunkers   **D** Dry Dock   **T** Towage
A Airport (within 100km)   **L** Lloyd's Agent (not including sub-agents)

GEOGRAPHIC INDEX

Column 1 — 145A

Punta Cuchillo 8 19 N 62 49 W
`P B T A`

Matanzas 8 17 N 62 51 W
`Y G B T A`

Ciudad Bolivar 8 08 N 63 33 W
`G`

Cabruta 7 40 N 66 16 W
Boca Grande Terminal 9 56 N 61 34 W
Gulf of Paria
Pedernales 9 58 N 62 15 W
River San Juan
   Guanoco 10 09 N 62 56 W
   Caripito 10 09 N 63 02 W
`P G B A`

Guiria 10 34 N 62 18 W
Puerto de Hierro 10 38 N 62 06 W
`Y G A`

Carupano 10 41 N 63 15 W
`G`

145B
Margarita Island
  San Juan Griego 11 05 N 63 59 W
  Pampatar 11 00 N 63 47 W
  Porlamar 10 57 N 63 51 W
  El Guamache 10 52 N 64 04 W
`P Q G A`

Los Hermanos Islands 11 45 N 66 28 W
Araya 10 34 N 64 15 W
`Y G`

Puerto Sucre 10 28 N 64 11 W
`Y G R B A`

Cumana 10 28 N 64 11 W
Mochima 10 21 N 64 20 W
Manare 10 25 N 64 21 W
Pertigalete Bay
  Pertigalete 10 15 N 64 33 W
  Pamatacual 10 14 N 64 34 W
  Pamatacualito 10 14 N 64 35 W
Guanta 10 15 N 64 36 W
`Y G`

El Chaure 10 15 N 64 37 W
Guaraguao 10 14 N 64 38 W
Puerto la Cruz 10 13 N 64 38 W
`P G B T A`

Bergantin 10 15 N 64 39 W
Barcelona 10 08 N 64 42 W
Puerto Jose 10 06 N 64 51 W
Piritu 10 05 N 65 04 W
Tortuga Island 10 54 N 65 20 W
Puerto Carenero 10 32 N 66 07 W
La Guaira 10 36 N 66 56 W
`P Y G C R B T A`

145C
Catia la Mar 10 36 N 67 02 W
Turiamo 10 29 N 67 51 W
Borburata 10 29 N 67 55 W
Puerto Cabello 10 29 N 68 00 W
`G B D T A`

El Palito 10 29 N 68 07 W
Moron 10 31 N 68 10 W
Tucacas 10 48 N 68 19 W
Chichiriviche 10 55 N 68 16 W
`Y`

145D
Tucupido 11 31 N 69 20 W
Cumarebo 11 30 N 69 21 W
`Y G`

La Vela de Coro 11 28 N 69 34 W
Paraguana Peninsula
  Amuay Bay 11 46 N 70 15 W
`P Q Y G B T A`

Las Piedras 11 43 N 70 13 W
`P T A`

Punto Fijo 11 41 N 70 16 W
Guaranao Bay 11 40 N 70 14 W
`G C T`

Punta Botija 11 37 N 70 14 W

Column 2

Punta Cardon 11 36 N 70 15 W — 146A
`P G B T A`

Lake Maracaibo
  Punta Gorda 10 46 N 71 34 W
  Puerto Miranda 10 46 N 71 36 W
`P Q B T`

El Tablazo 10 45 N 71 32 W
`Q Y G C B T A`

La Estacada 10 43 N 71 32 W
Punta Camacho 10 33 N 71 32 W
Punta Icotea 10 24 N 71 29 W
Cabimas 10 22 N 71 29 W
La Salina 10 22 N 71 28 W
`P Q B T A`

Tia Juana 10 15 N 71 22 W
Las Morochas 10 13 N 71 20 W
Lagunillas 10 07 N 71 16 W
Bachaquero 9 57 N 71 08 W
San Lorenzo 9 47 N 71 04 W — 146B
La Ceiba 9 28 N 71 04 W
`Q Y G`

Coloncha 9 12 N 71 45 W
Punta Palmas 10 27 N 71 38 W
`P B T A`

Bajo Grande 10 31 N 71 36 W
`P Q B T A`

Punta Piedras 10 34 N 71 36 W
Maracaibo 10 39 N 71 36 W
`Y G C B T A L`

COLOMBIA — 146C
Puerto Bolivar 12 15 N 71 58 W
`P Y G R T`

Rio Hacha 11 33 N 72 55 W
Santa Marta 11 15 N 74 13 W
`Y G C R T A`

Pozos Colorados Terminal 11 09 N 74 15 W
`P A`

Puerto Prodeco (Puerto Zuniga) 11 09 N 74 13 W
`Y T A`

Cienaga 11 01 N 74 15 W
Magdalena River
  Barranquilla 10 58 N 74 46 W
`P Y G C R B T A`

  Puerto Colombia 11 00 N 74 58 W
  Savanilla 11 00 N 74 58 W — 146D
Cartagena 10 25 N 75 32 W
`P Q Y G C B D T A`

Mamonal 10 19 N 75 31 W
`P B D T`

Tolu 9 16 N 75 35 W
Covenas 9 25 N 75 41 W
`P T A`

Puerto Cispata 9 24 N 75 47 W
Turbo 8 04 N 76 44 W
`G A`

ARUBA (Dutch)
Druif 12 32 N 70 04 W
Oranjestad 12 31 N 70 00 W
`G C R B T A`

Barcadera 12 29 N 70 00 W
`G T A`

San Nicolas Bay 12 26 N 69 55 W
`P Q Y G B T A`

Column 3

NETHERLANDS ANTILLES (Dutch) — 147A
Curacao Island
  Bullen Bay 12 11 N 69 01 W
`P Q G B T A`

St. Michiel's Bay 12 09 N 69 01 W
Willemstad 12 07 N 68 56 W
`P G C R B D T A`

St. Anna Bay
  Emmastad 12 08 N 68 56 W
Caracas Bay 12 04 N 68 52 W
`P T A`

Fuik Bay 12 03 N 68 50 W
`Y G T A`

Bonaire Island
  Goto 12 13 N 68 23 W
`P B A`

Kralendijk 12 09 N 68 17 W
`Y G C R B T A`

Salina 12 05 N 68 17 W
`Y A`

TRINIDAD AND TOBAGO — 147B
Trinidad
  Point Fortin 10 11 N 61 41 W
`P B A`

Brighton 10 15 N 61 38 W
`P Y B`

San Fernando 10 17 N 61 28 W
Pointe a Pierre 10 19 N 61 28 W
`P Q G B T A`

Claxton Bay 10 21 N 61 28 W
Point Lisas 10 24 N 61 30 W
`P Q Y G C R B T`

Port of Spain 10 39 N 61 31 W
`G C R B T A L`

Tembladora 10 41 N 61 36 W
`Y G B T A`

Carenage Bay 10 40 N 61 37 W
Cronstadt Island 10 39 N 61 38 W
Chaguaramas Bay
  Chaguaramas 10 40 N 61 39 W
`Y B A`

Galeota Point Terminal 10 08 N 61 00 W
`P G A`

Tobago — 147C
  Scarborough 11 11 N 60 44 W
`P G`

Sandy Point 11 08 N 60 52 W
Crown Point 11 09 N 60 51 W
Pigeon Point 11 10 N 60 50 W
Plymouth 11 13 N 60 46 W

GRENADA — 147D
St. George's 12 03 N 61 45 W
`P Q Y G C B A L`

ST. VINCENT and the GRENADINES
Kingstown 13 09 N 61 14 W
`G B L`

Georgetown 13 14 N 61 10 W

BARBADOS
Bridgetown 13 06 N 59 36 W
`P Q Y G C B D T A L`

Speightstown 13 17 N 59 37 W

GEOGRAPHIC INDEX

Code	Meaning	Code	Meaning
P	Petroleum	Q	Other Liquid Bulk
Y	Dry Bulk	G	General Cargo
C	Containers	R	Ro-Ro
B	Bunkers	D	Dry Dock
T	Towage	A	Airport (within 100km)
L	Lloyd's Agent (not including sub-agents)		

ST. LUCIA — 148A

Vieux Fort 13 44 N 60 57 W
`P Q G C R B A`

Soufriere 13 53 N 61 04 W
Port Marigot 13 58 N 61 02 N
Cul de Sac 13 59 N 61 02 W
`P Q G B A`

Castries 14 00 N 60 59 W
`Y G C R B T A L`

MARTINIQUE (French)

Fort de France 14 38 N 61 04 W
`P Q Y G C R B D A L`

St. Pierre 14 44 N 61 11 W
La Trinite 14 48 N 61 00 W

DOMINICA

Roseau 15 17 N 61 24 W
`P Q G C R B A L`

Portsmouth 15 32 N 61 29 W

GUADELOUPE (French) — 148B

Marie Galante
  Grand Bourg 15 53 N 61 19 W
Basse Terre
  Basse Terre 16 02 N 61 45 W
`P Q G T`

Grande Terre
  Pointe-a-Pitre 16 13 N 61 32 W
`P Y G C R A L`

MONTSERRAT (British)

Plymouth 16 42 N 62 13 W
`G C R A L`

ANTIGUA and BARBUDA

Antigua
  St. John's 17 07 N 61 52 W
`P Y G C R B T A L`

Barbuda 17 38 N 61 49 W

ST. KITTS-NEVIS — 148C

St. Kitts (St. Christopher)
  Basseterre 17 18 N 62 43 W
`Y G C R A L`

Nevis
  Charlestown 17 08 N 62 37 W

NETHERLANDS ANTILLES (Dutch)

St. Eustatius 17 29 N 62 59 W
`B T A`

Saba 17 38 N 62 14 W
St. Barthelemy (French)
  Gustavia 17 55 N 62 50 W
`G R A`

St. Maarten/St. Martin (Dutch/French) — 148D
  Groote Bay (Dutch)
    Philipsburg 18 02 N 63 03 W
`G C R B A`

  Marigot (French) 18 04 N 63 06 W

ANGUILLA (British)

Anguilla 18 15 N 63 00 W
Sombrero 18 36 N 63 28 W

BRITISH VIRGIN ISLANDS (British)

Tortola
  Road Harbour 18 25 N 64 37 W
`P G C R B A L`

U.S. VIRGIN ISLANDS (American) — 149A

St. John 18 21 N 64 40 W
St. Thomas 18 23 N 64 56 W
`G R T A L`

St. Croix
  Christiansted 17 46 N 64 41 W
`G C R B T A`

  Frederiksted 17 43 N 64 53 W
`G C R B T A L`

  Krause Lagoon
    Port Alucroix 17 42 N 64 46 W
`P Y T`

  Limetree Bay 17 42 N 64 45 W
`G C R B T A`

    Hovic 17 42 N 64 45 W
`P B T A`

PUERTO RICO (American) — 149B

Humacao 18 10 N 65 45 W
Naguabo 18 12 N 65 43 W
Ensenada Honda 18 12 N 65 38 W
Vieques Sound
  Roosevelt Roads 18 10 N 65 32 W
Ceiba 18 16 N 65 40 W
Fajardo 18 20 N 65 38 W
San Juan 18 28 N 66 07 W
`P Y G C R B D T A L`

Arecibo 18 28 N 66 43 W
`Y G`

Aguadilla 18 22 N 67 10 W
`Q`

Mayaguez 18 12 N 67 09 W
`G`

Mona Passage
  Mona Island 18 05 N 67 57 W
Guanica 17 58 N 66 55 W
`G B T`

Guayanilla 17 59 N 66 45 W
`G B T`

Tallaboa Bay 17 59 N 66 44 W
Ponce 17 58 N 66 37 W — 149C
`P Y G C R B T A`

Jobos 17 58 N 66 17 W
`P Q`

Aguirre 17 57 N 66 13 W
`G`

Las Mareas (Guayama) 17 57 N 66 08 W
`P Q G`

Yabucoa 18 04 N 65 48 W
`P`

DOMINICAN REPUBLIC — 149D

Manzanillo 19 43 N 71 45 W
`G B`

Monte Christi 19 52 N 71 39 W
Cape Isabela 19 55 N 71 02 W
Puerto Plata 19 49 N 70 42 W
`Y G C R B A`

Bergantin 19 47 N 70 38 W
Sosua 19 48 N 70 29 W
Samana Bay
  Samana (Santa Barbara de Samana)
  19 12 N 69 20 W
  Arroyo Barril (Puerto Duarte) 19 12 N 69 26 W
`Y G B`

  Sanchez 19 14 N 69 36 W
Cape Engano 18 36 N 68 19 W
La Romana 18 25 N 68 57 W
`Y G C B T A`

DOMINICAN REPUBLIC (cont.)

San Pedro de Macoris 18 26 N 69 18 W — 150A
`Y G B T A`

Andres Bay
  Andres 18 26 N 69 38 W
  Boca Chica 18 27 N 69 35 W
`G C A`

Santo Domingo 18 28 N 69 53 W
`P Y G C R B D T A L`

Rio Haina 18 25 N 70 00 W
`P Q Y G C R B T A`

Palenque Terminal 18 14 N 70 09 W
`P T`

Azua (Puerto Tortuguero)
18 25 N 70 40 W
Puerto Viejo de Azua 18 20 N 70 49 W
`G R B`

Barahona 18 12 N 71 04 W
`Y G T`

Cabo Rojo 17 54 N 71 40 W
`Y`

HAITI — 150B

Jacmel 18 13 N 72 31 W
Aquin 18 16 N 73 23 W
Aux Cayes 18 11 N 73 44 W
Cap Tiburon 18 21 N 74 27 W
Anse d'Hainault 18 28 N 74 27 W
Jeremie 18 39 N 74 07 W
Miragoane 18 28 N 73 06 W
`Y G T`

Petit Goave 18 26 N 72 52 W
Leogane 18 31 N 72 38 W
Port au Prince 18 33 N 72 21 W
`P Q Y G C R B T A L`

Laffiteau 18 43 N 72 26 W
Fond Mombin 18 45 N 72 28 W
Pointe de Mont Rouis 18 57 N 72 42 W
St. Marc 19 07 N 72 42 W
Gonaives 19 27 N 72 42 W
Port de Paix 19 57 N 72 50 W
Tortuga Island 20 01 N 72 38 W
Cap Haitien 19 46 N 72 12 W
`G C R B A`

Caracol 19 44 N 72 07 W
Fort Liberte 19 41 N 71 51 W

JAMAICA — 150C

Port Morant 17 53 N 76 20 W
Morant Bay 17 52 N 76 24 W
Port Royal 17 56 N 76 51 W
`G T`

Kingston 17 58 N 76 48 W
`P Y G C R B D T A L`

Old Harbour Bay 17 54 N 77 06 W
Port Esquivel 17 53 N 77 08 W
`Y G B A`

Salt River 17 50 N 77 10 W — 150D
Rocky Point 17 49 N 77 09 W
`P G A`

Alligator Pond 17 52 N 77 35 W
Port Kaiser 17 53 N 77 36 W
`Y G A`

Black River 18 01 N 77 53 W
`G A`

Bluefields 18 10 N 78 02 W
Savanna la Mar 18 12 N 78 08 W
Negril 18 16 N 78 22 W
Green Island 18 25 N 78 18 W
Lucea 18 27 N 78 10 W
Montego Bay 18 28 N 77 56 W
`P G C R B A`

Falmouth 18 29 N 77 39 W

P Petroleum   **Q** Other Liquid Bulk   **Y** Dry Bulk   **G** General Cargo
C Containers   **R** Ro-Ro   **B** Bunkers   **D** Dry Dock   **T** Towage
A Airport (within 100km)   **L** Lloyd's Agent (not including sub-agents)

151A

Rio Bueno 18 28 N 77 27 W
`G A`

Discovery Bay
    Port Rhoades 18 28 N 77 26 W
`Y G A`

St. Anns Bay 18 26 N 77 12 W
Ocho Rios 18 25 N 77 07 W
`Y G A`

Oracabessa 18 25 N 76 59 W
Port Maria 18 23 N 76 55 W
Annotto Bay 18 17 N 76 45 W
Buff Bay 18 14 N 76 39 W
Hope Bay 18 13 N 76 35 W
Port Antonio 18 11 N 76 27 W
`G B A`

Manchioneal 18 02 N 76 17 W

CAYMAN ISLANDS (British)   **151B**

Grand Cayman Island
    George Town 19 18 N 81 23 W
`P Q G C R B A L`

Little Cayman Island 19 40 N 80 07 W
Cayman Brac
    Creek 19 45 N 79 44 W
`G C R A`

CUBA

Punta de Maisi 20 15 N 74 08 W
Puerto Baitiqueri 20 01 N 74 51 W
Guantanamo Bay
`Q Y G T`

    Guantanamo 20 08 N 75 11 W
    Boqueron 19 59 N 75 07 W
    Caimanera 19 59 N 75 09 W
    Deseo 19 58 N 75 08 W
Daiquiri 19 55 N 75 38 W
Siboney 19 57 N 75 42 W
Santiago de Cuba 19 59 N 75 52 W
`P Q Y G B T A`

Nima Nima 19 57 N 75 59 W
Pilon 19 54 N 77 18 W
Niquero 20 03 N 77 36 W
Media Luna 20 10 N 77 26 W
San Ramon 20 13 N 77 22 W
Ceiba Hueca 20 13 N 77 19 W
Campachuela 20 14 N 77 17 W   **151C**
Manzanillo 20 21 N 77 07 W
`P Y G T A`

Guayabal 20 42 N 77 37 W
`G`

Manopla 20 39 N 77 52 W
Santa Cruz del Sur 20 42 N 77 59 W
Boca Grande 21 33 N 78 40 W
Jucaro 21 37 N 78 51 W
`G T`

Palo Alto 21 36 N 78 58 W
Tunas de Zaza 21 38 N 79 33 W
Casilda 21 45 N 79 59 W
`G T`

Cienfuegos 22 08 N 80 27 W   **151D**
`P Q Y G B T`

Batabano 22 41 N 82 18 W
Isla de Pinos
    Nueva Gerona 21 55 N 82 46 W
`G`

Rio Coloma 22 15 N 83 34 W
Arroyos Anchorage 22 21 N 84 23 W
Santa Lucia 22 41 N 83 58 W
`Y T`

Bahia Honda 22 58 N 83 10 W
`G`

Orozco 23 08 N 83 02 W
Cabanas 23 00 N 82 59 W
`Q Y G T`

152A

Mariel 23 01 N 82 45 W
`P Y G T`

Chorrera Bay 23 08 N 82 24 W
Castillo del Morro 23 09 N 82 21 W
Havana (Habana) 23 08 N 82 21 W
`P Q Y G C R B D T A L`

Regla 23 08 N 82 20 W
Matanzas 23 03 N 81 34 W
`Q Y G A`

Cardenas 23 03 N 81 12 W
`G T A`

Rio Sagua la Grande
    Isabela de Sagua 22 57 N 80 01 W
`G B T`

    Sagua la Grande 22 51 N 80 05 W
Caibarien 22 32 N 79 28 W
`G T`

Cay Frances 22 38 N 79 13 W
Nuevitas 21 33 N 77 16 W
`P Q Y G B T A`

Puerto Tarafa 21 34 N 77 15 W   **152B**
Bufadero 21 34 N 77 14 W
Pastelillo 21 33 N 77 13 W
Manati 21 22 N 76 49 W
`Q Y G T`

Puerto Padre 21 17 N 76 32 W
`P Q G`

Chaparra 21 12 N 76 33 W
Gibara 21 07 N 76 08 W
Vita 21 05 N 75 57 W
`P Q G`

Sama 21 07 N 75 46 W
Banes 20 55 N 75 42 W
Nipe Bay
    Antilla 20 50 N 75 44 W
`G B T`

    Preston 20 47 N 75 39 W
    Felton 20 45 N 75 36 W
Nicaro 20 43 N 75 33 W
`G`

Tanamo 20 42 N 75 20 W
`G A`

Cayo Mambi 20 40 N 75 17 W   **152C**
Cananova 20 41 N 75 06 W
Cayo Moa 20 41 N 74 54 W
`G T`

Punta Gorda 20 38 N 74 51 W
Baracoa 20 21 N 74 29 W
`G T A`

TURKS and CAICOS ISLANDS (British)

Grand Turk Island
    Grand Turk (Cockburn Town)
    21 28 N 71 09 W
`Y G G C B A L`

Caicos Islands
    Providenciales Island
        Providenciales 21 44 N 72 17 W
`Q Y G C R B A`

BAHAMAS   **152D**

Great Inagua Island
`Y G A`

    Matthew Town 20 57 N 73 41 W
Little Inagua Island 21 30 N 73 00 W
Ragged Island 22 14 N 75 45 W
Long Island 23 41 N 75 21 W
San Salvador Island 24 00 N 74 30 W
Little Exuma Island 23 23 N 75 30 W
Great Exuma Island
    Exuma 23 34 N 75 49 W

153A

Little San Salvador 24 34 N 75 56 W
Eleuthera Island 25 23 N 76 33 W
New Providence Island
    Nassau 25 04 N 77 21 W
`P Q G B T A L`

    Clifton Pier 25 00 N 77 33 W
Andros Island 24 43 N 77 47 W
Berry Islands 25 49 N 77 57 W
Ocean Cay 25 25 N 79 13 W
`Y`

Bimini Islands 25 45 N 79 19 W
Great Abaco Island
    Hole in the Wall 25 51 N 77 10 W
    Marsh Harbour 26 31 N 77 05 W
Grand Bahama Island
    Freeport 26 31 N 78 47 W
`P Y G C R B T A L`

    Lucaya 26 32 N 78 40 W
    South Riding Point 26 36 N 78 13 W
`P T A`

PANAMA   **153B**

Gulf of San Blas 9 34 N 79 01 W
Puerto Bello 9 33 N 79 39 W
Las Minas Bay
    Payardi Island 9 24 N 79 50 W   `p.59`
`P G C R B T A`

Manzanillo 9 22 N 79 52 W
Coco Solo 9 22 N 79 53 W
Colon 9 22 N 79 55 W
Cristobal 9 21 N 79 55 W
`P G C B T A L`

Panama Canal
    Gatun 9 16 N 79 55 W
    Gamboa 9 07 N 79 42 W
    Balboa 8 57 N 79 34 W
`P Q Y G C B D T A L`

Chiriqui Grande Terminal
8 58 N 82 08 W   `p.60/61`
`P`

Almirante 9 17 N 82 23 W
`P G A`

Bocas del Toro 9 20 N 82 15 W

COSTA RICA   **153C**

Puerto Vargas 9 44 N 82 48 W
Puerto Limon 9 59 N 83 01 W
`P Q Y G C R B T A`

Puerto Moin 10 00 N 83 05 W
Barra Colorado 10 47 N 83 35 W

NICARAGUA

San Juan del Norte 10 57 N 83 43 W
El Bluff 12 01 N 83 44 W
`P G R B A`

Las Perlas 12 20 N 83 40 W
Man of War Cays 13 02 N 83 23 W
Isla San Andres (Colombian)
    San Andres 12 33 N 81 41 W   **153D**
`G C B A`

Isla de Providencia (Colombian)
13 23 N 81 22 W
Puerto Benjamin Zeledon 13 19 N 83 37 W
Puerto Cabezas 14 02 N 83 23 W
`G B A`

Puerto Cabo Gracias a Dios
15 00 N 83 10 W
Serrana Bank (American/Colombian)
14 28 N 80 17 W
Quita Sueno Bank (American/Colombian)
14 29 N 81 08 W

HONDURAS

Swan Islands 17 25 N 83 55 W
Santa Rosa de Aguan 15 55 N 85 40 W

GEOGRAPHIC INDEX

P Petroleum	Q Other Liquid Bulk	Y Dry Bulk	G General Cargo
C Containers	R Ro-Ro	B Bunkers	D Dry Dock	T Towage
A Airport (within 100km)	L Lloyd's Agent (not including sub-agents)		

HONDURAS *continued*

Puerto Castilla 16 01 N 86 03 W
[Q][G][C][R][A][ ][ ][ ][ ][ ][ ][ ]

Trujillo 15 51 N 86 00 W
Guanaja Island 16 25 N 85 58 W
Roatan Island 16 16 N 86 40 W
La Ceiba 15 47 N 86 47 W
[G][A][ ][ ][ ][ ][ ][ ][ ][ ][ ][ ]

Utila Island 16 04 N 87 02 W
Tela 15 47 N 87 30 W
[P][Q][G][B][A][ ][ ][ ][ ][ ][ ][ ]

Puerto Cortes 15 51 N 87 56 W
[P][Q][Y][G][C][R][B][T][A][L][ ][ ]

Omoa 15 47 N 88 04 W

GUATEMALA

Puerto Barrios 15 44 N 88 36 W
[P][Y][G][C][R][T][A][ ][ ][ ][ ][ ]

Santo Tomas de Castilla 15 42 N 88 37 W
[P][Y][G][C][R][B][T][A][ ][ ][ ][ ]

Livingston 15 50 N 88 45 W

BELIZE

Big Creek 16 30 N 88 24 W
Riversdale 16 32 N 88 20 W
Dangriga 16 58 N 88 14 W
Belize City 17 30 N 88 11 W
[P][G][C][R][B][T][A][L][ ][ ][ ][ ]

Corozal 18 22 N 88 24 W

MEXICO

Chetumal 18 30 N 88 18 W
Dos Hermanos 18 35 N 88 06 W
Cozumel Island
    Cozumel 20 30 N 86 58 W
[G][B][ ][ ][ ][ ][ ][ ][ ][ ][ ][ ]

Puerto Morelos 20 50 N 86 54 W
El Cuyo 21 30 N 87 40 W
Dzilam 21 25 N 88 50 W
Progreso 21 17 N 89 40 W
[P][G][C][R][B][T][A][ ][ ][ ][ ][ ]

Yukalpeten 21 17 N 89 43 W

[G][B][A][ ][ ][ ][ ][ ][ ][ ][ ][ ]

Sisal 21 10 N 90 02 W
Cayo Arcas Terminal 20 11 N 91 59 W   p.59
[P][T][ ][ ][ ][ ][ ][ ][ ][ ][ ][ ]

Campeche 19 51 N 90 33 W
[G][T][A][ ][ ][ ][ ][ ][ ][ ][ ][ ]

Lerma 19 48 N 90 36 W
Carmen Island 18 31 N 91 52 W
Laguna de Terminos
    Ciudad del Carmen 18 39 N 91 51 W
[G][B][A][ ][ ][ ][ ][ ][ ][ ][ ][ ]

River Grijalva
    Frontera 18 35 N 92 39 W
[G][B][A][ ][ ][ ][ ][ ][ ][ ][ ][ ]

Dos Bocas 18 25 N 93 08 W

[P][T][A][ ][ ][ ][ ][ ][ ][ ][ ][ ]

Rabon Grande 18 13 N 94 24 W
Coatzacoalcos River
    Coatzacoalcos 18 09 N 94 25 W
[P][Q][Y][G][C][B][D][T][A][L][ ][ ]

Nanchital 18 04 N 94 25 W
[P][G][B][T][A][ ][ ][ ][ ][ ][ ][ ]

Minatitlan 18 00 N 94 32 W
[P][Y][G][B][T][A][ ][ ][ ][ ][ ][ ]

Alvarado 18 46 N 95 46 W
Veracruz 19 12 N 96 08 W
[P][Q][Y][G][C][R][B][D][T][A][L][ ]

Nautla 20 17 N 96 47 W

Gutierrez Zamora 20 27 N 97 05 W
Punta Cazones 20 45 N 97 11 W
Tuxpan 20 59 N 97 20 W

[G][C][B][D][T][A][ ][ ][ ][ ][ ][ ]

Tampico 22 13 N 97 53 W
[P][Y][G][C][R][B][D][T][A][L][ ][ ]

Altamira 22 25 N 97 55 W
[P][Y][G][C][R][B][A][ ][ ][ ][ ][ ]

Mezquital 25 08 N 98 21 W

U.S.A.

TEXAS (TX)

Rio Grande   p.54/55
    Brownsville 25 57 N 97 24 W
[P][Q][Y][G][C][B][T][A][ ][ ][ ][ ]

Port Isabel 26 04 N 97 12 W
[P][Y][G][B][A][ ][ ][ ][ ][ ][ ][ ]

Corpus Christi 27 48 N 97 23 W
[P][Q][Y][G][C][B][D][T][A][ ][ ][ ]

Ingleside 27 50 N 97 14 W
Harbor Island 27 52 N 97 04 W
Port Aransas 27 50 N 97 04 W

Port Lavaca 28 37 N 96 38 W
Point Comfort 28 38 N 96 34 W
[Y][G][B][D][T][A][ ][ ][ ][ ][ ][ ]

Brazos River
    Freeport 28 56 N 95 18 W
[P][Q][Y][G][C][R][B][T][A][ ][ ][ ]

Galveston Bay
    Galveston 29 18 N 94 48 W
[P][Y][G][C][R][B][D][T][A][ ][ ][ ]

Texas City 29 22 N 94 53 W
[P][Q][Y][G][B][T][A][ ][ ][ ][ ][ ]

Houston Ship Channel
    Bayport 29 37 N 95 01 W
    Barbours Cut 29 41 N 95 00 W
    Baytown 29 44 N 95 01 W
    Deer Park 29 44 N 95 08 W
    Port Adams 29 45 N 95 11 W
    Norsworthy 29 45 N 95 12 W
    Pasadena 29 43 N 95 13 W
    Deepwater 29 44 N 95 14 W

    Sinco 29 43 N 95 14 W
    Galena Park 29 44 N 95 16 W
    Houston 29 45 N 95 20 W
[P][Q][Y][G][C][R][B][D][T][A][L][ ]

Port Bolivar 29 22 N 94 47 W
Sabine Pass
Sabine 29 43 N 93 52 W
[P][G][B][T][A][ ][ ][ ][ ][ ][ ][ ]

Port Arthur Canal
    Port Arthur 29 52 N 93 55 W
[P][Y][G][C][B][D][T][A][ ][ ][ ][ ]

Sabine-Neches Canal
Neches River

    Atreco 29 59 N 93 53 W
[P][B][T][A][ ][ ][ ][ ][ ][ ][ ][ ]

    Port Neches 29 59 N 93 56 W
    Magpetco 30 02 N 93 59 W
    Smith's Bluff 30 00 N 93 59 W
[P][B][A][ ][ ][ ][ ][ ][ ][ ][ ][ ]

    Beaumont 30 05 N 94 06 W
[P][Q][Y][G][C][R][B][T][A][ ][ ][ ]

Sabine River
    Orange 30 06 N 93 44 W
[Q][G][B][D][T][A][ ][ ][ ][ ][ ][ ]

LOUISIANA (LA)

Calcasieu Lake
    Calcasieu River
        Lake Charles 30 13 N 93 15 W
[P][Q][Y][G][C][R][T][A][ ][ ][ ][ ]

West Lake 30 14 N 93 15 W
    Lockport 30 14 N 93 16 W

Intracoastal Waterway
    Morgan City 29 42 N 91 13 W
    Houma 29 35 N 90 43 W
LOOP Terminal (Louisiana Offshore Oil Port)
28 53 N 90 02 W
[P][B][ ][ ][ ][ ][ ][ ][ ][ ][ ][ ]

River Mississippi
    Southwest Pass 28 58 N 98 23 W
    South Pass 29 00 N 89 10 W
    Buras 29 22 N 89 32 W
    Empire 29 24 N 89 36 W
    Port Sulphur 29 28 N 89 41 W
    Myrtle Grove 29 38 N 89 57 W
    Alliance 29 40 N 89 58 W
    Belle Chasse 29 51 N 89 59 W
    Gretna 29 55 N 90 04 W
    Marrero 29 54 N 90 06 W
    Amesville 29 54 N 90 07 W
    Westwego 29 55 N 90 09 W
    Avondale 29 55 N 90 11 W
    Hahnville 29 58 N 90 25 W
    Taft 29 59 N 90 25 W
    Donaldsonville 30 05 N 91 00 W

    Plaquemine 30 17 N 91 14 W
    Port Allen 30 28 N 91 12 W
    Greenville (MS) 33 25 N 91 04 W
    River Arkansas
        Tulsa (OK) 36 07 N 95 58 W
    Baton Rouge 30 28 N 91 11 W
[P][Y][G][A][ ][ ][ ][ ][ ][ ][ ][ ]

    Geismar 30 13 N 91 01 W
    Burnside 30 08 N 90 55 W
    Convent 30 01 N 90 50 W
    Gramercy 30 03 N 90 41 W
    South Louisiana 30 06 N 90 29 W
    Norco 29 59 N 90 24 W
    Good Hope 29 59 N 90 24 W
    Destrehan 29 56 N 90 21 W
    St. Rose 29 56 N 90 20 W
    New Orleans 29 57 N 90 04 W
[P][Q][Y][G][C][R][B][D][T][A][L][ ]

    Chalmette 29 56 N 90 00 W

    Meraux 29 55 N 89 56 W
    Braithwaite 29 52 N 89 57 W
    Davant 29 36 N 89 51 W
    Ostrica 29 22 N 89 32 W
    Pilottown 29 11 N 89 15 W
    Port Eads 29 01 N 89 10 W

MISSISSIPPI (MS)

Bienville 30 13 N 89 35 W
Gulfport 30 21 N 89 05 W
[Y][G][C][B][T][A][ ][ ][ ][ ][ ][ ]

Ship Island 30 13 N 88 58 W
Biloxi 30 24 N 88 54 W
Pascagoula 30 21 N 88 34 W
[P][Q][Y][G][R][B][D][T][A][ ][ ][ ]

ALABAMA (AL)

Mobile 30 41 N 88 03 W
[Y][G][C][R][B][D][T][A][L][ ][ ][ ]

Fort Morgan 30 14 N 88 01 W

FLORIDA (FL)

Pensacola 30 25 N 87 13 W
[Q][Y][G][C][R][B][T][A][ ][ ][ ][ ]

St. Andrew Bay
    Panama City 30 08 N 85 39 W
[P][Y][G][C][R][B][T][A][ ][ ][ ][ ]

St. Joseph Bay
    Port St. Joe 29 49 N 85 18 W
Apalachicola 29 43 N 84 59 W
Apalachicola River
    Flint River
        Bainbridge (GA) 30 54 N 84 33 W
    Chattahoochee River
        Columbus (GA) 32 28 N 84 59 W
Carrabelle 29 51 N 84 40 W
St. Marks 30 09 N 84 12 W

GEOGRAPHIC INDEX

St. Petersburg 27 47 N 82 38 W   **157A**
Port Tampa 27 52 N 82 33 W
Tampa 27 57 N 82 27 W

`P Q Y G C B D T A L`

Port Manatee 27 30 N 82 33 W

`P Q Y G C R B T A`

Boca Grande 26 43 N 82 15 W
Pine Island 26 35 N 82 05 W
Tortugas Islands
   Tortugas Harbour 24 38 N 82 23 W
Key West 24 33 N 81 48 W

`P G R B D T A`

Sand Key 24 27 N 81 53 W
Sombrero Key 24 38 N 81 07 W
Miami 25 47 N 80 11 W

`G C R B D T A L`

Port Everglades 26 06 N 80 07 W

`P Y G C R B T A`

Fort Lauderdale 26 06 N 80 08 W
West Palm Beach 26 43 N 80 03 W   **157B**
Palm Beach 26 46 N 80 03 W

`P Q Y G C R B A`

Jupiter 26 57 N 80 04 W
Fort Pierce 27 27 N 80 19 W

`G C R B T A`

Port Canaveral 28 25 N 80 35 W

`P Q Y G C R B D T A`

Cape Canaveral (Cape Kennedy)
  28 28 N 80 33 W
Daytona Beach 29 11 N 81 01 W
St. Augustine 29 53 N 81 17 W
St. Johns River
  Mayport 30 23 N 81 26 W
  Jacksonville 30 23 N 81 38 W

`P Q Y G C R B D T A L`

Fernandina 30 41 N 81 28 W

`G C T A`

GEORGIA (GA)

St. Mary's 30 43 N 81 33 W
Kings Bay 30 49 N 81 31 W
Brunswick 31 08 N 81 29 W

`P Q Y G R B T`

Darien 31 23 N 81 25 W   **157C**
Sapelo Island 31 36 N 81 17 W
Savannah River
  Savannah 32 05 N 81 05 W

`P Q Y G C R B D T A L`

  Augusta 33 29 N 82 00 W

SOUTH CAROLINA (SC)

Tybee Roads 32 01 N 80 51 W
Port Royal 32 23 N 80 42 W

`Q Y G C B A`

Beaufort 32 26 N 80 40 W
Charleston 32 47 N 79 56 W

`P Y G C R B D T A L`

Georgetown 33 21 N 79 18 W

`Y G R B T A`

NORTH CAROLINA (NC)   **157D**

Southport 33 55 N 78 00 W   `p.58`
Cape Fear River
  Sunny Point 33 59 N 77 57 W
  Wilmington 34 14 N 77 57 W

`P Y G C R B T A L`

Cape Fear 33 50 N 77 58 W
Wrightsville 34 13 N 77 50 W
Morehead City 34 43 N 76 42 W

`P Q Y G C R T A`

Beaufort 34 43 N 76 39 W
Lookout Bight 34 37 N 76 33 W
Cape Lookout 34 37 N 76 32 W

Diamond Shoal Light 35 09 N 75 18 W   **158A**
Cape Hatteras 35 14 N 75 31 W

BERMUDA (British)

St. George's Island
  St. George's 32 23 N 64 40 W   `p.54/55`

`P Y G R B T A`

Main Island
  Hamilton 32 18 N 64 47 W

`G C R T A L`

Ireland Island
  Freeport 32 19 N 64 50 W

`P Y B T A`

U.S.A.

VIRGINIA (VA)

Chesapeake Bay
  Cape Henry 36 56 N 76 00 W   `p.58`
  Lynnhaven Roads 36 56 N 76 05 W
  Sewells Point 36 58 N 76 20 W
  Hampton Roads

`P Q Y G C R B D T A L`

    Elizabeth River   **158B**
     Norfolk 36 51 N 76 19 W
     Chesapeake 36 47 N 76 18 W
     Portsmouth 36 50 N 76 17 W
    James River
     Claremont 37 16 N 76 58 W
     Hopewell 37 18 N 77 17 W
     Richmond 37 32 N 77 26 W

`Y G C B T A`

    Newport News 36 58 N 76 25 W
  York River
    Yorktown 37 14 N 76 24 W
  Potomac River
    Piney Point (MD) 38 08 N 76 32 W
    Alexandria 38 48 N 77 03 W
    Washington (DC) 38 53 N 77 01 W

MARYLAND (MD)

  Patuxent River
    Hog Point 38 18 N 76 24 W
  Cove Point 38 23 N 76 23 W
  Annapolis 38 59 N 76 29 W
  Baltimore 39 17 N 76 35 W

`P Q Y G C R B D T A L`

  Sparrows Point 39 13 N 76 30 W
  Chesapeake & Delaware Canal   **158C**
    Chesapeake City 39 22 N 75 48 W
  Cambridge 38 34 N 76 04 W
  Salisbury 38 21 N 75 37 W

VIRGINIA (VA)

Cape Charles 37 16 N 76 01 W

DELAWARE (DE)   **158D**

Fenwick Island Light 38 27 N 75 03 W
Delaware Bay
  Cape Henlopen 38 48 N 75 06 W
  Delaware Breakwater 38 49 N 75 06 W
  Lewes 38 47 N 75 08 W
  Delaware River
    Reedy Island 39 30 N 75 34 W
    Reedy Point 39 34 N 75 34 W
    Delaware City 39 34 N 75 35 W
    New Castle 39 40 N 75 34 W
    Wilmington 39 45 N 75 30 W

`Y G C R B T A`

    Claymont 39 48 N 75 26 W

PENNSYLVANIA (PA)

    Marcus Hook 39 49 N 75 25 W
    Chester 39 50 N 75 22 W
    Hog Island 39 52 N 75 16 W
    Point Breeze 39 55 N 75 12 W
    Philadelphia 39 54 N 75 08 W

`P Q Y G C R B D T A`

Port Richmond 39 58 N 75 07 W   **159A**
Morrisville 40 13 N 74 46 W

NEW JERSEY (NJ)

  Trenton 40 11 N 74 45 W
  Burlington 40 05 N 74 51 W
  Pensauken 40 00 N 75 03 W
  Camden 39 56 N 75 08 W

`Y G C B A`

  Gloucester 39 53 N 75 08 W
  Westville 39 52 N 75 08 W
  Billingsport 39 51 N 75 15 W
  Paulsboro 39 50 N 75 15 W
  Carneys Point 39 43 N 75 29 W
  Salem 39 34 N 75 28 W
Cape May 38 56 N 74 58 W
Five Fathom Bank Light 38 47 N 74 35 W
Atlantic City 39 22 N 74 25 W
Tuckerton 39 36 N 74 20 W
Barnegat 39 46 N 74 06 W
Sandy Hook 40 29 N 74 01 W
Ambrose Channel Light 40 27 N 73 50 W
Raritan River   **159B**
  South Amboy 40 29 N 74 17 W
  Sayreville 40 28 N 74 21 W
Perth Amboy 40 30 N 74 16 W
Arthur Kill
  Sewaren 40 33 N 74 15 W
  Port Reading 40 34 N 74 13 W
  Chrome 40 35 N 74 13 W
  Carteret 40 36 N 74 13 W
  Grasselli 40 37 N 74 12 W
  Linden 40 38 N 74 12 W
  Bayway 40 39 N 74 12 W
Elizabethport 40 39 N 74 11 W
Port Newark 40 41 N 74 09 W
Kearney 40 43 N 74 07 W
Bayonne 40 39 N 74 05 W

NEW YORK (NY)

Staten Island
  Tompkinsville 40 38 N 74 05 W
  Stapleton 40 37 N 74 05 W
  Tottenville 40 31 N 74 15 W
  Port Mobil 40 32 N 74 14 W
  Port Ivory 40 38 N 74 12 W
  Howland Hook 40 39 N 74 11 W
New York 40 42 N 74 01 W   **159C**

`P Q Y G C R B D T A L`

Hudson River
  Jersey City (NJ) 40 43 N 74 02 W
  Hoboken (NJ) 40 45 N 74 02 W
  Weehawken (NJ) 40 47 N 74 01 W
  Edgewater (NJ) 40 49 N 73 59 W
  Stony Point 41 14 N 73 58 W
  Tomkins Cove 41 16 N 73 59 W
  Newburgh 41 30 N 74 05 W
  Roseton 41 34 N 74 00 W
  Kingston 41 52 N 73 58 W
  Catskill 42 13 N 73 53 W
  Coxsackie 42 20 N 73 48 W
  Ravena 42 28 N 73 48 W
  Albany 42 39 N 73 45 W

`P Q Y G R T A`

  Troy 42 44 N 73 41 W   **159D**
  Rensselaer 42 39 N 73 44 W
  Alsen 42 11 N 73 55 W
  Cementon 42 08 N 73 55 W
  Hyde Park 41 47 N 73 56 W
  Poughkeepsie 41 41 N 73 53 W
  Milton 41 36 N 73 57 W
  Jones Point 41 17 N 73 57 W
  Peekskill 41 15 N 73 55 W
  Buchanan 41 12 N 73 55 W
  Yonkers 40 57 N 73 50 W
East River
  Hunts Point 40 48 N 73 52 W
  Brooklyn 40 42 N 74 00 W
Long Island
  Gravesend Bay 40 36 N 74 00 W
  Jamaica Bay 40 36 N 73 54 W
  Fire Island Light 40 37 N 73 16 W
  Patchogue 40 46 N 73 01 W
  Sag Harbour 41 01 N 72 18 W
  Riverhead 40 55 N 72 40 W

`P A`

  Greenport 41 06 N 72 21 W
  Northville 40 59 N 72 39 W

GEOGRAPHIC INDEX

P Petroleum   **Q** Other Liquid Bulk   **Y** Dry Bulk   **G** General Cargo
C Containers   **R** Ro-Ro   **B** Bunkers   **D** Dry Dock   **T** Towage
A Airport (within 100km)   **L** Lloyd's Agent (not including sub-agents)

U.S.A. *continued* — 160A

NEW YORK (NY)

Port Jefferson 40 57 N 73 04 W
| P | | | | | | | | | |

Northport 40 56 N 73 22W
| P | | | | | | | | | |

Long Island Sound
City Island 40 51 N 73 47 W
Port Chester 40 59 N 73 39 W

CONNECTICUT (CT)

Stamford 41 01 N 73 32 W
Norwalk 41 05 N 73 24 W
Bridgeport 41 09 N 73 11 W
| P | G | T | A | | | | | | |

New Haven 41 15 N 72 54 W — 160B
| P | Q | Y | G | T | A | | | | |

Clinton 41 16 N 72 32 W
Saybrook 41 17 N 72 22 W
New London 41 24 N 72 06 W
| P | Q | Y | G | R | D | T | A | | |

Groton 41 21 N 72 05 W

RHODE ISLAND (RI)

Block Island 41 14 N 71 35 W
Point Judith 41 22 N 71 29 W
Narragansett Bay
Quonset 41 35 N 71 24 W
Davisville 41 37 N 71 24 W
Providence 41 48 N 71 23 W
| P | Q | G | C | R | B | T | A | | |

Bristol 41 40 N 71 16 W
Melville 41 35 N 71 17 W
Newport 41 29 N 71 20 W
| G | B | T | A | | | | | | |

Sakonnet River
Portsmouth 41 36 N 71 14 W
Brayton Point 41 42 N 71 12 W
Somerset (MA) 41 47 N 71 08 W
Fall River (MA) 41 42 N 71 10 W
| P | Q | Y | G | C | R | B | T | A | |

Tiverton 41 38 N 71 12 W

MASSACHUSETTS (MA) — 160C

Buzzards Bay
New Bedford 41 38 N 70 55 W
| G | B | A | | | | | | | |

Cape Cod Canal (W. Entrance)
41 44 N 70 39 W
Woods Hole 41 31 N 70 40 W
Marthas Vineyard Island
Vineyard Haven 41 27 N 70 36 W
Nantucket Island 41 17 N 70 06 W
Chatham 41 40 N 69 56 W
Cape Cod Light 42 02 N 70 04 W
Race Point 42 04 N 70 15 W
Provincetown 42 03 N 70 11 W
Sandwich 41 46 N 70 29 W — 160D
| P | | | | | | | | | |

Cape Cod Canal (E. Entrance)
41 47 N 70 30 W
Plymouth 41 57 N 70 40 W
| P | G | B | T | A | | | | | |

Scituate 42 12 N 70 43 W
Weymouth 42 16 N 70 55 W
Quincy 42 16 N 71 00 W
Boston 42 23 N 71 03 W
| P | Q | Y | G | C | B | D | T | A | L |

Everett 42 24 N 71 03 W
Chelsea 42 23 N 71 02 W
Revere 42 25 N 71 00 W
Lynn 42 25 N 70 56 W
Marblehead 42 30 N 70 50 W
Salem 42 31 N 70 52 W

Beverly 42 33 N 70 53 W — 161A
Gloucester 42 37 N 70 40 W
| G | R | B | T | A | | | | | |

Rockport 42 40 N 70 37 W
Annisquam Harbour 42 40 N 70 41 W
Newburyport 42 49 N 70 52 W

NEW HAMPSHIRE (NH)

Portsmouth 43 04 N 70 42 W
| P | Q | Y | G | C | D | A | | | |

MAINE (ME)

Portland 43 39 N 70 14 W   p.57
| P | Y | G | R | B | D | T | A | | |

Yarmouth 43 48 N 70 12 W
Bath 43 54 N 69 49 W
| G | D | A | | | | | | | |

Wiscasset 44 00 N 69 40 W — 161B
Boothbay 43 50 N 69 39 W
Rockland 44 06 N 69 07 W
| G | B | | | | | | | | |

Rockport 44 09 N 69 04 W
Belfast 44 25 N 69 00 W
Searsport 44 27 N 68 55 W
| P | Y | G | B | A | | | | | |

Stockton Springs 44 29 N 68 51 W
Penobscot River
Sandy Point 44 31 N 68 49 W
Winterport 44 38 N 68 51 W
| G | A | | | | | | | | |

Bangor 44 48 N 68 47 W
| G | A | | | | | | | | |

South Brewer 44 47 N 68 47 W
Bucksport 44 34 N 68 48 W
| P | G | T | A | | | | | | |

Castine 44 23 N 68 50 W
Bar Harbour 44 23 N 68 12 W
Machiasport 44 42 N 67 24 W
Eastport 44 54 N 66 59 W
| G | B | T | A | | | | | | |

Calais 45 11 N 67 17 W

CANADA — 161C

NEW BRUNSWICK

Grand Manan Island
Grand Harbour 44 40 N 66 45 W
Seal Cove 44 36 N 66 52 W
St. Stephen 45 12 N 67 17 W
Bayside 45 10 N 67 08 W
| G | B | | | | | | | | |

St. Andrews 45 04 N 67 03 W
| G | A | | | | | | | | |

St. George 45 09 N 66 49 W
L'Etang 45 04 N 66 49 W
Beaver Harbour 45 03 N 66 44 W — 161D
| G | B | A | | | | | | | |

Partridge Island 45 14 N 66 03 W
Saint John 45 16 N 66 04 W
| P | Q | Y | G | C | R | B | D | T | A |

Canaport 45 12 N 65 59 W
Quaco Bay
St. Martins 45 21 N 65 32 W
Alma 45 36 N 64 57 W
Herring Cove 45 35 N 64 58 W
Waterside 45 38 N 64 50 W
Grindstone Island 45 44 N 64 37 W
Harvey 45 42 N 64 43 W
Albert 45 45 N 64 40 W
Petitcodiac River
Hillsborough 45 56 N 64 39 W
Moncton 46 05 N 64 47 W
Memramcook River
Cole Point 45 52 N 64 33 W
Dorchester 45 53 N 64 32 W

Rockport 45 47 N 64 30 W — 162A
Sackville 45 53 N 64 21 W

NOVA SCOTIA

Amherst 45 50 N 64 13 W
Joggins 45 42 N 64 27 W
Advocate Harbour 45 19 N 64 47 W
Port Greville 45 24 N 64 33 W
Minas Basin
West Bay 45 22 N 64 21 W
Parrsboro 45 23 N 64 20 W
| G | B | | | | | | | | |

Economy 45 23 N 63 55 W
Maitland 45 19 N 63 30 W
Noel Bay 45 18 N 63 44 W
Walton 45 14 N 64 01 W
Cheverie 45 10 N 64 11 W
Windsor 45 00 N 64 09 W
Hantsport 45 04 N 64 10 W
| Y | G | B | T | A | | | | | |

Wolfville 45 06 N 64 22 W — 162B
Port Williams 45 06 N 64 24 W
Kingsport 45 10 N 64 22 W
Morden 45 06 N 64 57 W
Margaretsville 45 03 N 65 04 W
Port George 45 00 N 65 09 W
Annapolis Basin
Port Wade 44 40 N 65 43 W
Annapolis Royal 44 45 N 65 31 W
Clementsport 44 39 N 65 37 W
Deep Brook 44 35 N 65 38 W
Bear River 44 37 N 65 41 W
Digby 44 38 N 65 45 W
| G | B | | | | | | | | |

Tiverton 44 24 N 66 13 W
Brier Island
Westport 44 16 N 66 21 W
St. Mary's Bay
Weymouth 44 27 N 66 01 W
| G | A | | | | | | | | |

Belliveau Cove 44 24 N 66 03 W
Meteghan 44 12 N 66 10 W
| G | B | A | | | | | | | |

Cape St. Mary 44 05 N 66 13 W
Port Maitland 43 59 N 66 09 W
Yarmouth 43 50 N 66 07 W
| Y | G | C | R | B | T | A | | | |

Chebogue 43 46 N 66 06 W — 162C
Abbot Harbour 43 40 N 65 50 W
Pubnico 43 36 N 65 47 W
Clarks Harbour 43 25 N 65 38 W
Cape Sable 43 23 N 65 37 W
Baccaro Point 43 27 N 65 28 W
Port La Tour 43 30 N 65 28 W
Negro Harbour 43 33 N 65 24 W
Shelburne 43 40 N 65 19 W
| G | B | | | | | | | | |

Lockeport 43 42 N 65 07 W
| G | B | | | | | | | | |

Port Herbert 43 47 N 64 54 W
Port Joli 43 50 N 64 52 W
Port Mouton 43 54 N 64 49 W
Liverpool 44 03 N 64 43 W — 162D
| P | Y | G | B | D | T | | | | |

Brooklyn 44 03 N 64 41 W
Port Medway 44 08 N 64 34 W
| G | | | | | | | | | |

La Have River
La Have 44 17 N 64 21 W
Bridgewater 44 22 N 64 30 W
| Y | G | | | | | | | | |

Riverport 44 17 N 64 20 W
Lunenburg 44 22 N 64 18 W
| Y | G | B | T | | | | | | |

Mahone Bay
Mahone 44 27 N 64 22 W
Gold River 44 33 N 64 19 W
Chester 44 32 N 64 14 W

P Petroleum Q Other Liquid Bulk Y Dry Bulk G General Cargo
C Containers R Ro-Ro B Bunkers D Dry Dock T Towage
A Airport (within 100km) L Lloyd's Agent (not including sub-agents)

GEOGRAPHIC INDEX

163A

New Harbour 44 28 N 64 05 W
Ingramport 44 40 N 63 58 W
Prospect 44 28 N 63 47 W
Sambro Harbour 44 29 N 63 36 W
Ketch Harbour 44 29 N 63 33 W
Halifax 44 38 N 63 33 W

P	Q	Y	G	C	R	B	D	T	A	L		

Dartmouth 44 40 N 63 35 W
Jeddore 44 43 N 63 00 W
Ship Harbour 44 45 N 62 45 W
Tangier 44 48 N 62 42 W
Spry Harbour 44 50 N 62 35 W
Sheet Harbour 44 51 N 62 27 W

Y	G	B							

Beaver Harbour 44 52 N 62 24 W
Necum Teuch Harbour 44 55 N 62 17 W
Ecum Secum 44 57 N 62 09 W
Liscomb 45 00 N 62 00 W
Sherbrooke 45 09 N 61 59 W
Sonora 45 04 N 61 55 W
Fishermans Harbour 45 07 N 61 41 W
Isaac's Harbour 45 10 N 61 39 W
Country Harbour 45 13 N 61 44 W

163B

G	B								

Cole Harbour 45 15 N 61 17 W
Cape Canso 45 18 N 60 56 W
Canso Harbour 45 20 N 61 00 W

Q	Y	G	B						

Guysborough 45 23 N 61 30 W
Boylston 45 27 N 61 31 W
Mulgrave 45 36 N 61 23 W

P	G								

Cape Breton Island
  Port Hawkesbury 45 37 N 61 21 W

G									

  Point Tupper 45 36 N 61 22 W

P	Y	G							

  Arichat 45 31 N 61 00 W

G	B								

  St. Peter's 45 39 N 60 52 W
  Bras d'Or Lake
    West Bay 45 45 N 60 59 W
    Iona 45 58 N 60 48 W

163C

G	A								

    Little Narrows 45 59 N 60 59 W

Y									

    Whycocomagh 45 59 N 61 08 W
    Baddeck 46 06 N 60 44 W

G	B	A							

    Big Harbour 46 10 N 60 25 W
    Eskasoni 45 56 N 60 39 W
    Soldiers Cove 45 42 N 60 44 W
  Louisburg 45 55 N 59 58 W

B	A								

  Cape Breton 45 57 N 59 47 W
  Glace Bay 46 12 N 59 57 W
  Sydney 46 09 N 60 12 W

163D

P	Y	G	C	R	B	D	A	L	

  Point Edward 46 11 N 60 14 W
  North Sydney 46 12 N 60 13 W

G	R	T	A	L					

  Little Bras d'Or 46 19 N 60 17 W
  St. Ann's Harbour 46 15 N 60 36 W
  Ingonish 46 38 N 60 25 W
  Neil Harbour 46 48 N 60 19 W
  Dingwall 46 54 N 60 27 W
  Cape North 47 02 N 60 24 W
  St. Paul Island 47 11 N 60 10 W
  Cape St. Lawrence 47 03 N 60 35 W
  Cheticamp 46 38 N 61 01 W
  Margaree 46 26 N 61 07 W
  Mabou 46 05 N 61 24 W
  Port Hood 46 01 N 61 32 W
  Judique 45 53 N 61 29 W
  Port Hastings 45 39 N 61 24 W
Tracadie Harbour 45 38 N 61 38 W
Bayfield 45 38 N 61 44 W
Antigonish 45 42 N 61 53 W
Merigomish 45 39 N 62 27 W

164A

Trenton 45 37 N 62 38 W
New Glasgow 45 36 N 62 38 W
Pictou 45 41 N 62 43 W

G	B	D	A						

Wallace 45 49 N 63 28 W
Pugwash 45 52 N 63 40 W

G	B	A							

Tidnish 46 00 N 64 02 W

PRINCE EDWARD ISLAND

Port Borden 46 15 N 63 42 W
Victoria 46 12 N 63 30 W
Charlottetown 46 13 N 63 07 W

P	G	B	A	L					

Cape Bear 46 01 N 62 27 W
Murray Harbour 46 02 N 62 29 W
Montague 46 10 N 62 38 W
Georgetown 46 11 N 62 32 W

G	B	A							

Annandale 46 16 N 62 25 W
Souris 46 21 N 62 15 W

G	B	A							

East Point 46 27 N 61 58 W
St. Peter's Harbour 46 26 N 62 45 W
Savage Harbour 46 25 N 62 50 W
Tracadie 46 25 N 63 03 W
North Rustico 46 27 N 63 17 W
New London 46 31 N 63 29 W
Alberton 46 48 N 64 03 W
Tignish 46 58 N 64 00 W
North Point 47 04 N 63 59 W
West Point 46 37 N 64 23 W
Summerside 46 24 N 63 47 W

G	B	A							

NEW BRUNSWICK

Port Elgin 46 04 N 64 04 W
Cape Tormentine 46 06 N 63 46 W
Shemogue 46 10 N 64 08 W
Pointe du Chene 46 15 N 64 31 W
Shediac 46 14 N 64 32 W

164C

G	B	A							

Buctouche 46 29 N 64 41 W
Rexton 46 39 N 64 52 W
Richibucto 46 41 N 64 52 W
Miramichi Bay
  Escuminac 47 05 N 64 53 W
  River Miramichi
    Loggieville 47 05 N 65 23 W
    Millbank 47 03 N 65 27 W
    Chatham 47 02 N 65 28 W

P	Y	G	B	T	A				

    South Nelson 46 59 N 65 33 W
    Newcastle 47 00 N 65 33 W

P	G	B	A						

    Douglastown 47 03 N 65 32 W
Shippegan 47 45 N 64 42 W

164D

G	B								

Chaleur Bay
  Miscou 47 54 N 64 35 W
  Caraquet 47 48 N 64 56 W

G	B	A							

  Bathurst 47 37 N 65 38 W

G	B	A							

  Belledune 47 55 N 65 51 W

P	Q	Y	G	A					

  New Mills 47 57 N 66 10 W
  Dalhousie 48 04 N 66 22 W

G	B	A							

  Campbellton 48 01 N 66 40 W

QUEBEC

Cross Point 48 02 N 66 41 W
Carleton 48 06 N 66 08 W

G	A								

165A

Maria Harbour 48 10 N 65 59 W
New Richmond 48 10 N 65 54 W
Black Cape 48 07 N 65 49 W
Bonaventure 48 02 N 65 29 W
New Carlisle 48 01 N 65 18 W
Paspebiac 48 02 N 65 14 W

P	G	B	T						

Hopetown 48 03 N 65 08 W
Port Daniel 48 11 N 64 56 W
Chandler 48 21 N 64 40 W

G	B								

Perce 48 30 N 64 13 W
Magdalen Islands
  Amherst Harbour 47 14 N 61 50 W
  Grindstone 47 23 N 61 51 W
Barachois 48 37 N 64 16 W
Douglastown 48 46 N 64 23 W
Gaspe 48 50 N 64 29 W

165B

P	G	B	T	A					

Anticosti Island
  Heath Point 49 05 N 61 42 W
  West Point 49 52 N 64 32 W
  Ellis Bay
    Port Menier 49 49 N 64 21 W
River St. Lawrence
  Cape Rosier 48 51 N 64 12 W
  Fox River 49 00 N 64 24 W
  Fame Point 49 07 N 64 36 W
  Petite Vallee 49 13 N 65 02 W
  Grande Vallee 49 14 N 65 09 W
  Cape Magdalen 49 15 N 65 19 W
  Mont Louis 49 14 N 65 44 W

G									

  Martin River 49 13 N 66 11 W
  Ste. Anne des Monts 49 08 N 66 29 W
  Cape Chat 49 05 N 66 45 W
  Capucins 49 03 N 66 51 W
  Les Mechins 49 01 N 66 59 W
  Matane 48 51 N 67 32 W

Y	G	B							

  Little Metis 48 41 N 68 02 W
  Grande Metis 48 38 N 68 08 W
  Pointe au Pere (Father Point)
    48 31 N 68 28 W
  Rimouski 48 29 N 68 31 W

165C

P	G	B	A						

  Bic 48 22 N 68 45 W
  St. Fabien 48 19 N 68 51 W
  Cape Original 48 22 N 68 49 W
  Basque Island 48 08 N 69 15 W
  Trois Pistoles 48 07 N 69 10 W
  Apple Island 48 06 N 69 19 W
  Ile Verte 48 03 N 69 25 W
  Gros Cacouna 47 56 N 69 31 W

Y	G	B	A						

  Riviere du Loup 47 51 N 69 34 W
  St. Antoine 47 04 N 70 32 W
  Montmagny 46 59 N 70 33 W
  Berthier 46 57 N 70 44 W
  Orleans Island
    St. Francois 47 00 N 70 48 W
    St. Jean 46 55 N 70 54 W
    Ste. Petronille 46 51 N 71 08 W
  Lauzon 46 49 N 71 09 W
  Levis 46 49 N 71 11 W
  Ste. Croix 46 38 N 71 44 W
  Becancour 46 24 N 72 23 W

165D

Q	Y	G	C	R	B	A			

  Sorel 46 03 N 73 07 W

Y	G	B	D	T					

  Contrecoeur 45 53 N 73 12 W

Y	B								

St. Lawrence Seaway
  St. Lambert Lock 45 30 N 73 31 W
  Cote Ste. Catherine Lock
    45 24 N 73 34 W
  Beauharnois Lock 45 19 N 73 55 W
  Valleyfield 45 13 N 74 05 W

Q	Y	G	C	T	A				

GEOGRAPHIC INDEX

U.S.A. — 166A

NEW YORK (NY)

Snell Lock 44 59 N 74 46 W
Eisenhower Lock 44 59 N 74 51 W
Waddington 44 51 N 75 12 W
Ogdensburg 44 42 N 75 30 W

`Y G B T A`

Clayton 44 14 N 76 05 W
Cape Vincent 44 08 N 76 20 W
Tibbetts Point 44 06 N 76 22 W

GREAT LAKES

Lake Ontario
Oswego 43 28 N 76 32 W   [p.56]

`P Y G B A`

Rochester 43 17 N 77 36 W
Lake Erie
Tonawanda 43 01 N 78 53 W
Buffalo 42 53 N 78 53 W

PENNSYLVANIA (PA) — 166B

Erie 42 10 N 80 05 W

`Y G C B A`

OHIO (OH)

Conneaut 41 58 N 80 34 W

`Y G B T A`

Ashtabula 41 55 N 80 49 W

`Y G B T A`

Fairport 41 46 N 81 19 W
Cleveland 41 31 N 81 43 W

`Q Y G C R B T A L`

Lorain 41 28 N 82 10 W

`Y G B T A`

Huron 41 24 N 82 35 W

`Y G B T A`

Sandusky 41 27 N 82 44 W
Toledo 41 42 N 83 28 W

`P Q Y G C R B D T A`

MICHIGAN (MI) — 166C

Monroe 41 55 N 83 20 W

`G A`

Detroit River
Detroit 42 20 N 83 02 W

`P Y G C R B T A L`

St. Clair River
Marysville 42 55 N 82 29 W
Port Huron 42 59 N 82 26 W

`G T`

Lake Huron — 166D
Bay City 43 35 N 83 53 W

`Y G T`

Saginaw 43 27 N 83 55 W
Alpena 45 03 N 83 26 W
Thunder Bay 45 04 N 83 26 W
Cheboygan 45 40 N 84 28 W
Lake Michigan
Mackinaw City 45 45 N 84 44 W
Manistee 44 15 N 86 20 W

`Y B`

Ludington 43 58 N 86 27 W
Muskegon 43 11 N 86 14 W
Grand Haven 43 04 N 86 15 W

`P G T A`

Holland 42 47 N 86 13 W
South Haven 42 27 N 86 15 W
Benton Harbour 42 07 N 86 27 W
St. Joseph 42 05 N 86 30 W

INDIANA (IN) — 167A

Burns Harbour 41 38 N 87 11 W

`P Y G C R B T A`

Gary Harbour 41 36 N 87 21 W
Buffington 41 38 N 87 25 W
Indiana Harbour 41 40 N 87 30 W

ILLINOIS (IL)

Chicago 41 50 N 87 38 W

`Q Y G C R B T A L`

WISCONSIN (WI)

Kenosha 42 35 N 87 49 W

`G C R A`

Racine 42 44 N 87 48 W
Milwaukee 43 03 N 87 52 W — 167B

`P Q Y G C R B T A`

Sheboygan 43 45 N 87 42 W
Manitowoc 44 06 N 87 38 W

`Y G B A`

Sturgeon Bay 44 51 N 87 21 W
Green Bay 44 31 N 88 00 W

`P Q Y G B T A`

Marinette 45 07 N 87 37 W

MICHIGAN (MI)

Menominee 45 08 N 87 37 W
Escanaba 45 47 N 87 04 W
St. Marys River
Sault Ste. Marie 46 29 N 84 25 W
Lake Superior
Marquette 46 36 N 87 23 W
Lake Linden 47 13 N 88 23 W

WISCONSIN (WI)

Ashland 46 35 N 90 54 W

`Y G B A`

Superior 46 43 N 92 05 W

MINNESOTA (MN) — 167C

Duluth 46 44 N 92 09 W

`P Q Y G C R B D T A`

Taconite Harbour 47 30 N 90 55 W

CANADA

ONTARIO

Thunder Bay 48 25 N 89 13 W

`P Y G B T A`

Red Rock 48 56 N 88 15 W
Marathon 48 45 N 86 23 W

`G A`

Michipicoten Harbour 47 58 N 84 53 W

`Y A`

St. Marys River — 167D
Sault Ste. Marie 46 31 N 84 20 W

`P Y G B T A`

Lake Huron
Manitoulin Island
Gore Bay 45 55 N 82 28 W
Little Current 45 58 N 81 55 W
Sheguiandah 45 53 N 81 57 W
Blind River 46 12 N 82 54 W
Spragge 46 12 N 82 42 W
Killarney 45 58 N 81 31 W
Britt 45 47 N 80 38 W
Parry Sound 45 22 N 80 03 W

`P Y G A`

Port McNicoll 44 45 N 79 48 W

Midland 44 45 N 79 56 W — 168A

`Y G B A`

Penetanguishene 44 46 N 79 56 W
Collingwood 44 30 N 80 14 W

`Y G D A`

Meaford 44 38 N 80 37 W
Owen Sound 44 35 N 80 57 W

`P Q Y G A`

Goderich 43 45 N 81 44 W

`Y G B T`

St. Clair River
Sarnia 42 59 N 82 25 W

`P Y G B T A`

Corunna 42 53 N 82 27 W
Lake St. Clair
Wallaceburg 42 36 N 82 24 W
Detroit River
Windsor 42 19 N 83 03 W

`Q Y G C R B T A`

Amherstburg 42 06 N 83 05 W

`G A`

Lake Erie — 168B
Kingsville 42 03 N 82 44 W
Leamington 42 03 N 82 37 W
Port Stanley 42 40 N 81 13 W

`Y G B`

Port Burwell 42 38 N 80 48 W
Port Maitland 42 52 N 79 35 W
Fort Erie 42 56 N 78 57 W
Welland Canal
Port Colborne 42 52 N 79 15 W

`P Y G B A`

Humberstone 42 54 N 79 15 W
Welland 42 58 N 79 13 W

`G`

Thorold 43 05 N 79 10 W

`Y G`

St. Catharines 43 10 N 79 16 W

`Y G B A`

Port Weller 43 14 N 79 13 W

`Y G D T`

Lake Ontario — 168C
Port Dalhousie 43 12 N 79 16 W
Hamilton 43 14 N 79 51 W

`Y G C R B T A`

Burlington 43 19 N 79 45 W
Bronte 43 24 N 79 42 W
Oakville 43 26 N 79 40 W
Clarkson 43 30 N 79 36 W
Port Credit 43 33 N 79 36 W
Toronto 43 38 N 79 23 W

`P Y G C R B T A L`

Whitby 43 51 N 78 55 W
Oshawa 43 52 N 78 50 W

`Y G R A`

Port Hope 43 56 N 78 17 W — 168D
Cobourg 43 57 N 78 10 W
Belleville 44 08 N 77 22 W
Kingston 44 12 N 76 30 W

`Y G B D T A`

Gananoque 44 19 N 76 10 W
St. Lawrence Seaway   [p.57]
Brockville 44 36 N 75 38 W
Prescott 44 43 N 75 31 W

`Y G B T A`

Cardinal 44 47 N 75 20 W
Iroquois Lock 44 50 N 75 19 W
Morrisburg 44 56 N 75 11 W
Cornwall 45 01 N 74 43 W

`P Q G B T A`

P Petroleum   **Q** Other Liquid Bulk   **Y** Dry Bulk   **G** General Cargo
C Containers   **R** Ro-Ro   **B** Bunkers   **D** Dry Dock   **T** Towage
A Airport (within 100km)   **L** Lloyd's Agent (not including sub-agents)

QUEBEC — 169A

River St. Lawrence
Montreal 45 30 N 73 33 W

`P Q Y G C R B T A L`

Sutherland Pier 45 33 N 73 32 W
Pointe aux Trembles 45 38 N 73 29 W
Cap St. Michel 45 43 N 73 26 W
Lanoraie 45 58 N 73 11 W
Tracy 46 01 N 73 10 W
Three Rivers (Trois Rivieres)
46 21 N 72 33 W

`P Q Y G C R B T A`

Batiscan 46 31 N 72 14 W
Grondines 46 45 N 72 02 W
Pointe au Platon 46 40 N 71 51 W
Donnacona 46 40 N 71 46 W
Quebec 46 49 N 71 12 W

`P Q Y G C R B D T A`

Cape Brule 47 07 N 70 43 W
Cape Maillard 47 15 N 70 35 W
Baie St. Paul 47 26 N 70 30 W
Cape Goose 47 29 N 70 14 W
Pointe au Pic 47 37 N 70 08 W

169B

`G`

Murray Bay 47 39 N 70 09 W
Port au Saumon 47 45 N 69 57 W
Red Islet 48 04 N 69 33 W
Saguenay River
St. Etienne 48 11 N 69 54 W
St. Jean 48 15 N 70 11 W
Ha Ha Bay
Port Alfred 48 20 N 70 52 W

`P Q G B T A`

Bagotville 48 21 N 70 53 W
Chicoutimi 48 26 N 71 05 W

`P Q Y G B T A`

Tadoussac 48 08 N 69 43 W
Basque Cove 48 19 N 69 25 W
Les Escoumins 48 21 N 69 23 W
Pointe au Boisvert 48 34 N 69 08 W
Portneuf 48 37 N 69 05 W
Forestville 48 48 N 69 04 W
Comeau Bay (Baie Comeau)
49 13 N 68 09 W

169C

`Y G R B A`

St. Nicholas 49 19 N 67 47 W
Godbout 49 19 N 67 35 W
Trinity Bay 49 25 N 67 18 W
Egg Island 49 37 N 67 11 W
Lobster Bay 49 49 N 67 05 W
Port Cartier 50 01 N 66 52 W

`P Y G B T A`

River Ste. Marguerite
Clarke City 50 12 N 66 38 W
Pointe Noire 50 10 N 66 28 W
Seven Islands (Sept Iles) 50 06 N 66 23 W

`P Y G C R B T A`

169D

Moisie 50 12 N 66 05 W
Mingan 50 17 N 64 01 W
Romaine 50 18 N 63 48 W
Havre St. Pierre 50 14 N 63 36 W

`Y G B A`

Baie Johan Beetz 50 17 N 62 48 W
Natashquan 50 12 N 61 51 W
Cape Whittle 50 11 N 60 07 W
Bonne Esperance 51 24 N 57 37 W
Bradore Bay 51 29 N 57 14 W
Greenly Island 51 22 N 57 11 W
Blanc Sablon 51 25 N 57 08 W

NEWFOUNDLAND

Pistolet Bay 51 36 N 55 46 W
Flowers Cove 51 17 N 56 45 W
St. Barbe Harbour 51 12 N 56 46 W
St. Genevieve Bay 51 09 N 56 50 W
St. Margaret Bay 51 01 N 56 57 W
Ingornachoix Bay
Port Saunders 50 38 N 57 19 W
Hawkes Bay 50 37 N 57 10 W

170A

Mal Bay 50 33 N 57 23 W
Daniels Cove 50 14 N 57 35 W
Bonne Bay
Rocky Harbour 49 36 N 57 55 W
Lomond Cove 49 28 N 57 45 W
Bay of Islands
Cox Cove 49 08 N 58 02 W
Woods Island 49 06 N 58 10 W
Humbermouth 48 58 N 57 55 W
Corner Brook 48 57 N 57 56 W

`P Y G C B A`

Curling 48 58 N 57 59 W
Pleasant Cove 48 58 N 58 01 W
Lark Harbour 49 06 N 58 21 W
Port au Port Bay
Aguathuna 48 45 N 58 43 W
Stephenville 48 31 N 58 32 W

`G B T A`

Turf Point 48 26 N 58 28 W
St. George's Harbour 48 27 N 58 29 W
Flat Bay 48 24 N 58 35 W
Codroy 47 53 N 59 24 W
Cape Ray 47 37 N 59 18 W
Port aux Basques 47 34 N 59 07 W

170B

`G B`

Isle aux Morts 47 35 N 59 00 W
Rose Blanche 47 36 N 58 41 W
Barachois 47 35 N 57 45 W
Burgeo 47 36 N 57 37 W

`G B`

Ramea Island 47 31 N 57 25 W
Rencontre 47 36 N 56 40 W
Hare Bay 47 37 N 56 32 W
Bonne Bay 47 38 N 56 12 W
Pushthrough 47 38 N 56 11 W
Bay d'Espoir
St. Albans 47 52 N 55 51 W
Milltown 47 54 N 55 47 W
Hermitage Bay
Gaultois 47 36 N 55 54 W
Hermitage Cove 47 34 N 55 56 W
Harbour Breton 47 29 N 55 48 W

`G B`

Jerseyman Harbour 47 29 N 55 46 W
St. Jacques 47 28 N 55 25 W
Belleoram 47 31 N 55 25 W
Belle Harbour 47 40 N 55 20 W
English Harbour East 47 38 N 54 54 W
Grand Bank 47 06 N 55 45 W

170C

`G B`

Fortune 47 04 N 55 50 W

ST. PIERRE and MIQUELON (French)

Miquelon Island
Miquelon 47 08 N 56 22 W
St. Pierre Island
St. Pierre 46 47 N 56 10 W

`P G C R D T A`

CANADA — 170D

NEWFOUNDLAND

Lamaline 46 51 N 55 48 W
Placentia Bay
St. Lawrence 46 54 N 55 20 W
Burin 47 02 N 55 10 W
Mortier Bay 47 10 N 55 07 W
Marystown 47 10 N 55 09 W

`P G B D`

Rose au Rue 47 32 N 54 09 W
Come by Chance 47 48 N 54 01 W

`P B T`

Harbour Buffet 47 32 N 54 03 W
Long Harbour 47 27 N 53 49 W

`G B`

Ship Harbour 47 22 N 53 53 W
Argentia 47 18 N 53 59 W

`Q G C R B`

Placentia 47 15 N 53 50 W
St. Marys 46 55 N 53 34 W

171A

Trepassey 46 43 N 53 23 W
Cape Race 46 39 N 53 04 W
Renewse 46 54 N 52 54 W
Fermeuse 46 58 N 52 54 W
Aquafort 47 00 N 52 53 W
Ferryland Harbour 47 01 N 52 51 W
Witless Bay 47 17 N 52 46 W
Bay Bulls 47 18 N 52 44 W
St. John's 47 34 N 52 41 W

`P Y G C R B A L`

Conception Bay
Bell Island
Wabana 47 38 N 52 55 W
Long Pond 47 31 N 52 58 W

`P Y G B A`

Holyrood 47 24 N 53 08 W

`P B A`

Brigus 47 33 N 53 11 W
Port de Grave 47 36 N 53 12 W
Coley's Point 47 35 N 53 15 W
Bay Roberts 47 34 N 53 13 W

171B

`G B A`

Harbour Grace 47 41 N 53 13 W

`P G B`

Carbonear 47 44 N 53 14 W
Bay de Verde 48 05 N 52 54 W
Trinity Bay
Hearts Content 47 53 N 53 23 W
Dildo 47 34 N 53 34 W
Tickle Harbour 47 38 N 53 43 W
Clarenville 48 10 N 53 57 W

`P G B`

Bonaventure 48 17 N 53 26 W
Trinity 48 22 N 53 21 W
Catalina Harbour
Catalina 48 31 N 53 04 W

`P Y G`

Port Union 48 30 N 53 05 W
Bonavista 48 39 N 53 07 W
Charlottetown 48 26 N 54 00 W
Port Blandford 48 23 N 54 10 W

171C

Alexander Bay
Glovertown 48 39 N 54 00 W
Gambo 48 46 N 54 12 W
Butchers Cove 48 50 N 54 00 W
Indian Bay 49 02 N 53 52 W
Greenspond 49 04 N 53 36 W
Musgrave Harbour 49 27 N 53 56 W
Carmanville 49 24 N 54 17 W

`G A`

Fogo Island
Fogo Harbour 49 43 N 54 16 W
Change Island
Change Island Tickle 49 40 N 54 24 W
New World Island
Herring Neck 49 39 N 54 35 W
Twillingate Island
Twillingate 49 41 N 54 45 W

`G B A`

Exploits Bay
Lewisporte 49 15 N 55 03 W
Botwood 49 09 N 55 19 W

171D

`P Q Y G B A`

Badgers Quay 49 00 N 56 04 W
Glover Harbour 49 28 N 55 29 W
Tommy's Arm 49 26 N 55 47 W
Triton Island
Troytown 49 34 N 55 35 W
Roberts Arm 49 29 N 55 48 W
Hall Bay
Springdale 49 30 N 56 04 W

`G B`

Little Bay Island 49 39 N 55 47 W
Burlington 49 46 N 56 01 W
Nippers Harbour 49 48 N 55 51 W
Tilt Cove 49 53 N 55 37 W
Cape St. John 50 00 N 55 30 W
La Scie 49 58 N 55 35 W
Mings Bight 50 00 N 55 59 W
Baie Verte
Baie Verte 49 56 N 56 12 W

`P G B`

CANADA *continued*

NEWFOUNDLAND

    Coachman Harbour 50 03 N 56 05 W
Fleur de Lys 50 07 N 56 05 W
White Bay
    Hampden 49 33 N 56 50 W
    Sops Arm 49 45 N 56 50 W
    Jacksons Arm 49 51 N 56 45 W
    Williamsport 50 28 N 56 20 W
Canada Bay
    Roddickton 50 52 N 56 07 W
    Englee Harbour 50 43 N 56 07 W
Conche Harbour 50 54 N 55 56 W
Groais Island 50 59 N 55 31 W
Croc Harbour 51 03 N 55 47 W
Hare Bay
    Main Brook 51 10 N 56 00 W

G	B										

    St. Anthony 51 22 N 55 35 W
Quirpon 51 36 N 55 27 W
Strait of Belle Isle

    Forteau 51 28 N 56 56 W
    Pointe Armour 51 27 N 56 52 W
Belle Isle 51 55 N 55 21 W
Battle Harbour 52 16 N 55 35 W
St. Lewis Inlet 52 24 N 56 01 W
Granby Island
    St. Francis Harbour 52 33 N 55 41 W
Alexis Inlet
    Port Hope Simpson 52 33 N 56 18 W
    Occasional Harbour 52 40 N 55 45 W
Venison Tickle 52 58 N 55 46 W
Hawke Harbour 53 02 N 55 48 W
Domino 53 28 N 55 44 W   p.50/51
Spotted Island 53 30 N 55 44 W
Cartwright 53 42 N 57 01 W
Hamilton Inlet
    Rigolet 54 11 N 58 25 W
    Goose Bay 53 21 N 60 25 W

P	G	C	R	B	A				

Indian Harbour 54 27 N 57 13 W
Cut-Throat 54 29 N 57 07 W
Cape Harrison 54 56 N 57 56 W
Webeck Harbour 54 52 N 58 02 W
Tuchialic Bay 54 47 N 58 25 W

Adlavik 55 00 N 58 49 W
Makkovik 55 06 N 59 10 W
Hopedale 55 27 N 60 12 W
Ford Harbour 56 27 N 61 11 W
Nain 56 32 N 61 42 W
Hebron 58 12 N 62 36 W
Saglek Bay 58 29 N 62 34 W
Ramah 59 05 N 63 26 W
Cape Chidley 60 23 N 64 26 W

ALPHABETICAL INDEX

ALPHABETICAL INDEX

ALPHABETICAL INDEX

ALPHABETICAL INDEX

ALPHABETICAL INDEX

ALPHABETICAL INDEX

ALPHABETICAL INDEX

ALPHABETICAL INDEX

ALPHABETICAL INDEX

ALPHABETICAL INDEX

ALPHABETICAL INDEX

ALPHABETICAL INDEX

ALPHABETICAL INDEX